COMPARATIVE SOCIAL RESEARCH: METHODOLOGICAL PROBLEMS AND STRATEGIES

Comparative Studies in Behavioral Science:
A WILEY SERIES

Robert T. Holt and John E. Turner, *Editors*
Department of Political Science
University of Minnesota

The Logic of Comparative Social Inquiry
by Adam Przeworski and Henry Teune

The Analysis of Subjective Culture
by Harry C. Triandis

*Comparative Legislative Behavior: Frontiers
of Research*
edited by Samuel C. Patterson and John C. Wahlke

*Mass Political Violence: A Cross-National
Causal Analysis*
by Douglas A. Hibbs, Jr.

Cross-Cultural Research Methods
by Richard W. Brislin, Walter J. Lonner, and
Robert M. Thorndike

Unity and Disintegration in International Alliances
by Ole R. Holsti, P. Terrence Hopmann, and
John D. Sullivan

*Comparative Social Research: Methodological
Problems and Strategies*
edited by Michael Armer and Allen D.
Grimshaw

Comparative Social Research: Methodological Problems and Strategies

EDITED BY

MICHAEL ARMER
Indiana University

ALLEN D. GRIMSHAW
Indiana University

PUBLISHED UNDER THE AUSPICES OF THE
INSTITUTE FOR COMPARATIVE SOCIOLOGY

A WILEY-INTERSCIENCE PUBLICATION

JOHN WILEY & SONS
New York · London · Sydney · Toronto

Library of Congress Cataloging in Publication Data:

Main entry under title.

Comparative social research.

(Comparative studies in behavioral science)
"A Wiley-Interscience publication."
Selected papers from a seminar of the Institute for
Comparative Sociology held in Bloomington, Ind. in 1971.

1. Sociological research—Congresses. 2. Sociology—
Comparative method—Congresses.
I. Amer, Michael, ed. II. Grimshaw, Allen Day, ed.
III. Institute for Comparative Sociology.
[DNLM: 1. Research. 2. Social sciences. HM48 C737 1973.]

HM 48.C64   301'.01'8   73-7604
ISBN 0-471-03321-9

10 9 8 7 6 5 4 3 2 1

Participants in the Conference [a]

THEODORE ANDERSON, *University of Minnesota*

MICHAEL ARMER[b], *Indiana University*

JEANNIE BALDIGO, *Indiana University*

CHARLES BIRD, *Indiana University*

KENNETH BROWN, JR., *Indiana University*

GLADYS BUSCH, *Indiana University (Ohio State University)*

JOHN BUSCH, *Indiana University (Ohio State University)*

DAVID CHAPLIN, *Western Michigan University (University of Wisconsin)*

JOHN CLARK, *University of Minnesota*

PHILLIPS CUTRIGHT[b], *Indiana University*

RUSSELL DYNES, *Ohio State University*

JOSEPH ELDER[b], *University of Wisconsin*

HORACIO FABREGA, *Michigan State University*

KURT FINSTERBUSCH[b], *University of Maryland (University of Wisconsin)*

ROBERT FORD, *State University of New York, Buffalo*

WILLIAM FORM[b], *University of Illinois (Michigan State University)*

PAUL FRIDAY, *Ohio State University*

HAROLD GOULD, *University of Illinois*

ALLEN GRIMSHAW[b], *Indiana University*

A.O. HALLER, *University of Wisconsin*

LAWRENCE HAZELRIGG[b], *Indiana University*

RICHARD HILL[b], *University of Oregon (Purdue University)*

BYONG JE JON, *Indiana University*

[a]First institution named indicates affiliation as of Fall 1972; institutions in parentheses indicate affiliation in April 1971, if different from location in Fall 1972.
[b]Contributed a chapter to this volume.

v

DAVID JOHNSON[b], *University of Nebraska*

FRANK JONES, *McMaster University*

BERNARD KARSH, *University of Illinois*

PETER MANNING, *Michigan State University*

HUGH MEHAN[b], *University of California, San Diego (Indiana University)*

DARIO MENANTEAU, *University of Minnesota*

DELBERT MILLER[b], *Indiana University*

ALEJANDRO PORTES[b], *University of Texas (University of Illinois)*

ALLAN SCHNAIBERG[b], *Northwestern University*

KENT SCHWIRIAN[b], *Ohio State University*

MILES SIMPSON, *Stanford University*

KENNETH SOUTHWOOD, *University of Illinois*

MURRAY STRAUS, *University of New Hampshire*

FRED STRODTBECK, *University of Chicago*

SHELDON STRYKER, *Indiana University*

YUAN TIEN, *Ohio State University*

AUSTIN TURK[b], *Indiana University*

FRED WAISANEN, *Michigan State University*

JOHN WALTON[b], *Northwestern University*

[b]Contributed a chapter to this volume.

We dedicate this book to all the anonymous people the world over who have been subjected to comparative study. We hope that the book may help reduce occasional abuses of their hospitality, improve the quality of comparative social research and the quality of life, and, finally, hasten the day in which all people in all societies will understand one another better — and live in peace.

SERIES PREFACE

The last decade has witnessed the burgeoning of comparative studies in the behavioral sciences. Scholars in specific disciplines have come to realize that they share much with experts in other fields who face similar theoretical and methodological problems and whose research findings are often related. Moreover, specialists in a given geographic area have felt the need to look beyond the limited confines of their region and to seek new meaning in their research results by comparing them with studies that have been made elsewhere.

This series is designed to meet the needs of the growing cadre of scholars in comparative research. The emphasis is on cross-disciplinary studies, although works within the perspective of a single discipline are included. In its scope, the series includes books of theoretical and methodological interest, as well as studies that are based on empirical research. The books in the series are addressed to scholars in the various behavioral science disciplines, to graduate students, and to undergraduates in advanced standing.

Robert T. Holt
John E. Turner

University of Minnesota
Minneapolis, Minnesota

Preface[1]

William Graham Sumner, W. I. Thomas, E. A. Ross, amd Robert E. Park (all early presidents of the American Sociological Society) were among the more notable early American sociologists who exhibited substantial interest in the comparative study of other societies. Some early sociologists assembled masses of secondary ethnographic data, from which they tried to derive general sociological principles; others traveled widely on several continents to observe the variety of social life; nearly all were convinced of the importance of developing concepts or theories that could transcend any particular society and that might guide following generations in their research on a world-encompassing scale. Between the 1930s and 1950s, however, these concerns seemed marginal to American sociologists, who were focusing attention primarily on analyzing specific aspects of American society. This change is reflected in a study done by our colleague Frank R. Westie and was described by him in his Presidential Address to the Ohio Valley Sociological Society in May 1972. Westie's data include a list of American Sociological Society/Association (ASA) presidents from the Society's inception to the present. We note that (by contrast with the early period) of the 20 ASA presidents from 1931 to 1950, not one is known primarily or substantially for comparative work. Those who did some comparative work did so either incidentally (with respect to their main interests) or after their terms as president.

A converging set of scientific and national circumstances precipitated this constriction of interests. Politically, there was a national reaction against foreign involvements and a great upsurge of isolationism. Intellectually, the emergence of cultural relativity as a useful scheme for differentiating societies and the eclipse of the evolutionary model for comparing total societies fostered a theoretical reorientation to the study of society. (It is interesting to note that the reflorescence of comparative interests in the last two decades has, in its most recent phase, been accompanied by a reemergence of evolutionary themes in the

---

[1] The first part of this preface draws heavily on Useem and Grimshaw (1966; see references following Chapter 1 for full citation).

theoretical literature of the social sciences.) This pronounced shift reinforced a growing conviction that one of the first tasks in developing sociology as a discipline meeting acceptable, rigorous criteria of scientific investigation was to derive operationally manageable concepts and instruments. Demands during the Depression for sociological findings on social problems and, later, for effective administration of World War II further reinforced a natural concern with the domestic scene. Then, as now, a demand for relevance sometimes meant that the quest for understanding what was common to the life of all men in social groups was overshadowed by a demand for action that would better conditions for those close by. Whatever the judgement of later generations may be on the wisdom of the shift toward parochialism in sociology, the interaction of (1) sociologists' concerns about their scientific status, (2) constricting resources, (3) immediate social problems, and (4) political isolationism constrained sociologists (and other social scientists, anthropologists excepted) to turn away from other societies and focus their analytical skills on their own.

Even though the predominant concerns of American sociology in this period were largely within one societal and cultural context, the discipline consistently retained its traditional definition of its underlying objective: the discovery of uniformities in social behavior and social structures. The tacit presumption prevailed until well after World War II, however, that most sociological research could be pursued effectively without necessarily going beyond American society. An even more unwarranted, and sometimes damaging, assumption was that if someone did want to refine and apply, through work in other areas, generalizations about social life drawn from American-based studies, he could accomplish this task by simply transferring established concepts and technical procedures to foreign countries. This book offers convincing evidence against the reality of such a perspective, but standard treatises on sociological methods produced during the 1930s and 1940s remained largely silent on the design and conduct of comparative sociological research.

The long period of looking inward was terminated by World War II and the events of the postwar years. Servicemen traveled. Planners demanded information on the needs and strengths of specific countries and specific world areas. Military and political decision-makers discovered that they had no intelligence on distant and obscure peoples and places that suddenly had become very important. Their concern over defective intelligence resulted in substantial support for area programs, but there was no parallel upsurge of interest in comparative social research. Crash programs were initiated during the war to teach both foreign languages and information on the cultures and societies in which those languages were used. From their inception and for a period of some 15 years after the war, area programs were both well-financed and generally productive (for a comprehensive review of the current status of area programs, see Lambert, 1972; full citation included in references for Chapter 1). The initial demands for an understanding of foreign societies grew primarily out of pragmatic considerations, just as had the earlier emphasis on domestic sociology. A consequence of the multiplicity of cultural exchange programs, interuniversity contracts, technical-assistance endeavors, Peace Corps activities, foundation projects, and grants to advanced students and faculty for research and training, however, was that numerous sociologists became interested in, and acquired the resources to do, overseas studies; still others were encouraged to consider that possibility.

Some of these "foreign-returned" sociologists, smitten by culture shock or struck down by sloth, returned to more comfortable American surroundings, where they studied more familiar social behavior and drew on their overseas experience only for occasional illustrative comparisons or cocktail party ancedotes. Another set of sociologists, probably a considerably smaller one, struck by the richness of their newly discovered cultures and by the *differences* from American society, went into area research, immersing themselves more and more deeply in their new societies and possibly substituting a new parochialism for the old. A third set, smaller still initially, was impressed with the *similarities* in social behavior that appeared to emerge, after constraints due to social structure and cultural variation had been taken into account, and began to ask once again the questions of an earlier generation about the possibilities of transsocietal generalization and even about the possibilities for discovering universals. It is this latter group that, together with the even smaller one that had continued to ask comparative questions throughout the heyday of domestic sociology, constituted the core of a new group of explicitly comparative sociologists. In the early 1960s, this group grew rapidly; simultaneously, the pathways that could lead new recruits to sociology into comparative work expanded rapidly, as did the networks that would assure meaningful communication among those with mutual interests.

The middle of the 1960s saw the creation of a Social Science Research Council Committee on Comparative Sociological Research (which was unsuccessful for reasons unrelated to its timeliness); the appearance of the Institute for Comparative Sociology; the initiation of graduate training programs in comparative sociological research at many major institutions; the provision of regular sessions with comparative emphases at annual meetings of the ASA; a sharp increase in both journal and monograph publications with comparative foci; and the convergence of comparative interests across disciplinary boundaries. Another bit of evidence on the reemergence of comparative sociology as a major activity within the discipline can be found in the fact that, of the 10 most recent ASA presidents, 8 have had substantial comparative dimensions in their work.

During the summer of 1964 John Useem (Michigan State University) and Karl Schuessler (Indiana University), began discussing the possibility of a program in comparative sociology involving their own institutions and others in the

Midwest. In the fall of that year, representatives from the four universities (the other two being the Universities of Illinois and Wisconsin) in the Midwestern Universities Consortium for International Activities, Inc. (MUCIA) met; in the summer of 1966 the first seminar of the Institute for Comparative Sociology (ICS) was held in Bloomington, Indiana. In subsequent years the four schools were joined by five other (Committee on Institutional Cooperation) universities (Iowa, Minnesota, Northwestern, Ohio State, and Purdue) in sponsorship of the Institute. During its first five years the Institute sponsored five summer training seminars for advanced graduate students and for faculty beginning comparative work. During these seminars at Indiana, Ohio State, and Illinois, several hundred students, faculty, and visiting scholars representing nearly 50 American and foreign unversities participated in the Institute's activities. The range of topics in these summer seminars was considerable; the continuing emphasis, however, was on methodological problems.

Following the 1970 summer seminar in Urbana, Illinois, it was decided to convene faculty members of the participating departments to consider in greater depth the theme of methodological problems in comparative sociological research. Papers were solicited, submitted, and circulated in advance, and in the spring of 1971 the approximately 40 persons (most of them sociologists and most from ICS institutions) listed on pages v-vi met in Bloomington. Each set of papers was first discussed by someone who had prepared an extensive critique; general discussion then followed. This volume consists of a selected set of those papers (see discussion of the selection process below) and edited portions of the critique and general discussions.

Following this preface and the introductory chapters by each of the editors, the book is divided into five principal parts. In the first, "Relating to the Research Environment," are papers by Form, Elder, and Portes which reflect research experience in both Americas, Europe, and India; the researchers encountered problems of trust and communication with leaders in government, industry, and labor as well as with factory workers and villagers. In the second part, "Design Strategies in Comparative Research," Walton proposes a technique of standardized case comparison, and Miller reflects on the transferability of techniques for studying the community power structure of cities in four different countries. In the third part, "Approaches to Conceptual Clarification," are papers by Hazelrigg and by Armer and Schnaiberg. The first examines problems with the notion of class consciousness. The second tests the validity and universality of the concept and/or measures of individual modernity.

The final two parts examine problems in the "Comparative Applications of Qualitative Methods" and "Comparative Applications of Quantitative Methods." In Part 4, Turk reflects on the sociological relevance of historical data with particular reference to legal control in South Africa. Mehan analyzes sources of error in certain testing situations and reveals some of the advantages of incorporating videotaping into the technological inventory of comparative social research. In Part 5, Schwirian discusses the relative usefulness of alternative data-analysis techniques and models in comparative tests of ecological theories. Johnson and Cutright report on methodological problems in the use of aggregated data in the study of Latin American illegitimacy. Finally, Finsterbusch proposes a combination of inductive and deductive techniques for identifying types of nation-states. Following these chapters is a brief postscript by Hill, who comments on a noncomparative methodologist's reactions to the special problems outlined in the earlier chapters.

Each of the chapters in the five principal parts is followed by an abridged and edited version of the lively discussions that occurred at the conference itself. The table of contents, the detailed discussions in the introductory chapters, along with the name index will be sufficient enough to locate most topics cited in this text.

To an even greater extent than is usually the case with a symposium volume, this book has been a cooperative enterprise. Credit for the original idea of an ICS-sponsored faculty seminar belongs to Yuan Tien, of Ohio State University, Director of the ICS in 1970 and at the time of the conference. During the latter part of the time in which this volume was being prepared for publication, directorship passed to Bo Anderson, of Michigan State University, who has continued to provide the editors with support and encouragement. Acknowledgment is also due to members of the Executive Board of the ICS, who first approved the conference and subsequently approved preparation of the volume.

Financial support for the conference itself was provided by MUCIA, by the Graduate Research Committee of Indiana University, and by the Committee on Comparative Politics of the Social Science Research Council. Additional participant support was provided by the ICS and by individual universities. Logistic support for editorial work and typing was advanced to the ICS by Indiana University's Institute of Social Research; further financing was given by ICS itself. We are also grateful to our Indiana colleagues for their continued encouragement.

The stenotype transcript of the conference discussions was done by Mrs. E. R. Craft of Ace Federal Reporters, Inc., Washington, D. C. We are grateful for her perserverance and impressed at her skill in sorting out the discussion. We are also tremendously impressed with, and correspondingly grateful for, the editorial skills of Carolyn J. Mullins, who has been a help to all the contributors—some of whom must feel they know her well through extensive correspondence, and all of whom join us in our thanks for the improvements she has made in the chapters and related discussions. Completion of this book would have taken longer without her efficient work, which made us struggle harder to meet deadlines. We are also grateful to Donna Hancock, Sue Havlish, Betsy Hein, Joanne Hobson, Kevin Musser, Mary Olguin, Janie Richardson, and Lorie

Simmons who typed—and retyped—various portions of the book, and to Deanna Strom, who prepared the index.

The ICS conference, and consequently this volume, would not have been possible without the unselfish labors of our contributors and discussants, the thoughtful observations of other participants, and the critical intellectual contribution of those who acted as manuscript reviewers. Our contributors are literally that; they will receive no more for their efforts than additional entries to already respectable *vitae*; all proceeds from this volume will go to the ICS. Our reviewers (each paper was read by at least two and some by as many as four) will not even be able to add to their *vitae*; we are genuinely thankful to them. Their names are listed on page xvii.

Four of these papers, which were originally presented at the ICS Conference, have subsequently been published elsewhere. Chapter 3 (by Form) was published in *Studies in Comparative International Development,* Vol. 8, 1973. Chapter 5 (by Portes) was published in *Rural Sociology,* 37 (March 1972): 27-42. Chapter 7 (by Miller) was published in *Social Forces,* 51 (March 1973): 261-274. Chapter 9 (by Armer and Schnaiberg) was published in *American Sociological Review,* 37 (June 1972): 301-316. We are grateful to these authors and publishers for permitting publication of these papers here at no cost to the ICS.

Richard Hill has provided continuing wise counsel and encouragement and has, in his own ineffable way, made even subtler contributions. He also provided a rousing farewell address for the conference and a thoughtful concluding comment for the book.

The editorial division of labor was as follows: The topic of the Conference was selected by Grimshaw in consultation with Tien and the Executive Board of the ICS; Grimshaw solicited and selected papers presented at the Conference. Armer handled the complex logistics of the meeting itself. Following the Conference, Armer and Grimshaw requested evaluations of the Conference papers from the Executive Board members and from a set of outside referees especially chosen for each paper. They are jointly responsible for the final selection of chapters and discussion material and for other editorial decisions. Each has written an introductory chapter.

Michael Armer
Allen D. Grimshaw

Bloomington, Indiana
April 1973

ACKNOWLEDGMENTS

We are grateful to the following people for reviewing the manuscript:

Michael Aiken	David Mechanic
Carl Backman	Gilbert Merkx
Reinhard Bendix	Bernard Morris
George Bohrnstedt	Robert Perrucci
Charles Bonjean	Norman Ryder
Donald Carns	Leonard Savitz
Aaron Cicourel	Karl Schuessler
Irwin Deutscher	Michael Schwartz
Leonard Doob	Marshall Segall
John Gillespie	Gideon Sjoberg
Jerry Hage	Kenneth Southwood
Carl Harter	Arthur Stinchcombe
Pat Horan	George Stolnitz
Irving Horowitz	Gerald Strauss
Herbert Hyman	Sheldon Stryker
Richard Lambert	Richard Tomasson
William Labov	James Vaughn

CONTENTS

Introduction

CHAPTER ONE

Comparative Sociology: In What Ways Different From Other Sociologies?[1]

ALLEN D. GRIMSHAW

Indiana University

Introduction

There are many senses in which it can be said that all good sociology is comparative—that, as a matter of fact, sociology cannot be done without making comparisons. For this reason, one reader of an earlier version of this chapter expressed impatience with any lengthy discussion of the topic suggested by the title of this chapter, claiming that it was a waste of time and, further, that any decision to accept one rather than another definition would be arbitrary. Moreover, any such arbitrary definition could, by virtue of what it included or excluded, deter sociologists from undertaking some very necessary kinds of work.

There is merit in my colleague's complaint, and there are clearly many cogent reasons for "getting on with the work to be done." At the same time, however, there is a special activity that comparative social scientists carry out that differs in some specifiable ways from work in only one society. These differences are reflected in comparative sociology's goals, special methodological problems, and rewards in terms of intellectual discovery. In short, there *are* arguments about what comparative sociology is. The outcomes of these arguments have consequences for decisions about professional training; the allocation of possibly diminishing funds for social research; and the cumulative character of substantive findings, empirical generalizations, and theoretical development in sociology. The paraphrase of W.I. Thomas is obvious.

In this chapter, I will consider the "ways in which comparative sociology differs from all other sociologies." I will first make my own attempt at defining comparative sociology, noting some claims and counterclaims and commenting on some unanswered (and even unraised) questions. I will then discuss briefly the ways in which comparative sociology specifically differs from "area" sociology (for American sociologists a principal area specialization is the United States), observing the advantages and disadvantages of both approaches. Following this discussion, I will consider some of the particular benefits of comparative work (the testing of limits on generalizations and the asking of new questions about one's own society), using some of my own experience in research in India as illustrative material. Finally, I want to discuss one aspect—language—that has frequently been identified as one of the most difficult and methodologically problematic in cross-cultural and cross-national research. My argument is that while the problems involved are no different in kind from those involved in domestic research, they are of such great magnitude as to constitute an almost qualitative difference for comparative, as compared to noncomparative, research.

In What Ways Different from All Other Sociologies?

In attempting to answer the apparent conundrum posed by the title of this chapter, I have reviewed several attempts to define comparative sociology, particularly those that have appeared since John Useem and I (1966) made our preliminary attack on the issue. A number of thoughtful people have made some very interesting and provocative statements; a number of banal attempts have been made to resolve peripheral questions; no one has yet given a satisfactory answer. I shall therefore propose an answer and then discuss both how I came to it and how it may extend and clarify some previously made suggestions. I think that I can demonstrate that some issues previously deemed central to such a definition (e.g., whether or not comparative sociology requires the fielding of research on the same topic in more than one society by the same researcher[s] ; the relative merits of emphasis upon methods of agreement or difference a la Galton, or Mill, for that matter) become less critical if my definition is accepted.

All sociology, indeed all work directed toward understanding the behavior of men and women in social groups, is posited on the axiomatic assumption that that behavior is nonrandom and rule-governed in the sense that "natively competent" members of social groups behave in accordance with shared understandings that simultaneously govern their own behavior and their interpretations of the behavior of other members (for a fuller explication and sources, see Grimshaw, 1972a). The sociological task is to identify (1) system-specific (I will defer discussion of what constitutes a system), (2) empirical (substantive) universal, and (3) metatheoretical universal rules about social behavior (for a discussion of these terms and their use in moving toward a unified theory of human behavior, see Grimshaw, 1972b). *The particular task of comparative sociology is to distinguish between those regularities in social behavior that are system-specific and those that are universal* (in either the substantive or the metatheoretical sense). The search for universals has as its ultimate goal the statement of a universal grammar for social behavior. There are also grammars for social behavior in specific systems. The movement from the statement of specific grammars for specific social systems to the statement of *a* grammar for all social systems can proceed only through the comparison of rules for specific systems.

Most readers will recognize the analogy to the linguistic model of grammars of languages and *a* grammar of language. What I hope to do by introducing this model is to suggest a resolution for that persistent problem in the epistemology and the practice of comparative sociology, the question of generality versus uniqueness. Przeworski and Teune observe, "Social reality may be infinitely diverse. This belief leads some to conclude that social reality can be 'understood' only within the context in which it is observed, and can never be explained by general lawlike statements." They further observe that "those who accept the model of social science calling for general statements believe that, regardless of the extent of social diversity, it nonetheless can be expressed in terms of general theories" (1970: 12). I suggest that it should be no more dismaying for sociologists to say that social reality (behavior) is infinitely diverse than for linguists to say that it is possible, within any language, to generate an infinite number of sentences. These sentences, linguists have been able to demonstrate, are generated from a relatively modest set of basic phrase structure rules, another set of transformational rules, and a fairly substantial lexical inventory (Chomsky, 1965). Likewise, diverse social behaviors are also generated from a relatively modest set of rules (and probably transformations) and the interaction of large numbers of individuals.

The analogy must be pushed one step further if we are to discover an answer to at least one part of the uniquism problem. It is true that in any one language an infinite number of sentences can be generated. It is also true, however, that some sentences (those which violate syntactic rules) *cannot* be generated because ungrammatical (degrees of grammaticality need not be considered here; see Chomsky, 1965). Similarly, while an infinite number of social behaviors can be generated, it is also true that specific kinds of social behaviors cannot occur because they would violate the rules of social syntax. On the system-specific level, the effect of this situation is that categorical rules are not violated by competent native members;[2] on the extrasystemic level, roles are not randomly allocated nor events randomly ordered (for a fuller explication of this discussion, see Grimshaw, 1972b). In short, I agree with the Przeworski and Teune formulation that "whenever there is a system specific factor that seems to be necessary for explanation, the conclusion should not be that systems are unique but rather that it is necessary to identify some general factors so far not considered" and that, moreover, "this is indeed the primary function of comparative inquiry" (1970: 13).

I take this to be saying, in a slightly different way, exactly what Bendix (1963) said in his discussion of concepts and generalizations in comparative sociological studies. He observed that sociological concepts should be universally applicable and that such concepts (e.g., "division of labor") already existed. Moreover, such concepts can be used, according to Bendix, in an interrelated and "deductively elaborated" systemic framework applicable to all social units. The fact remains, however, that these general principles have different manifestations in the empirical reality of different social systems because there are different degrees of, for example, social differentiation, based on different values or different allocations of resources in various societies. Bendix asserts that it is the differences in manifestations of universal characteristics rather than the simple presence or absence of the characteristics themselves that provide an "entering wedge" (John Useem's term) into sociological analysis of the infinite variety of actual social behavior.

Bendix characterizes comparative sociological studies as representing "an attempt to develop concepts and generalizations at a level between what is true of all societies and what is true of one society at one point in time and space," asserting that, "in fact, many sociological concepts imply such an 'intermediate level' of analysis, though frequently they are used as if they applied universally" (1963: 532). I find his distinction between "generalizations. . . true of all societies" and "what is true of one society at one point in time and space" congruent with my identification above of types of rules. Moreover, his "level between" represents a matter of difference in emphasis rather than one of substance. He observes, for example, that stratification and authority are social patterns present in all societies (i.e., are universals) but that particular "socio-historical configurations" produce specific manifestations such as "class" or "bureaucracy" (p. 533). He emphasizes, for example, the successes of students of comparative law and comparative administration in identifying societally specific constraints (social transformations?) in generating diverse social behaviors out of fundamentally identical underlying patterns of social relations. His focus is on the "level between," mine on the universal-specific distinction. The two perspectives are only analytically separable. I believe that we would both accept Form's (1972) observation that "most studies have both universalistic and specific (in terms of local societies) generalizations. It is the moving back and forth to decide whether a generalization of theory is specific or universal which makes comparative sociology exciting."

Before turning to the question of emphases on differences or on similarities, I want to note one additional way in which a look at the activities of linguists can be instructive to us in deciding what comparative sociology is. For some time linguists have been able to identify universal attributes of languages; in the past they were less interested in relational statements and tended to discard as irrelevant those aspects of language behavior that could not easily be incorporated into their descriptions of languages as entities. This tendency, in turn, has reflected a characteristic emphasis on "competence," in contrast to "performance," in the work of the generative grammarians.[3]

Sociologists, on the other hand, have only occasionally attempted to identify characteristics that hold for all societies (see, e.g., the fairly general descriptions of sociological concepts like status and role that are found in introductory texts or the invocation of "universal" concepts like social differentiation) and have generally believed that the behavior they study is so complex that they can make only contingent, relational (probability) statements. This has not been an unprofitable posture for sociologists; much is known about social behavior in social structures. Sociologists have been reluctant, however, to claim knowledge of the laws underlying social behavior even though such laws must exist for social behavior, just as for any other behavior, in an ordered universe.

Recent work by linguists has shown an increasing interest in variable behavior; note the current discussion of "presuppositions." Recent work by sociologists has shown an increasing interest in the possibilities of discovering invariant behavior in social interaction; the work of some ethnomethodologists is one reflection of this trend. I submit that an increasingly sophisticated comparative sociology has been simultaneously both source and benefactor of this trend (these perspectives may converge in sociolinguistics; see Grimshaw, 1971a and 1972b).

A considerable proportion of past discussion about the special nature of comparative sociology has centered upon different interpretations of, and resolutions suggested for, "Galton's problem" (really Tylor's, but Tylor has not complained; in this volume see, especially, Elder, p. 123). This issue, focusing on differences versus similarities, has at least two critical facets. First, limited resources may necessitate a methodological choice: Should units studied be as similar as possible so that, in the natural experiment implied by comparative work, as many as possible of the diverse structural and other factors conditioning social behavior can be held constant? Or should the strategy of the "critical test" be invoked? (Both "tests" are, of course, necessary for "proof" in Mill's sense.) Andrejewski (1954: 4-5) provides a strong formulation of the latter point of view: "The connection between two or more phenomena can be proved not to be accidental only if it obtains when all other circumstances are different. For this reason, the more distant, unrelated and different are the societies under observation, the more instructive is their analysis." I will turn briefly to this point below; it clearly has implications for strategies related to distinguishing between those regularities in social behavior that are system-specific and those that are universal.

The second question also has implications for agreement as to what comparative sociology is all about. The question here is one of goals, however, and it has been nicely articulated by Scheuch. He argues that two versions of the comparative method can be distinguished, differing primarily "in the goal of comparisons (i.e., in what is shown to be different from what) and in the logic of accounting for the differences that are found" (1968: 197). In a first instance, the goal may be no more than to establish the different identities of the units being compared and the identification of those observed characteristics that are indicators of particular configurations of properties distinguishing those units (Scheuch, 1968: 197). In such a case, sheerly descriptive work might be included, and a comparison of literacy rates in several different societies might, along with other societal characteristics, be used to identify types of societies. (Later in this section I will discuss whether or not solely descriptive research constitutes comparative sociological research or, for that matter, sociology.) Scheuch (1968) cites Redfield's work as an example of this sort of activity (clearly a more sophisticated enterprise than the simple collection of descriptive indices): Redfield's search was simply for that set of attributes of different societies that characterized "folk," in contrast to "urban," societies.

I would argue that the creation of such typologies contributes to the task of a specifically comparative sociology in two ways. First, their very creation contributes to an ordering of the infinitely diverse varieties of social behavior mentioned above. Taxonomic activity is always a first step toward codification and interpretation. Second, most typologies are constructed around the variable presence of different societal attributes—for example, folk-urban, sacred-secular, status-contact, traditional-transitional-modern. I submit that the identification of such dimensions can contribute either directly or indirectly to the identification of universal characteristics or relationships to be found in all societies.[4]

Scheuch continues by remarking that collecting the same data under different conditions serves as an analogue to experiment. In such an instance:

"Experiments may be defined as the creation of different conditions that should lead to differences in the phenomena that are to be accounted for; in the comparative method, the differences in conditions are not created but selected and viewed as causative agents. Choosing different cultures (or nation-states) is an attempt to magnify the differences in conditions. . . . A main problem in this version of the comparative method results from the lack of control over the conditions of differential observations: it is difficult to establish whether it is merely the set of factors deemed relevant by the researcher that really accounts for the observed differences in the dependent variables" (1968: 197).

At first glance this seems no more than a restatement of the methodological position referred to above, that is, an invocation of notions of control in the context of a natural experiment. But something quite different is implied: The critical question is whether the units observed are themselves to be treated as entities (configurations) or whether their several characteristics are to be seen as constituting sets of constraints on social behavior. Table 1.1 shows Scheuch's attempt to apprehend the interaction of characterizations of units and purposes of research in comparative sociology (Scheuch credits Inkeles with inspiring this formulation). For Scheuch, identifying universals refers to discovering, in all cultures or societies, consistent empirical patterns (he uses the incest taboo as his example). In the text Scheuch (1968: 198) notes that research directed to testing the applicability of conceptual schemes (the example he suggests is Levy, 1952) would also be located in this cell. The simple identification of empirical universals implies no attempt to provide a theoretical argument (justification, explanation) for that regularity nor does it imply a perspective that seeks to distinguish such empirical regularities from system-specific rules.[5] The second entry in this column, distinguishing among societies (characterized above as typology construction), has already been discussed.

Most of the chapters in this volume represent either contributions that would be located in one of the two second-column cells in Scheuch's paradigm or attempts to provide adequate concepts, designs, or methods for such contributions. The authors variously seek (1) to demonstrate how conditions present in all units that might be investigated generate regularities in behavior common to all units (e.g., papers as disparate in focus as Form's analysis of the politics of distrust or Schwirian's on the interaction of ecological variables); (2) in Scheuch's terminology, to "specify time-space coordinates of propositions"

Table 1.1   Characterization of Unit of Analysis and Purpose of Comparison

	Treatment of "culture"	
Purpose of Comparison	"Culture" as an Entity and as Analytic Unit	"Culture" as a Set of Conditions for Units in Analysis
Show similarities	Identify universals	Demonstrate generality of propositions
Show differences	Distinguish among societies	Specify time-space coordinates of propositions

Source. Adapted from Erwin K. Scheuch, "The cross-cultural use of sample surveys: problems of comparability," in Stein Rokkan (Ed.), *Comparative Research Across Cultures and Nations,* The Hague: Mouton, 1968, p. 200.

(e.g., the chapters by Elder, Mehan, and Johnson and Cutright); (3) to provide suggested research designs, conceptual clarification, and the like which will permit other students to attack directly problems of generalization and/or specificity (since this volume is directed to methodological problems, most of the chapters address these issues in one way or another). It is precisely in the interaction implicit in this search for both generalization (universals) and specification that the task of comparative sociology is located.

Marsh (1967), whose interests lie solely in the second column of Scheuch's paradigm, offers a further specification. He has settled on a single dimension—the degree of social differentiation in cultures or societies—that he considers an adequate codifier for most comparative studies (he emphasizes, however, on pp. 42-43, the preliminary character of his work). While differences in amount or degree of social differentiation are then expected to explain much variation in social behavior, he nonetheless recognizes instances in which relationships among social variables will vary independently of this characteristic of social units. He suggests three possible reasons for such independence: (1) chance or sampling variations, (2) experimental artifacts, and (3) failure of the phenomena under study to correlate with degree of differentiation (Marsh, 1967: 40-41). He considers the last situation particularly critical for the comparative sociologist. It is rich in possibilities for identification of general propositions or specification of time-space coordinates for propositions, that is, the comparative activities mentioned in the second column of Scheuch's taxonomy (Marsh does not mention this specific possibility; I believe it follows from his argument).

Marsh claims that each criterion for codification of any comparative study can be expressed as a question with only two possible answers. Table 1.2 shows Marsh's assignment of labels to the codification categories generated by answers to three questions. He further notes that types of comparative studies other than those identified in his schema are not logically possible (Marsh, 1967: 42).

Thus far I have not directly addressed the matter of identifying units to be compared in comparative sociology (in addition to sources cited below, see Marsh, 1967: 11-15, and Przeworski and Teune, 1970). In part this omission is because I subscribe in spirit to the notion that we should "get on with doing comparative sociology" in the manner implied in a comment by Andreski (1965: 66):

"Comparisons (verbal or numerical) enter into all deduction, but *by common acceptance comparative method designates only comparisons which draw upon data from different societies.*[6] To be precise we should have to define what we mean by a society; but let us leave this problem for the moment and follow the vague current usage, as its vagueness does not matter for the purpose of the present argument." (emphasis added)

Table 1.2   Marsh's Codification Schema for Comparative Studies

Codification Category	Are societies compared similar or dissimilar in degree of differentiation?	Do phenomena to be explained vary among societies compared?	Do phenomena to be explained vary with, or independently of, degree of differentiation?
Replication	Similar	No	–
Universal generalization	Dissimilar	No	–
Contingency generalization	Dissimilar	Yes	Vary with differentiation
Specification	Similar Dissimilar[a]	Yes	Vary independently of differentiation

Source. From *Comparative Sociology: A Codification of Cross-Societal Analysis* by Robert M. Marsh, copyright, 1967 by Harcourt Brace Jovanovich Inc. and reproduced with their permission.

[a]For our purposes, it makes no difference in this category whether the societies compared are similar or dissimilar; the crucial factor is that in both cases the phenomena to be explained vary independently of differentiation.

In part, also, however, I am concerned that to raise the issue of what constitutes a meaningful unit for comparative analysis is to open the lid of a Pandora's box: to do so may frighten off potential comparativists by prematurely demanding answers to an extremely complex question. Nonetheless, a characterization of comparative sociology must say something about what is to be compared, if only to avoid the dangers of what Hyman (1964) has designated as pseudocomparative sociology (the result when one unit is investigated and compared with imagined results from some other, mentally constructed, unit).[7]

Some comparativists will accept a general characterization of comparative sociological research as including studies involving complex societies or segments of complex societies and specifying for inclusion *only* those instances in which data from two or more societies are compared.[8] Warwick and Osherson (1973), for example, "use the term 'comparative method' to refer to social scientific analyses involving observations in more than one social system, or in the same social system at more than one point in time." Unfortunately, the notion of social system is only slightly less vague than that of the more abstract "unit." Frey (1970: 178-179) notes that "cross-systemic" and "cross-social unit" are generic terms that subsume, at the least, the notions of cross-cultural and cross-national and suggests a distinction between these two more "specific" terms:

"Cross-cultural research essentially refers to research in social units that differ to some usually specified degree in shared patterns of behavior and orientation. A nasty problem in this connection is that of designating the *amount* of sharing and the specific *kinds* of behaviors and orientations that need to be examined in order to determine whether one is dealing with a single culture. Cross-national research, on the other hand, refers to research in social units of a given political level, regardless of the homogeneity, similarity, or difference in their cultures, although it is commonly.assumed that nations always differ culturally to some degree."

While Frey concludes that the specific topic under investigation will determine whether the emphasis will be on national or cultural comparisons and that in many instances the distinction is not problematic, there still exists a problem that becomes particularly salient if we agree that distinguishing between system-specific and universal rules is the central task of a comparative sociology.

Consider the problem of establishing system boundaries. Elder's study in this volume is clearly not cross-national (at least not in terms of separate nation-states). It could be argued with considerable cogency that this study is cross-cultural. However, while language and many social customs differ between North India and Tamilnad, it can also be argued more broadly that all of India shares in a single cultural "Great Tradition." The boundary problem is not easy to resolve. Can it be argued that northern and southern India are more similar than Seattle and Bristol (see Miller's chapter in this volume)? Than the many countries in Latin America (see Johnson and Cutright)? Than South Africa two hundred years ago and South Africa today (see Turk)? Clearly, the resolution depends on the topic under investigation. This problem can be nicely illustrated with another linguistic example. It might be suggested that the relevant system for linguistic analysis is the "homogeneous speech community."[9] But is this definition satisfactory? In the case of English, do we mean the "English-speaking community" of the world (with the directly implied inclusion, for example, of language systems as different as those of Great Britain, India, and Jamaica)? Do we mean American English? Do we mean American Standard? Do we mean that so-called black dialect (Black Vernacular English) constitutes a system? How do we handle regional and class dialects? Do we handle the case of Indian English by including only native speakers as members of the speech community? Obviously not, because the categorical (system-specific) rules of English hold for all competent English speakers, however exotic their dialects may be.[10] In the case of bilinguals, do we attempt to establish some quantitative measure of interference and simply state that if more than some specified amount of interference occurs, a speaker is not a member of a specified community, subject to the categorical rules of that community's system? Such a solution is unsatisfactory both because we have no adequate measures of this sort (this situation holds for biculturalism as well as bilingualism, of course) and because of the tautological dangers introduced (i.e., competent speakers do not break categorical rules; those who break categorical rules are not competent speakers).

It is equally clear that national boundaries cannot, in many cases, be used as social-system boundaries. Many nations include large numbers of specific social systems within their boundaries. Consider Elder's Indian case. He makes no specific argument that his two broad samples were drawn from separate social systems; he asserts only a cultural difference (p. 119). He might, however, see certain tribal groups as constituting social systems distinguishable from the larger Indian society. In the case of the United States there are native American societies that clearly do not, for example, share rules about silence, questioning behavior, or definitions of success with the dominant white majority. On the other hand, there are dangers in suggesting that each subculture constitutes a separate system, since it is always possible to find differences and we could well end up finding individual families or even dyads in the final "Chinese box"; families do indeed have special rules that they always follow and that are not followed by all other families. The boundary problem can become even more complicated when we consider that different researchers sometimes come to very different conclusions about the characteristics of the *same* society or social system.[11] While increasingly satisfactory discovery procedures for identifying the boundaries of meaningful social units are being developed (see Labov, 1972a), most scholars interested in comparative problems will continue to make decisions with reference to the problem under consideration—choosing nation-states (as Johnson and Cutright and Finsterbusch have done), subpopulations of nation-states (as Armer and Schnaiberg have done), factories in different countries (as Form has done), national subregions (as Elder has done), single nations over time (as Turk has done), speech communities in multilingual situations (as Mehan has done), or cities in different countries (as Miller and Schwirian have done)—as the logic of the particular research requires. In any event, resolution of this problem is not yet critical for comparative researchers; the differences being examined are still gross, and much work can be done without completely resolving the boundary problem.

Before discussing the ways in which comparative sociology differs from area studies, I must return to a question raised earlier: What is the status of primarily descriptive studies within a comparative framework? Scientists engage in three analytically separable kinds of activity: description, explanation, and replication. Although explanation (or, at minimum, prediction or forecasting; see Schuessler, 1968) is presumably the ultimate goal of the sociological enterprise, description and replication are equally critical—the former as a first step in theory construction (see note 5, above), the latter in testing the generality of description and explanatory statements.

The interaction of description and replication in creating theoretical frames that simultaneously identify and distinguish characteristics of social behavior that are either system-specific or common to men in all societies is complicated indeed. Part of the difficulty in determining whether description alone can be comparative results from the fact that there are different kinds (note that I do *not* say levels) of societal description. Two principal varieties are measurements of aggregated individual attributes (e.g., the percent literate mentioned above) and determination of the presence or absence of some societal characteristic (e.g., class as a manifestation of stratification, or bureaucracy of authority; see discussion above, p. 6). Description of the first variety assumes the distribution of individual societies—or the same society at different times—on continua (all societies fall within a range from 0 percent to 100 percent). Description of the second variety assumes that societies either will or will not have the attribute in question; this latter difference is that between variables and attributes.[1 2]

Replication and confirmation or disconfirmation, or empirical descriptions of these two sorts, have different consequences for the construction of a universal grammar of social behavior. This difference also holds for intrasystem replication, for replication within some sample of systems, and for replication across the universe of social units (see the discussion of Smelser immediately below). In the case of percent literate, there will always be a value, whether in the same society over time or in different societies. Only the magnitude of the measurement can change. A difference in magnitude within the same society implies either bad measurement originally or in the remeasurement—or unexplained social change. Across societies this difference implies nothing unless the measurement is set within some relational context (e.g., literacy is posited as a function of some other variable). If differences are found, either within or across societies, one must assume that the aggregated individual attribute under examination is related to other describable characteristics, and an explanatory effort is implied.

If, on the other hand, a societal attribute's presence is confirmed or disconfirmed within a society or across societies, the implications can be quite different. Within a society the appearance or disappearance of such a societal characteristic again is interpretable as reflecting either bad research or social change. Across societies, however, confirmation of presence can lead the researcher to attempt specification of a substantive or empirical social universal. If, on the contrary, an attribute of one society cannot be found in at least one other, the researcher is led rather to attempt specification of an intrasystemic categorical rule.

The situation with explanatory statements is more complicated but essentially analogous. Two principal kinds of explanatory statements directly parallel the two types of descriptions suggested above: (1) There are statements that say, "*a* is a function of *b*" or "*a* varies as *b* varies." (2) There are also statements that say, "*x* is present when *y* is present and not present when *y* is not." Confirmation or disconfirmation within a society has the same interpretation as that for replications with regard to strictly descriptive statements about variables and attributes: Confirmation does not mean much, while disconfirmation again implies bad research or social change. In the case of relational statements tested across social units, confirmation implies movement toward the possible identification of a substantive universal. Failure to confirm should direct the researcher to search for the specification of additional constraints on the relationship that operate differently in the different societies; his eventual goal should be to engage in multifactorial analyses. In the case of the concomitant presence or absence of paired attributes, confirmation again suggests the possibility of universals, while disconfirmation suggests that the original finding may possibly be interpreted as a system-specific, categorical rule.

Smelser (1966, 1967) suggests three dimensions for a typology of comparative analysis: (1) the types of dependent variables, (2) the number of units to be compared, and (3) static or dynamic analysis. There are four "levels" of dependent variable: (1) aggregated attributes (used in the same way as in my discussion immediately above), (2) behavioral precipitates (rates of behavior such as voting or crime), (3) patterned social interaction (roles or social structure; Smelser uses the term "relational" but with a different meaning from mine), and (4) cultural patterns (e.g., values and the like). In ascending order these levels are less amenable to treatment as parameters and increasingly problematic for interpretation. Finally, the number of units interacts with the mode of analysis in a manner such that Smelser, to a greater extent than many comparativists, considers designs comparing a single unit over time to be critically important.

Smelser presents a chart (Table 1.3) that is helpful both in illustrating his paradigm and in drawing together several themes from the discussion above. When these elements are juxtaposed in this way, it can be seen that Smelser admits several different kinds of studies to comparative status. Careful study will reveal, however, that each of the studies cited as an illustration is directed toward the purposes delineated in the second column of Scheuch's paradigm (Table 1.1 above), that is, demonstration of the generality of propositions and/or specification of time-space coordinates of propositions. Thus we come full circle!

The particular importance of comparative social research is that it permits the discovery of possible universals, the specification of which empirical regularities are system-specific, the reassignment of rules not only as intrasystemic or extrasystemic but within those categories (e.g., substantive universals can become metatheoretical; categorical rules can become semicategorical or variable rules), and, finally, the reexamination of concepts and methodologies that is

Table 1.3 Levels of Comparative Analysis

	Same Social Unit		Different Social Unit	
	Static	Dynamic	Static	Dynamic
Aggregated population attributes	What factors account for the different composition of the American labor force in 1870 and 1950?[a]	What institutional conditions underlie the steady population decline of rural Ireland?[b]	What factors account for the different shape of the age pyramids of the populations of India and the United States?[c]	What conditions account for the peculiar course of the "demographic transition" in Holland, as compared with most other Western countries?[d]
Behavioral precipitates	Why has the rate of church attendance been higher in mid-twentieth century America than in mid-nineteenth century America?[e]	Why has the American divorce rate shown a steady upward climb, with peaks around wartime periods, during the past century?[f]	Why are divorce rates lower in Australia than in the United States?[g]	What conditions account for the different rates of economic recovery of the United States after the Civil War, Russia after World War 1, and Germany and Japan after World War II?[h]
Social structure	Why is the nuclear family stronger in Israeli collective settlements than it was a generation ago?[i]	By what processes did the British family become a more specialized social unit during the years of the Industrial Revolution?[j]	What are the conditions underlying unilateral cross-cousin marriage?[k]	Why did technological innovation proceed at a more rapid pace in the United States than in Great Britain during the nineteenth century?[l]

Cultural patterns "other"	Why have American values become more "other-directed" and less "inner-directed"?[m]	By what processes does a communitarian social experiment become secularized?[n]	What are the social conditions underlying the rise of extremist, totalitarian social movements?[o]	By what processes are revolutionary ideologies routinized after successful revolutionary overthrows?[p]

Source. Adapted from Smelser (1973). Used by permission of author and of Prentice-Hall, Inc.

[a]Philip M. Hauser. "Labor Force." In *Handbook of Modern Sociology.* Robert E. L. Faris, Ed. (Chicago: Rand McNally, 1964), pp. 167-72.

[b]Conrad M. Arensberg and Solon T. Kimball. *Family and Community in Ireland* (Cambridge, Mass.: Harvard University Press, 1954). Chap. 6.

[c]Kingsley Davis. *The Population of India and Pakistan* (Princeton, N.J.: Princeton University Press, 1951).

[d]William Peterson. "The Demographic Transition in Holland." *American Sociological Review,* 25 (1960): 334-47.

[e]Seymour M. Lipset. *The First New Nation* (New York: Basic Books, 1963).

[f]P. H. Jacobson. *American Marriage and Divorce* (New York: Rinehart, 1959).

[g]Lincoln H. Day. "Patterns of Divorce in Australia and the United States." *American Sociological Review,* 29 (October 1964): 509-522.

[h]Jack Hirshleifer. *Disaster and Recovery: A Historical Survey* (Santa Monica, Calif.: Rand Corporation, 1963).

[i]Melford E. Spiro. *Children of the Kibbutz* (Cambridge, Mass.: Harvard University Press, 1958).

[j]Neil J. Smelser. *Social Change in the Industrial Revolution* (Chicago: University of Chicago Press, 1959). Chaps. 8-10.

[k]George C. Homans and David M. Schneider. *Marriage, Authority, and Final Causes: A Study of Unilateral Cross-Cousin Marriage* (Glencoe, Ill.: Free Press, 1957).

[l]H. J. Habbakuk. *American and British Technology in the Nineteenth Century: The Search for Labour-Saving Inventions* (Cambridge: Cambridge University Press, 1962).

[m]David Riesman, Nathan Glazer, and Reuel Denney. *The Lonely Crowd* (New York: Doubleday, 1953).

[n]Charles Nordhoff. *The Communistic Societies of the United States* (New York: Harper and Bros., 1875).

[o]William Kornhauser. *The Politics of Mass Society* (Glencoe, Ill.: Free Press, 1959).

[p]Crane Brinton. *The Anatomy of Revolution* (New York: Vintage, 1958). Chaps. 7-9.

mandated by the discovery of exceptions. To note only one example: Form's early work (pp. 84, ff.) led him to a bargaining model of social research. This model worked well enough for some of his analyses in this country. Identifying the broader notion of political distrust in the research situation (a concept that may very well prove to be a universal of some sort) became imperative only when he tried to stretch the bargaining model to fit situations for which it was not adequate.

In sum, then, comparative sociology is not fundamentally different from other sociologies in either its goals or its methods. All sociological research involves description, explanation, and, through replication, confirmation or disconfirmation. Comparative sociology involves attempts to explain similarities or differences in social behavior through references to differences in structured social relationships and the testing of limits on generalizations of propositions derived through research in different societies. The purpose of such work is the movement from contingent propositions of the "When a and b and c, then, if x, then y" variety to propositions that state "If and whenever x, then y"; or determination that the latter type of statement can be made only for specific societies. (Austin Turk, 1972, cautions that we are not so much "moving away" from contingent propositions as coming to understand the contingencies "in terms of more general concepts and variables instead of system-specific ones." He continues by observing that "our a, b, c conditionals are of a different order, not abandoned or eliminated.") This shift will be possible, ultimately, only through transsocietal replication.[13]

In What Ways Different from Area Sociology?

For an interesting comment on the differences between comparative and area sociology, see Przeworski and Teune (1970: x-xi). Some scholars argue that research in a society other than one's own is by its very nature comparative. From a methodological point of view there is much to such an argument. It is frequently stated that comparative sociology is no different from one-country sociology other than in that methodological problems are sharply exacerbated and, in the case of language, possibly of a magnitude sufficiently greater to warrant acceptance of a claim of qualitative difference. In the case of one-country area sociology, particularly in the non-English-speaking nations, the methodological problems *can* be identical. Given the definition I have essayed above, however, I would claim that area sociology and comparative sociology are not the same on the grounds that *studies in which a country is the unit of study cannot forward the search for distinctions between system-specific and universal regularities in social behavior.*[14] The counterargument that a number of single-country studies can do so is meaningless, since the net outcome in such an instance meets comparative requirements. In stating that area and comparative sociology are different, I do not mean to suggest that there are not substantial benefits to be garnered from country-specific sociology. Holt (1971: 143) has clearly stated the conditions for good area research:

"In working toward a general science of society, comparative studies are absolutely essential. But they must include analyses of great detail to provide for the proper elaboration of the internal structure of theory, and they must be alert to the fact that boundary events and related mechanisms must be adequately conceptualized and researched."

It is necessary, however, to remind ourselves continually of the differences between the two perspectives and of the consequences resulting from these differences.

In defining comparative sociology I drew heavily on analogies with linguistics; in distinguishing comparative from area sociology, I will invoke another analogy, that between clinical and statistical prediction in psychology (Meehl, 1954). Directing his attention to psychological issues, Meehl defines the clinical enterprise as one in which an attempt is made to learn one case in such depth that, in a kind of *verstehende* operation, we find ourselves able to predict the behavior of the subject under study. Individuals are so complex, however, that the expectation is that the particular interaction of characteristics and attributes of individuals will seldom if ever be repeated in precisely the same manner in other individuals—a position that some historians and many other humanists find most congenial.[15]

In like manner, students of Bengali or Brazilian literary traditions are able to forecast with some accuracy new developments in those traditions in much the same manner that specialists on Kerala or Malaysian politics are able to understand the unique interactions of literacy, poverty, religion, and politics in those places. Such activities are interesting in their own right and ultimately can provide resources in a search for more general patterns in either literary or political behavior. Familiarity with developments in a single literature or on one political stage does not, however, provide the generalized understanding that would permit the scholar to anticipate developments of a literature in Vietnam or of a political movement in the Soviet Ukraine. (This assertion does not imply, of course, that there are no patterns in such developments wherever they occur. That there *are* patterns is the argument of the comparative scholar.)

Statistical prediction is based on analysis of the interaction of a relatively restricted number of variables or characteristics or attributes over a relatively large number of cases.[16] Similarly, the comparativist does not purport to be able to forecast social patterns in individual units but rather looks for possibilities of generalization about larger social processes. He is not concerned with the mechanics of bureaucracy in the particular case but rather with the interaction of variables such as autonomy, accountability, authority, and responsibility over larger numbers of cases. These and other variables will permit him to understand a great deal about bureaucracy and to make limited forecasts about the consequences of the interaction of these and other variables; they will not permit him to make specific statements about outcomes to be expected in bureaucratic behavior for which variables *not* included in the original analysis may have greater importance. (Sheldon Stryker, 1972a, comments "that critics of generalization make the generalization that there will *in fact* be variables of great import not included!") It is not possible to understand the structure and functioning of bureaucracy in India today without reference to the historical experience of the Indian Civil Service (just as contemporary law in South Africa cannot be understood without familiarity with earlier events in that country; see Turk, Chapter 10 below).

To reiterate, comparative and area sociology are both different and necessary. In brief, only through comparative studies is it possible to make propositional statements of an "if. . .then" character. However, only through intensive examination of individual cases is it possible to explain the failure in some instances of the "if. . .then" statements to hold true (see Holt, 1971). We are once again back to the linguistic analogue with its emphasis on system-specific and universal rules.

In What Ways Differently Beneficial?

Ten years ago I did research in India on the response of an Indian city (Poona) to the trauma of a major flood disaster. To a substantial extent my research was replicative in the sense described above; I wanted to know whether the kinds of generalizations and propositions developed from disaster studies in Western societies, particularly the United States, held as well for a society with quite markedly different social structural relationships (or so I thought as I left for India). I was particularly interested in learning whether patterns of convergence, the emergence of sets of latent decision-makers, and other social behavior reported for Western societies occurred in Poona. (One completed study on the disaster is Brahme and Gole, 1967.) At the same time, however, I was interested in attempting to identify the interaction of political preferences, awareness of current events, disaster experience, reported response to the disaster itself and to the government (which in some persons' minds was at least partly responsible for the disaster because the flood occurred when a nearly completed dam being constructed by the government collapsed), and other variables (or indicators of variables). This second set of activities presumably could be classified as explanatory in nature; to my knowledge no previous students had been interested in these interactions.

The following is not a review of my findings. Let me simply report that in the attempt to test limits on findings reported from studies done in Western settings,

I found that convergence behavior did occur but that there was no emergence of a latent power structure that took over either administrative responsibility or decision-making powers. The failure of such a structure to appear resulted from the distribution of resources between Government and the larger society in the Indian city studied. In brief, only the government in Poona had sufficient resources or managerial skills to engage in relief and rehabilitation on a large scale (Grimshaw, n.d.a).

I am more interested, for the purposes of this chapter, in the ways in which *comparative research can generate new research problems and new perspectives on sets of relationships within domestic settings that we come to take for granted.* I will be brief (I will discuss this example in fuller detail elsewhere). Like many other students of India, I had been very impressed with the central importance that the institutions of caste and family have in Indian society. I fully expected that victims of the flood in Poona would turn to these traditional networks for help. Yet it early became obvious that the Government had played a crucial, even critical, role in relief and rehabilitation (Brahme and Gole, 1967). I then decided to ask two questions: "In time of major personal or family difficulties, for example, sickness, retrenchment, and so forth, from whom do you have a moral right to expect assistance?" and "From whom would you actually expect help?" An attempt was made to emphasize the individual (i.e., family) character of the hypothetical problem; in the context there were doubtless some respondents who had the flood and its aftermath in mind when they answered.

I do not have the space to review the full findings here (Grimshaw, n.d.b); suffice it to say that in answer to the first question the largest single response category was not, as I had anticipated, family or caste but Government. Family followed; caste and other responses (including "God") were given by substantially smaller proportions of respondents. The difference between the moral right and the actual expectation was not in the rank ordering of potential sources; rather all declined in approximately equal proportions, and the proportion expecting help from no source increased markedly. This finding, like that of the nonoccurence of latent power structures, can be explained quite straightforwardly by examining the distribution of resources among responding groups. When class (as measured by income, occupation, education, and so on, and various combinations of these indicators) was held constant, it became obvious that poor people responded "Government" (this response seems to have reflected a perception of reality rather than ideology) and that the better-off respondents stated that family (or at least person-linked) sources should and could be expected to help.

And now the benefit from comparative work. It seemed to me that if resource distribution provided an explanation for this unexpected finding in a specific setting, this same factor might have equal explanatory powers in other settings. Hence, it might be worthwhile to try to determine what patterns of response would emerge in the United States. When I returned, I asked some experts on the American family what expectations might be reported in this country. Each of these experts suggested that American respondents would be far more likely to assert reliance on family; they also suggested that the "family" response would be most typical among middle-class respondents. Through the graciousness of a colleague I was able to ask questions with the *same intent* (as my Indian questions) of a sample of respondents in Indianapolis (a city no more or less typical of the United States than Poona is of India, I trust) and to compare their responses by class.[17] This study has not yet been completed, but preliminary analysis shows that government was infrequently mentioned. Family was often mentioned as were such sources as private insurance (not a factor in India) and (in greater proportions than in Poona) God and the church (in the Poona sample, only 17 out of 1015 respondents mentioned God as either owing them any obligation to help or as likely to help them in any event).

I find this an unusually interesting set of findings. In India, a society that has been characterized as sacred and traditional (albeit with some modernizing sectors), there is a modal response that seems, on first reading, to be characterizable as modern and secular. In the United States, a society that is clearly among the most modernized in the world and that is usually characterized as highly secular and rational, the responses could be characterized as traditional, if not sacred. I do not believe these findings should be interpreted to mean that individual Indians are less pious than citizens of this country. However, I do think we can infer that (at least in India and the United States) the structural arrangements affecting access to resources are more important than so-called cultural values in determining responses to questions like those I asked.[18] What we learn is that, in both societies, people with access to helping resources within personal networks are (1) less likely than those without to assign moral obligations to the government and (2) more likely to assign these obligations and to expect their fulfillment from person-linked sources.[19]

In this case we have an illustration of an instance in which comparative research has had, as an unanticipated by-product, the raising of some substantive theoretical questions about the organization of familial obligation structures; the answers to these questions suggest that there may be greater similarities within classes across societies than within societies across classes. The finding in itself is not terribly profound; what impresses me is that without the startling revelation of the Indian experience the question might not have been asked. More generally, the Poona research suggests three special benefits of comparative research: (1) confirmation of a pattern already found in other societies with concomitant movement toward the statement of a substantive universal (e.g., convergence patterns in the post-impact period); (2) the raising of questions about one's own society (e.g., what is the character and perception of familial obligation structures in an American city); and (3) movement toward the identification of a new, possibly metatheoretical, universal (e.g., the priority of class membership over cultural or societal membership in influencing expectations of support). The last of these may be a metatheoretical universal since an underlying explanation probably can be found in the structure of resource distributions.

In What Ways Differently Problematic: Some Problems of "Meaning"[20]

The chapters in this volume demonstrate that the sharpening of methodological acuity is another profitable by-product of comparative sociological work. Just as contrasts in social structures and associated social behavior may be more marked across than within societies, similarly, some general research problems that are always present appear in exacerbated form when researchers work across cultures and across societies. Indeed, some authors have suggested that this exacerbation constitutes the principal difference between comparative and other sociologies (e.g., see Holt and Turner, 1970: 6; Frey, 1970: 183- 184; compare, however, Scheuch, 1968: 176-179).

People who have worked in other societies have shown that there are some fundamental difficulties involved in doing good domestic research that go unnoticed until we have confronted them when they are obvious—namely, in comparative research. Readers will find evidence to support this observation in several of the chapters below. Scholars working across languages encounter particularly severe difficulties in achieving comparability. Indeed, I suggested above that these problems may be of sufficiently greater magnitude as to warrant the claim that on this methodological dimension comparative sociology may be qualitatively different. Some researchers have long been aware of the difficulty of working across languages (although the number who have paid explicit attention to the difficulties involved is only a miniscule proportion of all those who have worked across societies). Some researchers, particularly survey researchers, have claimed that they are aware of the problems and have resolved them (this claim does not hold for all survey researchers; see especially Scheuch, 1968; and Frey, 1970). Fewer people today than in the past judge the methodological problems of working across languages and interrogative systems as resolved; I see this fact as a direct consequence of learning from failures in comparative work. An additional benefit has been the growth of awareness that the same kinds of problems hold for work across subcultures and other groups *within* societies—including our own (Grimshaw, 1969a, 1969-1970, 1971a).

When I did field work in India a decade ago, I fielded a survey. The schedule was originally prepared in English, translated into Marathi (with modest corrections introduced through back-translation), and taken in Marathi. Answers were translated back into English—or at least those parts of answers that translators *decided* I needed for my research (another question that I would like to elaborate on sometime)—and coded from the English translation. Cards were punched in Bombay and repunched and cleaned in Bloomington. Analysis was done in Bloomington. I realized that each stage of this long process provided opportunities for the introduction of error. I failed to realize, however, the potential importance of a class of observations like the one I made during my first week in India but that did not register fully until several years later (after I had begun to scrutinize more carefully the effects of language differences on the research process). The particular observation was that it is very difficult (if not impossible) to say "Thank you" in Marathi.[21] My failure to read the significance of this linguistic-cultural cue was not a lapse due solely to ignorance of cultural norms but reveals also a general characteristic of much past comparative work: a failure to consider fully the sociolinguistic dimensions of working across groups, communities, or nations.

Each contributor to this volume has confronted the language problem at some level. In several instances a sociolinguistic dimension has been critical in the work reported. Elder, in his work in India, had to contend not only with the problem of semantic equivalence (see, e.g., pp. 127 ff. below, his discussion on the concept of "trust"; see also discussion of Elder, pp. 144 ff. below) but also with cultural values regarding the appropriateness of different codes (colloquial and formal) in spoken and in written language (for a richly detailed analysis of language and dialect diversity and its meaning, see Gumperz, 1971: sec. 1). Hazelrigg discusses the difficulties of trying to make the imprecise and multidimensioned theoretical concept of class meaningful for members of different societies with quite different lexical and semantic sets. Armer and Schnaiberg directly confront the now familiar problem of acquiescent response set. Mehan, in his specifically sociolinguistic study of communicative competence, identifies a number of problems, attending particularly to failures in cross-cultural interpretations of paralinguistic and kinesic cues. Each of these problems will be noted in the following discussion; readers will find details in the papers themselves.

Two sets of problems are related to the need to use language (speech) in social research. The first set has to do with what some people have been calling the "ethnography of interrogation":[22] the identification of, and taking into account of, rules for asking questions and interpreting answers within speech communities (see note 9, above). The second set of problems, more closely associated with traditional concerns of linguists, includes questions of lexical, syntactic (including paralinguistic), and phonological variation—and the semantic dimensions of that variation.[23] I should like to say something briefly about both of these sets of problems.

Special Talk

Social scientists must acquire much of their knowledge about the objects of their inquiries from listening to people talk and interpreting what people say (see Mehan, Chapter 11 below). This assertion holds, of course, for all people in all of their everyday activity. What is true of most people, however, is that the talking and listening they do is usually done with other members of their own speech communities, that is, with people who share with them sets of rules for that talking and that listening. *As* frequently as not, social scientists *engaged in research* must listen to people who are not from their own speech communities (a truth that holds within, as well as across, societies). *More* frequently than not, social scientists cannot be satisfied with everyday, casual talk or conversation but must elicit special talk. To a substantial extent, the talk is special simply because a stranger—the social scientist or his helper—is present (Gumperz, 1971: 172). The talk becomes even more special when questions are asked. Respondents may be requested to talk about things that are either taken for granted (and therefore not talked about) or private (and therefore not talked about) or incomprehensible, threatening, improper, forgotten, or unimportant (and therefore not talked about). My comments here are directed explicitly to the special talk that occurs in interrogative encounters and to the methodological problems that, while present in all uses of spoken language, are particularly critical in such encounters.

Among the many potential sources of misunderstanding in interrogative (or any other) speech transactions, two sociolinguistic factors are particularly important. These are (1) the history of relationships between persons or groups prior to the particular interaction in which communication is to be attempted and (2) the normative expectations about language that are held by speakers and listeners.

Past History. Either outright hostility or simply the absence of trust between parties in an encounter can prevent successful communication from taking place (for a convincing demonstration of this problem in communication between black children and their teachers, see Labov, 1972b). There need not be (but frequently are) sharp discrepancies of status or power among those interacting. Hostility or distrust among even those of equivalent formal status or power can cause substantial distortions. Thus, international encounters characterized by suspicion or dislike can occur between equals at the international bargaining table (whether those interacting are ex-colonials and citizens of new societies negotiating assistance pacts or representatives of great powers negotiating arms reduction treaties) as well as between haves and have-nots within societies.[24] Every interaction has some past history. The situation of the comparativist in a hostile or fearful society can be difficult indeed (see, e.g., the Form, Elder, and Portes chapters in this volume).

Normative Expectations. There are at least three kinds of normative expectations about talk that, if not shared, can make communication difficult. First, subcultures within societies and societies as wholes differentially evaluate the importance of speech skills and differentially value speech performance.[25] In our own society there are teachers who value "proper English" more than skilled metaphor and effective communication. In other societies politeness may be valued more than understanding or the transmission of information (note the so-called acquiescent bias; see Armer and Schnaiberg, Chapter 9 below, and relevant citations in Frey, 1970); apt expressiveness more than factual exchange; or silence more than speech (for a thought-provoking treatment of silence among the Apache, see Basso, 1970). Some people use words in play; others, primarily instrumentally.

Second, there are different norms, both within and across cultures and subcultures, about privacy and its violation. Middle-class strangers in India will casually ask foreigners their income in much the same way that we will ask seatmates in planes or bars, "What do you do?" These differences in what people are willing to tell about themselves can be quite revealing of important group values; yet they are seldom mapped either as indicators of salient status concerns or as potentially problematic in asking questions. At the same time, cultural values in one society may define certain facts as problematic, while in another these same facts are taken for granted. To follow a question on age with one on marital status can constitute an egregious social lapse in a society that defines as derelict parents whose children are not married at the proper age.[26]

Finally, and related to considerations of privacy, there are norms about proper ways of getting information. In the "survey culture" of white America, there are few questions that cannot be asked directly (although there are some). In other societies, however, direct questioning in many matters is simply not tolerated among unrelated adults (see Grimshaw, 1969a, for references). Moreover, even when direct questioning is considered legitimate, there will always be respondents who cannot be expected to have information on certain items or who, even if they have it, are not willing to talk about it. Thus, questions about requirements for the roles of others or, more generally, hypothetical questions about unlikely events ("What would you do if you were the leader of your country?") may simply be meaningless.

In general, comparative researchers have attended neither to the realities of differentiated speech systems nor to the necessity of developing theories for the adequate and correct interpretation of utterances. Such a theory would be concerned, minimally, with identifying social norms for the maintenance of interpersonal boundaries in discourse—defining the proper initiation, carrying-on, and termination of interrogative encounters. What are the rules for initiating interaction with strangers? What linguistic or other violations disrupt interaction once initiated? In our society interaction may be disrupted if an interlocutor demands explicitness when shared meanings should be assumed (Garfinkel, 1967)—or offers it when it implies that the other person lacks the wit to understand. This description may hold for other societies as well, but we are a very long way from being able to formulate a general theory of universal rules for obtaining information.

Variations Within Language Itself

Social scientists engaged in comparative work have not resolved the research issues implied by acknowledgment of different histories of intergroup relations and different norms about speech and its use; nevertheless, at least the kinds of problems just discussed are familiar to sociologists. Problems of intended meaning and of understanding resulting from linguistic variation have also been recognized by at least some sociologists, but the full implications of these problems, frequently seen as arcane and inaccessible, have been even less comprehended and systematized. I want now to suggest some linguistic dimensions of the language problem. I will conclude by asserting that they are not as inaccessible to understanding by nonlinguist social scientists as some of us have sometimes thought.[27]

The Lexical Dimension. The most obvious semantic differences associated directly with language itself (and those most familiar to sociologists) are of lexical variation: the need to search for words that, at a particular point in time, mean the same or very similar things in different languages or in different subcultures. The lexical dimension of semantic variation, particularly across languages, has been attacked primarily along three lines: use of the semantic differential, back-translation, and componential analysis.[28] Each of these techniques has been useful; each has its shortcomings. Unfortunately, researchers too frequently neglect the facts: (1) Even within a single speech community there can be quite different meanings for the same word (not just in the sense of homonyms but also in the sense of different interpretations of the "same" semantic intent). (2) Meanings alter over time (even within the span of a single interaction). (3) Meanings for the "same" word vary across subcultural groups. (4) Meanings change as a result of shifts in topic or setting in interaction involving only members of the same subgroups. Moreover, there are words whose cognitive referents may be quite constant over time but whose expressive meaning may change quite sharply (Grimshaw, 1969-1970). The problem can be severe within a single language; it is manifestly compounded when more than one language is involved.

The Syntactic Dimension. For many years linguists themselves seemed reluctant to confront directly the question of semantic consequences resulting from syntactic organization. In the last 15 years, in substantial part because of the "Chomskyan revolution,"[29] increasing attention has been directed to semantic issues in syntax. Much of this discussion has been directed specifically to the question of whether or not transformations "preserve" meaning (Partee, 1971). The implications of this controversy for social scientists who must use talk for data are as yet only vaguely adumbrated, but there are at least three semantic issues in syntax that we can ignore only at very considerable risk.

An increasingly familiar example of the first of these problems can be identified in the syntactic differences between Black Vernacular English and Standard English (American variety) within our own society. Utterances such as "He go downtown," "He father," "He be busy," or "He busy" sound alien to most white, middle-class Americans. More important, there is a semantic difference between the last two phrases (immediate present as contrasted to continuous present) that is unknown to most whites and could in some circumstances engender critical misunderstandings. Since all living languages are continually changing, there is every reason to believe that similar differences occur in every situation characterized by divergences between standard speech and dialect. Since comparative researchers very frequently use standard speakers to interview dialect speakers (see Elder, Chapter 4 below), it is highly probable that we are continuously introducing interpretive errors of *unknown dimensions.* The problem is further exacerbated when interviews are done in a dialect but transcribed in a standard.

Paralanguage includes, among other items, phenomena such as intonation (raising and lowering of the voice), loudness, rhythm, and sequencing. Another syntactic-semantic problem arises from the fact that it is possible for phrases to be structurally identical (i.e., to have the same words in the same order) but simultaneously to represent different syntactic organization and substantial semantic variation. Paralinguistic variation, which follows a set of transformational rules (as yet unwritten), is syntactic and is lost in all casual, and even most careful, transcriptions (although frequently preserved as critical in fictional accounts)—a fact easily verified by comparing transcripts and audio- or videotapes of the same communicative encounter. For confirmation of the importance of this usually neglected variable without reference to mechanical reproductions, one need only remind oneself of the variety of ways in Standard English in which military personnel can say "Yes, sir," or spouses, "Yes, dear" (see Grimshaw, 1969-1970). Similar variation occurs in other languages.[30]

Phonological Variation. An increasing number of sociologists are becoming familiar with the possibilities of using phonological variation as speech data (see, among others, references to Labov and to Crockett and Levine in Grimshaw, 1969b, 1972d); even the "man in the street" is quick to identify—and usually to scorn as affectation—a speech pattern that seems discongruent with other known attributes of a speaker. Differences in meaning are both consciously and unconsciously conveyed by differences in pronunciation. Patterned differences in phonological production that are associated with different regional or class dialects can be either intentional or unintentional. Put simply, listeners who control a language (usually, but not always, native speakers) sort speakers, in part, according to pronunciation; speakers are sorted by region, class, and even ideology.[31] "Social ranking" factors, which operate in each of the three kinds of sorting, can substantially influence listeners' interpretations of intended and unintended meanings. To my knowledge, no scholars have as yet systematically investigated this phonologically based semantic variation.

Kinesics and Proxemics. Kinesics (defined as the body motion aspects of human behavior) and proxemics (which has to do with the spatial contextualization of communication, among other things; see especially, Hall, 1963, 1966) have not yet been sufficiently formalized to permit their incorporation into syntactic or semantic structures. There is, in fact, some doubt that they will be.[32] Yet, just as the tone of an utterance can contradict its "surface" content, we all know what is meant when someone states that another did not *look* as if he meant what he said (see Hymes, 1967, on "Key"). We know also, at least in American culture, that a look of great interest directed to an interlocutor *can* be intended for the amusement of an audience. Furthermore, gestural modes of assent and negation, greeting, contempt, beckoning, politesse, and so on vary across cultures—in brief, that one man's yes is another's no, that one culture's "Come here" is another's "Go away" (LaBarre, 1964, remains the most comprehensive review of materials on this topic; Mehan, Chapter 11 below, provides rich empirical documentation). Comparative researchers should be aware that failure to take these behaviors into account may totally vitiate the interpretation of talk in interrogative encounters, particularly between cultural strangers.

Some Additional Questions and Some Reasons for Optimism

This last section presents a truncated outline of some of the principal sociolinguistic dimensions of the problem of meaning in interrogative encounters and, more generally, in cross-language and cross-code communicative encounters. I want to emphasize the problematic character of language. The language problem is not always of the same magnitude; moreover, even the most difficult questions may become tractable once they are recognized. Austin Turk (1972), who read an earlier version of this chapter, raised some very important questions:

"After making what I think is a solid case for social structure (e.g., resource availability and control) as more fundamental a shaper of behavior than is culture (values and all that), you then go on to emphasize language as data and communication in interviewing as very nearly *the* crucial methodological problem area for comparative researchers. Query: What factors produce variation in the *seriousness* of the language problem? What kinds of research problems, research objectives, target populations, etc.? For instance, perhaps high-status, powerful, relatively cosmopolitan authorities and influentials in more modern (complexly and formally organized, developing but past "bush" and "isolation") polities are found to operate with an analytical. . . framework quite similar to that of the inquiring scientist. It seems to me that the language problems identified in research on disadvantaged, primitive, dominated, parochial, etc., populations *may* not be as great—or not the same, anyhow—for advantaged, educated, dominant, cosmopolitan, etc., populations. Another point might be that the language problems stuff has been generated in large part out of work with relatively naïve (complex, abstract, remote concerns, not salient) rather than sophisticated (in this sense) people. Still another point may be that language problems are more crucial in research on relatively unique aspects of culture and social organization, as distinguished from research on more fundamental and obvious (to authorities) and maybe universal social relational facts of life (such) as political control, coordination of economic investment, etc. (This point is probably more significant where we are dealing with more modernized polities.)"

Satisfactory answers to all Turk's questions will not be possible until much more research has been completed (much of it has not even been started); a review of what is already known would extend this short section into a monograph. The following comments should be viewed as only a preliminary outline for a fuller answer.

Turk's first question is misleading in one sense and incomplete in another. It is misleading in that it poses a contradiction between a social structural explanatory perspective for an understanding of human social behavior and the identification of language as a critical methodological problem. Clearly, there is a difference between explanation of events and factors influencing the collection of data needed to construct that explanation. Moreover, while all data and their collection and analysis are in some way affected by the problematic character of language, there are, as Turk himself suggests, numerous factors that affect the differential *seriousness* of the language problem. There are, as the papers by Johnson and Cutright, by Schwirian, and by Finsterbusch demonstrate, analyses which strongly support social-structurally based interpretations but which to a significantly lesser extent than other research (e.g., much survey research) are directly and continuously affected by language problems. To single out a particular methodological problem as critical implies neither support for nor retreat from any given theoretical perspective.

Turk's question is incomplete in that it hints at, but does not explore, the richness of the interpenetration of social structure and social interaction, on the one hand, and of language and speech behavior, on the other. There are four perspectives on the causal relationship between social structure and language (Grimshaw, 1969b), the most persuasive of which sees speech (language) and other social behavior (and social structure more generally) as co-occurring and codetermining. According to this view there is a fundamental embedding of the two structures and the two sets of behaviors, and the two structures are so inextricably interrelated as to require integrated study as one phenomenon (Grimshaw, 1969b). If this view is held, it will be seen that (1) control over language and variation in speech reflect location in the social structure (meaning, among other things, that factors like status and modernity affect the range of contexts within which persons can communicate effectively) and (2) simultaneously and obviously, language skills are themselves an important resource, differently distributed according to social structural regularities.

Turk is right, of course, in his supposition that the seriousness of the language problem varies with the population under study and with the topic being investigated. There is, as Useem and associates (1963) have shown, for example, a "Third Culture" community of scientists and other specialists who seem to communicate effectively in a variety of interactional contexts. As Portes observes in his paper and as most comparativists know from their own experience, there are in almost every country some people who understand a researcher's purpose. Moreover, as Form (1972) has observed and as Schwirian demonstrates in his paper, questions about ecology (and by extension, numerous other areas, e.g., in science and engineering) are easy (or easier) to translate. The language problem doubtless is more serious in work with Elder's *sādhāran lōg* ("everyday people") and Mehan's teachers and school children than with factory managers (at least some factory managers) or community influentials (at least some community influentials). Even with such groups as the latter, however, the investigator would be foolish to forget that there are different rules for talking generally and for questioning more specifically—in every society and in subgroups within societies.

I myself have noted a number of problematic aspects in working across languages and communication codes; Turk has suggested additional facets of the general communicative problem. Nonetheless, I do not believe we need despair. As I have said, as sociologists we know how to work on the sociolinguistic aspects of the communication problem, and even the more purely linguistic dimensions of the problem are not inaccessible to understanding. I have three reasons for my confidence.

First, it seems to me that (after many years of neglect, avoidance, and even occasional denial of the problem) increasing numbers of our colleagues (in sociology and in other disciplines) are now preparing themselves for direct confrontation with the issues outlined, while only a rapidly diminishing rear guard continues to insist either that there is no problem or that it has already been resolved. While Mehan most directly confronts the problem of communicative competence in his paper, many of the contributors to this volume have explicitly acknowledged language problems (e.g., Armer and Schnaiberg, Elder, and Hazelrigg, among others), and the discussions reported have also turned often to language-related issues. Here, as elsewhere, problem recognition (and definition) is the first step toward problem resolution.

Second, while I have emphasized the lack of systematic investigation in the past, I am confident that, once initiated, research will reveal that social behavior in this area, like that in every other area we have investigated, is not random but patterned and consistent (for demonstrations of this patternedness, see Gumperz and Hymes, 1972; and Bauman and Sherzer, forthcoming). We will have to learn how to find the patterns, but we are not going to uncover unordered congeries of idiosyncratic behavioral variation.

Finally, I believe that some useful models are already available to us. I am not so naive as to expect that the findings or methods of colleagues in other disciplines can be incorporated without revision into our own. But my own work on universals (1972b), my reading of work in the various hyphenated "ethno" fields (medicine, botany, possibly methodology), the work on micro-interaction of scholars like Goffman (see references in Grimshaw, 1972a), the rich and growing corpus of sociolinguistic research—all encourage me to believe that the problems I have outlined are tractable. The successes reported in the chapters below give me further assurance. Frey's comment at the end of his excellent discussion of comparative survey research (1970: 294) can serve as an envoi for this chapter:

"Although this long essay has necessarily focused on all kinds of difficulties and problems, they should be taken in perspective: I would simply repeat that none of these is distinctive in cross-cultural research. On the contrary, cross-cultural research already has its modest success stories, established by careful scientists who overcame the difficulties. Fascinating international regularities in occupational prestige structures, the patterning of attitudes toward population control, national stereotypes, the impact of the mass media, structure of connotational meaning, political socialization, and the distribution of achievement aspirations have already been glimpsed. The problems discussed have their solutions, and the theoretical promise of cross-cultural . . . research to . . . [the] social sciences is truly exciting."

Notes

1. Among the numerous discussions of comparative social research in the literature I have found treatments by Andrejewski (1954), Andreski (1964), Bell (1971), Bendix (1963, 1969), Frey (1970), Haas (1971), Holt (1971), Holt and Turner (1970), Hyman (1964, 1967), Jacob (1971), Lambert (1964), Marsh (1967), Murdock (1949), Nadel (1953, 1957), Przeworski and Teune (1970), Riggs (1970, 1971),

Rokkan (1966, 1968), Scheuch (1968), Schapera (1953), Singer (1953), Smelser (1966, 1967), and Warwick and Osherson (1973) to be particularly stimulating and suggestive or provocative. I have also drawn heavily on my own earlier papers. I have benefited substantially from written comments on drafts of this paper by Michael Armer, Reinhard Bendix, Phillips Cutright, William Form, Lawrence Hazelrigg, Richard Lambert, Alejandro Portes, Karl Schuessler, Neil Smelser, Sheldon Stryker, Richard Tomasson, Austin Turk, John Useem, and John Walton. I have talked with many people about problems in comparative research; in acknowledging special debts to Michael Armer, Reinhard Bendix, Aaron Cicourel, John Gumperz, Herbert Hyman, Dell Hymes, Richard Lambert, Austin Turk, John Useem, and Fred Waisanen, I do not intend to slight others. None of those I have read or listened to can be blamed for my stubbornness and/or obtuseness.

Several readers have commented that this chapter puts an undue emphasis on survey methods in comparative research. I think their complaint is warranted in some measure. I also believe that the principles discussed in the section on defining comparative research hold for historical studies or research using aggregated data or intensive social ethnography as well as for surveys and that language problems will be met and must be confronted in *all* comparative research.

2. Sherzer (1972) asserts that the very identification of categoricals sometimes leads to their intentional violation in contrived ways (such as "experimental" violations of commonly shared understandings, in Garfinkel, 1967). It would be more precise to say that "categorical rules are not *naturally* violated." For discussion of categorical and semicategorical rules and their violation, see Grimshaw (1972b) and references there.

3. Chomsky (1965) distinguishes between "competence" (all native speakers by definition are competent in the grammar of their language) and "performance" (the actual ways in which the grammar is enacted in speech, subject to socially influenced differentiation and other "grammatically irrelevant conditions"). Linguists have been interested in grammar, not in performance. It might be said that sociologists have been primarily interested in performance. Both disciplines are changing now, becoming interested in both aspects. William Labov first called my attention to this apparent convergence.

4. There have been numerous attempts to systematize societal taxonomies. For one recent example, see Riggs (1970); for a general review, see McKinney (1966). These attempts should not be interpreted as an indication that these taxonomies have been empirically validated, although they are useful "sensitizing concepts" in Merton's sense. Unfortunately, they have sometimes been treated as validated empirical categories.

5. I have distinguished elsewhere (Grimshaw, 1972b) between metatheoretical and empirical (or substantive) universals. Until such time as they are given theoretical interpretations, the latter are interesting, but not terribly useful, in constructing theories of human social behavior. For an interesting perspective on routes to universals and unified theory starting from area studies and comparative studies, see Haas (1971: 123-126).

I will argue below that primarily descriptive studies, however many analytic units may be involved, are unlikely to contribute directly to the building of theories on social behavior. Nevertheless, the very choice of what is to be described is informed by theoretical notions; and descriptions, by allowing similarities and differences to be observed, are necessary first steps in taxonomy construction and subsequent writing of propositions. See, among others, Greer (1969); Kuhn (1962); Stinchcombe (1968);

and in this volume, Turk (Chapter 10).

6. Compare Andreski's "common acceptance" with Portes's comment on an earlier draft of this paper:

    "There seems to be consensus among researchers that the label 'comparative' is applicable to single-setting studies, provided that they are not oriented to the 'ideographic' description of the area but to the testing of general propositions that have been found to have some merit elsewhere. Thus, a study of the impact of status inconsistency on political attitudes in Ecuador would rank as comparative. There is no pseudo-comparativism involved here since the referent is not imagined processes in another society but a general theory" (Portes, 1972; emphasis added).

7. Hyman (1964) would accept Portes's Ecuadorian example as comparative research as he would accept all cases in which information on one or more of the units compared was obtained from rigorous secondary analysis.

8. I should note numerous scholars' strong claim that simply including more than one unit of analysis in a study—whether that unit be a culture, a society, a nation, or whatever—is not a sufficient condition to warrant the label of comparative. Przeworski and Teune (1970: 36-37) present this argument in perhaps its strongest form:

    "Comparative research is inquiry in which more than one level of analysis is possible and the units of observation are identifiable by name at each of these levels. Thus a study of local leaders sampled from local communities in a single country is comparative, since research can proceed at both the individual and at the community levels. But if supranational regions are not identifiable, according to this definition a study conducted exclusively at the level of countries is not comparative."

    These authors subsequently elaborate their point by stating that "even if the levels of observation are multiple but the levels of analysis are not, such studies will not be considered as 'comparative' " (p. 50). An example of a noncomparative cross-national study would be, presumably, one in which individual attributes of respondents were obtained and descriptive statistics presented for national samples without any relational analysis being done. That is, simply to say that nation A has more literates than nation B is not comparative. Comparison occurs only when literacy is related across nations to some output variable (e.g., political activity).

    At first reading this definition would seem to imply that factor-analytic studies using aggregated indices for nations are not comparative. Most such studies combine nations into sets or clusters on the basis of factor scores and then compare correlations of characteristics of clusters and dependent variables (or indicators). If I correctly interpret Przeworski and Teune, they seem to be saying that the simple identification of factors is itself not comparative.

9. A speech community has been defined tentatively as one sharing rules for the conduct and interpretation of acts of speech (considered to include writing as well) and rules for the interpretation of at least one linguistic code (Hymes, 1967; Gumperz, 1968). On interpretive procedures, see Cicourel (1970). For one approach to the difficult boundary problem, see Labov (1972a). On regional boundaries, see Grimshaw (1967).

10. No competent English speaker, regardless of dialect, violates categorical rules on, say, copula deletion (or reduction) or on the reflexive; for example, competent English speakers do not say "I'm smarter than he's," or "Go wash you." See Grimshaw (1972b).

11. One striking illustration of such differences is Lewis's (1951) restudy of Tepoztlan,

discussed also in Redfield (1955). The two ethnographers came to sharply divergent conclusions about the character of life in the community: "contented and well-integrated" (Redfield) and pervaded by "fear, envy and distrust" (Lewis). Also striking are Fischer's and Goodenough's quite different findings on residence rules in Truk (both reported in Goodenough, 1956). Differences in the investigator's own world view as well as social change or simply defects in research design or conceptual specification can cause such discrepancies (see below, pp. 14 ff.).

12. Since it is possible to transform literacy from a proportional measure to a dichotomous attribute (some-none; high-low) and since authority may be bureaucratized to different degrees, the claim may be made that there is ultimately no difference between these kinds of descriptions. The kinds of measures implied are subjected to different analytical techniques, however, and whatever the defects of my particular examples, the distinction is analytically necessary.

13. I do not mean to imply that comparative analysis will provide a simple route to causal analysis (on "cause," see, among others, Schuessler, 1968). I have suggested elsewhere (1972b) that there are many other problems to be resolved before causal claims can be made (at least with any assurance). I do mean to imply, however, that claims about categorical (intrasystemic) and universal rules must be subjected to comparative replication.

14. Single-country, "area experts" in the social sciences are a diminishing breed as the advantages of a comparativist perspective have become increasingly clear in the disciplines themselves. See, among others, Lambert (1972).

15. Riggs (1970: 87) warns against this perspective:

"Reference ought to be made in passing to a fallacy that is, logically, the opposite of reductionism, although we seem to lack a word for it—perhaps *inductionism* would serve the purpose. Academically this is the conventional logic of area studies. It involves the conception that every system is unique, that we cannot understand any political system as an example of a more general rule, but must view it as a whole, as distinctively different from any other polity."

16. I should note, of course, the existence of techniques, like factor analysis, that undertake to comprehend the interaction of *large* numbers of variables (or indicators of variables) over large numbers of cases. On possible dangers resulting from the uncritical use of quantitative materials, see Holt (1971).

Given the N's involved in most comparative research, an analogy with controlled experiment may be more persuasive than that with statistics. What is critical is the notion of interaction among variables over more than one case.

17. When I was actually engaged in arranging to have the questions asked, I simply said, "I want to ask the same questions." I now realize that it is probably not possible to ask the "same questions"; I am increasingly skeptical as to whether the same intent or "meaning" can be conveyed. Armer (Chapter 2 below) elaborates on this problem.

18. Reinhard Bendix (1968) offers the following cautionary note: "Concerning the interclass differentials in active family solidarity as a field of comparative study I would ask: Is poverty always decisive or only when disasters make the demands for help unreasonably large?"

19. There has been independent, if indirect, confirmation of this finding for India (and for other societies as well; see Bott, 1957; Firth, 1957; Firth et al., 1970; and, more generally, Stryker, 1972b). Anthropologists have, in recent years, begun to question the assumption, long dominant in the literature on India, regarding the kinds of claims that can be made by family members and castemates upon each other;

increasingly researchers have questioned whether groups low in the social hierarchy have ever supported a mutual obligation system to the extent true of more highly ranked groups. (At least part of the explanation for this misunderstanding can be found in the fact that generations of visitors to India have learned about Indian society from asking questions of Indians most like them, namely, those middle-class Indians who have been most integrated into systems of kin and caste obligations.)

Just as anthropologists in India are beginning to raise questions about the strength of the extended family in quite traditional settings (see also Goode, 1963), researches on kin networks and obligations in the urbanized West are raising questions about commonly held assumptions regarding the *decline* in importance of the extended family there (Goode, 1963; Stryker, 1972b).

20. Since this book is on methodological problems in comparative sociological research, I have emphasized problems in the treatment following. I want to emphasize here, however, that language and speech materials are a tremendously important and underused data resource for sociologists (comparative and otherwise). I have touched upon this more positive facet of language and speech in several papers (1969a, 1969b, 1972a, 1972b, 1972c, 1972d), and there are illustrative citations in those papers. I also urge the reader to look closely at the Hymes papers cited in the bibliography, especially Hymes (1970), which is a more complete treatment of the topic under discussion in this section.

21. I did manage to elicit some highly Sanskritized circumlocutions that provoked friendly hilarity when I tried to use them. A friend's father (not a native Marathi speaker) "explained" to me that "Thank you" couldn't be said in Marathi because Maharashtrians were "boors." Subsequent inquiry has shown that many Indians think that "Americans are hypocritical because they're always saying 'Thank you.' " The contrast in cultural norms is clear (but productive of social misunderstanding); Marathi speakers take it for granted that common courtesies should simply be done and need no acknowledgment. To remark on such courtesies is to suggest surprise that your benefactor has behaved properly. Gratitude for really substantial services – for example, assistance in finding employment–is shown in other ways.

22. This term bothers some people because it evokes an image of policemen and suspects. It may be replaced by "ethnography of asking questions."

23. There are other problems of phenomenal identity and conceptual equivalence that occur in work across social, cultural, and political boundaries. In the case of counting *things*–for example, Indian "goods wagons" as contrasted to boxcars" in the United States–standardization through metric equivalents can be calculated (although metric equivalents may not reflect society-specific impact and evaluations). In the case of observing some nonverbal behaviors–for example, "deference" or "skill level" (as in manufacturing)–the researcher is sometimes confronted with problems quite similar to those involved in working with language. For example, see Form (1966).

24. Austin Turk comments (1972):

"I very much doubt that international negotiators are as much creatures of their personalized likes and dislikes; on the contrary, the skills of duplicity and of game theoretic thinking and ploys have long been emphasized in the training and use of such people. Moreover, there *is* a 'language of diplomacy'; and the collapse of negotiations, resort to war, etc., are not adequately explained by recourse to the language problem line of explanation. As we know, both sides in Paris clearly do understand each other!"

Turk is partly right. There certainly is a language—or at least a rhetoric—of diplomacy. It is true, moreover, that international negotiators are not "creatures of their personalized likes and dislikes"; indeed, personal likes and dislikes may be suppressed at the bargaining table (although notions of variable trustworthiness of opposite parties interact with beliefs about "ability to deliver," to affect negotiation decisions made with different representatives of "the other side"). It would be hard to deny, however, that *past* duplicity and deceit influence current readings of what the other side says. American Indian suspicion of white representatives of the Bureau of Indian Affairs *does* influence Indian interpretations of what is said in negotiations. There *are* dangers in an overoptimistic response to "mutual understandings" in negotiations between the United States and the Peoples' Republic of China or between India and Pakistan. I am not convinced that we know that "both sides in Paris clearly [did] understand one another." Overconfidence about such understandings has produced tragedies in familial as well as in international relations. Past misunderstanding is a critical contextual variable in current interaction.

25. It can hardly be said that talking is as important for middle-class white Americans as it is for some other groups in the American population or for members of other societies (see, for example, Albert, 1972; and Bauman and Sherzer, 1973). Skills in speech performance are clearly valued; shifts in speech codes are used as boundary-maintaining devices. I believe, however, that black Americans are far more interested in speech than white Americans, far more aware of subtle differentiations in speech skills, and far more likely to use speech both in maintaining group solidarity and boundaries as well as inter- and intragroup conflict (Abrahams, 1972). There appears to be more covert content in black speech as addressed to whites than vice versa; there also appear to be more subtleties (and rewards for skills) within the community itself. However, these appearances may be only that. We may simply be more conscious of concern about talk in other groups and thus more alert to specializations (and this alertness is another reminder of the reflexive values of comparative work).

26. The issue here is more general. We sometimes tend to consider questionnaire items as independent interrogative events and to see probes from the viewpoint of our own culture. This error can be just as serious as that made by linguists when they study individual sentences as if they appeared *in vacuo* in the real world. There are no speech events that are not context-bound (or, as the ethnomethodologists might say, there are no nonindexical expressions). The significance of environing questions varies from group to group, but contexts always constrain semantic interpretation.

27. Nor are the linguists themselves as sure on some issues as some outsiders think. Many students of social behavior, unfamiliar with the details of linguistic work, have accorded to linguistics the status of the most precise, rigorous, and scientific of the social-science disciplines. This reputation rests in part upon the fact that linguists, in contrast to some other social scientists, deal with a level of behavior that is simultaneously inaccessible to common-sense description and interpretation and so patterned as to invite rigorous logical and inductive analysis. Linguists have done little to disabuse their colleagues about possible errors in this stereotype and have not infrequently been admired as masters of an arcane art who are additionally blessed with polyglottal fluency. It is a shock, therefore, to discover that linguists often do not even agree on the meaning of commonly used terms, let alone on fundamental relationships, such as that between talk and meaning.

28. Grimshaw (1969a) has some representative references. For a more thorough look at semantic problems by an anthropologist, see Burling (1970); for a linguist's view, see Lyons (1969: 400-481).

29.   Lyons comments:

> "There are at least as many recognizably different 'schools' of linguistics throughout the world as there were before the 'Chomskyan revolution.' But the 'transformationalist,' or 'Chomskyan,' school is not just one among many. Right or wrong, Chomsky's theory of grammar is undoubtedly the most dynamic and influential; and no linguist who wishes to keep abreast of current developments in his subject can afford to ignore Chomsky's theoretical pronouncements. Every other 'school' of linguistics at the present time tends to define its position in relation to Chomsky's views on particular issues" (1970: 1-2).

Lyons provides a clear and readable introduction to "transformational grammar." Another good introductory treatment is Thomas (1965).

30.   Ibrahim (1972), discussing greetings in the desert among the Tamachaq, a subgroup of Tuareg, observes, "The *salaam* can be pronounced with various intonations – each a key (Hymes, 1967) expressing familiarity, haste, seriousness, or threat." In actual production register, rhythm, and speed vary as well as intonation.

Some Americans think that paralinguistic shifts change American English into a universal language; for example, they believe that if they shout in English, native speakers in any society should be able to understand them (if they do not, they are simply thought to be willful). I once worked with a sergeant in the military who was convinced that if he raised his voice and added an "a" at the end of each word, monolingual Italian or Spanish speakers could understand him ("IF-a YOU-a DON'T-a LISTEN-a . . .").

31.   A somewhat fuller review of phonological variation and its interpretation can be found in Grimshaw (1969-1970). For an introduction to language and dialect diversity in one setting (Hindi-speaking North India), see Gumperz (1971, Part 1). The importance of ideology can be seen in instances where language has become a political issue. See, among others, Haugen (1966) and citations on language and social conflict in Grimshaw (1969b, 1972d).

32.   Birdwhistell (1970: 8) is more optimistic. He writes:

> "While the human face alone is capable of making some 250,000 different expressions, I have fifteen placement symbols plus eleven special markers sufficient to record the significant positions of all the faces I have ever seen. Less than one hundred symbols are all that are required to deal with any kinesic subject which I have yet studied – and this recording covers the activity of the whole body in its through-time activity."

For further discussion, see Grimshaw (1969-1970).

References

Abrahams, Roger.
    1972   A true and exact survey of talking Black. Paper presented at the Conference on the Ethnography of Speaking, University of Texas, Austin (April). In Richard A. Bauman and Joel Sherzer (Eds.), *The Ethnography of Speaking.* Cambridge: Cambridge University Press. In press.

Albert, Ethel M.

1972   Culture patterning of speech in Burundi. In John J. Gumperz and Dell Hymes (Eds.), *Directions in Sociolinguistics: The Ethnography of Communication.* New York: Holt, Rinehart and Winston. Pp. 73-105.

Andrejewski, Stanislaw.

1954   *Military Organization and Society.* London: Routledge and Kegan Paul.

Andreski, Stanislav (Andrejewski, Stanislaw).

1964   *The Uses of Comparative Sociology.* Berkeley and Los Angeles: University of California Press.

Basso, Keith H.

1970   To give up on words: silence in Western Apache culture. *Southwestern Journal of Anthropology*, 26 (Autumn): 213-230.

Bauman, Richard A., and Joel Sherzer (Eds.).

        The Ethnography of Speaking. Cambridge: Cambridge University Press. In press.

Bell, Wendell.

1971   Comparative studies: a commentary. In Fred W. Riggs (Ed.), *International Studies: Present Status and Future Prospects.* Philadelphia: American Academy of Political and Social Science. Pp. 56-73.

Bendix, Reinhard.

1963   Concepts and generalizations in comparative sociological studies. *American Sociological Review,* 28 (August): 532-539.

1968   Personal communication.

1969   *Nation-Building and Citizenship: Studies of Our Changing Social Order.* Garden City, N.Y.: Doubleday. Originally published 1964.

Birdwhistell, Ray L.

1970   *Kinesics and Context: Essays on Body Motion Communication.* Philadelphia: University of Pennsylvania Press.

Bott, Elizabeth.

1957   *Family and Social Network.* London: Tavistock.

Brahme, Sulabha, and Prakash Gole.

    1967   *Deluge in Poona: Aftermath and Rehabilitation.* Bombay and New York: Asia.

Burling, Robbins.

    1970   *Man's Many Voices: Language in its Cultural Context.* New York: Holt, Rinehart and Winston.

Chomsky, Noam.

    1965   *Aspects of the Theory of Syntax.* Cambridge, Mass.: MIT Press.

Cicourel, Aaron V.

    1970   Basic and normative rules in the negotiation of status and role. In Hans P. Dreitzel (Ed.), *Recent Sociology No. 2: Patterns of Communicative Behavior.* New York: Macmillan. Pp. 4-95.

Firth, Raymond W. (Ed.).

    1957   *Two Studies of Kinship in London.* New York: Humanities Press.

Firth, Raymond W., Jane Hubert, and Anthony Forge.

    1970   *Families and Their Relatives: Kinship in a Middle-Class Sector of London.* New York: Humanities Press.

Form, William H.

    1966   A cross-cultural exploration of a crucial concept: skill level. Paper presented to Institute for Comparative Sociology Summer Seminar, Bloomington, Indiana (June).

    1972   Personal communication.

Frey, Fred W.

    1970   Cross-cultural survey research in political science. In Robert T. Holt and John E. Turner (Eds.), *The Methodology of Comparative Research.* New York: Free Press. Pp. 175-294.

Garfinkel, Harold.

    1967   Studies of the routine grounds of everyday activities. In *Studies in Ethnomethodology.* Englewood Cliffs, N.J.: Prentice-Hall. Pp. 35-75.

Goode, William.

    1963   *World Revolution and Family Patterns.* New York: Free Press.

Haugen, Einar.

1966   *Language Conflict and Language Planning: The Case of Modern Norwegian.* Cambridge, Mass.: Harvard University Press.

Holt, Robert T.

1971   Comparative studies look outward. In Fred W. Riggs (Ed.), *International Studies: Present Status and Future Prospects.* Philadelphia: American Academy of Political and Social Science. Pp. 134-143.

Holt, Robert T., and John E. Turner (Eds.).

1970   *The Methodology of Comparative Research.* New York: Free Press.

Hyman, Herbert H.

1964   Research design. In Robert E. Ward (Ed.), *Studying Politics Abroad: Field Research in the Developing Areas.* Boston: Little, Brown. Pp. 153-188.

1967   Instrumentation: phenomenal identity and conceptual equivalence. Two lectures given at the Summer Seminar of the Institute for Comparative Sociology, Indiana University, Bloomington (June).

Hymes, Dell.

1966   Two types of linguistic relativity (with examples from Amerindian ethnography). In William Bright (Ed.), *Sociolinguistics: Proceedings of the UCLA Sociolinguistics Conference, 1964.* The Hague: Mouton. Pp. 114-167.

1967   Models of the interaction of language and social setting. *Journal of Social Issues,* 23 (April): 8-28.

1970   Linguistic aspects of comparative political research. In Robert T. Holt and John E. Turner (Eds.), *The Methodology of Comparative Research.* New York: Free Press. Pp. 297-341.

1972a   Models of the interaction of language and social life. In John J. Gumperz and Dell Hymes (Eds.), *Directions in Sociolinguistics: The Ethnography of Communication.* New York: Holt, Rinehart and Winston. Pp. 35-71. (An elaboration and revision of 1967.)

1972b. Editorial introduction to *Language in Society. Language in Society,* 1 (April): 1-14.

Ibrahim, Ag Youssouf.

1972 Encounters in the desert: Tamachaq greetings. Tape recorded term paper, Indiana University.

International Studies of Values in Politics.

1971 *Values and the Active Community: A Cross-National Study of the Influence of Local Leadership.* New York: Free Press.

Jacob, Philip E.

1971 Values and public vitality: the political dynamics of community activeness. In International Studies of Values in Politics, *Values and the Active Community: A Cross-National Study of the Influence of Local Leadership.* New York: Free Press. Pp. 3-39.

Kuhn, Thomas S.

1962 *The Structure of Scientific Revolutions.* Chicago: University of Chicago Press.

La Barre, Weston.

1964 Paralinguistics, kinesics and cultural anthropology. In Thomas A. Sebeok et al. (Eds.). *Approaches to Semantics: Transactions of the Indiana University Conference on Paralinguistics and Kinesics.* The Hauge: Mouton. Pp. 191-220.

Labov, William.

1972a Where do grammars stop? Paper presented at the 23rd Annual Georgetown Roundtable on languages and linguistics, Washington, D.C. (March). Georgetown University Monograph Series on Languages and Linguistics. In press.

1972b Academic ignorance and black intelligence. *Atlantic,* 229 (June): 59-67.

Lambert, Richard D.

1964 Comment: comparativists and uniquists. In William T. De Bary and Ainslie T. Embree (Eds.), *Approaches to Asian Civilizations.* New York: Columbia University Press. Pp. 240-245.

1972 *Language and Area Studies Programs Review.* Draft report for Social Science Research Council. Xerox.

Levy, Marion J., Jr.

1952 *The Structure of Society.* Princeton, N.J.: Princeton University Press.

Lewis, Oscar.

1963 *Life in a Mexican Village: Tepoztlán Revisited.* Urbana, Ill.: University of Illinois Press. (Originally published 1951.)

Lyons, John.

1969 *Introduction to Theoretical Linguistics.* Cambridge: Cambridge University Press.

1970 *Noam Chomsky.* New York: Viking.

McKinney, John C.

1966 *Constructive Typology and Social Theory.* New York: Appleton-Century-Crofts.

Marsh, Robert M.

1967 *Comparative Sociology: A Codification of Cross-societal Analysis.* New York: Harcourt, Brace Jovanovich, Inc.

Meehl, Clifford.

1954 *Clinical vs. Statistical Prediction: A Theoretical Analysis and a Review of the Evidence.* Minneapolis: University of Minnesota Press.

Murdock, George P.

1949 *Social Structure.* New York: Macmillan.

Nadel, S.F.

1953 *The Foundations of Social Anthropology.* Glencoe, Ill.: Free Press.

1957 *The Theory of Social Structure.* Glencoe, Ill.: Free Press.

Partee, Barbara H.

1971 On the requirement that transformations preserve meaning. In Charles J. Fillmore and D. Terence Langendoen (Eds.), *Studies in Linguistic Semantics.* New York: Holt, Rinehart and Winston. Pp. 1-21.

Portes, Alejandro.

1972 Personal communication.

Przeworski, Adam, and Henry Teune.

1970 *The Logic of Comparative Inquiry.* New York: Wiley.

Redfield, Robert.

1955 *The Little Community: Viewpoints for the Study of a Human Whole.* Chicago: University of Chicago Press.

Riggs, Fred W.

1970 The Comparison of whole political systems. In Robert T. Holt and John E. Turner (Eds.), *The Methodology of Comparative Research.* New York: Free Press. Pp. 75-121.

Riggs, Fred W. (Ed.).

1971 *International Studies: Present Status and Future Prospects.* Philadelphia: American Academy of Political and Social Science.

Rokkan, Stein.

1966 Comparative cross-national research: the content of current efforts. In Richard L. Merritt and Stein Rokkan (Eds.), *Comparing Nations: The Use of Quantitative Data in Cross-National Research.* New Haven, Conn.: Yale University Press. Pp. 3-25.

Rokkan, Stein (Ed.).

1968 *Comparative Research Across Cultures and Nations.* The Hague: Mouton.

Scheuch, Erwin K.

1968 The cross-cultural use of sample surveys: problems of comparability. In Stein Rokkan (Ed.), *Comparative Research Across Cultures and Nations.* The Hague: Mouton. Pp. 176-209.

Schapera, I.

1953 Some comments on comparative method in social anthropology. *American Anthropologist,* 55 (August): 353-362.

Schuessler, Karl.

1968 Prediction. In *International Encyclopedia of the Social Sciences,* vol. XII. New York: Macmillan and Free Press. Pp. 418-425.

Scherzer, Joel.

1972 Personal conversation.

Singer, Milton B.

1953 Summary of comments and discussion. *American Anthropologist,* 55 (August): 362-366.

Smelser, Neil J.

    1966   The methodology of comparative analysis. Paper presented to the Summer Seminar of the Institute for Comparative Sociology, Indiana University (July).

    1967   Notes on the methodology of comparative analysis of economic activity. In *Transactions of the Sixth World Congress of Sociology,* vol. II. Louvain: International Sociological Association. Pp. 101-117.

    1973   The methodology of comparative analysis. In Donald P. Warwick and Samuel Osherson (Eds.), *Comparative Research Methods.* Englewood Cliffs, N.J.: Prentice Hall.

Stinchcombe, Arthur.

    1968   *Constructing Social Theories.* New York: Harcourt, Brace and World.

Stryker, Sheldon.

    1972a Personal communication.

    1972b The small group and industrialized society. Paper presented to Symposium on Comparative Analysis of Highly Industrialized Societies, Villa Serbelloni, Bellagio, Italy (August 1-7, 1971).

Teune, Henry.

    1971   The strategy of comparative inquiry: methods of assessment and analysis. In International Studies of Values in Politics, *Values and the Active Community: A Cross-National Study of the Influence of Local Leadership.* New York: Free Press. Pp. 40-64.

Thomas, Owen.

    1965   *Transformational Grammar and the Teaching of English.* New York: Holt, Rinehart and Winston.

Turk, Austin.

    1972   Personal communication.

Useem, John, and Allen D. Grimshaw.

    1966   Comparative sociology. *Items,* 20 (December): 46-51.

Useem, John, Ruth Useem, and John Donoghue.

1963   Men in the middle of the Third Culture: the roles of American and non-Western people in cross-cultural administration. *Human Organization,* 22 (Fall): 169-179.

Warwick, Donald P., and Samuel Osherson.

1973   Comparative analysis in the social sciences. In Donald P. Warwick and Samuel Osherson (Eds.), *Cross-Cultural Research Methods.* Englewood Cliffs, N.J.: Prentice-Hall. In press.

CHAPTER TWO

Methodological Problems and Possibilities in Comparative Research[1]

MICHAEL ARMER

Indiana University

Introduction

The chapters and discussions included in this report of the 1971 ICS Conference proceedings deal with an impressive range of methodological and substantive issues in comparative sociological research. It will be useful, therefore, to outline some of the most important methodological concerns as a backdrop against which the contributions in this volume can be viewed. The purpose of this chapter is to provide such a framework in order to give perspective to both the general topic of methodological problems in comparative sociology and the particular chapters and discussions that follow.

At the outset, I want to acknowledge the several good discussions of methodological problems in comparative research from which I have drawn ideas and illustrations.[2] These discussions vary in their selection and categorization of methodological issues, owing in part to the different purposes and different research interests and experiences of their writers. Those discussions, which are focused on specific problem areas, offer much more of the detail and complexity of methodological difficulties than is possible in a brief overview. I have footnoted such discussions where relevant.

Previous discussions of comparative methodology generally agree in their conceptions of (1) the field of comparative sociology and (2) the relationship of comparative methods with those employed in noncomparative research. In general, comparative sociology refers to studies of human behavior that involve comparisons of social-cultural phenomena in two or more societies. This conception approximates common usage as well as the definitions used in previous reviews and is compatible with Grimshaw's definition (preceding

49

chapter), which stresses the objectives, rather than the form, of comparative research. Testing the spatiotemporal limits of generalizations and identifying a universal grammar of social behavior requires studies that compare evidence across societies. Because the emphasis is on comparison across societies, terms such as "cross-cultural," "intersocietal," "cross-national," and "between-society" may be used as reasonable categories of comparative sociology.

There is also general agreement that the methods of comparative sociology do not differ in principle from those of other branches or fields of sociology. Comparative sociology follows the canons of scientific research, as do other areas of sociology, and it suffers from all of the methodological difficulties and handicaps that affect social research in general. There are, however, two obvious ways in which comparative research differs from most sociological research, and these differences frequently accentuate the methodological problems and force greater concern with all aspects of the research process. First, comparative research usually involves one or more cultures that are foreign to the investigator; second, it usually involves comparisons across different social-cultural systems. This chapter examines the varying consequences of these differences for the research process and concludes with some general observations on comparative research problems and prospects.

Appropriateness and Equivalence Within the Research Process

The first major difference is that the comparativist usually works within one or more cultures other than his own. In such settings the investigator cannot assume that the behavioral regularities, conceptions, language, social-cultural environments, and physical realities to which he is accustomed characterize the foreign cultures that provide the setting for his research. In fact, he can usually assume they are *not* the same and that his understanding of them is considerably inferior to that of his own culture. Of course, even within his own culture some variations will occur, but he is likely to be more familiar with these subcultural variations than with intercultural variations. As Grimshaw notes, one of the benefits of comparative research is that it sensitizes the larger discipline—and individual researchers—to analogous methodological problems and findings in single-society studies.

The primary methodological implication of foreign settings is that theoretical problems and concepts, strategies for gaining access and cooperation, sampling methods, measuring techniques and instruments, data-collection and analysis procedures, and other aspects of the research process that are appropriate for research in one's own culture will often *not* be appropriate and valid for research in foreign cultures. Indeed, it should be assumed that research methods will have to be adapted or newly devised for each culture. Thus, a major methodological problem facing comparative sociological research is the *appropriateness* of conceptualizations and research methods for each specific culture. Appropriateness requires feasibility, significance, and acceptability in each foreign culture as a necessary (but not sufficient) condition for insuring validity and successful completion of comparative studies.

In short, one important task of comparativists is to select theoretical problems, conceptual schemes, methodological strategies, and research techniques that are appropriate for specific foreign cultures. This task is shared with anthropologists, area specialists, and other researchers whose investigations typically involve foreign cultures. Indeed, it is these specialists who have helped to sensitize comparativists to parochial, misleading, and invalid methods, which may affect cross-cultural research.

The second major difference from most noncomparative research is that comparative sociology by definition involves comparisons among societies. Since the emphasis on appropriateness of methods in each particular society ultimately means that methods are rarely, if ever, phenomenally identical across societies because of variation in social-cultural conditions, comparativists must inquire whether there is sufficient equivalence in the research concepts and methods to permit meaningful comparisons across societies. Even if the concepts and methods in different societies are outwardly identical, the meanings or implications may not be. The same word in two languages may have different connotations (in this volume see Grimshaw, p. 24; Elder, pp. 127ff; Hazelrigg, pp. 234; and Mehan, pp. 234ff). The same sample may have a different position with respect to the total society (e.g., communities of 25,000 may be cities in some societies but towns or villages in others; 18-year-olds may be adults in some societies but not in others). The same measurement technique in two societies may measure different aspects of reality (see Schnaiberg's and my discussion of modernity measures; Johnson and Cutright's discussion of illegitimacy measures; Schwirian's discussion of truebound versus overbound areas). As a result of such problems, differences observed in the data for the two societies may be artifacts of method rather than valid differences. In short, a second major methodological task in comparative research is to devise and select theoretical problems, conceptual schemes, samples, and measurement and analysis strategies that are comparable or equivalent across the societies involved in a particular study.

Identity Versus Equivalence

This notion of conceptual or functional equivalence has received considerable attention in the comparative sociological literature. Briefly, the distinction between phenomenal identity and conceptual equivalence is not one of opposite poles on a single dimension but rather of two separate dimensions. Phenomenal identity or, more precisely, phenomenal similarity refers to the extent to which methods are duplicated in each society in a comparative study. For example, in measuring a conceptual variable such as intelligence or political participation, how similar are the indicators, data collection, and scoring procedures in the societies studied? If they are the same, the measurement across societies is said to be based on phenomenally identical methods. Alternative examples could be considered with respect to phenomenally similar sampling methods, archival research methods, statistical analysis methods, field work administration methods, experimental methods, and so on. However, we know from the difficulties that researchers have had in developing culture-free intelligence tests (see Straus, 1969, for elaboration of this example) that phenomenally indentical measures of concepts may be confounded with other factors in some countries (e.g., exposure to the Western world, in the case of intelligence tests). Hence, tests may actually be measuring different concepts in the different societies (e.g., intelligence in one society; exposure to the Western world in another) and thereby lack conceptual equivalence.

In short, conceptual equivalence with respect to measurement refers to whether the instruments used in separate societies in fact measure the same concept, regardless of whether the manifest content and procedures are identical or not. Conceptual equivalence is based on the assumption that measuring a concept requires choosing indicators that are believed to indicate with some degree of accuracy the conceptual properties we wish to measure; in different societies, these theoretical properties may be more accurately measured by different, than by identical, indicators. Thus, the language and referents used in intelligence test items and the behaviors used as indicators of political participation must often differ in order to be conceptually equivalent in different social-cultural contexts. Likewise, sampling (e.g., of minorities, community leaders, or factories), research sponsorship, observational criteria, and other methodological features may necessarily differ between societies in comparative research in the interests of conceptual equivalence. It follows, then, that the criterion for asserting comparability is not whether methods (sampling, sponsorship, etc.) are phenomenally identical but rather whether they are conceptually equivalent *for the purposes of the research.*

The heightened importance of clarity about the theoretical purposes and conceptual variables in comparative research is evident from these considerations. It is essential that the investigator define precisely the conceptual property that he seeks to observe or measure, the theoretical population that he wants to sample, the researcher image that he wants to convey, and so forth. Contrary to the emphasis in many methodological discussions on detailed standardization of methods and procedures, comparativists maintain that literally translated questions, identical sampling procedures, and carefully copied methods and procedures in other aspects of the research enterprise are justified *only* when they lead to conceptual equivalence across societies for the particular research objectives.

Appropriateness Versus Equivalence

Before considering problems at each stage of the research process, several general features of appropriateness and equivalence should be noted. The concepts and/or methods employed in two societies may conceivably be equivalent and yet inappropriate in one or both societies, in which case the results will be meaningless or misleading. For example, the use of the questionnaire method may be conceptually equivalent in two closely related societies but inappropriate if either or both have a high proportion of illiterates in the population to be studied. An interview team of university students may provide conceptually equivalent images but be inappropriate in societies that have culturally restricted conversation patterns between younger and older persons. Observational categories may be conceptually equivalent but inappropriate if the behavior to be observed is secret or sensitive in one or more societies. Census data on age and sex distribution may be conceptually equivalent but inappropriate if not reported for the subpopulation being compared across societies. Conversely, even if the research procedures are appropriate for each society, they may not be equivalent and may thus require modification.

In fact, these two objectives may contradict each other to the extent that maximizing the appropriateness of methods for a particular culture makes them culturally specific (i.e., less amenable to comparative study) and vice versa. For example, Form (Chapter 3 below) had to use different strategies for access and sponsorship; Elder (Chapter 4) had to use two different sampling designs; and Portes (Chapter 5) notes that different data-collection methods are obtrusive in different societies. The requirements of appropriateness and equivalence may conflict with each other sufficiently to produce a potential dilemma in comparative research. This issue will be raised again at the end of this chapter.

I should reemphasize that these two requirements are not unique in principle to comparative sociology. Researchers conducting intracultural studies must also be sensitive to the subpopulations and subcultures with which they are dealing and tailor their methods accordingly. Shifts may be required in the language of questions, sex of observers or interviewers, observational techniques, sampling designs, and so on, depending on such variations within cultures as those between subjects who are young or old, male or female, urban businessmen or rural farmers. In short, questions of appropriateness and equivalence across cultures are analogous to those present, but often less salient, across subcultures within single-society studies. These difficulties are of greater magnitude and complexity in most comparative research, because distinctively foreign and separate societies are involved. As Hudson and associates (1959:6) note: "The methods of cross-cultural research are not in principle unique. They are different primarily in the sense that procedural precautions become more critical and some problems more difficult to identify and to solve than for within-culture studies."

The Research Process

Problems of appropriateness and equivalence are encountered at almost every stage, from formulation to data analysis, of the comparative research process. In actual practice, of course, there is no simple sequence of steps in comparative or other sociological studies; an investigator moves back and forth among aspects of the research operation, making decisions and taking actions that will have effects on subsequent decisions, until his study is completed. Nevertheless, an overall organization of the research enterprise can be identified, and this framework is useful for examining the methodological difficulties of appropriateness and equivalence in comparative research.

For purposes of discussion I have divided the research process into four general stages that correspond approximately to the sequence of operations involved in comparative studies:

1. Formulation of problems and conceptualization of variables
2. Selection of societies and research sites
3. Design and administration of fieldwork: negotiation of access, sampling of units of analysis within societies, development of measuring instruments and indexes, collection of data
4. Analysis of data and interpretation of results.

The following sections elaborate some of the difficulties in comparative research with respect to appropriate and equivalent methods at each of these stages of the research process. Although I have illustrated my discussion of the research process with reference to sections of the chapters and discussions, I should note that the chapters and discussions deal with a much larger variety of methodological and substantive issues in comparative sociological research than does this overview. In addition, some aspects of the research process receive only brief mention because problems of appropriateness or equivalence are either less applicable or less explored.

Formulation of Problems and Conceptualization of Variables

Appropriateness. The need to identify appropriate concepts for comparative research is suggested in several of the chapters. Hazelrigg notes that conceptions of class can be expected to vary from one society to the next. Other chapters indicate that American or Western conceptions of labor unions and how they operate (Form), community power (Miller), marriage (Johnson and Cutright), modernity (Armer and Schnaiberg), political participation (Walton), and so forth are inappropriate in particular societies.

Indeed, an important payoff of comparative research is the revelation of parochialisms and cultural biases in the conceptual definitions chosen for research. Smelser (1966:22) has called attention to limitations in Western conceptions of economic institutions when applied to other nations, especially to small, rural-agrarian societies. Others have noted limitations in Western conceptions of mental illness (Murphy and Leighton, 1965) and socioeconomic development (Frank, 1967; and Myrdal, 1968), not to mention such culturally differentiated concepts as deviant, liberal, unemployed, educated, and adult. All of these nominally identical categories may be defined quite differently across societies.

Moreover, some concepts are virtually absent in certain societies; note the translation problems reported by Grimshaw (pp. 23ff.) and by Elder (pp. 127ff.). Examples of nonuniversal phenomena include civil service, retirement, caste, graduate study, and plural marriage. Thus, it would be generally inappropriate to propose research on cultural pluralism in Somalia (one of the few culturally homogeneous societies in Africa) or on polygamous marriage in Great Britain.

In addition to conceptual limitations, some theoretical subjects may be too unfamiliar or too threatening for investigation in particular societies, even though the concepts are meaningful. For example, topics in the areas of sex and politics (see Portes's paper, p. 158) are widely sensitive across cultures. Other topics are more culturally specific; for example, Form's questions on union identification were sensitive in Italy where unions are politically oriented. (For further discussion and examples, see Mitchell, 1965; and Warwick and Osherson, 1973.) These limitations are especially relevant in connection with the selection of societies for comparative research and with negotiation for access and cooperation in conducting fieldwork (see below).[3]

Equivalence. The other side of problem formulation and conceptualization is the need to identify problems and concepts with cross-cultural utility. In particular, concepts tend to have different connotations in different societies, and these differences, if not controlled, may well account for the pattern of research results observed when a concept is used cross-culturally. Concepts in cross-cultural studies need to be "non-culture bound" (Sjoberg, 1955) or "transcultural" (Sears, 1961; and Whiting, 1968). At minimum, they should be comparable for the cultures that are to be included in the research or to which generalizations will be made.

One common procedure for reducing cultural specificity is to raise the concepts involved to a higher level of abstraction. The value dimensions cited by Elder and by Schnaiberg and me illustrate high-level abstractions in the realm of attitudes, and Hazelrigg provides an in-depth conceptual analysis of class consciousness in an effort to identify a level of abstraction that will enable comparative research. On the other hand, raising the level of abstraction to achieve universal applicability must not "do violence to the events and situations we wish to compare" (Smelser, 1966:21); that is, the concepts should remain appropriate for each society being compared. Moreover, there is the tendency, when moving from the theoretical level to more specific, operational levels, to revert to parochial and noncomparable conceptions. "Modernity" has often been defined conceptually in terms of Western achievement values; "political behavior," in terms of voting; "national development," in terms of economic productivity and political stability.

Hazelrigg's chapter demonstrates the difficulty of defining a concept in both a theoretically meaningful and a transcultural fashion. Even concepts that are successfully conceptualized at a cross-cultural level can be difficult to operationalize. Hazelrigg describes a measurement technique intended to permit the concepts of "class" and "class consciousness" to be operationalized empirically in each society. This technique requires comparing citizens' conceptions of class structure and their role in it with an investigator's records of these phenomena for the same citizens. This approach inevitably raises questions about how adequately the resulting culture-specific operations will fit into the original transcultural conceptions of class and to what extent cross-cultural comparability is gained or lost in the process. In the final section of his chapter, Hazelrigg considers whether an investigator can determine if the similarities or differences between societies in class structures or class consciousness are valid or, instead, are artifacts of faulty or inequivalent conceptualization, language use, and methods. Thus, his chapter forces us to consider a complex question that has yet to be answered adequately in comparative research: How can we *demonstrate* the appropriateness and equivalence of our concepts and procedures?

Related to the difficulty of conceptual identification and clarification is that of identifying meaningful problems and hypotheses. Finsterbusch illustrates a descriptive or taxonomic approach to theory construction by identifying (from an essentially functionalist framework) a set of important components for the concept of nation-state. He then postulates the direct influence that each component has on the others and produces a list of multivariate equations to explain nation-building.

The utility of Finsterbusch's set of variables and equations for comparative research depends in part upon the validity of the variable indicators and the availability of data; both conditions, Finsterbusch acknowledges, are highly problematic. In addition, one must inquire about the equivalence of concepts across cultures. Do "differentiation" and "competition" have equivalent meanings, much less operationalizations, in different societies? This problem becomes particularly acute when Finsterbusch (see Figure 14.1) combines concepts into higher and higher levels of abstraction, distilling from his original list of 23 items a final list of 7 factors. How does a researcher convincingly define and operationalize a concept like "modernization," which includes such notions as "knowledge-skills," "capital," and "centralization," among others? Can we assume that the "democratic egalitarianism" of one society is equivalent to that of another? If such equivalence cannot be ascertained in advance, how meaningful are comparisons among societies on such conceptually fluid variables?

A major implication of these considerations is that the range of dimensions upon which nations (or other social units) can be compared is virtually limitless. There is no single list of concepts with established and equivalent meanings that are useful for all research purposes. Hence, conceptual and operational equivalence depend upon a clear understanding of the theoretical and analytical rationale of the research to be undertaken as well as of the societies and cultures in which it is to be carried out.

Selection of Societies and Research Sites

Appropriateness. Closely involved with the formulation of a theoretical problem for comparative research is the selection of societies to be compared. Indeed, in some cases such as Nadel's (1952) analysis of witchcraft among the Nupe and Gwari, the societies largely determine the problem. These two societies exist side by side and share closely related languages, identical kinship systems, and very similar social, political, economic, and belief systems with one intriguing exception: Witches among the Nupe are believed to be female but among the Gwari may be of either sex. Nadel sought to explain this difference in witchcraft beliefs and its implications through comparative analysis.

Nadel's study illustrates a selection strategy that maximizes similarities between societies except for the phenomenon to be explained. This strategy seeks to control as many potential determinant variables as possible in order to identify the critical determinants more easily. Such a strategy is also useful for sampling when an investigation seeks to test the effects of a particular variable or set of variables. For example, Johnson and Cutright restricted their national sample to those Latin American countries in which Spanish is the major national language and for which archival data were sufficient for analytic purposes.

An altogether different sampling strategy may be called for when the research objective is to test the universality of a phenomenon or relationship. In such cases, maximum difference between societies may be appropriate, or societies may be selected to provide critical tests by virtue of their special features (or lack of them) when compared with societies used in previous research. For example, Schnaiberg and I note that the concept of individual modernity is claimed to be universally applicable even though the research using modernity measures has been restricted to a rather narrow range of semideveloped societies. By investigating that concept and measures of it in the United States, a highly industrialized nation, we provide a more critical test of their universality.

In actual practice, most comparative research is conducted in societies that have been selected in large part because of convenience, available contacts, expected satisfactions, and other fortuitous or irrelevant considerations (regardless of disclaimers or ex post facto rationalizations to the contrary). This situation is not altogether unreasonable or illegitimate, and frequently a researcher must choose between no research at all or research in a society that has been chosen in part by the consideration of extraneous circumstances. Researchers owe it to their readers, however, to acknowledge honestly their constraints in selecting societies and to identify as directly as possible the advantages and disadvantages of the resulting selection.

As for the ideal strategy in society selection, some comparativists prefer random or stratified samples. However appropriate this strategy may be for certain research purposes, it is nevertheless fraught with theoretical and technical problems. In particular, it would theoretically require that every society of the world—large and small, past and present, nation and tribe—be included in the sampling frame from which a study sample is to be drawn. Obviously there is no such complete listing, and even a listing of all contemporary societies (if they could be satisfactorily identified) would present limitations with regard to adequate data and research feasibility.

Equivalence. In the context of sampling of societies, the problem of equivalence has little relevance insofar as it refers to using comparable sampling strategies in selecting each society included in a study. The importance of equivalence is increased if it is interpreted as referring to the maximization of similarity across societies on those extraneous factors that could theoretically disturb the hypotheses being tested. Random sampling designs provide one means of achieving this result within measurable levels of error but, as noted above, are rarely feasible.

A more realistic approach to achieving both appropriateness and equivalence (as just redefined) in the selection of societies is purposive sampling. This strategy is generally more likely than others currently available to provide appropriate variation in the key variables as set by the research hypotheses and reasonable equivalence on other theoretically relevant factors. For example, Johnson and Cutright restrict their sample to Spanish-speaking Latin American countries. Thus they control for many possible cultural, geographical, and other differences but retain considerable variation in illegitimacy rates, their major dependent variable. However, the difficulty of obtaining and demonstrating the appropriateness and equivalence of the selected societies with respect to the critical variables required by the research remains as in other aspects of comparative research. (For further discussion of society sampling difficulties, see Hyman, 1967; Naroll, 1968; Whiting, 1968; and Frey, 1970.)

Design and Administration of Fieldwork: Negotiation of Access

The difficulties of gaining access to, and cooperation from, individuals and groups in host societies are always experienced but rarely acknowledged by comparative researchers. Gaining access and making arrangements to conduct an investigation in each society require that the researcher obtain approval and cooperation from those individuals in the host culture who control access to the social units involved in the research. The need for access and cooperation generally continues throughout a research operation and, if inadequately handled, can sabotage a project in midstream. The following discussion is focused primarily on practical considerations, but it is important to note that there are also underlying moral issues that must be considered by the comparativist (see Portes below, Chapter 5; also Sjoberg, 1967).

Appropriateness. Specific problems connected with this task involve knowing what agencies and individuals should be contacted, what procedures are appropriate for making research contacts, what is required to maintain goodwill both throughout present research and for future research, and what effects these arrangements will have on the quality and comparability of research. Unfortunately, there are no simple formulas available for dealing with these problems in a society, and appropriate tactics will vary from one society to another. Indeed, the matter of access and cooperation is such a nebulous area of concern that many past comparative-research reviews have failed to discuss it at all. On the other hand, there is ample evidence in the research literature to indicate the critical importance of dealing satisfactorily with these issues, and several of the chapters in this volume (especially those by Form, Portes, and Elder) focus explicitly on such concerns (see also Frey, 1970:202-214).

The appropriateness of different strategies of access is affected by variation in the degree to which relevant individuals in a foreign society understand and are receptive to social science research. Receptivity to nonindigenous, especially United States-sponsored, research may be particularly problematic in some societies (see Portes below). The variation in understanding and receptivity occurs both between cultures and between different collectivities within cultures. Portes systematizes these variations in a way that makes them more salient and that will, it is hoped, encourage efforts to analyze and prepare appropriate strategies for undertaking future cross-cultural research. He also suggests that the crucial factors in facilitating access, cooperation, and continued goodwill for future research are (1) minimization of sensitive research topics (see discussion above) and (2) maximization of unobtrusive research methods.

Thus, a specific problem faced by the comparativist is to determine whether his proposed research would, in fact, be too sensitive or otherwise inappropriate for one or more of the societies or publics with which he wants to deal. Assuming that reasonable and appropriate topics have been defined for investigation, the cross-cultural researcher must then reduce to tolerable levels the remaining inconvenience and threat created by his research. Cross-cultural research is often highly visible and many societies or groups in societies have reasons to be suspicious of "outside" researchers or even xenophobic. The degree of threat is largely a function of how members of the host society perceive a researcher, and their perception is affected by his research sponsorship, the nature of his inquiries, and his personal appearance (including aspects that vary from ethnic or class identity to the length of hair). Since none of these factors produce uniform images either across societies or across different collectivities within societies, the strategies for gaining access and cooperation must be appropriate for the particular societies and groups in the study. Such strategies are difficult to determine in advance of the research itself.

Form's candid chapter on the politics of distrust details his own experiences in seeking access and cooperation for comparative research, and it is instructive both in clarifying problems and suggesting possibilities for solutions. He shows that the researcher is invariably cast into role relationships with respect to the host society that critically affect both access and cooperation. In discussing Form's chapter (pp. 114ff.), Gould reiterates that the comparativist is not working with passive subjects who are unperturbed and unaffected by the investigations of social scientists from other nations but rather with purposeful, active members of the host society who inevitably develop images of, and relationships to, the researcher that greatly affect his success or failure. The researcher should therefore try to emphasize a role definition that will provide satisfaction with minimum threat or disturbance to the host society and without misrepresenting or compromising his major research objectives (see Elder, p. 135; Portes, p. 154ff.).

These problems of appropriateness with respect to strategies of access and cooperation are shared with area specialists and other foreign area researchers. They are also shared with those conducting American research, as Form's El Paso and Lansing researches clearly indicate, but such problems are especially acute in cultures less familiar to an investigator. At the present time, such questions are only beginning to receive systematic attention with respect to particular cultures and research operations. Form's paper provides a stimulating contribution to this concern. (For further discussion of investigator sponsorship, identity, and role-relationship problems, see Warwick and Osherson, 1973; and Frey, 1970.)

Equivalence. From the perspective of cross-cultural equivalence, the investigator's next concern is to achieve conditions of access and cooperation that are comparable across cultural settings. In the process of designing appropriate strategies for access, he may have been required to modify his research objectives and methods in different ways for different societies, thus reducing the possibilities for comparative research. For example, Oldsmobile management's lack of cooperation with Form restricted his possibilities for doing comparative research on management behavior and other matters elsewhere. Indeed, Frey (1970: 210) has noted that conditions in the most sensitive society included in a study often determine the level and range of investigation for all societies; that is, comparative research is often reduced to the lowest common denominator of research acceptable to all societies in the study.

From the foregoing discussion of access and cooperation, it is clear that methodological difficulties in single-society studies are increased by more than just an additive factor in comparative research. Not only is there the cumulation of access and cooperation difficulties in each society, but there is also difficulty in achieving comparability in the nature and degree of access and in the resulting research problem and methods after single-society adjustments have been made.

Design and Administration of Fieldwork: Sampling of Units of Analysis within Societies

Regardless of the nature of a comparative research project or its major data sources, unit sampling is generally required at one or more stages of the research. Further, comparative research usually involves sampling intrasocietal units at more than one level (e.g., communities, political districts, factories, families, individuals). For example, Walton (Chapter 6) selected from a large number of communities, individuals and document sources in his research; Elder sampled communities, residences, and individuals; Mehan sampled schools, classes, and students.

Appropriateness. At each level within societies, an investigator must decide which sampling design (e.g., random or nonrandom, stratified or nonstratified, accidental or purposive) is most appropriate for his research conditions and objectives. Of course, random or probability sampling is the preferred method, but it is often not feasible. Elder (pp. 121ff.) demonstrates the considerable difficulties involved in drawing random samples of individual populations in foreign settings, especially in the absence of adequate records or materials to use as sampling frames. He finally took his own censuses in the villages outside Madurai and Lucknow as a basis for constructing a sampling frame, but this solution is costly in time and resources and is often not feasible (e.g., in large cities or dispersed populations). An alternative that may be more appropriate in some settings is multistage area sampling in order to reduce units to a size for which sampling frames may be available or more easily constructed.

At the level of supra-individual units, several of the chapters report using samples consisting of only one or two cases—for example, one school (Mehan, Chapter 11), one city per nation (Miller, Chapter 7), or one factory per nation (Form, Chapter 3); such studies are subject to all of the limitations normally associated with unitary or small samples. Of course, the nature of the research or available resources often precludes large random samples, and in such situations Walton stresses purposive sampling as an appropriate strategy. In the discussion following his chapter (6 below), he describes how Almond and Verba's (1963) sampling design in Mexico, which concentrated on large urban centers, led to (1) a misrepresentation of overall Mexican political culture, which is quite different in rural (as opposed to urban) areas, and (2) a lack of equivalence in the Mexican data with the data from other societies in their study.

A second sampling concern is the appropriateness of individual or intrasociety samples for the particular research purposes of a study. A sample must provide sufficient variation on key variables to enable meaningful analysis. Clearly, the research problem determines which units or groups in a society should be investigated, but it is also clear that the appropriate group (in terms of significance, availability, and feasibility) may vary from one society to the next. A study of money income might concentrate on men in one society (e.g., America in the 1920s) and women in another (e.g., an African setting in which women may sell goods in the marketplace, while men engage in subsistance agriculture). A study of community power might focus on businessmen in one community and public officials in another (for example, see Miller's chapter, pp. 196, 205).

Related to the issue of sampling appropriateness is the question of whether individuals are meaningful units of analysis, especially in societies that lack the individualistic, participatory characteristics of Western societies. It is sometimes mistakenly suggested that survey research has an inappropriate individualistic bias and that units of investigation should be restricted to leaders of collectivities. Nevertheless, it is an empirical question whether individuals in collectivities share a collective opinion or differ among themselves, whether or not their opinions parallel those of their official leaders, and whether or not they demonstrate more communal and less individualistic orientations. Of course, the appropriate interview subjects for certain studies (e.g., studies of decision-making and political power) may be public officials and opinion leaders rather than ordinary citizens (see the discussion of Chapter 10 below, p. 306), but this fact does not rule out the utility of surveys with other publics for other research purposes (e.g., see Mitchell, 1965:672-675; also Stryker's comments, pp. 280 below)

Equivalence. In addition to intrasociety sampling appropriateness, the researcher must also consider sampling equivalence across the societies included in a study. As Frey (1970:196) observes, "The true counterpart for a given group in one society may be a nominally very different group in another society." He notes that comparativists are often interested in matching social roles or personality types across societies and that it is important to recognize that "high status" in one society may be quite different (e.g., in level of absolute wealth or education) from "high status" in another society. Thus, sampling based on identical (i.e., absolute) criteria may result in (1) quite inequivalent samples in some societies or (2) no sample at all in societies lacking populations that meet the particular criteria. (As an example of one effort to deal with these problems, see Straus, 1970.)

At the same time it should be noted that absolute, rather than relative, position may sometimes be fully appropriate as a sampling criterion. For example, random samples of students may be equivalent for a comparative study of student orientations but lacking in equivalence for a study of youth orientations, since in some societies large proportions of young people do not attend school and are likely to differ from students in important respects. (Although the example is obvious, the number of comparative and foreign area studies of "youth" based on student samples is testimony to the relative importance of convenience over appropriateness and equivalence in sampling designs.) Different sampling designs would be required if a comparative study were focused on *actual* family size versus *relative* family size, on communities with *absolute* versus *relative* levels of urbanism, on industries with over 2500 employees versus *relatively* large industries, and so on. In short, the selection of samples on the basis of either absolute or relative position should be dictated by the research objectives. These considerations affect the sampling of subjects and events in observational studies and the sampling of records, census categories, and such in archival studies, as well as sampling in survey and experimental research.

A further difficulty in achieving sample equivalence can be illustrated with the investigation by Schnaiberg and me of the validity and cross-cultural utility of individual modernity measures. We selected males in a high-migration, lower-middle-class urban setting of the United States as most equivalent to the males in urban settings in developing countries who had participated in previous studies. However, one substantive purpose of our research was to examine family-planning values and practices; this necessarily required concentration on married men and tended to reduce sampling equivalence for the modernity-testing objectives of the study. The implication is not only that the researcher must be conceptually clear about his research objectives and critical variables in order to maximize sampling equivalence across societies but also that multiple research objectives in a study (a common occurrence) may pose conflicting requirements for the selection of equivalent samples. Those samples most equivalent for one research purpose may not be for another. Similar contradictions and inconsistencies in achieving appropriateness and equivalence may also occur in other phases of the research process when multiple research objectives are involved. As with other aspects of comparative research, accentuating the problems of appropriateness and equivalence forces the comparativist to be clear in his purposes, conceptualization, and methods. (For further discussion of sampling in comparative research, see Scheuch, 1968; Frey, 1970; and Warwick and Osherson, 1973.)

Design and Administration of Fieldwork: Development of Measuring Instruments and Indexes

Measurement problems have been among the most extensively discussed in the comparative-methods literature, and numerous examples of inappropriate and inequivalent measures have been reported. In general, intracultural measurement efforts have been primarily concerned with identifying appropriate indicators (e.g., questionnaire items, observational units, documentary information) for the intended theoretical variables in a study. Required, of course, are valid measures with sufficient variation in scores to enable meaningful analysis.

Appropriateness. As Schwirian notes, measurement is especially problematic for archival research because the data are often either unavailable or collected for other purposes and are, therefore, inadequate. Mitchell (1965:673-674) calls attention to some of the measurement problems in cross-cultural surveys that result from the prevalence of questions on "(a) topics about which the respondent has no opinion or is unable to give an adequate factual answer, (b) topics which are culturally sensitive, and (c) topics which need greater conceptual, linguistic, and measurement sophistication in order to draw out information." The first category frequently leads to respondent answers reflecting cultural or individual response sets (e.g., acquiescence, social desirability, and courtesy biases) rather than valid data, while the second and third categories often lead to either missing or meaningless data.

The third category of problems is emphasized by the research reported in Mehan's chapter. Among the factors contributing to distortions in the measurement of language skills in the school testing program which he investigated were test-administration errors, recording errors, contextual effects, respondent language effects, and erroneous test assumptions about logical response patterns. Moreover, Mehan's findings with respect to measurement difficulties among subcultures within a U.S. school system suggest that even greater difficulties can be expected in cross-cultural settings, especially in research involving respondents, investigators, and test (or measurement) creators who do not share common cultural assumptions.

Measurement difficulties such as these plague not only interview and paper-and-pencil testing techniques but also observational techniques (see Mehan's evidence on the test administrator's difficulty in interpreting the children's hand responses). Using documents and records, Schwirian shows differences in measurement results depending on whether sector or zonal techniques are used to study an area; similarly, different segregation indexes can produce different pictures of the ecological structure of the same community. Thus, the theoretical purposes and assumptions underlying a given research project and situation may dictate that one measurement technique or index is more appropriate than another.

Equivalence. The problem of measurement equivalence is pervasive in cross-cultural research and is dealt with at one point or another in many of the chapters and discussions in this volume. To note a few examples, Elder discusses difficulties in attaining equivalent item wording and translation; Hazelrigg discusses the difficulties cross-cultural researchers will have in operationalizing measures of class consciousness; Walton notes (pp. 189ff., in the discussion of his paper) the difficulty of finding equivalent indicators of political behavior in different cultures; Finsterbusch acknowledges the absence of equivalent data and measures for many of the variables in his conceptual framework, an absence that becomes even more problematic when he combines variables into higher-order abstractions; and Johnson and Cutright emphasize the superiority of illegitimacy *rates* over illegitimacy *ratios* as a measure with cross-cultural equivalence. The general point stressed in these papers and in the comparative literature is that phenomenally identical measures do not necessarily provide equivalent measurement; different indicators are often needed to tap equivalent concepts in different settings.

Given this perspective, the questions then become how to achieve measurement equivalence and how to assess whether it has, in fact, been achieved by a particular set of indicators in different societies. Several suggestions have been made regarding the attainment of measurement equivalence (e.g., by Ramsey and Collazo, 1960; Suchman, 1964; Straus, 1969; Przeworski and Teune, 1966-1967, 1970). The elaborate technique proposed by Przeworski and Teune (1970) begins with a large pool of items, some identical across societies and others specific to particular societies, that are intended to measure a theoretical concept. Then they select out, as an index in each society, those items that cohere in a similar fashion in all societies and those items that correlate within each society with the common set. The technique must be repeated for each critical variable and appears limited in applicability to those studies in which correlation analyses are meaningful (i.e., those utilizing large samples with appropriate distributional characteristics). For example, it is not clear how the technique would be used for assessing or increasing the equivalence of community power measures in studies involving less than a half dozen communities (e.g., Walton's or Miller's) or the equivalence of measures of management-labor relations in a handful of industries (e.g., Form's research). Other limitations of this procedure are discussed by Frey (1970) and Warwick and Osherson (1973).

Frey (1970:244-245) suggests that an ideal, although difficult, strategy for obtaining equivalent measuring instruments in cross-cultural research would be to gather a team of first-rate scholars who are indigenous to the cultures intended for inclusion in a study. Those scholars would discuss the research objectives and come to a common understanding of the theoretical concepts to be measured. They would then return to their respective countries and develop the most culturally valid indicators possible. Although the specific methods and instruments might be expected to vary from culture to culture, a high level of equivalent measurement across societies is assumed to result. (Although expensive and difficult, there are examples of such efforts, e.g., the International Studies of Values in Politics, 1971, and the Multinational Comparative Time Budget Research Project reported by Szalai, 1966.)

Even though such elaborate procedures are often impossible, it is clear that cross-cultural equivalence is enhanced by any means that increases the clarity and uniform understanding of concepts across cultures and that strengthens the validity of measuring instruments and techniques in each society. Accordingly, efforts to maximize and demonstrate measurement equivalence would be aided by techniques that test the consensus on conceptual domains and the validity of measures within cultures. Such validation efforts would contribute to equivalence through a single development and evaluation process. Assessment of conceptualization and measurement validity can be used to reevaluate and revise conceptual meaning and measurement until equivalence at some level of satisfaction is demonstrated.

My chapter with Schnaiberg demonstrates one method of making such an assessment of the value of concepts and scales in comparative research. Although the several available modernity measures have been developed with about as much technical sophistication as any cross-cultural measure, we found evidence of low discriminant validity, which suggests that either the measurement or the conception of modernity is inadequate: Clearly, existing measures are not universally applicable. Similar efforts at validity assessment of other common concepts would contribute to the attainment and demonstration of cross-cultural equivalence. For observational research, data-quality assessment methods such as those advocated by Naroll (1962, 1968) may be useful (see Walton, p. 177). As a further aid in measurement assessment, Mehan suggests the use of videotaping, which permits an investigator to have retroactive access to the numerous factors affecting any given interview or observed event.

Design and Administration of Fieldwork: Collection of Data

Comparative research uses a variety of designs, data, and methods. There are longitudinal and cross-sectional studies, case studies and surveys, historical analyses and contemporary studies, bicultural and multicultural studies, rigorous experiments and impressionistic essays, to mention just a few variations (see Walton for one classification scheme; for a narrower conception of comparative methods, see Smelser, 1966; and Gould, 1964). Contrary to the view that comparative research should develop a distinctive method (see Porter, in Walton, p. 173), comparative methods, like methods in noncomparative research, should be expected to vary depending upon the nature of the problems and cultures being investigated. One of the comparative methodologist's tasks, then, is to determine the best data-collection methods for his research objectives.

Appropriateness. This perspective suggests two general principles that should guide intersocietal, as well as intrasocietal, research: (1) Data-collection designs and methods should be tailored for the specific research problem and specific cultures being investigated. Every method can be varied and modified in different ways, and researchers should be creative in the selection, modification, and development of methods for each particular study. (2) Since every method has limitations and weaknesses (e.g., those identified by Walton for three categories of inquiry — archival research, case studies, and systematic surveys), the most appropriate strategy is generally one employing a combination of methods and data types that counterbalance each other's limitation. This strategy underlies Walton's suggested "standardized case comparison" approach as well as Turk's strong encouragement of the use of historical data and Schnaiberg's support (see discussion of Turk's chapter) for greater use of "kookie" (i.e., unconventional) data. Mehan's suggested use of videotaping is also clearly related to the need for cross-validation and triangulation of methods.

These suggestions are directed primarily to the difficulty of finding appropriate methods for particular cultures. There are extensive cultural variations in the suitability and difficulty of methods. For example, historical research may be welcome in one society or group (e.g., the British Parliament) and not in another (e.g., the Soviet politburo); interview questions with structured response alternatives may be considered "too brutal" (Hunt et al., 1964:65) in one culture and quite appropriate in another; content analysis of newspapers may provide meaningful data on political issues in one country (e.g., the United States) and not in another (e.g., in countries with a state-controlled press); and interviewers may be mistaken for tax collectors, salesmen, CIA agents, or military conscriptors (see Elder, p. 135) in different societies with different consequences for data collection and analysis. In contrast to these generally unfavorable images, Portes (pp. 154-155) found himself perceived by the people in his research sample as a high government official capable of improving their housing situation; this perception posed a different sort of research difficulty—unrealistic expectations and demands.

Interviewing problems are particularly acute in societies (or groups) that are divided into antagonistic factions, especially if interviewers can be identified with one of the factions (see Form's difficulties with labor versus management, pp. 94ff) or if interview questions happen to bear on divisive issues (see Form on the subject of union identification, pp. 95ff; for further discussion, see Warwick and Osherson, 1973).

In addition to interviewing difficulties, Elder discusses a number of other data-collection difficulties encountered in his research—for example, problems with the recruitment, training, and honesty of interviewers, problems in wording and translation of interview questions, and problems in arranging for transportation and accommodations for interviewers in rural areas. His primary concern is to call attention to the particular nature of comparative research problems encountered in less-developed societies and to report on his efforts to cope with them. Since the problems and resources varied in some respects within and between the two Indian research settings, different solutions to problems were sometimes considered appropriate; for example, the cooperation of school authorities in Melur (but not elsewhere) made it possible for interviewers to take boys out of class and use an empty school office for interviews, thus insuring privacy (Elder, p. 135).

A further difficulty may be the complete absence of appropriate data. Schwirian notes the present lack of adequate data for many kinds of cross-national studies on ecological issues. Form, supplementing this observation, comments that the type of data available may distort results. On the basis of his own field observation of Mayaquez, for example, he suggests that it is highly stratified and not "undifferentiated" as reported in Schwirian's analysis based only on census data (see pp. 375ff.). The value of triangulation or multiplication of data sources and methods of analysis is again underscored by this exchange.

Equivalence. In addition to feasibility and appropriateness, the comparative researcher must also consider the equivalence of data-collection methods across societies. As Suchman (1964:135) has noted, "A good design for the collection of comparative data should permit one to assume as much as possible that the differences observed among the groups being compared cannot be attributed to the differences in the method being used." It is clear from the previous comments that identical methods and techniques are often not feasible in different cultures. Even if they were feasible, method effects (Campbell, 1960) might differ from one society to the next and produce noncomparable data. In short, slavish insistence on phenomenally identical data-collection methods and techniques across cultures is less important than conceptual equivalence. (It should be noted that some scholars tend to disagree with this perspective and to favor identical methods. Related to this latter view is Miller's statement, p. 194, endorsing "frozen" or standardized research designs.)

And yet, if different data-collection methods are used in different societies, how does the researcher determine that the methods are, in fact, equivalent and therefore not responsible for the observed differences among societies? For example, it may be argued that structured interviews in one society are functionally equivalent to unstructured interviews in another (see Hunt et al., 1964) or that use of official records in one society is functionally equivalent to conducting a survey in another (e.g., one lacking official records), but how can this equivalence be demonstrated? Is Mehan's interviewing of white students in the classroom functionally equivalent to his interviewing of Mexican-Americans in their homes? Are Form's combinations of data sources and collection methods functionally equivalent for his automobile-company studies in the

United States, Italy, Argentina, and India? Are Elder's interviewer effects and quality in Tamil Nadu functionally equivalent to those in Uttar Pradesh? The fact is that we lack objective criteria for assessing the equivalence of methods in different situations.

All methods presumably have method effects, but unfortunately we have not yet been able to determine these precisely, much less how they vary across cultures. Until more systematic information is available on the utility and biases of different methods in different cultural settings (e.g., the courtesy bias in some cultures) or until independent, objective criteria for assessing equivalence are available, determination of functional equivalence will be largely a matter of individual, professional judgment. It follows that, in the absence of other information, methods should be as similar as is feasible while still retaining their appropriateness for the particular cultures in which they are being used. In general, the emphasis should be on selecting those methods that provide the most reliable and valid data in each setting. To this end, researchers should make greater efforts (1) to include measures to detect potential method effects that may reduce validity and (2) to incorporate combinations of methods and data to measure the same variables for cross-validation purposes.

One chapter that explicitly includes both theoretically relevant method-effect measures (e.g., acquiescent response set) and combinations of methods measuring the same variable is the modernity study by Schnaiberg and me. Our methods for measuring modernity are not as different as would be desirable for most cross-validation purposes and certainly do not approach the variation involved in Walton's standardized case-study approach. Nevertheless, the study illustrates the value of such validational procedures.

Design and Administration of Fieldwork: Analysis and Interpretation of Data

Closely related to problems of measurement and data collection in comparative research are those of data analysis. Fundamentally, the two key issues continue to be whether the analytical methods are appropriate for the particular purposes, data, and setting of the research and whether the methods are equivalent across cultures.

Appropriateness. The question of whether analytic methods are appropriate or not requires, among other things, a familiarity with the assumptions underlying different analytic methods and with the kinds of effects different methods have on actual results. Schwirian's chapter compares a variety of statistical and data-manipulation techniques in order to demonstrate the effects of the assumptions underlying different techniques. For example, he argues that both zone and sector tests of spatial distribution generate similar general results for Columbus, Ohio, but that this result may not hold for cities in other societies. Also, he shows that the assumptions of oblique solutions as opposed to orthogonal solutions are generally more appropriate for the factor analysis of ecological data. Johnson, in discussing Schwirian's study, calls attention to alternatives to the standard factor analytic approaches that are less well known but more theoretically meaningful. In particular, he stresses the appropriateness of having investigators build their theoretical predictions into the factor-analytic procedures and use the analysis to test the predictions.

Johnson and Cutright's study of Latin American illegitimacy provides an excellent illustration of how to make good analytical use of data sources. By explicitly challenging Goode's methods and thesis that illegitimacy is a function of societal integration, they clearly differentiate appropriate and inappropriate analytic techniques. Among the special features of this paper is the authors' use of historical evidence as the basis for suggesting an equally plausible alternative thesis that variation in illegitimacy rates results from national differences (1) in the degree of sexual exploitation by the early Spanish conquerors and (2) in the subsequent in-migration patterns. The theoretical interpretation is generalized on the basis of historical information and is then supported by statistical analysis of historical census materials available for a subsample of countries in the study.

Equivalence. The issue of equivalence in comparative research analysis stems from the fact that the assumptions about the variables and data implicit in different analytical techniques may not be equally well met in different societies. Also, if different analytical techniques and procedures are used in different societies (which is likely if different samples, measures, or data-collection techniques have been employed), analytic equivalence may be lacking and may lead to spurious results. For example, Johnson and Cutright use path analysis to examine alternative causal models of variations in illegitimacy rates for their sample of Latin American nations; however, their assumptions regarding relevant variables, direction of effects, and uncorrelated terms may not be equally applicable for a different set of societies and, in fact, may not even be equivalent if considered separately for each society in their study.

Thus, questions of equivalence arise in connection with numerous aspects of data analysis: Are the same methods of analysis really equivalent if, in one society, a particular variable (e.g., "Catholic Institutional Strength" in Johnson and Cutright's study) is absent or irrelevant and therefore not entered into an analytic model, or if, in one society, the range, variety, or distribution of scores (e.g., types and frequencies of marital unions) is different from the range, variety, or distribution in a second society? Likewise, should cutting points in the analysis of nominal or ordinal variables be identical across societies or relative to the distributions in each society? For example, standard differentiation between literate and illiterate respondents or between those communities with more and those with less than 100,000 population may fail to show any variation on these variables in societies that have, respectively, negligible illiteracy or very few large cities. Therefore, in such societies, the measurement of relationships between these variables and other variables in cross-cultural research may be misleading. In sum, analysis and interaction problems are extensive in cross-cultural research, but as is evident in the following chapters and discussions, these problems are now being identified and solutions are being proposed.

Comparative Research Possibilities

We now have an overview of the difficulties involved in achieving culturally appropriate and cross-culturally equivalent methods in comparative research. Let us return to the question raised earlier: Do these two requirements pose an insoluble dilemma? To the extent that an investigator tailors such things as his research objectives, conceptualization, sampling, and measurement so that they are maximally appropriate for a particular society and then repeats the process of tailoring for a second society, does he not run the risk of reducing equivalence of the research between the two societies? Conversely, to the extent that he concentrates on equivalence of objectives and operations across societies, is he not likely to do so at the expense of not finding the most appropriate conceptualization and methods for each particular society?

For illustrative purposes, let us consider the measurement of the concept of social class. In one society, the principal determinant of social class may be wealth and occupational category; in another, the determinants may be religious knowledge and age. In the first society, data on annual income and occupational title may be needed; in the second, data on religious knowledge and age-group membership may be necessary. To what extent can an investigator then treat the measures as equivalent and make social-class distribution comparisons between the two societies? Even if data on all four factors were collected by identical methods in both societies, to what extent would cross-cultural equivalence have been achieved and intracultural appropriateness maintained?

Although this deliberately chosen example accentuates the potential dilemma, on close examination I find the inconsistency more apparent than real. Theoretically, if conceptualization and methods are valid within each culture, cross-cultural equivalence automatically follows. In other words, if an investigator has a clear idea of his research objectives and the critical dimensions of his concepts and if he is successful in devising appropriate methods to obtain valid measurement of concepts in each society, then his measures across cultures will be equivalent even though the operations differ.[4]

Second, perfect equivalence is never obtained between individuals or subunits of a single society, much less between societies, but the nonequivalent portions, if small, may sometimes be treated as unlikely to distort results and interpretations seriously. For example, if a researcher finds a similar pattern of relationships across societies, he may assume greater confidence in the equivalence of methods across societies or in the persistence of the relationships despite methodological limitations.

Third, there are usually several alternative methods that can be used and that vary in degree of intrasocietal appropriateness and intersocietal equivalence. Thus, choices are often possible, and these allow for both maximization of appropriateness and equivalence and reduction of incompatibility between the two. The dilemma persists only in the unlikely situation that the appropriate method alternatives *cannot* produce valid information on the research problem at hand.

Fourth, cross-cultural comparisons can often be made even when equivalence in methods is not high, providing the nature of the nonequivalence is known. In such cases, the interpretation of results can take the lack of complete equivalence into account and qualify interpretations accordingly.

Other difficult questions remain unanswered and in need of further attention: (1) How does the comparativist determine *in advance* of his research what concepts and methods will be both appropriate and equivalent in particular societies? (2) How does he demonstrate *after* the research has been conducted that the concepts and methods he employed were, in fact, appropriate and equivalent? In short, it is important to review the conceptual and methodological pitfalls in comparative research, but it is even more important to know how to avoid them and how to test or demonstrate the extent to which they have been avoided.

With respect to the first of these questions, it is not enough to say that a researcher needs to be multicultural and able to use good judgment. Comparativists also need to know what kinds of advance knowledge about societies are critical and then begin systematically compiling such information. In what societies is one most likely to encounter acquiescent bias (such as investigated by Schnaiberg and me), and how does it vary by subpopulation? In what societies is one most likely to encounter unreliable illegitimacy or fertility records (such as investigated by Johnson and Cutright), and what is the nature of that unreliability? In what societies and among what groups are alien researchers most likely to be viewed as hostile foreign undercover agents or as political benefactors (as discussed in Portes's chapter)? We have only begun the systematic identification of problems related to feasibility, meaningfulness, receptivity, and other aspects of appropriateness, reliability, and validity that are associated with different societies or types of societies. In fact, at this stage in the development of comparative methods, the comparativist often cannot know about the appropriateness and equivalence of his methods in advance of his research. This situation provides one reason for doing the research. Comparativists must be prepared to explore methods, make mistakes, and record successes and failures in different social and cultural contexts so that a systematic body of information can develop to guide future research. Indeed, studies may sometimes need to be designed with no other purpose than to discover transcultural concepts and equivalent methods for studying them across societies.

With respect to the second question, several attempts have been made in the past to develop strategies for assessing equivalence (Suchman, 1964; Straus, 1969; Przeworski and Teune, 1970; Frey, 1970; and Warwick and Osherson, 1973). Some of these attempts focus on patterns of item correlations shared across societies, while others focus on patterns of correlation and validity within societies. All tend to be relevant primarily, if not exclusively, to *measurement* equivalence rather than more generally to *method* equivalence and to survey data rather than to observational, archival, or other forms of data. In this domain, comparative sociological research needs much further attention and progress.

Finally, it is important to balance this overview of difficulties in comparative research by recognizing that all methods have limitations and that no research study generates 100 percent confidence in results. Findings and interpretations are always subject to change through replication, new evidence, new insights, and so on. Therefore, we should consider the possibilities of comparative research and encourage greater research efforts beyond the boundaries of our own society even though the task is more difficult and time-consuming than single-society, indigenous research. In particular, we should consider some of the benefits (noted above by Grimshaw) and methodological advantages of comparative research.

In the first place, cross-cultural research forces comparativists to pay greater attention to conceptual clarity and to the appropriateness and equivalence of methods across societies. As a result, it has also made increasingly salient *within* societies the problems of clarity, appropriateness, and equivalence, which are too often ignored. Mehan's study in particular calls attention to the naïve assumptions of cultural homogeneity underlying standardized testing and data-collection procedures in much single-society research. In short, it should be noted that the methodological problems reviewed above are not unique to comparative research but may pose equally serious problems for other modes of research. They belong to a family of methodological and technical problems affecting the social sciences in general, and the sensitivities and solutions developed in comparative research should benefit the discipline as a whole.

Other methodological benefits of comparative research are that it can be useful in extending the range of critical variables, which are often insufficiently distributed within single societies (see Whiting, 1968:694-696, for an excellent discussion and illustration), and it enables investigation of societal variations and effects that cannot be done effectively with single-society studies. In particular, as is illustrated by many of the chapters in this volume, comparative research enables testing of the cultural limits within which measurement instruments are effective, and it contributes to reconceptualization and operationalization of theoretical variables.

The chapters and discussions in the present volume give testimony to the breadth and vitality of comparative research as well as to the difficult problems that hinder research progress. For the most part, the contributions have helped to clarify and increase the salience of methodological issues, and a variety of strategies and techniques for dealing with them have been suggested. Walton's standardized case comparison, Form's analysis of the politics of distrust, Schnaiberg's and my use of convergent-discriminant validity analysis, Mehan's illustration and speculation on the uses of videotaping, Schwirian's comparisons and tests of alternative analytical techniques, and Johnson and Cutright's illustration of measurement and analytical techniques for dealing with a difficult theoretical problem—all are examples of strategies and methods discussed at the conference that hold promise of contributing to the solution of methodological problems found in comparative sociological research and of bringing into clearer focus methodological issues that affect the discipline as a whole but that are frequently ignored.

As Frey (1970:187)-notes, "Although the problems of cross-cultural surveys are not in principle different from those of within-cultural surveys, in both particulars and severity they *are* different. Methodological studies specific to the particular problems of cross-cultural research are sorely needed." The chapters and discussions in this book have been directed precisely to this purpose and should contribute not only to the betterment of comparative research but of the social sciences in general.

Notes

1. I am greatly indebted to Carolyn Mullins, Allen Grimshaw, William Form, Lawrence Hazelrigg, and Fred Waisanen for helpful criticisms and suggestions on earlier drafts of this chapter, and to the Center for Innovations in Human Resource Development (CENFINN), Indiana University, under the direction of Michael Chiappetta, for the support that enabled me both to prepare this chapter and to continue my comparative research with the center.

2. Mitchell (1965), Marsh (1967), Whiting (1968), Scheuch (1968), Holt and Turner (1970), Frey (1970), Przeworski and Teune (1970), and Warwick and Osherson (1973). For additional relevant discussions, see Rommetveit and Israel (1954), Sjoberg (1955), Wilson (1958), Hudson et al. (1959), Moore (1961), Chance (1962), Zelditch (1962), Almond and Verba (1963), Bendix (1963), Suchman (1964), Strodtbeck (1964), Smelser (1966), Verba (1967), Naroll (1968), Rokkan (1968), Etzioni and Dubow (1970), Vallier (1971), and Manaster and Havighurst (1972) as well as other references cited in this paper. For a classified bibliography of comparative methods literature up to 1970, see Przeworski and Teune (1970) and Garfin (1971)

3. It is important not to overstate the problem of sensitivity. With ingenuity, care, and special effort, it is often possible to conduct research that local observers or area

experts might initially consider impossible. For example, consider the investigations of Kinsey et al. (1948) and note the efforts in circumventing sensitivity problems reported in Form's chapter.

4. This statement does not mean that valid methods and cross-cultural equivalence are identical; cross-cultural equivalence may also be achieved for invalid methods.

References

Almond, Gabriel, and Sidney Verba.

    1963   Some methodological problems in cross-national research. In *The Civic Culture: Political Attitudes and Democracy in Five Nations.* Princeton, N.J.: Princeton University Press. Pp. 56-72.

Bendix, Reinhard.

    1963   Concepts and generalizations in comparative sociological studies. *American Sociological Review,* 28, no. 4: 522-539.

Campbell, Donald T.

    1960   Recommendations for APA test standards regarding construct, trait or discriminant validity. *American Psychologist,* 15 (August): 546-553.

Chance, N.A.

    1962   Conceptual and methodological problems in cross-cultural health research. *American Journal of Public Health,* 52: 410-417.

Etzioni, Amitai, and Fredric L. Dubow.

    1970   *Comparative Perspectives: Theories and Methods.* Boston: Little, Brown.

Frank, Andre G.

    1967   Sociology of development and the underdevelopment of sociology. *Catalyst,* 5 (Summer): 20-73.

Frey, Frederick W.

    1970   Cross-cultural survey research in political science. In Robert T. Holt and John E. Turner (Eds.), *The Methodology of Comparative Research.* New York: Free Press. Pp. 173-294.

Garfin, Susan B.

    1971   Comparative studies: a selective, annotated bibliography. In Ivan Vallier (Ed.), *Comparative Methods in Sociology: Essays on*

Trends and Applications. Berkeley and Los Angeles: University of California. Pp. 423-467.

Gould, Julius.

1964   Comparative methods. In J. Gould and W.L. Kolb (Eds.), *A Dictionary of the Social Sciences.* New York: Free Press. Pp. 116-118.

Holt, Robert T., and John E. Turner (Eds.).

1970   *The Methodology of Comparative Research.* New York: Free Press.

Hudson, Bradford B., Mohamed K. Barakat, and Rolfe LaForge.

1959   Problems and methods of cross-cultural research. *Journal of Social Issues,* 15, no. 3: 5-19.

Hunt, W.H., W.W. Crane, and J.C. Wahlke.

1964   Interviewing political elites in cross-cultural comparative research. *American Journal of Sociology,* 70 (July): 59-68.

Hyman, Herbert H.

1967   Strategy for selection of countries and research sites. Lecture given at the Summer Seminar of the Institute for Comparative Sociology, Indiana University, Bloomington (June).

International Studies of Values in Politics.

1971   *Values and the Active Community.* New York: Free Press.

Kinsey, Alfred C., Wardell B. Pomeroy, and Clyde E. Martin.

1948   *Sexual Behavior in the Human Male.* Philadelphia: Saunders.

Manaster, Guy J., and Robert J. Havighurst.

1972   *Cross-National Research: Social-Psychological Methods and Problems.* Boston: Houghton Mifflin.

Marsh, Robert M.

1967   *Comparative Sociology: A Codification of Cross-Societal Analysis.* New York: Harcourt, Brace and World.

Mitchell, Robert E.

1965   Survey materials collected in the developing countries: sampling, measurement, and interviewing obstacles to intra- and international comparisons. *International Social Science Journal,* 17, no. 4: 665-685.

Moore, F.W. (Ed.).

1961   *Readings in Cross-Cultural Methodology.* New Haven, Conn.: HRAF.

Murphy, J. M., and A. H. Leighton (Eds.).

1965   *Approaches to Cross-Cultural Psychiatry.* Ithaca, N.Y.: Cornell University Press.

Myrdal, Gunnar.

1968   *The Asian Drama.* New York: Twentieth Century Fund.

Nadel, S. F.

1952   Witchcraft in four African societies: an essay in comparison. *American Anthropologist,* 54 (January-March): 18-29.

Naroll, Raoul.

1962   *Data Quality Control—A New Research Technique: Prolegomena to a Cross-Cultural Study of Culture Stress.* New York: Free Press.

1968   Some thoughts on comparative method in cultural anthropology. In H. M. Blalock, Jr., and A. B. Blalock (Eds.), *Methodology in Social Research.* New York: McGraw-Hill. Pp. 236-277.

Przeworski, Adam, and Henry Teune.

1966-1967   Equivalence in cross-national research. *Public Opinion Quarterly,* 30 (Winter): 551-568.

1970   *The Logic of Comparative Social Inquiry.* New York: Wiley-Interscience.

Ramsey, Charles E., and Jenaro Collazo.

1960   Some problems of cross-cultural measurement. *Rural Sociology,* 25, no. 1: 92-106.

Rokkan, Stein (Ed.).

1968   *Comparative Research Across Cultures and Nations.* The Hague: Mouton.

Rommetveit, Vagner, and Joachim Israel.

1954   Notes on the standardization of experimental manipulation and measurements in cross-national research. *Journal of Social Issues,* 10, no. 4: 61-68.

Scheuch, Erwin K.

1968   The cross-cultural use of sample surveys: problems of comparability. In Stein Rokkan (Ed.), *Comparative Research Across Cultures and Nations.* The Hague: Mouton. Pp. 176-209.

Sears, R. E.

1961   Transcultural variables and conceptual equivalence. In B. Kaplan (Ed.), *Studying Personality Cross-Culturally.* Evanston, Ill.: Row, Peterson. Pp. 445-456.

Sjoberg, Gideon.

1955   The comparative method in the social sciences. *Philosophy of Science,* 22, no. 2: 106-117.

Sjoberg, Gideon (Ed.).

1967   *Ethics, Politics, and Social Research.* Cambridge, Mass.: Schenkman.

Smelser, Neil J.

1966   The methodology of comparative analysis. Presented at the 1966 Summer Seminar of the Institute for Comparative Sociology, Indiana University (June).

Straus, Murray A.

1969   Phenomenal identity and conceptual equivalence of measurement in cross-national comparative research. *Journal of Marriage and Family,* 31 (May): 233-239.

1970   Methodology of a laboratory experimental study of families in three societies. In Reuben Hill and Rene Konig (Eds.), *Families in East and West.* Paris: Mouton. Pp. 552-577.

Strodtbeck, Fred L.

1964   Considerations of meta-method in cross-cultural studies. In A. Kimball Romney and Roy G. Andrade (Eds.), *Transcultural Studies in Cognition.* Special publication of *American Anthropologist,* 66 (June): 223-229.

Suchman, Edward A.

1964   The comparative method in social research. *Rural Sociology,* 29, no. 2: 123-137.

Szalai, Alexander.

1966   Multinational comparative social research. *American Behavioral Scientist,* 10, no. 4: 1-41.

Vallier, Ivan (Ed.).

1971   *Comparative Methods in Sociology: Trends and Applications.* Berkeley and Los Angeles: University of California.

Verba, Sidney.

1967   Some dilemmas in comparative research. *World Politics,* 20 (October): 111-127.

Warwick, Donald P., and Samuel Osherson.

1973   Comparative analysis in the social sciences. In Donald P. Warwick and Samuel Osherson (Eds.), *Cross-Cultural Research Methods.* Englewood Cliffs, N.J.: Prentice-Hall. In press.

Whiting, John W. M.

1968   Methods and problems in cross-cultural research.In G. Lindzey and E. Aronson (Eds.), *Handbook of Social Psychology,* vol. II. Reading, Mass.: Addison-Wesley. Pp. 523-531.

Wilson, Elmo C.

1958   Problems of survey research in modernizing areas. *Public Opinion Quarterly,* 22, no. 3: 230-234.

Zelditch, Morris, Jr.

1962   Some methodological problems in field studies. *American Journal of Sociology,* 67, no. 5: 556-576.

PART ONE

Relating to the
Research Environment

CHAPTER THREE

Field Problems in Comparative Research: The Politics of Distrust

WILLIAM H. FORM

University of Illinois

Early Experiences with Informant Distrust

Why should anyone trust a snooping sociologist? In my first comparative study along the U.S.-Mexican border, I became aware that informants in each country responded differently to the same research strategy. In subsequent comparative studies, I concluded that these differences resulted from informant distrust and that this factor varied enormously from one country to another. Systematic research on informant distrust is desperately needed to enable us to conduct effective comparative research. This paper reviews my encounters with distrustful respondents in several countries. I hope that these accounts will stimulate others to present their field protocols on the subject, because analysis of a large number of protocols might suggest some principles helpful to future researchers confronting problems of distrust in the field.

I first became aware of national differences in distrust when I went to the Rio Grande border to study how persons and organizations in an American and a Mexican community behaved during a severe flood (Form and Loomis, 1956; Clifford, 1956). Flood victims and officials of organizations in the two countries responded differently to being interviewed, but the researchers were so intent on gathering data that they did not record *how* informants reacted to being studied. In retrospect, two observations may be made. First, immediately after the flood's impact, the social routines of the victims were so disrupted that the researchers encountered little difficulty in gaining their cooperation; on the contrary, victims on both sides of the river were eager to talk about their often tragic experiences. Second, the researchers encountered more difficulty in establishing rapport with officials of organizations than with private persons. The officials' cooperation seemed to depend on their successful handling of problems during and after the crisis: the less their success, the less the cooperation. Also, the more bureaucratic the organization, the more its officers resisted the interviewers; officers of large American organizations showed more distrust than officers of smaller Mexican organizations. Other factors may also have been relevant, but they remain unknown.

I began to think systematically about field problems in comparative research shortly after returning from Italy in 1962. My colleagues had invited me to report on my findings in a departmental colloquium. Since the data had not been processed, I decided to describe the trying problems I had encountered in the field. In Italy, Dr. Paolo Ammassari and I were constantly trying to persuade reluctant organizations to cooperate. Perhaps because of my interest in industrial sociology, I analyzed our relationships with these organizations using a bargaining metaphor. The paper was ambitiously entitled, "The Bargaining Model of Social Research," but it had to be set aside at the time because it identified persons who had helped or blocked our research effort.

A little later Professor Camillo Pellizzi asked me to submit a paper to be translated into Italian and published in the *Rassegna di Sociologia.* I decided to compare my field experience in the United States and Italy at a level of abstraction that would avoid identifying individuals (Form, 1963). In doing that paper, I found that the bargaining framework, which was useful for organizing the Italian data, was inadequate for U.S. data. A more complex political model using social-systems terms provided a more fruitful framework for both sets of data. The ideas in the Italian paper were subsequently elaborated in English (Form, 1971). I shall summarize them briefly because they constitute a point of departure for this paper's discussion of the respondent distrust encountered in five different countries.

In the study of social behavior, a temporary set of relationships exists among researchers, their sponsors, and their informants. While informants may be thought of as playing host to the researchers, the latter usually want their hosts to play compliant roles. When hosts are not accommodating, researchers try to make them so. Success in this venture depends on many factors, for example, the amount of influence that research sponsors have over hosts; the common and/or conflicting values of hosts, researchers, and sponsors; the relative sophistication of the three concerning the subject being investigated; the usefulness that the research has for each party; and specific historical and situational factors. The tactics that the parties use depend on their resources, their skills, the complexity of the system (personal relations, organizations, organizational relationships), the extent to which the subject being studied threatens the parties, the type of instruments being used by the researchers, and other variables.

In situations in which researchers need the cooperation of hosts who distrust each other, researchers face the difficult task of restructuring relationships within the system. Often they have insufficient substantive knowledge of the system to design a successful strategy of intervention; moreover, intervention may affect the very processes and relationships they are trying to study. Yet most methodology texts furnish no guidance on what to do in these difficult situations.

The problems inherent in gaining the research cooperation of persons and organizations in conflict may now be analyzed using the political exchange model discussed above. The research on the Rio Grande flood had interrupted a study of community power in two other border cities, El Paso and Ciudad Juárez. The field problems encountered in those two cities were analyzed in a monograph (D'Antonio and Form, 1965: 259-267), but I shall reexamine them here along with my experiences in three American studies of automobile workers and a later comparative study dealing with the social and occupational integration of automobile workers in four nations: the United States, Italy, Argentina, and India.

The Comparative Study of Community Power

One phase of the research along the border called for interviewing political and economic influentials in El Paso and Ciudad Juárez. We needed a local sponsor to introduce us to knowledgeables as well as influentials. Figure 3.1 outlines the steps we took in both communities to gain access to influentials and associational officers. In El Paso we first approached university professors and officials of the Chamber of Commerce and asked them to provide names of influentials and introductions to them. They politely refused. Newspaper reporters, a social scientist in the city planning bureau, and a Spanish-speaking secretary to the Mayor gave us the names of some political and economic influentials, but these informants were unable to act as sponsors or intermediaries (D'Antonio and Form, 1965). We were forced to approach each influential directly, introduce ourselves, and explain the objectives of the research.

Most of the informants were suspicious of Michigan social scientists doing research in Texas. Further, the interview explored sensitive areas, such as covert community decision-making, contacts with Mexican influentials, and comparisons of Mexican and American business and political practices. Despite repeated assurances of anonymity, many informants remained guarded. While most persons agreed to be interviewed and answered all questions about themselves fully, they hesitated to elaborate accounts of the activities of others or to attribute attitudes to them. When they did attribute motives to others, they emphasized that this information was confidential. The subject matter of the interview was clearly interesting to the informants, but they seemed relieved

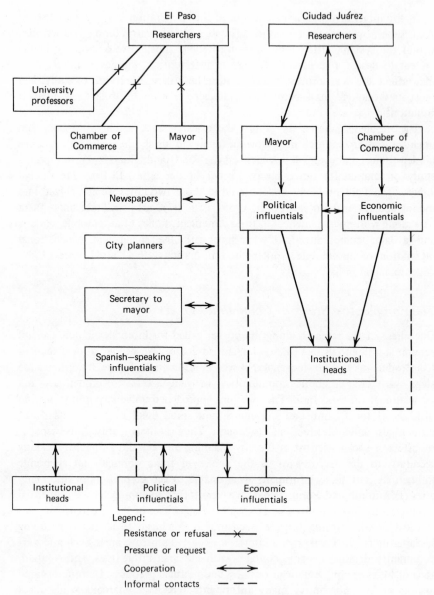

El Paso   Ciudad Juárez

Legend:

Resistance or refusal   ⟶✕⟶

Pressure or request   ⟶

Cooperation   ⟷

Informal contacts   – – –

Figure 3.1 Process of research entry: Ciudad Juárez and El Paso.

when the interview was finished. That we did not gain their complete confidence is indicated by the fact that no informants would introduce us to other influentials who were their friends.

We encountered a different type of reception in Ciudad Juárez. We went directly to the Mayor and the President of the Chamber of Commerce and asked them to name influential persons in their sectors and to introduce us to them. Both the Mayor and the Chamber President gave us their calling cards, on which they wrote brief notes urging their friends to give us full cooperation. Not only did we have easy access to the top influentials in business and government, but the influentials in turn sponsored us to the heads of local organizations.

The interviews in Ciudad Juárez contrasted markedly with those in El Paso. Informants seemed to understand the purpose of the research, they answered the questions fully, and they did not hesitate to describe the activities of their friends and foes or to attribute attitudes to others. Most informants were not concerned with anonymity; some even asserted that they wanted their views widely publicized. The interviews resembled informal conversations and, on the whole, contained fuller information than the El Paso interviews.

An important research goal had been to compare the institutional network of the two cities. The differences we experienced in gaining access to influentials in the two cities provided data on this very problem. Ties between business and government influentials in El Paso were informal, indirect, and invisible to most persons. Only a few had intimate knowledge about the integration of business and political activities, and these persons did not want strangers to have this information (Form and D'Antonio, 1959). While each sector of the Mexican city exhibited a high degree of internal cohesion, factionalism characterized relations between the economic and political sectors; that is, interpersonal trust was strong within, but weak between, sectors. This situation facilitated research sponsorship *within* sectors (which I noted above) but inhibited it *across* sectors. The two sectors were tied at important points, a fact not generally known in Ciudad Juárez, but sponsorship into this network across sectors was very difficult to obtain.

The American Automobile Studies

Four studies of automobile workers were done in Lansing, Michigan. Although only the fourth was part of a comparative study, I have included the access problems experienced in the first three, because they shaped the field strategy of the fourth study. All of the American studies shared some research requirements with the Italian, Argentine, and Indian studies. The interview was used to gather data from the workers, who were interviewed in their homes. The original plan was to draw samples of work teams in various departments from official rosters. Management and union officials were required to give at least passive consent to the study to assure interviewers an unprejudiced reception by the workers. Moreover, workers had to be assured that the research was independent of union and/or management influence. In every instance management refused to provide names of work group members, so random samples were taken of individuals within departments.

Figure 3.2 diagrams sequences of action in research access in these early studies. The purpose of the labor mobility research was to discover how social origins (foreign, Southern white, Negro, and rural and urban) affected the occupational allocation process (Form and Geschwender, 1962; Nosow, 1956). The Oldsmobile Division of General Motors (GM) in Lansing, Michigan was selected because it was large enough to have sufficient workers (for research purposes) in each category. We approached Oldsmobile's management for permission to conduct the study and for access to their employment records. Management refused. We then asked prestigious professors at Michigan State University who allegedly had contacts with Oldsmobile management to intervene on our behalf and ask management to draw a sample of workers for us. Management again refused. Forced to change the research design, we resorted to an area probability sample of workers living in the Lansing area.

The second study, on union integration, examined the economic, political, and social integration of workers into the union and the relationship of union participation to neighborhood and community involvement (Form and Dansereau, 1957). A sample of workers in a large union was needed. We asked the officers of the Oldsmobile union local for permission to do the study and for access to their seniority list to draw the sample. The company was not approached because it had earlier refused access to its records. Even though we had obtained initial approval from union officers, the members in an open meeting voted against endorsing the study, because the faction out of power suspected that the researchers were company spies. The officers then told us that only the United Auto Workers (UAW) headquarters in Detroit could grant permission for a study. I asked a colleague at Wayne State University who knew officers at the International Headquarters to intervene on our behalf. He did and we were granted permission, but we were advised not to approach the local that had earlier refused cooperation (see Figure 3.2).

Detroit officials suggested we approach Local B, an amalgamated-type local that contained seven subunits. The officers of Local B had been in contact with the Oldsmobile local, and they were suspicious about the research. The meeting with the officers convinced me that I had to demonstrate my loyalty to unionism in order to gain access to the seniority list. Even after I had convinced them of my union sympathies, though, the officers insisted that workers be told that the study was sponsored jointly by the union and the university. In sum, certain compromises in research design were forced upon us: a different type of union local was selected, the researcher had to demonstrate his commitment to

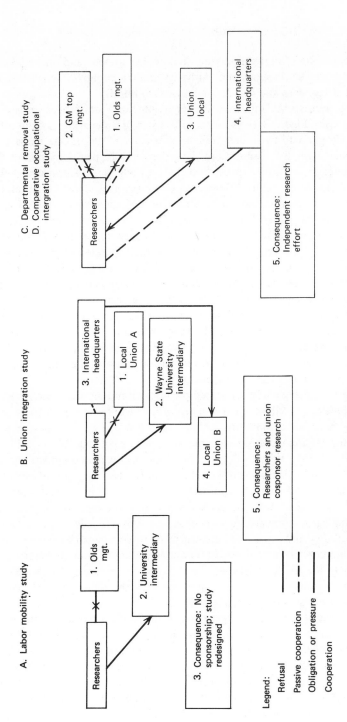

A. Labor mobility study

B. Union integration study

C. Departmental removal study
D. Comparative occupational intergration study

Figure 3.2 Research access in four American field studies. (Numbers represent sequence of

89

unionism, questions in the interview had to be altered, and the study was defined as partly union-sponsored. Although the compromises were fewer than in the first study, they affected future research in the city.

Research access problems were similar in the third and fourth studies. The third study (see Figure 3.2) investigated transfer of a department from a local Fischer Body plant to two other communities (Bloch, 1965). One phase of the research dealt with the reallocation of workers in GM plants located in three communities, and the other focused on the methods that management and the union used to settle their differences. Obviously, the cooperation of both organizations was needed, but the managers of the local plants refused. I sought permission for the study from top GM officials in Detroit, but after some hesitation they also refused. The local union agreed to cooperate, and so did UAW headquarters in Detroit. A list of the workers affected by removal of the department was obtained from the union, and they were interviewed. Although this study was independent of union control, it was incomplete because I could not interview foremen or gain access to company records.

For the first three Lansing studies, then, I was forced by the distrust of either the union, management or both to change research plans. My situation was different in each study. In the first, management denied me access to company records; in the second, the union placed me on probation; in the third, I was defined as pro-union and antimanagement.

The fourth Lansing study replicated the research in Italy. Its objective was to study the impact of technology on the behavior of workers on the job and in the union, neighborhood, community, and nation (Form, 1969). The research design called for identifying workers in specific departments who had certain skills that matched those of the Italian workers. Therefore, rosters of department members were needed from management because seniority lists are not organized by departments or skill level. I approached local management and asked for permission to do the study and access to departmental records. Predictably, it refused, and again I sought approval from top GM officials in Detroit. They refused, but they did direct local management to give me an extended tour of the plant and covertly agreed not to discourage workers from cooperating with the study. On the tour, we selected the departments for study. The local union provided the seniority list; we then succeeded, by a complex and devious method, to select an appropriate sample.

When I reviewed my field experiences with the four American studies, the Italian experience was still fresh in my mind. Research access in Italy had resembled a collective bargaining process. I concluded that over the years in Lansing, I had learned to bargain with increasing effectiveness; labor had come to accept me and management had begun to trust me despite my labor sympathies. I am now not certain that this conclusion was correct. Perhaps calm labor-management relations are more important than personal trust for research access. In 1948, at the time of the first study, relations between the union and GM were tense. A long, bitter strike had recently been terminated and the parties felt hostile toward one another. By 1963, though, when the fourth study was done, labor-management relations had calmed down and both camps had little to fear from research that required only their passive cooperation.

Research Bargaining in Italy

Gaining research access in Italy was a more difficult task than in the eight other studies reviewed in this paper. An important reason for including Italy in the comparative study of automobile workers was to ascertain the importance of technology and ideological unionism to the social relationships of workers. Italian unions are more ideological than American unions because they are tied to various political parties. Figure 3.3 locates the political sympathies of the unions, management, and other participants in the research social system. The Confederazione Generale Italiana del Lavoro (CGIL) is the allegedly Communist -controlled union; the Confederazione Italiana Sindicati Lavoratori (CISL) is the Catholic union, supported by the Christian Democratic party, then (1962) in power; the Unione Italiana del Lavoro (UIL) is the social democratic union, reputedly supported by U.S. interests; and the Sindicato Italiano dell'Automobile (SIDA) is an independent union, modeled along American lines but accused of being a company union. All four unions were represented at FIAT, the company selected for study.

Successful execution of the research required cooperation from the University of Turin, the company, and the four unions prior to our arrival in Italy. Access to the University was provided by an American colleague who had been in Italy; he wrote to an industrial sociologist at the University of Turin, who agreed to sponsor me locally. Establishing contact with FIAT proved more difficult. A colleague who had worked in Italy knew an Italian physician studying in the United States who had worked for FIAT and knew the general manager. I wrote to the physician, described my project, and asked him to write the general manager of FIAT on my behalf. He did so. In his response, expressing a desire to cooperate, the manager asked for a brief description of the research. From the sociologist at the University of Turin, I had obtained names of the chief officers of the local unions at FIAT. I then solicited their cooperation. The first reply came from the Fascist union, which did not have a representative on the plant's *Commissione Interna* ("Internal commission");[2] the second, from the CISL; the third, from the UIL; and the last, from the SIDA. All agreed to cooperate in the study. The CGIL did not reply to either the first or the second letter. Upon arriving in Turin, I planned to make contact first at the University, then to spend two months studying local institutions, then to involve the unions from (political) left to right, and finally to bring the finished

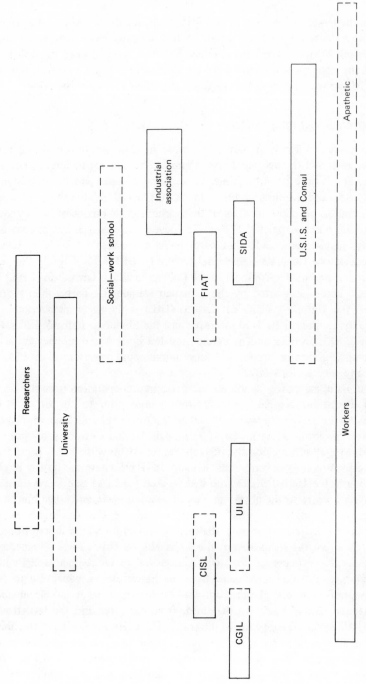

Figure 3.3 Political orientations of participants in the Italian research social system. (Length of bar denotes range of ideological flexibility.)

research proposal to FIAT management.

Initial Contacts with Unions: Ideological Dialogues

The reception at the University was cordial. My Italian co-worker, Paolo Ammassari, and I met top officials of the unions to explain the purpose of the research. All, including the Communist, promised cooperation and introduced us to union leaders at FIAT. The first interviews with local officials, which lasted about two hours, were designed to obtain the history of local industrial relations, current issues, and bargaining objectives. Several patterns immediately became clear. First, we spent considerable time discussing the political and ideological concerns of all the unions and of management. Second, officials wanted to test our knowledge about these conflicts, and they inquired about our own political beliefs. Third, all officials had such detailed knowledge of the problems facing the other unions that it appeared that they had informers in the other unions. Fourth, no union had a list of the workers in FIAT. Last, although all officials had firm ideological commitments, they appeared capable of analyzing the local industrial and political scene rather dispassionately.

Contacts with Management: Indoctrination, Inquiries and Bargaining

Figure 3.4 summarizes the chronology of events at FIAT. The first meeting with the Industrial Relations Department, in which we described the broad research objectives, was formal but cordial. In the second meeting, we listed research needs (e.g., information on union elections, visits to selected departments, and data on the labor force). To our surprise, we were asked to specify our research aims and told that the cooperation of the company in the study was contingent on its evaluation of our research plan. In the meantime, officials suggested that we get to know each other better.

About a week of systematic indoctrination ensued. The company apprised us fully of FIAT's services to its workers with regard to health, recreation, technical schools, social security, housing, homes for the retired, hospitals, cultural events, psychological testing, and so on. We sent the company the research proposal that had been submitted to the National Science Foundation and the Social Science Research Council. The third meeting, in which the research proposal was discussed in detail, was concluded with a meal at an exclusive restaurant. Before parting, we were asked to submit a *written* document listing in detail all the information we wanted.

The delaying tactics of the company, the lack of trust, and the threat of research surveillance were aggravating. We prepared a document that specified departments to be studied, size of the sample, kinds of questions we intended to ask, people who would do the interviewing (advanced university students), necessary union election data,[3] and the right to visit specific departments. At

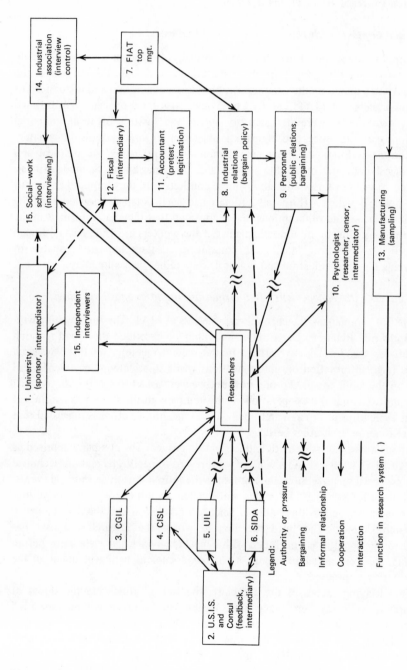

Figure 3.4 Stages of research access in Italy (FIAT). (Numbers represent sequence of actions.)

94

the conclusion of the fourth meeting, in which each item was discussed in detail, the company asked for the final interview, the names of the interviewers, and the name of the company that would publish the interview schedule. Reluctant to comply, we asked professors at the University and union officers what to do. "You'll never get it," they said. "No one else has ever gotten in; you're getting the runaround."

There seemed to be no alternative but to yield to the company's demands. We feared that we were being captured by FIAT; we were being indoctrinated, we were visiting company officials frequently, and we were under constant surveillance. Fearful that our relations with the unions might be endangered, we inaugurated a "balance of visits" scheme: each time we visited FIAT, we visited all four unions. This decision was very costly in time and energy. We also decided to assume a less compliant posture toward the company by trying to anticipate its moves and preparing to counter them. Thus questions were inserted in the interviews that could be discarded in future bargaining. A draft of the interview was sent to the company along with a request for a meeting.

We waited anxiously for a week. Finally, the company informed us that it had provisionally approved the study. FIAT's representative at the meeting generously offered to select the departments that fitted our specifications, to provide us names of the 200 people to be interviewed, to help clarify some of the interview questions, to eliminate perhaps some questions that might endanger our rapport with workers; to alter some questions to fit the local scene; and to locate experienced interviewers at the local school of social work.

At this point in the negotiations, the Industrial Relations Department turned us over to the Personnel Department to work out final arrangements. We decided that the unions should be provided with any information we gave management, so we gave all four unions copies of the interviews and informed management of this. We assured the company that we had already selected competent interviewers at the University, but we were told that the social workers were better qualified.[4]

FIAT wanted to eliminate interview questions dealing with evaluation of the company, of foremen, and of the industrial relations situation. More important, management did not want us to question workers about their union preferences. Fortunately, one of the people who participated in these sessions was an academic man who shared our values. Although management had put him in the stressful position of monitoring our research, outside the bargaining room he gave us helpful suggestions.

We complied with many of management's suggestions with some important exceptions. We demurred on employing "their" interviewers. We proposed that questions on union preference remain in the interview, but management insisted that asking the question would damage rapport with workers and invalidate the entire study. I proposed to settle the issue by a pretest, but management insisted that workers would learn about the pretest via the grapevine. The issue remained unresolved. We could not permit the company to select the sample, force us to abandon questions on union preference, and provide interviewers who could act as company informers. Negotiations were stalled.

At this point I asked a friend who was respected by FIAT to mediate. I asked him to determine whether interviewers from the school of social work could be trusted and whether conversations had been going on among the school, the Industrial Association, and FIAT. He learned that, although the school had been approached by FIAT, its personnel were professionally oriented and could be trusted. We permitted FIAT officials to introduce us to officers of the Industrial Association, who in turn introduced us to the head of the school of social work (whom we had previously met). The Association offered to print the interviews, a generous gesture that could hardly be refused. Obviously, the Association and the school could monitor our activities and inform the company whether we were living up to our agreements.

We asked our friend to persuade FIAT to be more flexible regarding the anonymity of workers to be sampled and the inclusion of questions on union preference in the interview. Our friend had no contacts with the Industrial Relations Department, but he did know other officials on the same authority level. He was able to convince the officials that a neutral and unbiased study should be permitted. He pointed out that past studies of FIAT were critical because they had been done by political radicals who had an ax to grind. He also suggested that we might be willing to drop the question on union identification. After waiting two agonizing weeks, we were informed that most of our demands could be met. The company agreed to let us draw a large sample, from which we would in turn select an anonymous subsample if we dropped the question on union identification from the interview.

Bargaining and Mediation with the Unions

During this mediation stage, we attempted to clarify our relations with the unions. As in the past, we approached them from the left to the right and asked each to furnish two or three typical workers on whom we could pretest the interview. All the unions sent workers who had been members of the internal commission. As befitted trusted union lieutenants, they answered every question with statements of the official union position. We asked them to give their own position rather than that of the union, but they insisted that there could be no difference. Yet the encounters were not completely useless, because the workers criticized the ideological slant of some questions and offered suggestions to improve the interview. After about an hour of parrying, most workers agreed to answer the questions as they thought their fellow workers might.

During these pretests we became aware of an undercurrent of hostility from the representatives of the two nonradical unions: the social democratic UIL and the "nonpolitical" SIDA. We therefore wanted both the company and the unions to approve a letter to be sent to the workers describing the study and referring to the fact that both had agreed to the research. During the meetings with the union officials, we asked them how they thought workers would respond to the question, "Which union do you identify with most?"[5] The officials' responses "scaled" perfectly, from left to right: radical CGIL officials insisted that the question should be asked and thought that all workers would answer it; Catholic CISL officials thought the question should be asked and that most workers would answer it; social democratic UIL officials thought the question was sensitive and that some workers might not answer it; and the president of SIDA, the independent union, thought the question was threatening and that most workers would not answer it.

Rapport with the unions was opposite to our expectations; we had expected the greatest cooperation from the conservative unions, which were now showing the greatest resistance. We decided to reexamine our relations with the unions and to get feedback on their attitudes toward us and their willingness to cooperate in the study. We suspected that the two conservative unions might be colluding with the company in opposing either some questions or the study itself. SIDA and UIL together dominated the internal commission, and they were being attacked by the two radical unions as promanagement.

Over the years the two conservative unions had allegedly been supported by the United States in their fight against CGIL. The United States Information Service (USIS) had a labor section in Turin that was in constant contact with the "non-Communist" unions. I was on good terms with the director of USIS as well as with an Italian employee in the USIS Labor Section and an American economic attaché who knew the local labor scene. I asked them to ascertain the attitudes of the unions toward the research and urged them to persuade reluctant unions to cooperate in the study. It would hardly do for an American professor to be "invited" to Turin to do a study only to return home because the unions refused to cooperate!

The reports from USIS revealed that our suspicions had been justified: SIDA, which was obligated to management, was hostile toward the study, and UIL was uncertain whether it should cooperate. USIS officials urged both unions to cooperate. When we next met with UIL's officers, we were greeted warmly and assured of cooperation; the meeting adjourned to the bar and to rounds of toasts. SIDA officials were formal and polite; they agreed to cooperate with the study because certain issues had been "clarified." Catholic CISL had lost confidence in FIAT management and had always been inclined to cooperate in the study. When its officers discovered that one of my friends was related to a high CISL official in Rome, there were no more questions. Students at the University who were members of the Communist party reassured us of CGIL's cooperation. The end result was that the four unions and management had agreed to the study, the interview, and the letter to be sent out to prospective informants. Such cooperation was unheard of in local annals.

Sample Selection and Administration of Interview

To select the sample, we needed intimate knowledge of the technology of various departments. The head of automobile production, second in FIAT's organizational structure only to the general manager, conducted us on a tour of the departments we wanted to inspect, including the highly secret experimental department where new models were being built. After we selected the departments, the Personnel Department offered to provide the names of 200 workers to be interviewed. We asked for 400 names to be selected at random, so that a subsample of anonymous respondents could be selected. To our surprise they agreed, but insisted on being involved in the selection of the sample. The researchers, the head of production, his assistant, and the plant psychologist sat around a table and, with a table of random numbers, selected the 400 names from departmental rosters.

Interview training sessions were arranged with the faculty and students at the school of social work. We had by this time pretested the interview on typical workers and found it satisfactory. All of the interviewers were mature women who had had considerable experience interviewing working-class people. We were pleased with the results of the first training session. The critical item on union preference had been dropped from the interview as a concession to management. Because we knew they could figure it out anyway, we told the interviewers that a series of filter questions would in most cases stimulate the respondent to reveal his union preference. We felt that their success in obtaining this information would test their skill and loyalty to the researchers. We asked the interviewers to conduct preliminary interviews in sections of the city where they would do subsequent interviewing.

After three days we examined the interviews. Not a single interviewer had obtained information on union preference, and other sensitive questions were left unanswered. We called a meeting of the interviewers. The interviewers admitted their reluctance to press for answers to the sensitive questions. They also indicated that they were encountering resistance from workers who had not been reassured about the positions of labor and management toward the study.

A number of quick decisions had to be made. We decided to instruct the interviewers to ask the workers directly for their union preferences. We stressed that the clinical style of interviewing was inappropriate for gathering the direct information we wanted. Uncertain whether to trust the social workers, we decided to employ "control" interviewers to provide a basis for comparing the quality of the interviewing.[6] We then asked the unions to identify informal leaders in the departments under study and to send them to a meeting. We informed these leaders about the research, the agreement with management and the unions, the guarantees of anonymity, and the need to encourage workers to cooperate with the interviewers. The meetings were well attended; only the independent union, SIDA, did not send a representative, but it agreed to urge workers in the departments to cooperate in the study. The interviewing was resumed, and we waited anxiously for the results. The gambles paid off. Both sets of interviewers performed well, and they were well received by the workers. Ninety percent of the workers answered the questions on union identification.[7]

In sum, we have used a bargaining metaphor to analyze fieldwork problems encountered in Turin. Distrust was so ubiquitous among the parties that we had to bargain for many things that are under researchers' control in most studies. The areas of bargaining included:

1. Sponsorship by management and the unions
2. The contents of the letter of introduction to informants
3. Questions in the interview
4. The departments to be studied
5. The number of workers to be interviewed
6. The anonymity of the informants
7. The interviewers to be hired
8. The cooperation of the interviewers
9. The reception workers accorded the interviewers (this factor depended upon management and the unions' urging workers to cooperate with interviewers).

The Argentine IKA Study

The research in Argentina was conducted at the Córdoba plant of Industrias Kaiser Argentine (IKA). We had hoped that the Institute of Sociology at the University of Córdoba would provide us local sponsorship. Professor Delbert C. Miller who had previously done research in Córdoba, graciously agreed to write to the Institute members on our behalf, and personnel there agreed to help us. The plan was to send Dr. Richard E. Gale, then my research assistant, to Córdoba to do preliminary work; I would arrive just before the interviewing was to begin. Gale was to obtain cooperation from management and the union. Letters describing the study were sent to the Institute, IKA officials, and labor union leaders before Gale departed (see Figure 3.5).

When he appeared in Córdoba, Gale found the Institute staff split according to preference for a philosophical or empirical research style. He asked a professor who appeared to be playing a mediating role to introduce him to IKA management. After the introduction, Gale was left to his own devices. He hired a research assistant from the psychology faculty, an act that some Institute members regarded as inappropriate. Others who regarded Gale more as a student than a colleague would occasionally ask when I was to arrive.

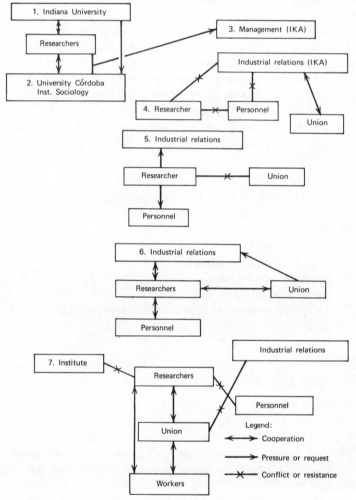

Figure 3.5 Stages of research access: Córdoba, Argentina (IKA). (Numbers represent sequence of actions.)

Gale early noted that he needed the cooperation of two officials at IKA: the industrial relations manager, who had access to local union officials, and the personnel manager, who had access to employee records needed to draw the sample. Unfortunately, the two were competing for the plant manager's favor; neither was convinced that Gale was a mature social scientist; both were apprehensive about cooperating with a foreign social scientist; and both were unconvinced that this study would be useful to them. As long as I was not there and the Institute could not provide Gale support, he was held in suspicion.

Gale decided to visit both the industrial relations manager and the personnel manager with equal regularity so that neither could accuse him of favoring the other. In order to demonstrate the utility of social science to the personnel manager, Gale decided to study personnel turnover. Since he had nothing to offer the industrial relations manager, though, ties with him weakened as they improved with the personnel manger. Whenever Gale asked the industrial relations manager for an introduction to the union officials, he was told that the time was not appropriate. Gale feared that he was being captured by management and that he would be so defined by the union. I decided to go to Córdoba, but just before my arrival Gale forced the issue by visiting union headquarters on his own. This act produced a meeting between Gale, the industrial relations manager, and union leaders. The latter, who wanted to demonstrate their independence from management, readily agreed to cooperate in the study. However, the industrial relations manager became more hostile and may have influenced the union president to withhold cooperation.

When I arrived in Córdoba, the professor who had introduced Gale to IKA management visited me. Since conflicts within the Institute were erupting and I did not want to be identified with any faction, I hurried to pay my respects to all members of the Institute. Professors introduced me to IKA managers, who gave me a tour of the plant, but the latter withheld permission to launch the study. Gale and I immediately completed the research on labor turnover and presented it to the personnel director, who forwarded it to the plant director. The report was well received, and the personnel director agreed to cooperate in the study. We already had obtained access to the files for the turnover study and had drawn the sample we needed. The only obstacle remaining was union agreement on a letter of introduction to be sent to prospective informants.

The president of the union, who had been working closely with management, had succeeded over the years in obtaining good contract terms. However, a faction was being organized against his reelection. We interviewed the president three times and had the impression that he had approved the study. During the next two weeks we worked on the final interview. However, when we returned to show him the letter of introduction to be sent to the workers, he was irked because we had not communicated with him for two weeks. His evasiveness in approving the letter constituted a denial of cooperation.

We had no alternative but to cultivate second-line officials, some of whom were leading the opposition faction. We also asked the industrial relations manager to persuade the union president to cooperate in the study. Apparently we convinced lower echelon officials that the union should approve the study. With the grudging consent of the industrial relations manager, all parties finally agreed on a letter to be sent to the workers. The letter simply indicated that both management and labor were aware of the study, that the study was being conducted by university professors, and that the workers could be assured of anonymity.

One consequence of the uncertainty about permission for the study was that we dropped from the interview questions that dealt with politics and ideology. We also alienated some members of the institute either because we did not involve them sufficiently in the study or because we did not heed local deference patterns. As in the other studies, we learned something about labor-management relations and union factionalism from our attempts to obtain permission for the study. We concluded that in such a highly personalistic environment, verbal agreements would remain binding only if personal relationships were constantly reinforced.

The Indian Premier Automobile Study

The last site was Premier Automobiles Limited in Bombay, India. I did not visit the plant, so the following account is based exclusively on materials provided by Dr. Baldev R. Sharma, who was completing his doctoral work under my direction in 1965. Prior to his departure for India, Sharma and I discussed the problems of research access, and he read my diaries and reports on the subject. He promised to keep a diary of his experiences.

Before leaving he obtained the usual documents given fieldworkers, including letters of introduction from professors in the United States and the Shri Ram Institute of India. The Institute, which conducts research in industrial relations, is highly respected in India. Since the institute had provided some support for the project, Sharma could refer to it as a sponsor. After inspecting several plants, Sharma decided to study the Premier plant in Bombay. His immediate concern was to find someone who would introduce him to a plant official. He first approached sociologists at a local university and presented himself as a doctoral student in the United States and as a research associate in the Shri Ram Institute. Since these sociologists had not typically engaged in fieldwork and had no contacts in industry, they were reluctant to sponsor Sharma to a local industrialist.

He next approached the Tata Institute of Social Science, a social-work training agency. This Institute trained welfare workers and regularly sent some of them to Premier for fieldwork experience. Institute members received Sharma warmly and permitted him to use the institute's facilities, but they were unable to introduce him to Premier officials (see Figure 3.6).

The Bombay Labor Institute, a state-supported institution, was approached next. Its director tried to establish contacts for Sharma at Premier, but his contacts were at too low a level to be useful. Sharma then approached union headquarters in Bombay. Although he was given considerable information about industrial relations at Premier, no official was willing to introduce him to

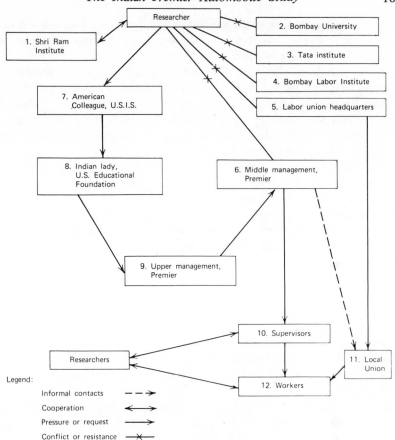

Figure 3.6   Stages of research access: Bombay, India (PAL). (Numbers represent sequence of actions.)

Premier management or to local union leaders. In desperation, Sharma decided to approach middle management directly. He went to the factory and obtained an appointment with the deputy staff manager. He was told that he did not have sufficient sponsorship or government authority to attempt such a large study. However, he was given an appointment to explore the subject at a later time.

Finally, Sharma encountered an employee of the USIS whom he had met as a student in the United States. He asked his American friend whether he knew anyone at Premier. Sharma was referred to a well-known Indian woman who was associated with an American educational agency. During a visit, she asked Sharma to write her a letter describing precisely what he wanted to do in the plant. The letter and her recommendation were submitted to a member of Premier's Board of Directors.

While waiting for a reply, Sharma returned to the deputy staff manager of the plant. This time he was well received and given permission to work with personnel records. The manager defined Sharma's presence in the plant in the same way that he defined that of social-work students from Tata Institute. The manager informed Sharma that he would recommend to higher authorities "that Sharma be permitted to do research in the plant." Somewhat later, the secretary to the deputy staff manager showed Sharma a four-word letter from the director of the company to the deputy staff manager that simply said: "I see no harm" (in Sharma's doing the study at Premier).

The final hurdle was apparently surmounted. Middle-management personnel presented Sharma to supervisors in various departments and urged them to cooperate in the study. Company relations with the local union had become so peaceful that Sharma did not hesitate to ask local union officials to cooperate in the study. In a series of interviews he gathered data on industrial relations in the company. He then asked for union backing to interview 300 workers. An interview was arranged with higher union officials in Bombay. When they were convinced that the study had no connections with the government, the company, or the rival union, they told local officials to give Sharma whatever help he needed for his survey.

The last problem was to convince the workers to cooperate in the interviewing. After considerable indecision, Sharma decided to interview them in the "time office" assigned to him on the factory floor. In general, he was able to enlist cooperation by telling the workers that he needed their help to write a book to complete his education. The fact that workers were critical of the factory, the union, and the government suggests that they were not intimidated by being interviewed in the plant.

Summary and Reflections

Not enough cases of research access in conflict situations have been described to allow identification of all factors that affect it. Systematic research on the politics of access should take into account the major characteristics of the host systems, the social attributes of the research unit, how the proposed research threatens or helps those involved in the research, and the resources available to participants in the research system for working out their exchanges. I shall try to consider these variables in analyzing the cases described above (see Glazer, 1972). To simplify analysis, I shall focus primarily on situations in which distrust of the researcher is high and conflict and suspicion exist among the informants. In such situations, hosts have the capacity to withhold cooperation from the researcher. It is therefore important to consider what tactics the researcher may use to overcome distrust.

His tactics are shaped by many factors. One of the most important is the social structure of the system being studied. For example, research access is easier into a community than into a bureaucracy because no one has the authority to deny researchers access into a community, while permission must be obtained to study a bureaucracy, especially if observable research techniques are used. The more and the stronger are the linkages between agencies being studied and external organizations, the more easily researchers can gain research access simply because more potential research sponsors exist. Even when research access is achieved, however, especially in a bureaucracy, some subjects are more difficult to study than others. For example, the study of managerial control is resisted more than the study of attitudes held by randomly selected individuals at the lowest level of an organization (Form, 1971:25-26).

Paradoxically, it may be easier to gain research access into organizations marked by internal conflict rather than stability. In either case, second-level, rather than first-level, officials cooperate with researchers more readily because officials at the second level most keenly resent the denial of power. In communities marked by internal conflict, the weakest parties tend to cooperate most with researchers because the weak have the least to lose and the most to gain. Intimate knowledge of the ongoing conflict can become.the researcher's most useful resource in persuading reluctant informants to cooperate. Especially in situations where it is difficult to contain conflict within the system, parties will often cooperate with a researcher to avoid giving the opposition credibility. However, conflict can be structured in so many different ways that researchers should be acquainted with its precise patterns before designing access strategies. For example, in the United States, industrial conflict tends to be situational, focusing on bread-and-butter issues; in much of Europe, by contrast, it is often part of the more general political conflict.

Another important variable affecting access in conflict situations is the extent to which parties feel that the research findings may change their power relationships. The amount of cooperation researchers need from informants is also important; where it is high, researchers are more dependent, and informants can manipulate them for their own ends. In such situations researchers need the aid of influential sponsors, high social status, and an ability to use whatever knowledge they have accumulated about the system under study. Where the level of ideological conflict is high, the ideological location of researchers affects the extent of informant cooperation. I shall consider all these factors in the review of the cases below.

Institutional Integration and Segmentation

In El Paso, the guarded attitude of the business and political influentials toward the researchers appeared to derive from a desire to protect private knowledge of how they informally set community policies. Their power depended upon their ability to keep this knowledge secret. Recent political challenges had made the influentials sensitive to accusations of community domination (D'Antonio and Form, 1965:131-141). Understandably, they wanted the researchers to believe that local decision-making was democratic and uncentralized. In no instance did an influential reveal that someone had informed him of our presence in the community. We could not have been so anonymous, though, given the importance of the subject being studied and the subsequent findings that influentials (1) knew each other professionally and socially, (2) cooperated in community projects, and (3) agreed on the tactics to follow on community issues.

Although the influentials could have refused to be interviewed, they did not; to refuse might have underlined an impression that they had something to hide. We had few weapons to combat the influentials' hesitancy at being interviewed and their tendency to omit detailed information in the interviews. Soon after arriving in El Paso, we held interviews with newspapermen, top officials of some institutions, and leaders of the Spanish-speaking community who provided information on the behavior of influentials relative to important community projects. Some of these informants were critical of the behavior of some influentials in community projects. When we first asked top influentials for interviews, we mentioned that our informants had suggested we make contact with them, hoping that this tactic would tempt them to give us their interpretation of community events.

Perhaps the most important factor enabling us to overcome the influentials' suspicion was the community's structure. El Paso, like most large cities, is a loose conglomeration of organizations with no central point of authority. The researcher can penetrate this relatively open and amorphous structure at many points. He can use the information that he systematically gathers to extract even more in subsequent interviews. Not infrequently, he knows more about the total community than any person interviewed (Blau, 1964).

In Ciudad Juárez, business and government were deeply split but each was highly integrated internally (Form and D'Antonio, 1959). Influentials felt that they could sponsor us to persons within their sectors but not to those in the opposing sector. No one claimed to have ties to the other sector, even though ties existed; the admission of ties would have exposed persons to accusations of ideological defection. Even when distrust of a researcher is high, as in a factionalized community, the researcher can use community knowledge as a lever. Antagonists do not want to run the risk of having researchers report a biased view of a conflict, and enemies are unlikely to agree on withholding information from a neutral party. On the contrary, antagonists sometimes want to present their views to a high-status outsider to get favorable publicity. Distrust of the researcher was not a problem in Ciudad Juárez because community conflict gave him resources to use in exchanges.

Bureaucratic Distrust

In studying automobile workers, I was seeking cooperation from companies and unions that had centralized authority structures. Tactics of research access useful in community research were not effective in studying organizations. In total institutions, managers have enormous power; if they distrust research, it will not be done. Researchers typically experience most resistance in studying top levels of organizations, where decisions are made. Managers have power to deny researchers access to the organization, and they often do so because they realize that research exposes how managers use their power and authority.

Thus, in Lansing I was never able to study areas over which management had control, but I was permitted to study areas over which management shared control with labor unions. Access was denied to study the behavior of work groups, the occupational allocation of workers according to social origins, and the transfer of the cut-and-sew department to other cities. Management resisted my requests to study its behavior with impunity; it had nothing to gain by permitting an outsider to examine its decisions. Management did permit others to study the morale of individual workers (selected at random), but it would not permit anyone to study its personnel decisions. For over 20 years, I could not persuade Oldsmobile's management to trust me. Yet it did not use all of its weapons to stop my research: it never advised workers to refuse to be interviewed, nor did it ask the unions to honor the contract clause that forbids outsiders access to the seniority list. Possibly management tolerated this violation because I did not study "important" issues and because I did not feed damaging data about the company to the unions or others. However, research can threaten management; during a strike, for example, information on derogatory attitudes of employees toward the company could be released. Even here, though, the company could respond that during strikes it is normal for workers to have imaginary grievances against the company.

But why did local unions cooperate with me? First, I demonstrated my ideological attachment to unionism by letting them know that I had indirect contacts with top union leaders in Detroit. Second, the research I proposed did not examine internal union problems; it did not threaten the authority of union officials, who are as fearful of studies on union democracy as managers are of studies on personnel decisions. Third, and perhaps most important, it is the almost universal tendency for the weakest party in a conflict to cooperate with outsiders who might be able to help it (Form, 1971:31). Labor unions felt weak vis-a-vis management power and saw no harm in cooperating with educators.

Ubiquitous Conflict, Ideology, and Bargaining

The FIAT case shows the relevance of social conflict and political ideologies for research access. Clearly, like Oldsmobile, FIAT could have refused to permit the research and the effort would have terminated immediately; only FIAT had the list of workers that I needed to draw a sample. I can only speculate why the company agreed in principle to cooperate (e.g., as a gesture of goodwill, a public-relations gesture, or the hope of a favorable study). Since the company agreed to cooperate, two factors about the environment explained much of its behavior: (1) general distrust of organizations over which it had no control, and (2) the conflict that existed among the unions and between them and management. For a number of years FIAT had fought the Communist-dominated CGIL. After the company had reduced the union's influence in the plant, it was able to dominate labor-management relations (Ornati, 1963). Management profited from the continuing union rivalries because their conflicts threw the power balance into management's favor.

Once FIAT had agreed to the research, two conditions became inevitable. First, the company was determined to exert maximum surveillance over the research to assure itself a "neutral" study; second, the researchers were given bargaining powers because they too could use the factionalized environment to advantage. In the ensuing bargaining, the company had the clear advantage; it had more resources, it could withdraw from the arrangement, it had contacts with the school of social work and the Industrial Association, and it dominated the weak unions. However, for the company to withdraw from the research might suggest to the unions that it had something to hide, so the company chose to monitor rather than to oppose the research.

The unions' behavior is easier to explain. As the weaker parties in industrial bargaining, the radical unions had nothing to lose and possibly something to gain from the research. They were convinced that a neutral scientist would produce findings that would support their contention that management's union policies were repressive. The hesitation of the conservative unions in power to cooperate in the research reflected their ties to management; aggravating the company by pleasing the researchers was not a risk worth taking. To withhold cooperation, however, would give credibility to the radical unions' charges that the conservative unions favored management. Their decision to cooperate was made easier by the company's ultimate consent and the good offices of U.S. agencies.

The main resource available to the researchers in the bargaining was their ability to take advantage of conflict. As long as a single party was willing to cooperate in the study, reluctant parties found it difficult to provide convincing reasons why they should withdraw. To do so would be a sign of weakness or collusion with management. The status of a foreign educator and sponsorship from the local university and U.S. agencies were other resources of the researchers.

Distrust and Opportunism

Inability to gain research access in Argentina was caused as much by conflict within management and unions as by conflict between the two. Distrust and opportunism seemed to be structural features of the system. Only in Argentina did factions within management and the union find the threat of cooperating with the researchers useful to their internal politics. Perhaps this condition was responsible for the fragile nature of the agreements with the researchers; the latter felt it necessary constantly to reinforce their personal contacts. Once an agreement was made, it had to be executed immediately because it might not endure. Sponsorship from the outside was not sufficiently strong to overcome pervasive distrust within and between the parties.

Bureaucracy, External Linkages, and Personal Sponsorship

The Indian research environment was distinctive. Labor and management had relatively few linkages to the external community, and their internal relationships were informal but hierarchical. This situation made it difficult for Sharma to find suitable research sponsors. Distrust of outsiders was so strong that research access could only be achieved by finding persons who had strong particularistic ties with company officials. Once permission was given by a powerful official in the company, the researcher could count on the cooperation of people in the lower echelons. The same situation applied for union consent. Overcoming distrust was a problem only during the early stages of field research in India, while in Italy and Argentina distrust tended to be endemic and ubiquitous.

Persistent Issues

These impressions on the relevance of social structure to research access are tentative. Two important questions remain: (1) Were the problems encountered due to societal differences or situational factors? (2) Can a strategy of research access be developed on the basis of knowledge about the social systems one is studying? My limited experience suggests that the problems reported here were not uniquely situational. In American industrial relations, labor and management operate rather independently of each other, except in formal bargaining. They are not concerned about each other's internal operations (Dunlop, 1970:94-128). In Italy industrial relations are part of the larger political scene, so the parties are concerned about issues in various contexts (La Palombara, 1957:71-104). Argentine society is fragmented, and labor is trying to establish its legitimacy (Alexander, 1962:210-222). Unions in India are weak bargaining agencies, more interested in national politics than in what is going on in management and in the plant (Myers, 1959:19-74).

Thus, research can be conducted with union sponsorship in the United States without arousing management's hostility, and it can be sponsored by management in India without arousing undue suspicion from labor. In the factionalized industrial relations climate of Italy, though, researchers encounter great difficulty in maintaining a neutral stance; their activities are assigned ideological significance by all parties. And the unsatisfied demand for recognition on the part of labor in Argentina results in their withholding cooperation from any effort until the claim for status is validated. Lack of confidence in organizational decisions adds to the complications (Filliol, 1961). Obviously, one can improve tactics of access by taking account of these social structural differences in industrial relations.

But researchers face a dilemma when studying social systems about which they have little previous knowledge. It is precisely the absence of this knowledge that motivates them to undertake the research. The challenge in the field is to obtain reliable knowledge about social systems rapidly enough to anticipate access problems and to design tactics to meet them. The inability of many researchers to accomplish this task accounts for the high mortality rate for cross-national studies and the shifting of research problems in midstream.

Unfortunately, knowledge acquired from failures to gain access usually remains private and unsystematic. It is now possible to design comparative studies to accumulate systematic knowledge on research as a social process. Alternative field strategies can be planned and records kept on the outcomes of those strategies. Comparative research offers sociologists quasi-experimental conditions in which to study the effects of local social systems on field strategy; the problems, instrumentation, and other research variables are similar even though the host communities differ. Materials commonly found in field-methods courses have not been tested in the context of comparative designs. Studies must be designed that make different types of organizational settings (bureaucracies, institutions, communities) the central research variables. In the meantime, social scientists should publish their field experiences to enable scholars to profit from them prior to departure for the field.

Notes

1. I am grateful to the following agencies for supporting this research: the National Science Foundation, the School of Labor and Industrial Relations and International Programs (Ford Foundation) at Michigan State University, the American Fulbright Commission, the Social Science Research Council, and the Institute of Labor and Industrial Relations at the University of Illinois (Champaign-Urbana). I am also indebted, intellectually and otherwise, to the field directors of the four studies reported in this paper: Dr. Paolo Ammassari, Italy; Dr. Steven E. Deutsch, United States; Dr. Richard P. Gale, Argentina; and Dr. Baldev R. Sharma, India.

2. A worker-elected body dealing with grievances, local bargaining, and related problems. The Fascist union (CISNAL) lacked sufficient votes to have representation on the commission, so we ignored it, as Figure 3.3 indicates.

3. Union elections were held in the plant. Slates of candidates of all unions are presented to workers, who elect the members of the internal commission according to the principle of proportional representation. The research design called for a sample that would accurately represent union preferences of the labor force.

4. Later we learned that philosophy students at the University had initiated critical studies of FIAT. Obviously, the company did not want them to be interviewers.

5. The question was needed because only 15 percent of the workers were union members. Union membership was not a requisite for voting; in fact, over 90 percent of the workers voted.

6. Earlier,we had wanted to hire a group of women who did interviewing commercially, but the social workers, we learned, competed for the same business. Since we could not meld the two groups into a single interviewing team, members of each team were assigned different sections of the metropolitan region.

7. Three weeks after termination of the interviewing, FIAT experienced its first strike in 13 years. We know of no connection between our study and the occurrence of the strike.

References

Alexander, Robert J.

    1962   *Labor Relations in Argentina, Brazil and Chile.* New York: McGraw-Hill.

Ammassari, Paolo.

    1969   The Italian blue-collar worker. *International Journal of Comparative Sociology,* 10 (March and June):3-21.

Blau, Peter M.

    1964   The research process in the study of the dynamics of bureaucracy. In Philip E. Hammond (Ed.), *Sociologists at Work.* New York: Basic Books. Pp. 24-32.

Bloch, Heinz.

    1965   *Some Sociological and Economic Consequences of a Departmental Shutdown.* Winterthur, Switzerland: Keller.

Clifford, Roy A.

    1956   *The Rio Grande Flood: A Comparative Study of Border Communities in Disaster.* Washington, D.C.: National Academy of Sciences – National Research Council.

D'Antonio, William V., and William H. Form.

1965   *Community Influentials in Two Border Cities.* Notre Dame, Ind.: Notre Dame University Press.

Dunlop, John T.

1970   *Industrial Relations Systems.* Carbondale, Ill.: Southern Illinois University Press.

Filliol, Thomas Roberto.

1961   *Social Factors in Economic Development: The Argentine Case.* Cambridge, Mass.: MIT Press.

Form, William H.

1963   Sulla sociologìa della ricerca sociale. *Rassengna di* Sociologìa 4 (Settembre):463-481.

1969   Occupational and social integration of automobile workers in four countries: a comparative study. *International Journal of Comparative Sociology,* 10 (March-June):95-116.

1971   The sociology of social research. In Richard O'Toole (Ed.), *The Management, Organization and Tactics of Social Research.* Boston: Schenkman. Pp. 3-42.

Form, William H., and H. Kirk Dansereau.

1957   Union member orientations and patterns of social integration. *Industrial and Labor Relations Review,* 11 (October):3-12.

Form, William H., and William D'Antonio.

1959   Integration and cleavage among community influentials in two border cities. *American Sociological Review,* 24 (December): 804-814.

Form, William H., and James A. Geschwender.

1962   Social reference basis of job satisfaction: The case of manual workers. *American Sociological Review,* 27 (April): 228-237.

Form, William H., and Charles P. Loomis.

1956   The persistence and emergence of social and cultural systems in disasters. *American Sociological Review,* 21 (April):180-185.

Form, William H., and Sigmund Nosow.

1958   *Community in Disaster.* New York: Harper.

Gale, Richard P.

    1969   Industrial development and the blue-collar worker in Argentina. *International Journal of Comparative Sociology,* 10 (March-June):117-150.

Glazer, Myron.

    1972   *The Research Adventure.* New York: Random House.

La Palombara, Joseph.

    1957   *The Italian Labor Movement: Problems and Prospects.* Ithaca, N.Y.: Cornell University Press.

Myers, Charles A.

    1959   India. In Walter Galenson (Ed.), *Labor and Economic Development.* New York: Wiley. Pp. 19-74.

Nosow, Sigmund.

    1956   Labor distribution and the normative order. *Social Forces,* 35 (October):25-33.

Ornati, Oscar.

    1963   The Italian economic miracle and organized labor. *Social Research,* 30 (Winter):519-526.

Sharma, Baldev R.

    1969   The Indian industrial workers. *International Journal of Comparative Sociology,* 10 (March-June):161-177.

Discussion

Mr. Gould.   Portes's paper [see below] reports the necessity of a basic change in the assumption that the milieu being investigated in social science research is essentially passive. We must now inquire how what we are affects what we know as social scientists. Portes points out that the passivity of the milieu can no longer be assumed in international sociological research; Form shows quite as much change right here at home. Neither the Oldsmobile corporation nor the unions representing the workers see any particular virtue in being studied unless they can influence the outcome of the findings. There is no such thing as objective sociological research, they say, and in holding this opinion they apparently agree with FIAT in Turin, with the automobile manufacturers of Córdoba in Argentina, and also with Premier of India.

We need to face the fact that the social science community has a political image as well as an academic one; further, this image has not been passively acquired. On the contrary, it derives from the selective process by which most of us ended up in social science rather than, say, the clergy or business community or the Ku Klux Klan. Form shows how he found it necessary, at one point in Lansing, to invoke his own ideological roots in order to get anything accomplished. The fact that he was identified more heavily with labor than with management obviously explains why he moved in the direction that he did when the injunction to get something done made some kind of ideological move necessary on his part. If not, why didn't he tell management that he was a Republican, a believer in the free-enterprise system, and a supporter of the NAM [National Association of Manufacturers] as a means of getting management-controlled doors opened?

What is important is that we recognize these facts about ourselves and build them into our research, thereby abandoning to that degree the paradisiacal illusion we once held that our work is value free (although I'm not sure any of us even initially believed that).

Form has presented us with a tremendously useful notion in his beautifully honest and well-designed study: Our research enterprise must be the focal point of a social system largely compounded of the very social stuff we endeavor to study. *We* are not passive observers any more than *they* are passive objects. We become a substructure of the total social system we investigate. This fact must influence the parameters of our scientific perceptions of that system.

In a sense, we are back to Marx in a crude sort of a way. This image of an interplay between binary social systems intrigues me; ultimately the "what" is profoundly determined by the "who." Awareness of the power structure, the cultural idioms, etc. is clearly fundamental to any penetration of a social institution, community, or other unit of inquiry. Most anthropologists have been quite aware of this necessity. For example, those of us who have worked in India have known that we can't just walk into an Indian village, visit the untouchable quarter, and say, "I want to study the oppression that you people are having inflicted upon you by these higher castes." We learned very quickly that the villages had a power structure, and if we were to get anything done, we had to work diplomatically with that power structure even if we did identify with the untouchables.

Put differently, the researcher must fashion a role for himself that conveys validity of some kind to the key individuals and groups in the milieu to be investigated. Both Form's and Portes's papers have implications for the way in which we develop a role vis-a-vis the institutions we want to study; the researcher's goal is to become a window on these institutions.

This concern is basically ethical. It requires deciding to be aware of other people's feelings, sensibilities, problems, and needs, and then organizing research which can be satisfying to us while simultaneously being capable of and willing to do something for the people, the subject matter, whom we study.

Mr. Form.   I appreciate Gould's comments because he has extended the kind of conceptual anxiety that I had in dealing with this material. He has taken some of the raw data that I had put down and cast it into still another framework. There is a history to my interest. While I have reworked these case studies three or four times, this is the first time I have put them all together. Each time I work with the material I seem to come back to the original research data with a somewhat different conceptual frame.

My first conceptual frame was the one that I put on the Italian material; I labeled that first analysis "A Bargaining Model for Social Research." My colleagues told me immediately that I didn't know what a model was, and I now guess they were right. My second notion was of a bargaining metaphor, a perspective which has seemed more appropriate. However, as I continued to work, I began to realize that, in addition to the exchange dimension of bargaining, we must also deal with the distrust which is basic to conflicts of an ethical character. So I superimposed a metaphor of trust and distrust over the bargaining metaphor and began once again to rework my material. I have concluded that the distrust metaphor is more useful because it permits more than one way of analyzing the rich sets of interrelationships that emerge as researchers interact with ongoing social systems.

There are other theoretical perspectives which should be explored. Fred Waisanen has suggested one fruitful possibility. It is different from mine because he is primarily concerned with social psychology as a frame of reference. He suggests handling these materials through conceptualizing the degree to which each of the participants in these systems perceive threat from significant others.

Mr. Gould.   Form is to be commended for the honesty of his self-scrutiny; I don't think anybody has tried to be this honest with himself since Gandhi wrote [his *Autobiography;* or *The Story of My Experiments with Truth.* Moreover, he has been successful and has provided a convincing demonstration of how researchers affect the workings of the organizations they are trying to study. Strictly from a conceptual viewpoint, however, I think it has ever been thus. I think we have always affected the institutions we studied. However, we have not always acknowledged this fact and have not built it sufficiently into our research, perhaps because we suffered from an inferiority complex or perhaps because we don't think we are as respectable, as important, as capable of impact as the natural sciences. The difference now is simply that these truths have become more obvious. Our subject matter talks back to us all the time now.

There is another, more subtle, point which should be made. It seems to me that we social scientists are much more responsible for this change than we have realized. We, as sociologists and anthropologists, have been teaching in universities, writing our books and articles, and generally influencing this population with our ideas for quite a long while, particularly since the end of World War II. Our motive has been to make people more sociologically aware. Form's experience in Lansing shows that, ironically, something else has also happened: In many cases we have succeeded in making more people aware of sociology in ways which enable them to block our capacity to do sociological research. Our subjects know us too well. They know too much about us and how our findings may affect their lives.

The most impressive general point that Form makes in this paper is that sociologists need to study research as a process and as a social system. This is a very important point; it excites me as an anthropologist.

One final observation. When he studied the FIAT factory, Form wanted information on union membership. He was not allowed to obtain this information officially, but he couldn't resist digging out the information anyway. This fact points up a very fascinating ethical dimension in the research we do. There is a structural strain between two systems – the research social system, on the one hand, and the social system we want to study exclusively, on the other. There are two ethics operating here, and sometimes they are not mutually compatible. Form obviously decided that he just had to have this information, and to a certain degree he violated the ethics of his contract with the FIAT factory. That violation, however, was legitimized on the ground that *he* would not hurt their interests even if *they* thought he would.

Mr. Form.   Let me comment on this ethical dilemma. As I look back I can find all kinds of good reasons why I did what I did. I suppose one way to answer Gould is to inquire whether I would do it again if I were confronted with the same situation. Would I again be the bastard that I was? Probably so, because I really believe that there is a legitimacy of our own that we need to consider.

Many social scientists seem to carry around a great sense of guilt nowadays. They feel guilty, domestically, about not working hard enough to recruit minorities or for failing to be sensitive to respondents' needs and feelings. Those who do comparative research feel guilty about "mining" data from their foreign counterparts. We have almost come to a point where we just assume our guilt, feeling that if we violate someone else's sense of dignity we are morally culpable and should give up our own work.

Well, there are foreign social scientists who will take advantage of such a political climate to attempt to blackmail you: to get you to write an article with them for which they haven't done any work, to invent or find employment for them, to leave all your data (which you haven't really had a chance to codify or work over) for their use. Cooperation *is* a reciprocal process and responsibility, a mutual obligation. I suggest that, in our international and regional meetings, social scientists rigorously examine cooperation within the profession.

Mr. Chaplin. I attended a conference not long ago at which people identically concerned with what the U.S. has done beat their breasts about our collective guilt. The leaders wanted to convene another meeting and invite Latin Americans to tell us how bad we were. At least in the Latin American case, this idealization of our counterparts is myopic. The pathological demoralization of the social science community in Latin America *is* to some extent our fault—in the sense that we provided research funds which came to be defined as "spoils" by some of our colleagues there. However, we are dealing with universities and professional climates in which, because of the university reform movement, the politicization of the universities is such that our colleagues simply cannot function freely. We should not be surprised that demoralization generates academic behavior, including blackmail, that we label as deviant. We must share the blame; we should also remember, however, that corrupt practices in many societies existed before the first American researcher ever arrived.

CHAPTER FOUR

Problems of Cross-Cultural Methodology: Instrumentation and Interviewing in India

JOSEPH W. ELDER

University of Wisconsin[1]

Introduction

If sociology aims at developing a body of theory free from specific time and place, it follows that theories generated and tested in one society must be retested in other societies.[2] Does the retesting of theories in other societies involve any unique methodological problems, or is the research methodology within single societies directly transferable to cross-cultural research? A number of writers have argued that there are only quantum differences between intrasocietal and intersocietal methodologies. Thus Hudson, Barakat, and LaForge (1959:6) state, "The methods of cross-cultural research are not in principle unique. They are different primarily in the sense that procedural precautions become more critical and some problems more difficult to identify and to solve than for within-culture studies." Frey (1970:183) takes essentially the same position when he asserts, "There are no fundamental differences in principle or in logic between cross-cultural survey research and within-culture survey research, under most conceptions of culture." Holt and Turner (1970:6) declare, "In principle there is no difference between comparative cross-cultural research and research conducted within a single society."

This paper examines some methodological problems of a research project I conducted in two regions of India in 1963. Although both regions were within the political boundaries of India, the project could be considered cross-cultural. The regions used unrelated languages—Hindi and Tamil. They contained divergent caste hierarchies. Their ethnic groups were differently arranged. They showed markedly dissimilar marriage practices and kinship relations. They reflected contrasting festival, musical, and literary traditions. They were separated by 1000 miles of intervening countryside. And one region's economic life had little effect on the economic life of the other.

In focusing on methodological problems, this paper asks whether there are qualitative differences between intrasocietal research and cross-cultural research or whether the differences are only a matter of degree. Implicit in the first question is a second: Must a sociologist engaged in cross-cultural research acquire additional research skills? Or are the skills of intrasocietal research sufficient for cross-cultural research?

My four years in India during the 1950s convinced me of the complexity of the interrelationships among people's attitudes. I had met "emancipated" Hindu reformers working on radical social legislation who, at the same time, observed the rituals of a vegetarian kitchen and were opposed to any but the most conservative form of arranged marriage for their children. I had talked with shrewd and calculating farmers, the first to adopt tractors and send their children to college, who, at the same time, stoically insisted, "Man proposes; God disposes." I knew of engineers who regularly took the advice of astrologers, civil servants who were planning to renounce the world and enter monasteries, and radical ex-untouchables who wanted equal treatment for themselves while refusing to eat food cooked by castes lower than themselves. The picture was anything *but* a simple one of people falling neatly along some continuum of attitudes from traditional to nontraditional, conservative to liberal, sacred to secular, *Gemeinschaft* to *Gesellschaft,* or any of the other continua devised and utilized by Western social scientists.

From my interest in the interrelationships among attitudes in India grew three research hypotheses: (1) There are various identifiable dimensions within which attitudinal change can occur (e.g., religious beliefs, caste practices, capacity to empathize, etc.); (2) Attitude change can occur differentially along these various dimensions; (3) Different independent variables can be associated with changes on different attitude dimensions.

The Research Strategy

India, with its complex geographic and linguistic regions, provided in itself a setting for testing these hypotheses cross-culturally. For two years I had been a high school teacher in Tamil Nadu, where Tamil is the regional language; for another two years I had done field research in Uttar Pradesh, where Hindi is the regional language. During those periods, I had noted marked differences between the two regions: the family structures and preferred marriages differed; the ratio of Brahmans to non-Brahmans differed; the outlines of the caste system differed; and so on (for specification of some of the differences between the two regions, see Elder, 1967:232-257). Testing propositions in two different sections of India might enable generalizations (with appropriate qualifications) to all of India; for example, if Brahmans in both the Hindi and the Tamil sections are strongly committed to educating their children, one might suspect that Brahmans elsewhere in India would be similarly committed. Furthermore, if the propositions being tested contained variables identifiable outside of India, it might be possible to generalize (again, with appropriate qualifications) from Uttar Pradesh and Tamil Nadu to the rest of the world; thus, if in both sections of India the belief that phenomena are "caused by fate" decreases with higher education, one might suspect that the same belief elsewhere in the world would decrease similarly with higher education.

Problems of Unit Comparability.

My research strategy required comparison between two regions of India. But what should be my unit of comparison? A random sample of each state's adult population would reflect certain differences in population characteristics. For example, my Uttar Pradesh sample would have contained 55 percent males contrasted with Tamil Nadu's 50 percent; 7 percent of Uttar Pradesh's sample would have come from cities over 100,000, by contrast with 11 percent of Tamil Nadu's sample; and so on. Before comparing random samples of the two states' adult populations, I would have to identify and control for these and other differences in population characteristics. Furthermore, a strictly random sample would pose complex logistical problems, with interviewers traveling throughout both states. Perhaps a more pertinent difficulty stemmed from the fact that, even if I had wanted a random sample of each state's population, no list existed from which I could draw such a sample. In the end, for strategic as well as practical reasons, I abandoned the idea of a random sample from both states.

Instead, I designed the research to maximize the comparability of the Uttar Pradesh and Tamil Nadu samples. The samples would be drawn equally from villages, small towns, and cities in the two states. Further, the villages should be small (less than 2000 population), the towns should approximate each other in size and should be *tahsil (taluk)* headquarters (like county seats in the United States), and the cities should be political—administrative centers—either state capitals or large district headquarters. In selecting the sites, I drew upon my previous experiences in India: my teaching had been done in the city of Madurai, Tamil Nadu (Madurai was a large district headquarters), and while living in Uttar Pradesh, I had visited the capital, Lucknow. Both cities seemed admirably suited for my purpose.

Once I had selected the two cities, the towns and villages were relatively easy to designate, since, for interviewing purposes, I wanted them within reach of the cities. In the end, the six interview sites included the following:

1. Uttar Pradesh (North India)

   City: Lucknow, population 656,000, capital of the state of Uttar Pradesh

   Town: Malihabad (15 miles west of Lucknow), population 8000, headquarters for Malihabad *tahsil*

   Villages: Utraitia and vicinity (8-12 miles east of Lucknow), population of each village less than 2000

2. Tamil Nadu (South India)

   City: Madurai, population 425,000, headquarters for Madurai district and partial headquarters for Ramanathapuram (Ramnad) district

   Town: Melur (20 miles east of Madurai), population 15,000, headquarters for Melur *taluk*

   Villages: Chittampatti and vicinity (9-11 miles east of Madurai), population of each village less than 1000.

The selected locations narrowed, but did not eliminate, the problem of unit comparability. How could I guarantee that a cross section of Lucknow's population, for example, was comparable to a cross section of Madurai's? Lucknow was the seat of Lucknow University; a purely random sample would have included a disproportionate number of undergraduate and postgraduate students. Lucknow also attracted young men who were pushed from the countryside by economic forces and frequently left their wives and children behind in their home villages. How could I control for these "atypical" cases?

In the end, I chose to focus on family units within the six interview sites. These might provide the comparability that seemed virtually impossible with strict randomization. I decided that my sample would include at least 100 families from each of the six locations. The family unit would consist of approximately 11-year-old boys plus their fathers, mothers, and any resident grandparents. I designated 11-year-old boys in the hope that this age would introduce certain general controls over the ages of the parents, since it would eliminate couples married less than a dozen years as well as those whose last children were approaching marriageable age. I also hoped that 11-year-old boys would be young enough to describe ongoing child-rearing patterns in their homes yet old enough to answer certain attitude questions. One reason for selecting boys *and* their parents was to permit intrafamily analyses of attitude-transmission (e.g., on what dimensions do boys and their mothers agree? Boys and their fathers? All three?). One reason for selecting three generations was the hope that they might provide rough indications of how attitudes had changed over time.

The units I finally compared, then, were families of 11-year-old boys from three locations within each of the states of Uttar Pradesh and Tamil

Nadu—a major city, a neighboring town, and nearby villages. For practical purposes, I had solved my problem of unit comparability. In a more abstract sense, though, I had no way of knowing whether or not I had actually solved the problem. My selection automatically ruled out important elements of the population: university students, workers who had left their wives and children in the villages in order to find jobs in the cities, the wives and children back in the villages of those workers who had migrated, the elderly, and so on. My selected units may have eliminated key explanatory groups from my sample population.

The unit comparability problem bedevils cross-cultural research. What are the minimal criteria for a society, tribe, region, culture? How do we know we are comparing the same things? Ever since E.B. Tylor's (1889) work, cross-cultural researchers have been required to defend their choice of cases they wish to compare. Even if they can defend their choice of cases and go on to discover correlations within them, however, what guarantee do they have that those cases really provide independent trials of the correlation? This so-called Galton's problem (Sir Francis Galton chaired the meeting in which Tylor read his paper) asks if the correlations might not exist because the cases have a common cultural ancestor or have borrowed from the same culture center, rather than because the variables are actually linked in some empirical association. The problems of unit comparability and unit independence promise to remain with cross-cultural research for many years.[3]

Problems of Sampling

The next step was to draw random samples from the universe of families of 11-year-old boys in the six designated locations in India. No sampling frame existed for such a universe; I had to generate one.[4] The villages and towns were small enough that census-takers could cover the entire location.[5] After receiving their instructions on the requirements of the sampling design, the census-takers went from door to door seeking 11-year-old boys. If the parents were not sure of a boy's age (as was often the case), the census-taker was instructed to guess. If the boy passed muster as being (more or less) 11 years old and neither his father nor his mother proved to be dead or away on an extended trip, the census-taker recorded the boy's name, his father's name, and some form of neighborhood address. In the villages and towns, we used as house addresses the orange, malaria-control numbers that the public health people had painted by each doorway. Despite these efforts to specify the location of given families, we still "lost" a few respondents between the census-taking and the interviewing a few weeks later.

In the cities we faced considerably greater difficulties. It was obvious from the size of both Lucknow and Madurai that a door-to-door census was out of the question. In the city of Madurai I was able to obtain street maps of the 33 census zones and information on the percentage of total city population living in each zone. On the basis of this information, I determined how many of my 100 Madurai families should come from each zone. Then I measured with a string the total street frontage on each zone's map, dividing with knots the measured length of string into as many parts as there were to be families drawn from that zone. Next I measured the map's street frontage again, placing an x on the map wherever I reached a knot. I then sent a census-taker to those x's, having instructed him to obtain the name of the 11-year-old boy living closest to the x. Occasionally the census-taker found the x's to be in the middle of a paddy field or factory compound. But, on the whole, the system worked effectively in providing us with a reasonably random cross section of the Madurai population of 11-year-old boys living with their parents. As for recording the addresses in Madurai, we often had street names and house numbers by which to go, although we were occasionally reduced to such addresses as "house over grain shop beside water tap."

Only after the project had been completed did I discover that, especially in the wealthier sections of Madurai, a slight selection bias had crept in. When standing on the approximate location of an x and facing a choice between going up to a grand mansion and asking whether or not an 11-year-old boy lived there or going around to the servants' quarters in the back and asking if an 11-year-old boy lived *there,* the census-takers had preferred to go around to the back. Given their relative youth (mostly in their twenties) and lack of social status (few were regularly employed), that was the easier course to take. As a result, the Madurai sample had a slight underrepresentation of sons of college-educated and wealthy families. Since most of the final tabulations controlled for education, that problem was more or less eliminated. Nonetheless, in future projects it would be useful to eliminate even that small element of choice available to the census-takers, in order to keep the sampling as random as possible.

The city of Lucknow posed more serious problems than Madurai. The 1962 Chinese invasion had swept most maps and census information out of public circulation for security reasons. However, Lucknow had a compulsory-education bill, so I decided to use school registers as my population source. After obtaining the names of as many primary and secondary schools as we could from the education offices, the Lucknow telephone directory, and the general knowledge of Lucknow residents, the census-takers went to the schools, perused the school registers, and recorded the name and address of every fifteenth boy born in 1952. By this method we obtained about 400 names and addresses of 11-year-old boys in Lucknow. We were aware that our sampling procedure automatically ruled out any boys not enrolled in school (despite the compulsory-education bill) or enrolled in private-tuition "sidewalk schools" and that it probably skewed our sample toward the higher castes and occupations.

One of the most serious deficiencies in our Lucknow census related to street addresses. The school register might carry something like "Ram Lal, son of Roshan Singh, Aminabad Park." Several thousand people live in the area known as Aminabad Park. How was one to find Ram Lal, son of Roshan Singh? In the end we were forced to abandon nearly three-fourths of our Lucknow sample frame because we could not trace the addresses. We hoped the one-fourth who remained were typical of the three-fourths we lost, but we had no way of knowing.

Problems of Instrument Construction

In trying to identify potentially independent dimensions within which attitude change might occur, I listed 14 separate dimensions for analysis:

1. Need achievement: the commitment to excel (for further discussions of this dimension, see McClelland et al., 1953; McClelland, 1961; McClelland and Winter, 1969)

2. Civic confidence: the belief that governmental agencies operate fairly and impartially (intended to correspond somewhat to the equality-of-treatment dimension in Almond and Verba, 1963:106ff.)

3. Concepts of causation: the belief that events occur in a haphazard and fortuitious way, contrasted with the belief that events occur in some morally or divinely-determined way or with the belief that events occur in an empirically-determinable way, and so on (this dimension corresponds somewhat with the distinction between pre-Newtonian and post-Newtonian attitudes toward the physical world described in Rostow, 1961:4)

4. Generalized empathy: the ability to imagine oneself in another person's position, especially a person with whom one has no kinship relations[6]

5. Authoritarianism: the concern over a dominance-submission axis, including the view that one's own life is shaped by dominating forces and that those outside one's own dominance-submission axis are threatening and should be punished[7]

6. Status concern: a felt need to enhance one's status or honor, even at the cost of other potential benefits[8]

7. Caste concern: a felt need for the "correct" observance of caste-avoidance taboos, especially regarding castes lower than one's own[9]

8. Mobility aspirations: degree of upward occupational or educational aspirations for one's offspring or for oneself

9. Competition approval: the acceptance of competition as a legitimate and desirable means for stimulating progress

10. Dependency-versus-autonomy orientation: the preference for dependency training and behavior versus autonomy training and behavior

11. Intrafamily orientation: attitudes toward preferred parent roles, preferred child roles, and so on

12. Relatives-versus-neighborhood orientation: degree of commitment to relatives' needs contrasted with degree of commitment to neighborhood needs

13. Regional-versus-national orientation: degree of commitment to one's linguistic region contrasted with degree of commitment to one's nation

14. Cultural choices: preference for particular festivals, religious personages, and so on.

In the early 1960s there were few tested cross-cultural instruments to deal with the above dimensions. Charles Morris (1956) had developed his "13 Ways to Live" scale and had used it on students from the United States, China, Japan, Canada, and Norway. However, each "way to live" consisted of a complex paragraph containing many parts, requiring advanced literacy, and aimed at the intellectual sophistication of college students. I was certain that Morris's scale could not be used on my less-literate Madurai and Lucknow samples. Srole (1956) had published his anomia scale as a tool for measuring the psychological state corresponding to a societal condition of anomie. However, this scale touched only peripherally on one of my dimensions, civic confidence. Kluckhohn and Strodtbeck (1961) had described an instrument that had the advantage of being applicable to peasant societies. However, again the dimensions in which I was interested overlapped only partially with their five dimensions. And other specific instruments, such as Inkeles and Smith's (1966) Overall Modernity Scale and the University of Michigan Institute of Social Research's compendia of tested questions, from which I might well have borrowed, were still being devised and standardized in 1963 (see Robinson et al., 1968; Robinson and Shaver, 1969). One extant instrument that seemed to fit into my dimensions was the "F scale" as a measure of authoritarianism. Consequently, from the "F-Scale Clusters: Forms 45 and 40" (Adorno et al., 1950:255ff.), I developed a seven-item abridgement, selecting and, if necessary, modifying those items that seemed to fit most readily into the Indian context. Aside from that scale, I was forced to compose my own questions to tap the dimensions in which I was interested.

During some earlier interviewing of illiterates, I had discovered that open-ended attitude questions often elicited only confusion. The very abstractness of the questions gave the respondent little to grasp. In the same way, closed-ended questions with more than three alternatives were also confusing. Respondents had trouble remembering all the alternatives, even when the questions were repeated several times. Respondents seemed best able to answer attitude questions when they were presented with two or three closed alternatives in the form of a short story.

I had also observed that direct requests for opinions often threatened respondents, especially those with little or no education. A question such as

"Which do you prefer—the past, the present, or the future?" might bring the response, "Sir, I'm an illiterate man. What's the use of my opinion?" One technique I had learned to circumvent respondents' reticence was to provide them with a "psychic ally." Thus I had learned to ask the past-present-future question in the following fashion:

"One man says, 'the things of the present are best. Things of the past are forgotten, and nobody can tell what the future holds.' A second man says, 'The practices and customs of our fathers and grandfathers are best. The modern age is not good.' A third man says, 'The future is what is important. That is what we must prepare for.' Which of these three men do you think is correct? the first? the second? or the third?"

By having the respondent identify the "correct person" rather than give his "own opinion," I automatically provided him with some ego protection. By the time my interview schedule was ready for field use, fully 55 percent of the questions were of the short-story, psychic-ally sort.

Problems of Instrument Translation

According to Bruce Anderson (1967:124), "Translation is involved whenever research requires asking the 'same' question of people with different backgrounds."[10] He further suggests that only a matter of degree separates "translating" for different subcultures using basically the same language and translating for different tribes or states using completely different languages. Is such indeed the case?

An immediate, and sometimes unresolvable, problem in cross-cultural instrument translation is that of lexical equivalence. Even the cumbersome, but essential, procedures of "back-translation" (having one person translate a question from language A to language B, having a second person translate the question "back" from language B to language A, and comparing the two versions of language A) may not overcome the problem of basic nonequivalence, even when the translation is lexically "correct." Take *friend* in English, *Freund* in German, and *amigo* in Spanish. Technically, they translate identically. Yet the German *Freund* refers to a few deep, personal associates; the English *friend* refers to a somewhat less intense and wider range of acquaintances; and the Spanish *amigo* refers to a very wide range of persons, some of whom might have been met only that day. Thus the question, "How many friends do you have?" is asking something different in all three languages. A strict back-translation would miss this fact. To make the questions more nearly comparable in the three languages, one would need to specify, with illustrations, how close a friend one meant with *Freund, friend,* and *amigo.* Grimshaw (1969:317) illustrates one way to achieve the needed specificity.

Sometimes lexical equivalence cannot be achieved. A concept can be sufficiently untranslatable and the process of explaining it in another language so laborious that the effort must be abandoned. Let me illustrate with one of my questions. In the original English, it read:

"For a country to progress, it is necessary to find people whom the public can trust. I shall read you a list of different people. Please tell me which of these you would trust completely, which you would trust a little, and which you would not trust at all:

1. An illiterate	10. A high government official
2. A college graduate	11. A government clerk
3. A man with no relatives	12. A government office-boy
4. A man with many relatives	13. A schoolteacher
5. A man from you own religion	14. A headmaster
6. A man who follows another religion	15. A foreigner (e.g., Englishman)
7. A relative	16. A resident of Uttar Pradesh (or
8. A non-relative	Tamil Nadu)
9. The prime minister	17. A resident of another state."

My hope was that answers to these questions would reveal "built-in" categories of who is trustworthy and who is suspect in Indian society. But when it came time to translate the question, I was chagrined to discover that Hindi has no ready equivalent for the concept of trust. *Visvas* typically connotes "belief" or "faith," with religious overtones. *Bharosa* typically connotes "dependence" or "reliance," with financial overtones. Other more esoteric Hindi terms are so unfamiliar to most listeners that they have to be translated into simpler Hindi terms; hence, little is gained. For the field pretest, we settled for including both *visvas* and *bharosa* in the first sentence: ". . . to find people whom the public can trust; and then using *visvas* for: "trust completely . . . trust a little, and . . . not trust at all."

The results of our field pretest showed that our efforts had been to no avail. What were we, the questioners, trying to find out? Were we asking if illiterates or relatives spoke the truth all the time? Were we asking if such people could support their dependents all the time? The questions remained—for most people—incomprehensible, despite the fact that the interviewers in the field pretest spent as much as 15 or 20 minutes trying to explain the questions to the respondents. In the end, we were forced to abandon that question entirely, leaving untapped an area that still may contain some revealing insights.

The literature is replete with illustrations of other English terms that, in the final analysis, cannot be accurately translated into other languages. For example, Blanc (1956:205-209) had considerable difficulty in maintaining distinctions among "very many," "too many," and other similar phrases when conducting multilingual interviewing and questionnaire translation in Israel. Hunt, Crane, and Wahlke (1964:66) indicate that such a deceptively simple phrase as "may or may not" can be virtually untranslatable cross-culturally. Mitchell (1965:677) found the term "aggressive" difficult if not impossible to translate out of English, as did Frey (1963:348) the term "loyalty" when he tried to translate it into Turkish. Phillips (1959-60:190ff) discovered in constructing his sentence-completion tests in Thailand that certain English concepts simply would not translate into Thai. For example, in Thailand there is no notion of a "good" (i.e., "cathartic") quarrel. Hence Phillips's sentence segment "Sometimes a good quarrel is necessary because," could not be translated. Phillips ran into another problem when he wanted to translate the English phrase "to be angry." Thai contains two terms expressive of anger: *chiw*, meaning "to feel anger in one's heart toward another person, but to conceal its expression"; and *moo-hoo*, meaning "to be angry at the situation in which one finds oneself, rather than toward another person." Which of these did Phillips mean by "to be angry"? In a technical sense, neither one. Yet the Thai language forced him to make a choice or to combine both, neither of which implied what he actually meant.

Along with the problem of lexical equivalence is that of contextual equivalence. Even if a term is technically translated correctly, the context within which the terms will be interpreted by hearers may alter its intended meaning. For example, neither Hindi nor Tamil has a generic pronoun for "you." The "you" pronoun coupled with the "you" verb endings instantly reflects whether a speaker feels he is socially higher or lower than his listener. *Tum* in Hindi and *ni* in Tamil imply that the speaker regards himself higher than, or intimate with, the listener. I used the *tum* and *ni* forms on the sons interview schedules. On the other hand, *āp* in Hindi and *ninkal* in Tamil imply that the speaker regards himself lower than, or distant from, the listener. I used the *āp* and *ninkal* forms on the fathers-grandfathers and mothers-grandmothers interview schedules. In none of the interviews would the respondent have seen the pronoun "you" as a neutral, nonhierarchical term.

As with such other Indo-European languages as French, Hindi changes verb endings to match the gender of the verb's subject. This complicated the translation process. For example, the question "Who do you think was correct?" differs not only if the "you" is higher or lower but also if the "you" is male or female. That question addressed to an 11-year-old boy reads: *Tum kisko thīk samajhte ho?* Addressed to his mother or grandmother, it reads: *Āp kisko thīk samajhti hai?* And addressed to his father or grandfather, it reads: *Āp kisko thīk samajhte hai?*

Since my short-story questions frequently provided the respondent with a psychic ally, it seemed potentially useful to make the ally the same gender as the respondent. Thus, the boys schedule read: "One boy said this. One boy said that. Which boy do you think was correct?" The mothers-grandmothers schedule read: "One woman said this. One woman said that. Which woman do you think was correct?" And the schedule for the fathers and grandfathers read: "One man said this .... One man said that .... Which man do you think was correct?"

Between the gender requirements of Hindi and the desire to provide respondents with psychic allies, entire working days went into proofreading both the Hindi and the Tamil schedules to eliminate incorrect gender carry-overs from one schedule to another, leaving three "pure" schedules. Even then, I could be grateful that Japanese was not one of the languages into which I needed to translate my schedule, since it contains even more structural gradations according to age and sex, thus posing even more complex translation problems (see Ervin and Bower, 1952:598).

The fact that some of my respondents were Hindus and others Muslims posed further problems of contextual equivalence. For example, in the question beginning "One man says, 'Priests and sacred books contain all truth . . .,' " the Hindi term *pandit,* although technically meaning "priest," connotes "Hindu priest," and *dharmik kitābe,* although technically meaning "sacred books," connotes "Hindu sacred books." In the straightforward translation the sentence using the Hindi words reads (by implication): "One may says, 'Hindu priests and Hindu sacred books contain all truth . . . .' " Such a statement might lead a Muslim respondent to give quite a different answer from a Hindu respondent, even if the Muslim felt that Muslim priests and Muslim sacred books did indeed contain all truth. We resolved the problem by including alternate sets of Hindi terms, one for Hindus, the other for Muslims: *pandit* ("Hindu priest") and *mullā* ("Muslim priest") and *dkārmik kitābe* ("Hindu sacred books") and *majahabī kitābe* ("Muslim sacred books"). The same problem (and same solution) applied to the question including the statement "One must work hard, but the results are in God's hands." In the Hindi schedule, we used two different terms for "God," *Iśvar* (Hindu) and *Khudā* (Muslim).

The Tamil language does not retain such sharp differences in Hindu and Muslim terminology. True, *pucāri* means "Hindu priest" and *maulvī* means "Muslim priest" (a difference I failed to note in settling on the single term *pucārī*). But *purāna pustakam* means "sacred books," either Hindu or Muslim. And *Katavul* is the generic term for "God." In these respects, the Tamil schedule involved fewer contextual complications than the Hindi schedules.

One of the seven items I retained in my modified version of the F scale was the statement "A great many things can be predicted by astrology." I saw no problem in including this, given the prevalence of astrologers in India. It was only after the interviewers were in the field that a dismaying fact was brought to my attention: Muslims are prohibited from believing in astrology. To ask one if he believed in astrology would be tantamount to asking whether or not he took the Islamic injunction seriously. I tried to think of some other statement I could substitute for the astrology item, at least for the Muslims. But the fieldwork was too far along for me to substitute at that point. There was nothing to do but wait for the results to come in and then run a special check to see if Muslims consistently answered that statement differently from Hindus. If they did, I was prepared to introduce some further controls on the Muslims' F-scale scores to make up for the inappropriate item.

I was much relieved when the special item check revealed no significant differences between Muslims and Hindus. Islam may officially disavow astrology, but, at least in India, this disavowal does not mean that Muslims do not believe that a great many things *can* be predicted by astrology.

In still another portion of the interview schedule I faced a further problem of contextual definition. Vegetarianism holds a peculiar place among Hindus. It is recommended in the scriptures, it is practiced by high castes more rigorously than by low castes (with important exceptions), and, in general, it is observed more by women than by men. Currently, in certain Hindu groups, it is enjoying a renaissance. In other groups it is being abandoned. In trying to understand attitude change in contemporary India, it seemed useful to include a set of questions concerning vegetarianism.

Yet vegetarianism plays no part in the life of Muslims. To the contrary, at certain Muslim festivals it is more or less expected that the main dish will be meat, even beef. To ask a Muslim if he is a vegetarian would be a mild insult. Therefore, in drawing up the vegetarianism questions, I looked for some set of questions (e.g., perhaps related to eating pork) for Muslims that might parallel the vegetarianism questions for the Hindus. In the end, I concluded that the Hindu vegetarianism did not sufficiently parallel the Muslim injunction against eating pork; hence the vegetarian questions appeared on the final interview schedule under a section labeled "For Hindus Only."

In still another area, that of caste, I faced a contextual definition problem. I was aware that, despite scriptural injunctions to the contrary, the Muslims had a general sort of caste hierarchy. But they appeared critical of Hindu caste, and it did not seem appropriate to ask Muslims the Hindu questions about caste observances (Would they eat food prepared by someone from a low caste? Would they marry their son or daughter to a boy or girl from a low caste? etc.). And I could not think of any equivalent questions to ask Muslims. So in the end, I assigned the caste questions to the section labeled "For Hindus Only," and the matter appeared to be settled.

Then one day an interviewer forgot and mistakenly took several Muslim respondents through the entire set of questions labeled "For Hindus Only." The Muslims responded to the caste questions with no difficulty. Moreover, in a number of cases, they indicated that they observed some of the Hindu caste proprieties. By then it was too late to rewrite the instructions. As a result, because I misperceived the context in which Muslims observe castes, I still do not know whether there are significant differences between Muslims' attitudes toward their castes and Hindus' attitudes toward theirs.

I faced one final translation problem when we began writing down the exact Hindi or Tamil wording that would be used during the interviews. There is a written form of English (in novels, magazines, etc.) and a spoken form of English (in small talk, conversations, etc.). When preparing interview schedules, one commonly writes the questions in the spoken form. Split infinitives, terminal prepositions, and various colloquialisms are all permissible if they keep the interview conversational and make the respondent less self-conscious.

In both Hindi and Tamil, the gap between the written and the spoken language is far greater than the gap in English. For centuries the written language has been the preserve of the high castes, while the spoken language has been used by the low castes and the illiterate. The result, at times, approaches two different languages, high Hindi (or Tamil) and colloquial Hindi (or Tamil).[11]

In Lucknow, I spent the better part of a week with four or five members of my research team, translating each question into Hindi. My instructions were that any question's final form should be immediately understandable when read to an illiterate 11-year-old village boy; anything fancier would have to be discarded. Even with these instructions and a research team most of whom had had some interviewing experience, I had difficulty achieving the simplicity I wanted.

In Madurai, the problem was even more severe. Tamil is highly polysyllabic (e.g., the Tamil equivalent for "now" contains four syllables; the equivalent for "is" contains five syllables; and the equivalent for the imperative "bring" contains six syllables). High Tamil insists that all the syllables be included; colloquial Tamil drops many of the intermediate syllables. Furthermore, high Tamil insists that only pure Tamil words be used; colloquial Tamil borrows without apology from Sanskrit, Hindi, or English (e.g., "ink," "station," "cycle," "hotel," "college," "judge," etc.). In ordinary times it would have been difficult to come up with a Tamil translation that would have been acceptable to all parties, but my research was aggravated by the fact that Tamil Nadu was undergoing a Tamil cultural renaissance. The major political party, the Dravida Munnetra Kalaham, had built part of its platform on Tamil purification, and Madurai's printing presses were competing among themselves to see who could publish the most "chaste" Tamil.

In Tamil Nadu, as in Uttar Pradesh, my translation instructions were that any question's final form should be immediately understandable when read to an 11-year-old village boy. For several days, the Tamil translation team wrote sentences that, because of their polysyllabic words and lengthiness, were clearly *not* understandable to such a boy. The breakthrough came when I took paper and pencil away from the translators and said, "Now, imagine I am an illiterate 11-year-old boy. Ask me the last question." They immediately asked the question using one-third the number of syllables they had been writing. "Write what you just said." They looked alarmed. "Tamil isn't written that way," they assured me. I insisted. Reluctantly, and with considerable amusement, they wrote down what they had said. When they read it back to me, I announced, "*That's* the way I want all the questions translated." For the next several days, bursts of laughter came from the room where the translators were working, as they read their "bad Tamil" to each other.

When I took the completed Tamil version to a third person to be backtranslated into Eglish, her first comment was, "This is terrible Tamil!" I acknowledged it might be, but asked her whether, if read aloud, its meaning would be clear to any listener. She said that it would be, adding, "It's written just as we speak."

The last hurdle came when I took the final Tamil version to the print shop—the "Temple of the Arts." The printer and I agreed on a price, then he began to read the copy. In a few moments he looked up and asked if he might be allowed to make some minor corrections. I insisted I wanted the copy just as it was. He pleaded that he had to uphold his reputation as a printer of quality Tamil. I invited him to redirect any blame to me. He was adamant. It was not until I had augmented our initially set price by 100 rupees that the printer agreed to print the copy unchanged. Even then it was with the understanding that the name of his print shop would nowhere appear on the final version.

Problems of Interviewer Selection and Training

In order to observe the local proprieties, I needed female interviewers to talk to the boys, their mothers, and their grandmothers, and male interviewers to talk to the fathers and grandfathers. In both Lucknow and Madurai my advertisements in the local papers and my inquiries in local colleges and universities had brought a large enough pool of experienced candidates that I could eliminate those with questionable talent, motivation, or energy. At the peak of operations, my Lucknow team included nine females and five males. My Madurai team contained five females and four males.

After an initial training session, I required all candidates to complete two practice interviews with the trial interview schedule. These trial interviews served two purposes: they helped eliminate a few more candidates, and they provided a pretest for earlier versions of the interview schedule.

As a result of the pretest, five questions were dropped from the interview schedule. The question dealing with "trust" was dropped because the English concept did not translate readily into Hindi. The abridged F scale was dropped from the sons interview schedule (although it was retained in the mothers-grandmothers and fathers-grandfathers schedules), since the 11-year-olds had considerable trouble figuring out what was wanted. The following question dealing with civic confidence was dropped because the mention of police seemed to threaten several of the pretest respondents.

134   *Instrumentation and Interviewing: An Indian Example*

"Which of these statements do you think is true?
1. People who break the law are always punished by the police.
2. People who break the law are usually punished by the police.
3. People who break the law are seldom punished by the police.
4. People who break the law are never punished by the police."

Two open-ended questions were dropped. "What things make you angriest?" too often produced the culturally approved answer that the respondent did not get angry. And "What things do you like the best?" turned out to elicit much the same response as another open-ended question that we retained: "If you had some extra money, what would you use it for?"

In both Lucknow and Madurai the interview teams consisted largely of young, well-educated, high-caste Hindus. The major exception in Lucknow was a Muslim lady (Muslims make a sharp distinction between "ladies" and "women") who, despite her somewhat lower education, was of inestimable value in interviewing the Muslim women living in seclusion in Malihabad; in fact, she and a lady from the Kayasth caste (a caste considered to have adopted Muslim characteristics while serving as bookkeepers and accountants for various Muslim rulers in India) completed the bulk of the Muslim women's interviews. The major exception in Madurai was a low-caste Christian lady who, nonetheless, was well educated and had had considerable interviewing experience. In a society so sensitive to caste and educational differences, one might speculate on possible interviewer effects on respondents' answers. However, I had set up no systematic way of identifying such effects, so speculations must remain unverified (for further discussion of interviewer problems in India, see Wilson and Armstrong, 1963:48-58; also Rudolph and Rudolph, 1958:235-244).

Problems of Field Response

The field operations in the Lucknow area began in late May 1963 and continued into early June. In Malihabad and the Utraitia village area we used public-works-department and irrigation-department inspection bungalows as our base, the male interviewers remaining in the bungalows throughout the period, while the females commuted from Lucknow every day by hired taxi. Public eating facilities were unavailable in these areas, so I had to hire cooks and arrange for utensils and food supplies to be transported to the bungalows. In both Malihabad and Utraitia the interviewers frequently had to walk miles between interviews. Special arrangements for bicycles and horse-drawn *ikkas* alleviated, but did not solve, the problem.

In Tamil Nadu, where we interviewed in July and August 1963, the logistics were considerably simpler. Melur contained numerous satisfactory "hotels" for meals, and buses constantly ran between Melur, Chittampatti, and Madurai. In the Chittampatti area there were still many miles between villages, but even so the problem was easier to deal with than in Uttar Pradesh, since one could rent a bicycle for a nominal sum near the bus stand.

Interviewers were instructed to conduct their interviews with as much privacy as possible. In certain cases in Melur, school authorities allowed the interviewers to take boys out of classes and use an empty school office for the interviews. However, in most cases the interviews were considerably more public. In respondents' homes the audience frequently expanded to include relatives and neighbors. At times the interviewers had to use considerable tact to discourage members of the audience from interjecting their own answers to the questions being asked. How private interviews might have differed from the public ones that were held is difficult to know. However, as a sociologist I was sure that the presence of others *did* affect the respondents' answers, even if I did not know the extent of that effect.

The field team was instructed to explain that the interviews were part of a large attitude study being done in two parts of India. However, it quickly turned out that people wanted answers about other aspects of the survey as well. Furthermore, upon checking one interviewer's answers against another's, they sometimes discovered discrepancies. For example, some of the interviewers, in their eagerness to elicit cooperation, promised that after the survey the neighborhood surveyed would receive schools, roads, and electricity; other interviewers denied that promise. The static began immediately. I called the interviewers together and insisted that they make no promises of government largess. The survey had to sell itself on its own merits.

Even more touchy was the matter of interviewers' salaries. Their wages depended on the number of interviews they completed satisfactorily. Early in the survey, some villagers overheard two interviewers totaling their day's interviews and figuring how much they had earned. The word was out. Respondents demanded that they receive part of the interviewers' pay. It took weeks for those demands to die down. In the meantime I informed the interviewers that, if questioned, they were to state that they were receiving subsistence and expenses. Beyond that, they were never to discuss their salaries while in the field.

Occasionally the interviewers met resistance. In Malihabad a Chamar (ex-untouchable) neighborhood insisted that after Independence they did not have to perform favors for anyone. No amount of discussion or explanation dissuaded the Chamars. In the end we were forced to abandon the neighborhood. In the town of Melur, the rumor started that the interviewing was part of a government program to recruit 11-year-old boys into the army to train them to fight the Chinese. In this case the interviewer set an 11-year-old boy in the midst of the questioning townsmen and asked them if they seriously believed the government wanted boys this size in the army. The townsmen had to agree it was unlikely, and there were no further objections to the study.

More often, the interviewers met with considerable cooperation. Respondents were eager to please, a situation that might pose another problem: response sets. Would too many of them answer whatever they thought the interviewer might want to hear rather than what they really felt? The short-story, psychic-ally question inhibited simple response acquiescence but may not have eliminated it totally (for a discussion of response-set problems, see Jones, 1963:70-76; also Landsberger and Saavedra, 1967:214-229).

To guard against dishonest reporting in both Lucknow and Madurai, I hired one person as a "back-checker." His job was to take a sample of completed interview schedules, return to each respondent concerned, and find out if the respondent had really been interviewed, and whether or not the date and length of interview time described by the respondent corresponded with the date and time recorded by the interviewer on the schedule. The back-checker also asked the respondent what questions he remembered and reasked half a dozen questions to see if the respondent's answers the second time tallied with the answers he was reported to have given the first time.

I described in advance to all the interviewers how the process of back-checking worked and informed them that they would be paid only for their satisfactorily completed interviews. On the whole, the knowledge that there was a back-checker discouraged dishonest reporting. However, in Madurai the back-checker uncovered one interviewer who had "coffee-housed" two dozen interviews. The offender was promptly sacked, and other members of the team completed the interviews he reported he had done.

Every day before going into the field, the interviewers received a list of the census-derived family members that they were supposed to try to interview that day. Even with the best of efforts, it was hard to keep the lists equal. One interviewer would spend the bulk of the day walking between distant villages in search of people who, it would turn out, were away. Another interviewer would find everyone he or she wanted within a few hundred yards of each other. In the course of time, certain interviewers came to feel that other interviewers consistently received "good" lists of names while they themselves consistently received "bad" lists. This was a difficult problem to solve, since it was hard to know before actually going into the field which lists were good and which bad. The most it seemed possible to do was to be sympathetic to complaints and, in cases where certain interviewers seemed to have had particularly bad luck for several days in a row, let the interviewer himself or herself pick his list for the next day.

In order to keep morale high, in both Lucknow and Madurai I held periodic, all-expenses-paid celebrations. These included such events as a special bus trip to a newly built dam, movies, dinners in the better restaurants, and mango and litchi fruit feasts. Within the contexts of Madurai and Lucknow, this "big daddy" approach seemed appreciated.

Single-Society and Cross-Cultural Research: A Return to the Questions

This paper's purpose has been to determine whether there are qualitative differences between intrasocietal research and cross-cultural research or whether the differences are only a matter of degree. In describing my Lucknow-Madurai study, I identified six methodological problems: unit comparability, sampling, instrument construction, instrument translation, interviewer selection and training, and field response. All but one seem no different qualitatively. My experience shows, however, that the problem of translation *is* qualitatively different. To be sure, a good interview schedule for use within a single society may provide several options for terms so that an interviewer can communicate readily with different age groups or subcultures within the same language pool. But the difference between supplying an occasional word-substitute and supplying an entire instrument in a different language is of sufficient quantitative magnitude to be considered qualitatively different. The sorts of lexical and contextual problems I experienced in my Hindi and Tamil translations can be found in translations between any languages. The Sapir (1931) and Whorf (1956) hypotheses that language shapes the cognitive structure of those who speak it are generally considered extreme today. However, no serious student of language would argue that different languages do not break up "reality" into different segments. And it is these segments from which interview schedules are composed. It takes skilled students of two languages, who know the segments of both languages as well as the contexts into which those segments fit, to carry out the translation processes accurately. In this dimension it seems that cross-cultural research *is* qualitatively different from intrasocietal research.

What implications does this finding hold for sociologists planning to engage in cross-cultural research? Must they become skilled students of two or more languages? In the best of all possible worlds, the answer might be yes. But given a world in which all sociologists are not gifted language learners and in which career patterns and research topics might not provide the necessary years for language learning prior to research, the answer must be no. However, if the sociologist himself is not familiar with the language subtleties of the cultures he plans to study, his responsibility is even greater to employ the most skilled linguists available. Otherwise he may never know which of the correlations he has found are spurious because they result from linguistic variability alone, or what correlations he has failed to find because they are concealed by linguistic noncomparability.

Notes

1.   The author wishes to thank the American Institute of Indian Studies and the

University of Wisconsin Office of International Studies, through whose financial assistance the overseas portions of the research described in this paper were conducted.

2. Among contemporary sociological theorists, Parsons (1949, chap. 1), Merton (1949, chap. 2), Zetterberg (1965, chap. 2), and Homans (1962, chap. 1) have stated that the goal of sociology is the development of general theory transcending specific societies or social systems. A.R. Radcliffe-Brown (1957:59ff.), the British anthropologist, has maintained that a theoretical science of human society must be built on systematic comparisons of societies of sufficiently diverse types. His position resembles that of such prominent social scientists as Karl Marx, Max Weber, and Emile Durkheim (all of whom systematically compared societies) and of more recent sociologists such as Andreski (1964) and van den Berghe (1967).

3. For a thorough review of the problem and a related bibliography, see Whiting (1968, vol. II, chap. 17). The problem of unit comparability exists for intrasocietal research as well, whether the units being compared are communities, complex organizations, social classes, ethnic groups, or individuals.

4. The problem of obtaining sampling frames is certainly not unique to cross-cultural research. For a discussion of this problem both cross-culturally and intrasocietally, see Riley (1963:285ff.).

5. Since the census-takers were recording only 11-year-old boys, their work was simpler than if they had been recording everyone in the towns and villages. Often, by talking with only one member of a family courtyard, they could determine whether or not there were any qualified 11-year-old boys in several related families. In both Uttar Pradesh and Tamil Nadu the census-takers were able to complete their operations in two to three weeks.

6. Although my operational measures differed from those of Daniel Lerner (see 1958:49ff.), the concept I identified approached at least his nominal definition of empathy.

7. For an early discussion of authoritarianism, see Adorno et al. (1950:224ff.). There has since been a growing body of literature dealing with the notion of authoritarianism (e.g., Christie and Jahoda, 1954).

8. During my earlier fieldwork in India, I had identified this dimension as having considerable impact on people's behavior; it could be quite helpful in interpreting otherwise apparently irrational behavior. Other field research in India has also suggested that status concern plays an important part in explaining behavior (e.g., Minturn and Hitchcock, 1963:esp. 218ff.).

9. There is a steadily growing body of literature on changing caste attitudes in India. One of the earliest reported studies is that of Professor Bangalore Kuppuswamy of Presidency College in Madras, reported in Murphy (1953:106ff.). A more recent view of how caste-avoidance patterns may be changing is described in Ross (1961).

10. For a sensitive analysis of instrument translation problems, see Deutscher (1968: 318-341).

11. For more specialized discussions of the differences between high and low usage, see Gumperz and Naim (1960:92-118) and Pillai (1960:27-42). This problem has also been discussed in relation to the English language; see Bernstein (1961:288-314).

References

Adorno, T.W., Else Frenkel-Brunswik, Daniel J. Levinson, and R. Nevitt Sanford.

1950   *The Authoritarian Personality.* New York: Harper.

Almond, Gabriel A. and Sidney Verba.

1963   *The Civic Culture: Political Attitudes and Democracy in Five Nations.* Princeton, N.J.: Princeton University Press.

Anderson, R. Bruce W.

1967   On the comparability of meaningful stimuli in cross-cultural research. *Sociometry,* 30 (June):124-136.

Andreski, Stanislav.

1964   *The Uses of Comparative Sociology.* Berkeley and Los Angeles: University of California Press.

Bernstein, Basil.

1961   Social class and linguistic development: a theory of social learning. In A.H. Halsey, Jean Floud, and C. Arnold Anderson (Eds.), *Education, Economy and Society: A Reader in the Sociology of Education.* Glencoe, Ill.: Free Press. Pp. 288-314.

Blanc, Haim.

1956   Multilingual interviewing in Israel. *American Journal of Sociology,* 62 (September):205-209.

Christie, Richard, and Marie Jahoda (Eds.).

1954   *Studies in the Scope and Method of "The Authoritarian Personality."* Glencoe, Ill.: Free Press.

Deutscher, Irwin.

1968   Asking questions cross-culturally: some problems of linguistic comparability. In Howard S. Becker, Blanche Geer, David Riesman, and Robert S. Weiss (Eds.), *Institutions and the Person: Papers Presented to Everett C. Hughes.* Chicago: Aldine. Pp. 318-341.

Elder, Joseph W.

1967   Regional differences in family and caste attitudes: north and south India. In Robert I. Crane (Ed.), *Regions and Regionalism in*

South Asian Studies: An Exploratory Study. Duke University Program in Comparative Studies on Southern Asia, Monograph and Occasional Paper Series, Monograph no. 5. Durham, N.C., Pp. 232-257.

Ervin, Susan, and Robert T. Bower.

1952   Translation problems in international surveys. *Public Opinion Quarterly,* 16 (Winter):595-606.

Frey, Frederick W.

1963   Surveying peasant attitudes in Turkey. *Public Opinion Quarterly,* 27 (Fall):335-355.

1970   Cross-cultural survey research in political science. In Robert T. Holt and John E. Turner (Eds.), *The Methodology of Comparative Research.* New York: Free Press. Pp. 173-294.

Grimshaw, Allen D.

1969   Sociolinguistics and the sociologist. *American Sociologist,* 4 (November):312-321.

Gumperz, John J., and C. M. Naim.

1960   Formal and informal standards in the Hindi regional area. In John Gumperz and C. A. Ferguson (Eds.), *Linguistic Diversity in South Asia.* University Research Center in Anthropology, Folklore, and Linguistics, Publication 13. Bloomington, Ind.: Pp. 92-118.

Halsey, A.H., Jean Floud, and C. Arnold Anderson (Eds.).

1961   *Education, Economy and Society: A Reader in the Sociology of Education.* Glenco, Ill.: Freee Press.

Holt, Robert T., and John E. Turner.

1970   The methodology of comparative research. In Robert T. Holt and John E. Turner (Eds.), *The Methodology of Comparative Research.* New York: Free Press. Pp. 1-20.

Homans, George C.

1962   *Sentiments and Activities: Essays in Social Science.* Glencoe, Ill.: Free Press.

Hudson, Bradford B., Mohamed K. Barakat, and Rolfe LaForge.

1959   Introduction to problems and methods of cross-cultural research. *Journal of Social Issues,* 15, no.3:5-19.

Hunt, William H., Wilder W. Crane, and John C. Wahlke.

1964   Interviewing political elites in cross-cultural comparative research. *American Journal of Sociology,* 70 (July):59-68.

Inkeles, Alex, and David H. Smith.

1966   The OM Scale: a comparative sociopsychological measure of individual modernity. *Sociometry,* 29, no. 4:353-377.

Jones, Emily L.

1963   The courtesy bias in South-east Asian Surveys. *International Social Science Journal,* 15, no. 1:70-76.

Kluckhohn, Florence, and Fred L. Strodtbeck.

1961   *Variations in Value-Orientations.* New York: Harper.

Landsberger, Henry A., and Antonia Saavedra.

1967   Response set in developing countries. *Public Opinion Quarterly,* 31 (Summer):214-229.

Lerner, Daniel.

1958   *The Passing of Traditional Society: Modernizing the Middle East.* Glencoe, Ill.: Free Press.

McClelland, David C.

1961   *The Achieving Society.* Princeton, N.J.: Van Nostrand.

McClelland, David C., John W. Atkinson, Russell A. Clark, and Edgar L. Lowell.

1953   *The Achievement Motive.* New York: Appleton-Century-Crofts.

McClelland, David C., and David G. Winter.

1969   *Motivating Economic Achievement: Accelerating Economic Development Through Psychological Training.* New York: Free Press.

Merton, Robert K.

1949   *Social Theory and Social Structure: Toward a Codification of Theory and Research.* Glencoe, Ill.: Free Press.

Minturn, Leigh, and John Hitchcock.

1963   The Rājpūts of Khalapur, India. In Beatrice B. Whiting (Ed.), *Six Cultures: Studies of Child Rearing.* New York: Wiley. Pp. 203-361.

Mitchell, Robert E.

   1965   Survey materials collected in the developing countries: sampling,
           measurement, and interviewing obstacles in intra- and inter-
           national comparisons. *International Social Science Journal*, 17,
           no. 4:665-685.

Morris, Charles.

   1956   *Varieties of Human Value.* Chicago: University of Chicago Press.

Murphy, Gardner.

   1953   *In the Minds of Men: the Study of Human Behavior and Social
           Tensions in India.* New York: Basic Books.

Parsons, Talcott.

   1949   *The Structure of Social Action: A Study of Social Theory With
           Special Reference to a Group of Recent European Writers.*
           Glencoe, Ill.: Free Press.

Phillips, Herbert P.

   1959-
   1960   Problems of translation and meaning in field work. *Human Organ-
           ization*, 18, no. 4:184-192.

Pillai, Shanmugam M.

   1960   Tamil—literary and colloquial. In John J. Gumperz and C. A.
           Ferguson (Eds.), *Linguistic Diversity in South Asia.* University
           Research Center in Anthropology, Folklore, and Linguistics,
           Publication 13. Bloomington, Ind. Pp. 27-42.

Radcliffe-Brown, A.R.

   1957   *A Natural Science of Society.* Glencoe, Ill.: Free Press.

Riley, Matilda White.

   1963   *Sociological Research: A Case Approach.* New York: Harcourt,
           Brace and World.

Robinson, John P., Jerrold G. Rusk, and Kendra Head.

   1968   *Measures of Political Attitudes.* Ann Arbor, Mich.: Institute of
           Social Research.

Robinson, John P., and Philip R. Shaver.

    1969   *Measures of Social Psychological Attitudes.* Ann Arbor, Mich.: Institute of Social Research.

Ross, Aileen D.

    1961   *The Hindu Family in its Urban Setting.* Toronto: University of Toronto Press.

Rostow, Walter W.

    1961   *The Stages of Economic Growth: A Non-Communist Manifesto.* Cambridge: Cambridge University Press.

Rudolph, Lloyd, and Susanne Rudolph.

    1958   Surveys in India: field experience in Madras State. *Public Opinion Quarterly,* 22 (Fall):235-244.

Sapir, Edward.

    1931   Conceptual categories in primitive languages. *Science,* 74 (December 4):578.

Strole, Leo.

    1956   Social integration and certain corollaries: an exploratory study. *American Sociological Review,* 2, no. 6:709-716.

Tylor, E.B.

    1889   On a method of investigating the development of institutions; applied to laws of marriage and descent. *Journal of the Royal Anthropological Institute of Great Britain and Ireland.* 18:245-269.

van den Berghe, Pierre L.

    1967   *Race and Racism: A Comparative Perspective.* New York: Wiley.

Whiting, John W.M.

    1968   Methods and problems in cross-cultural research. In Gardner Lindzey and Elliot Aronson (Eds.), *The Handbook of Social Psychology,* vol. II, 2nd ed. Reading, Mass.: Addison-Wesley. Chap. 17.

Whorf, Benjamin Lee.

    1956   A linguistic consideration of thinking in primitive communities. In John B. Carroll (Ed.), *Language, Thought, and Reality: Selected*

Writings of Benjamin Lee Whorf. Cambridge, Mass.: MIT Press. Pp. 65-86.

Wilson, Elmo C., and Lincoln Armstrong.

1963   Interviewers and interviewing in India. *International Social Science Journal,* 15, no. 1:48-58.

Zetterberg, Hans.

1965   *On Theory and Verification in Sociology.* 3rd ed. Totowa, N.J.: Bedminster.

Discussion

Mr. Waisanen. Elder's paper provides strong testimony to the difficulties encountered in comparative research and how these difficulties are compounded when one decides, as Elder did, to use a site-selection design which maximizes differences by enabling a search for sharp contrasts in normative patterns. As he shows, the sampling problems endemic to all research are compounded in comparative work. His discussion of sampling in the absence of sampling frames and of the problems that resulted is familiar to many of us. Elder further considers problems of unit comparability, instrument construction and translation, interviewer selection and training, and field response. Emphasis on the specifics of these several problems is, of course, justifiable, but I would have preferred more attention to the attempts he made to resolve these problems. For example, with regard to sampling [see p. 125], "we were forced to abandon nearly three-fourths of our Lucknow sample frame because we could not trace the addresses." What happened as a consequence? Did this stop the research? Or were strategies available that enabled some resolution of this kind of issue?

Elder also presents an interesting problem related to the concept of trust. This matter is interesting and important from the perspectives of both theory and methodology. The paper reports failure to resolve the translation problem for field application. One might ask, with regard to such difficulties, about the distinctions which can be made between conceptual equivalence and behavioral equivalents. Suppose we were trying to collect data on interpersonal trust among students at a university in the United States. We might use Elder's basic question and then ask a student to indicate his "degree of trust" in a man who follows another religion. In such a case, what would we be asking the student in this culture? Would he move toward or away from that person who follows another religion? Has he or would he lend him money? Has he or would he accept a stranger's counsel, etc.? As we use concepts of this kind in English in the United States, we ordinarily assume a common dimension of trust in each of these behavior indicators, and the word "trust" identifies this dimension.

There is an alternative strategy. We can decrease the number of stimulus subjects (i.e., the person who follows another religion; the government official; the person from another province) and increase the number of behavioral indicators of the concept (i.e., vote for; loan money to; ask to arbitrate a dispute; etc.). We might then achieve a higher validation level (by predictive power) for a variable, expressed by an index of behavioral indicators, rather than having to settle for attempts to measure that same variable by trying to translate a single term for which there may be no direct semantic equivalent.

Mr. Elder. Another interesting concept that I've been working with is that of "amount of education." I have just completed a content analysis of the textbooks that were used in these two different sections of India. Slightly more than 30 percent of the information conveyed in the language textbooks referred specifically to India's mythological or historical past. Clearly those who are educated received a heavy dose of the Ramayana, the Mahabharata, the Rigvedic legends, the stories of the greatness of India under the Emperor Ashok, and so on. I am not sure, though, that exposure to eight years of education in, say, Chicago [see Armer-Schnaiberg, paper below] is analogous to eight years' exposure in India. So creating comparable measures even for the concept "amount of education" poses real problems.

Mr. Waisanen. I think there is good reason to believe that the effects of equal amounts of education will *not* be comparable. The data I have worked with show not only differential impact but differential *point* of impact. These findings, of course, relate to the critical curvilinearity in the relationship of normal education to any behavioral or attitudinal indicator of modernity. This curvilinearity seems constant across cultures. The point of so-called attitudinal takeoff which seems related to education differs according to social and economic development. It seems true that in Costa Rica, for example, three or four years of formal education is functionally equivalent to no education.

Mr. Elder. One of the dimensions I played with was the concept of nationalism or patriotism. Testing that concept through the 10 years of schooling, I found a more or less straight increase. The longer a boy was exposed to school, the more his responses to certain questions showed a patriotic component. Similarly, the longer a boy had been in school, the clearer was his conception of the mythology behind a series of festivals. He knew the religious heritage better, and he could name the gods in the heavens better. There is also some evidence that students adopt patterns of increasing religious orthodoxy as they increase their amount of education. For example, a value of vegetarianism is presented in these textbooks, and there is some indication that exposure to education increases a type of religiously orthodox vegetarianism.

Mr. Waisanen. Elder's paper sensitizes the reader to yet another concept, a concern for modernity. He has observed shrewd and calculating farmers who were the first to adopt tractors and send their children to college and who yet insist that "man proposes, God disposes." He has also observed engineers who took the advice of astrologers with some consistency and regularity. What he is saying is that some compartmentalization of beliefs is accepted in India (as well as in the United States, where we have some Ph.D.'s who pray and doctors of divinity who prey).

We should ask whether these "exceptions" are actually predominant. And more important: Whatever the incidence of this compartmentalization at the time of the original observation (e.g., the percentage of engineers who consulted astrologers or the percentage of American Ph.D.'s who prayed in 1930), has this incidence changed since that time? If in India we find that a significantly reduced percent of engineers consulted astrologers regularly in 1970 (compared with 1930), that fact of change is as important and interesting, if not more so, as the fact that some engineers *still* consult astrologers. The process of change should be taken into account.

Mr. Elder. Mr. Waisanen gets right at the heart of the problem in trying to define the parameters of modernization (if, indeed, there is such a thing) when he says that the engineer who consulted astrologers was compartmentalizing. My question is, Who among us is entitled to decide that he is compartmentalizing? It certainly may be that, according to my logic of cause and effect, he is compartmentalizing; he understands the laws and principles, etc., of engineering, yet he utilizes astrologers regularly.

The intriguing thing to me about that engineer is that, in *his* logic of cause and effect, he is not compartmentalizing. When I asked him to explain these two apparently conflicting sets of activities, his explanation, within his context as both a Hindu and an engineer, made sense. Who of us has such a mastery of logic and illogic that we can say which behavior is illogical, and will presumably erode with time, and which is logical and will presumably continue indefinitely?

Mr. Waisanen. I don't want to imply that compartmentalization is "bad." I am saying, though, that we should observe whether an attitude or belief system is truly a system; whether its parts are interrelated and interdependent. If so, we can still accept compartmentalization, but we would also have to conclude that the inconsistencies will erode with time.

Mr. Chaplin. I have a clarifying question on this very point. Does compartmentalization depend on the areas of life that one is mixing together? Did you ask the engineer if he ever made an engineering decision on the basis of astrology or whether he only went to astrologers, say, when he wanted to decide who to marry?

Mr. Elder. Yes. In this case, the astrologer was a specialist in certain areas, such as when a factory should be opened. From the Indian engineer's viewpoint, since there are many uncontrollable factors in any venture, an astrologer is a good man to ask about the best date for signing a contract or starting operations in a factory. But the engineer wouldn't inquire about technical matters, such as how many workers to hire or which of several production techniques to use.

Mr. Waisanen. Let's propose some hypothetical data. If data from 1930 showed 50 percent of the engineers putting significant decisions into the hands of astrologers but only 40 percent doing so in 1970, what would be happening?

Mr. Elder. I don't have this sort of data, but I think it would reveal that the engineers were defining the astrologer's skill area more narrowly.

Ms. Busch. Given the social structure in India, is it normal and expected for an engineer to start work, stop work, marry his daughter, etc., according to astrologer's data? The expectation is not for just the last, but also the first two items?

Mr. Elder. Yes. In fact, my point is that it is as normal for an Indian engineer to decide on a factory's opening date in consultation with an astrologer as it would be abnormal for an engineer in Bloomington, Indiana, to do so. For us to speak of this as compartmentalization suggests that we feel there is only one "normal" pattern an engineer can follow—that pattern being what we do in the United States.

Ms. Busch. If this Indian engineer were living in Bloomington and made a decision about starting a factory here in the same way as if he were in India (i.e., using an astrologer), would you say then that his action reflected dependence on astrologers per se rather than dependence on social context?

Mr. Jones. That's an interesting question. A businessman here might consider an investment consultant the functional equivalent of an astrologer. There is a tremendous amount of hand-holding among businessmen.

Mr. Elder. I can't answer that question, but I do know there have been Indian graduate students here who have sent back to India for advice from their home astrologers regarding decisions they had to make here. These matters get very involved. It would be hard to make a general rule about the range and effects of social context.

Mr. Haller. The whole question of the relationship between rationality, use of evidence, and public use of evidence is fairly complicated and certainly involved here. I don't think we have the information necessary to carry this discussion further, though.

CHAPTER FIVE

Perception of the U.S. Sociologist and Its Impact on Cross-National Research

ALEJANDRO PORTES

University of Texas at Austin

Introduction

Of the five general stages of sociological development outlined by Timasheff (1961), the last two—between the two world wars and from World War II to the 1950s—were characterized by an increasing predominance of American sociology over early European schools. Had the Russian-born sociologist had the opportunity, he probably would have introduced a sixth stage, the last 15 years, in which American sociology has not only reached preeminence but has moved outside its borders, influencing other countries through the presence of researchers applying modern techniques of investigation.

The main goal of contemporary "cross-national" or "cross-cultural" research has seldom been the description of a foreign society for its own sake but rather the use of foreign areas to test the empirical validity or theories. This emphasis has been largely determined by the structure of American sociology, which emphasizes empirical instances more as reflections of general sociological regularities than as unique, peculiar occurrences. The impetus of international research has been such that, until recently, most U.S. sociologists have seen its main problems as straightforward extensions of methodological difficulties encountered at home and have had little concern for the social reactions and legal implications of this type of enterprise when carried out in a foreign country.

Thus the bulk of treatises on cross-national sociological research have dealt

149

with the technical issues of conceptual equivalence, measurement reliability, interviewer training and biases, nonresponse, the need for supervision of fieldworkers, difficulties of conducting data analysis in foreign countries, and so on.[1] Although valuable, discussion of cross-national research in these terms implicitly conveys the image of an active agent (the researcher) dealing with a relatively inert social body (the foreign population). Contrary to this orientation, two points appear to be increasingly true: (1) Research conducted by American or any other foreign sociologists in another country inevitably carries legal and political implications that transcend those of purely domestic investigation. (2) The final outcome of cross-national research is not solely dependent on the researcher's technical skill in dealing with a docile population but on the interaction between his presence and plans and the manner in which the country and specific population studied react toward them.

Johann Galtung (1966) noted some years ago that many U.S. researchers combine high methodological skill with a political naïveté which makes them assume that "good intentions" and candidness will be sufficient to dispell doubts and earn the goodwill of local scholars and citizens. This assumption, of course, fails to take into account the entire social setting into which the researcher and his project are supposed to fit: social and political currents operating at the time, dominant views of the United States and its activities within the national borders, and past experiences of the host country with foreign-sponsored research. Yet social science investigation is, if anything, more dependent than other disciplines on the consent of a country's population. In cross-national studies, dependence is accentuated by the researcher's need to be granted entrance into the countries and specific areas to be studied and to secure the cooperation of groups with whom he does not even share a common national identity (see Form's chapter above).

The reservoir of sympathy and willingness to cooperate with American investigators has been, until recently, relatively abundant. Despite the rarity of major scandals, though, the balance over the last few years shows that in many countries, reserves of goodwill have been depleted, rather than maintained or increased, by past experience with American sociological research (Whyte, 1969). Beyond the effects of international political relations, over which sociologists have little control, the main determinant of this trend has been the consistent absence of *reciprocity* in the conduct and results of cross-national research.

His own orientations and the value system of the U.S. academic establishment have led the typical investigator to take advantage of a favorable reception in order to test general hypotheses that, however important for theory development and interesting to the American sociological community, may nevertheless have only tangential relevance to the specific problems of the country in question (Roy and Fliegel, 1970). Moreover, the structure of this "experimental lab" approach to cross-national research easily leads to impressions of academic imperialism. Research is directed, usually hurriedly, by a passing scholar who selects the topic, general research design, and mode of analysis with little or no consultation with local scholars. Data are usually taken back to the United States without allowing time for even a preliminary report in the local language. Niceties and a conciliatory attitude on the part of the researcher do not hide the fact that the important decisions are made by a foreigner and only secondary, "manual" work is left for nationals.

As Blair (1969) has noted in the case of Guatemala, the result of the U.S. social scientist's interest in his own academic system has been the development of a brand of intellectual mercantilism in which Guatemalans are used as "hired hands" to gather data, which are then exported to the United States. Expressing the view of many Latin American sociologists, Graciarena (1965) has criticized the exclusive foreign origins of theoretical frameworks and research designs employed by U.S. cross-national researchers and the selection of topics that have little bearing on crucial priorities in Latin America.

The attractiveness of U.S.-sponsored research for many countries has been based on: (1) the general prestige of having scientific personnel come from an advanced country; (2) the possibility of learning research techniques and new theoretical developments, thus furthering the growth of local social science; and (3) the expectation that research results will be relevant to some important aspect of national reality. As the glamor of foreign researchers fades away under the cumulative impact of time and growing numbers and the other two expectations are but poorly fulfilled, initial positive orientations seem bound to change to a far more critical reception of future U.S. investigators. Within this context, the goals of the rest of this paper are:

1. To further illustrate the fundamental dependence of U.S. sociological ventures abroad on the orientations predominant in foreign countries and, hence, the impossibility of treating cross-national research problems as limited to methodological difficulties.

2. To outline the main types of cultural environments found in foreign countries and the basic problems which each presents to the conduct of research.

3. To continue the above analysis of features of U.S. cross-national research that have led to a deterioration of initial receptivity in many countries.

While much of the ensuing discussion seems applicable to most cross-national research, primary emphasis will be on the Latin American situation. Examples and references are thus aimed less at a general discussion of sociological ethics than at illustrating the current state of U.S. research in Latin America.

The Camelot Affair

It took a political confrontation with the magnitude of Project Camelot to impress on American social science that foreign countries are more than passive conglomerates of respondents waiting to be manipulated in whatever fashion research teams see fit. As described by Horowitz (1967) and Selser (1966), the purpose of Camelot was to evaluate the Chilean masses' potential for revolutionary political action and the most effective means of counteracting that action. While the topic was theoretically important, the form in which it was approached contained unacceptable aspects. Crucial among these were:

1. The lack of a legal framework for a project of such magnitude, sponsored by the U.S. government and with obvious political implications.
2. The subordination of social scientists and scientific interests to the political concerns of the U.S. military.
3. The value assymmetry of a theoretical framework that defined the political consequences of popular discontent as negative outcomes to be prevented, never as mechanisms promoting necessary change.
4. The deceitful manner in which the project was introduced to Chilean social scientists, who were confronted with the science-building aspects of the study, while the source of financing and final destination of results were hidden from them.

The significance of Project Camelot is that it uncovered a previously unsuspected image of U.S. social science and linked that image to U.S. political relationships with developing countries. As a recent survey of Chilean social scientists documents, a major result of that single project has been to change a relaxed and generally unquestioning acceptance of U.S.-sponsored research into a far more suspicious attitude (Schaedel, 1969).[2]

The general ethical implications of Project Camelot have not been entirely elucidated. Further discussion, however, must be bypassed here in favor of examining the difficulties of cross-national research in the post-Camelot era. Research problems in foreign countries can be defined as resulting from interactions between the cultural framework within which research is to take place and the topic and design brought by the investigator. Each of these factors is examined below.

General Cultural Settings

The attempt to abstract typical situations from the actual cultural plurality in which cross-national research occurs yields two main criteria for classification. Cognitively, cultural situations differ according to their degree of familiarity with the goals and procedures of sociological research. A population's familiarity can be defined as the closeness of consensual definitions of the activity to those that the investigators themselves hold. Familiarity applies to knowledge of technical means and their possible results but not to evaluations, which form a separate dimension. Expressively, cultural situations vary as to the level of favorableness to social science and, more specifically, U.S.-sponsored empirical research. Favorableness refers to the degree to which research is perceived as "good" and, hence, elicits cooperation.

While the reaction against Project Camelot was a consequence of its negative ethical implications, this reaction does not mean that exposure to legitimate research—or, for that matter, a total lack of exposure—will necessarily generate favorable attitudes. U.S. culture tends to assume the value of gaining information about some aspect of reality and, more deeply, the value of "doing something" about specific issues. The activity represented by empirical research is thus implicitly assumed to be positive and, hence, favorably received. This attitude is not expected to change unless technical or ethical mismanagements occur. In the case of Project Camelot, verbal arguments by U.S. social scientists in support of the study have often been based on the fact that participants were at least trying to "do something" while project critics were doing nothing and, for the most part, had never conducted any empirical research.

Most countries, however, do not seem to value scientific knowledge and an active approach to reality as much as American society does. There are cultural situations, some in Latin America, in which "doing something" is not necessarily defined as better than "doing nothing." Activity that is too extended, too intense, or too observable may be distasteful. The intrinsic positive quality imputed by this culture to information-gaining activity is thus often nonexistent in other settings, where, in the absence of additional considerations, the evaluation of empirical research per se may be entirely neutral.

Familiarity with, and favorableness toward, social research admit many empirical gradations. For heuristic purposes, however, it is possible to dichotomize each dimension (see the fourfold typology presented in Table 5.1). The labels assigned to cells synthesize fairly obvious aspects of each situation; they are intended only as guides to the ensuing discussion.

Lack of familiarity and unfavorable attitudes, producing *suspicion,* generally characterize situations in which researchers are "breaking new ground" in traditional areas.[3] Research among rural populations in developing countries is often of this nature. Sociologists studying these areas should learn much from the experiences of social anthropologists whose fieldwork seldom occurs under different conditions. Sociologists' tendency to collect data in a relatively short period of time and after no more than passing acquaintance with an area's culture should frequently give way to longer periods for cultural acclimatization. This change would serve the dual purpose of helping researchers "blend into the landscape," raising less fear and suspicion at the time of data collection, and clarifying the best strategy for obtaining the desired information.

Table 5.1   Cultural Settings of Cross-National Sociological Research

Expressive Dimension	Cognitive Dimension	
	Unfamiliar	Familiar
Unfavorable	Suspicion	Critical reserve
Favorable	Unrealistic expectations	Measured expectations

Traditional situations probably require the closest familiarity with the population involved. While the task of initiating scientific research in previously forgotten areas seems all to the good, failure to manage the situation properly may not only jeopardize the research project but also close opportunities for future investigations. Traditional populations tend to be structurally homogeneous and conscious of authority. Going directly to the people to obtain necessary information without consulting locally powerful individuals may doom a study. It is crucial in traditional situations to secure the support, or at least tolerance, of those endowed with authority. Their position and the closely knit social structure guarantee their ability, should they wish it, to prevent realization of the project. Interviewers from a recent project on fertility in Guatemala were effectively barred from a rural municipality by the single act of a local priest who warned his parishioners against the "red urbanites" who would prevent women from having children (Amaro, 1968).

Areas characterized by an uninformed, traditional reserve toward empirical investigation require, in short, a major shift in the conventional style of sociological research. Researchers must invest more time in acquiring familiarity with, and acceptance by, local groups.

Situations in which lack of familiarity with the methods of sociological research is coupled with favorableness toward it are those in which a population places *high*, and generally *unrealistic, expectations* on the researcher's presence and the results of his activity. Situations of this type may not be immediately obvious since interested individuals are often not willing or able to state exactly what they expect from the researcher. Such situations are generally characterized by excessive manifestations of deference.

During the first months of this writer's research in Santiago de Chile, he was invited to meetings of the *junta de vecinos* (neighborhood council) of a slum settlement in the city's northern periphery. Repeated displays of amiability were followed by invitations to the leaders' homes and insistence that the area be included in the study. For this purpose, Junta leaders provided a map of the settlement and took pains to demonstrate the cooperativeness of settlement dwellers. It took several weeks for the researcher to discover that his hosts thought he held a high government position and that, through him, the settlement's situation would be well publicized, thus accelerating their resettlement in new government projects.

Such situations place the researcher in a dilemma. Mistaken impressions of his power may be quite useful in securing a population's cooperation. Were he to set the record straight at the start, ensuing disappointment could result in a hostile reaction, thus closing the area to his research. On the other hand, reinforcing an erroneous image is not only unethical but may bias the information he receives, since respondents may answer according to what they imagine will please the researcher most or would be best for their interests. Moreover, repeated reinforcement of what amounts to a lie will infuriate local groups when they discover the truth, thus jeopardizing any prospect of future research. Hence, solutions to this dilemma must be found in either clarifying matters from the start, risking rejection, or clarifying them gradually over a short period of time, refusing to reinforce a mistaken impression and presenting the whole matter openly as soon as minimal rapport has developed.

In the above case, the problem was to reduce an overly favorable image of one's work. Situations characterized by high familiarity but negative evaluation of sociological research present the opposite difficulty: how to counteract an impression that is excessively (and, one believes, unjustly) negative. This *critical reserve* is often, although not necessarily, the result of bad experiences with past research projects. At the national level, this situation is exemplified by the case of post-Camelot Chile. At the local level, it is found in heavily researched areas. To take one example, a model zone in the Christian Democratic Agrarian Reform Program in Chile had been researched by no less than 10 U.S. economists, water-law experts, engineers, and sociologists in less than three years; in addition, the Chileans themselves had conducted studies. By 1969, the end of that period, farmers were reportedly refusing to answer new questionnaires, arguing that they had invested too much time in this kind of activity without any tangible improvements in their situation.

Conducting a successful research project under these conditions, clearly the most difficult among those outlined in Table 5.1, requires a strategy in which discretion must be a key element. Since a conventional presentation of researcher and research proposal may yield instant failure, the investigator must search for alternative paths. Secretiveness, however, must be avoided. Hiding one's identity and purposes runs contrary to professional ethics. Further, such behavior will eventually reinforce a negative image of research work by linking it with duplicity and untrustworthiness. Schaedel (1969) reported that in Chile a number of individuals interviewed under such conditions were extremely resentful, their experience tending to reinforce the general suspicion of Americans created by Project Camelot.

Although the rule applies to all cases, researchers in these situations should take special pains to make the exact nature of their topic and research design known to all interested parties. It is often of great importance to conduct research in cooperation with an established academic institution in the target country and to leave copies of the data and at least a preliminary report of results with that institution (Roy and Fliegel, 1970).

One of the most serious consequences of the assumption that foreign countries can be employed as passive, nonreactive research settings has been the veritable invasion of many countries by "free-floating" researchers—often graduate students—sent by their home universities to fend for themselves in an unfamiliar environment. This practice should be discouraged since it neither yields effective research nor improves the deteriorating image of U.S. social science abroad. Without experience or guidance, the tendency among such researchers is often to engage in precisely the kind of secretive information gathering that can only produce negative reflections on American social science.

Discretion in carrying out research in unfavorable situations requires that, after relevant parties have been informed of an investigation's purpose and a minimum of acceptance has been secured, the researcher proceed in such a way as *to minimize the costs* to a population wary of this type of activity. This requirement challenges the researcher to employ techniques other than questionnaires and formal interviews (e.g., previously collected data and other secondary sources, systematic observation, informal conversations when other participants are aware of the researcher's goals).

The fourth situation, that of *measured expectations* based on familiarity with sociological research and a favorable orientation to it, requires little comment since it is obviously the ideal setting for investigation. Developed nations such as those of Western Europe probably provide more such settings than do the underdeveloped countries of Latin America. In the latter, one of the main long-run goals of sociological research is precisely to generate this type of orientation. High professional standards, relevance of U.S. research to national problems, and a concern for training local groups should ideally lead to high levels of familiarity with, and favorableness toward, scientific work. As was noted above, though, the experience in several countries and the current trend of events run far short of these expectations.

Specific Cultural Levels

The situations summarized in Table 5.1 apply not only to the general culture of a country but can also be used to describe specific segments of that culture. At minimum, research in a foreign country is confronted with one or another of the above orientations at four levels:

1. Generalized cultural themes permeating "public opinion"
2. Attitudes of the local scholarly community
3. Government interests and policies
4. Attitudes of the specific universe to be studied.

Obviously the last three levels partially overlap the first; the last could also overlap with the government, the scholarly community, or both.

The four alternatives described above do not appear with equal frequency at different levels. In fact, for any given research situation, one or more cells in Table 5.1 can be presumed empty in several categories. General public opinion is, in most cases, not characterized by high levels of familiarity with the goals and techniques of sociological research. Attitudes are formed on the basis of superficial reports provided by the mass media, with one well-publicized positive or negative instance creating a stereotype, which is then applied to all social investigation. Thus in most cases the four-cell classification is reduced, at this level, to two: favorableness or lack of favorableness in similar low-familiarity situations. At the other extreme, the alternatives portrayed above apply equally unevenly across local scholars and especially social scientists since, in most cases, familiarity with sociological research is relatively high. Thus the question is reduced to favorableness or the lack of it in similar high-familiarity situations.

The importance of government's familiarity with, and favorableness toward sociological research varies from situations in which governmental agencies may only admit, bar entrance of, or expel researchers from their country, to those in which government approval and supervision are required at each step of the research. In practically all cases, however, the overwhelming power of governments means that, in reality, cross-national researchers are confronted with only two of the four situations outlined above; strongly negative attitudes by a foreign government generally imply a project's demise. Thus, actual cross-national research takes place under and because of favorable government orientations, ranging from mild indifference to high expectations.

While high governmental favorableness toward, and familiarity with, sociological research represent the ideal, those situations in which favorability is produced by excessive expectations yield not only an unstable research environment but potential danger. Backward regimes of a dictatorial character are prone to loud displays of "modernity," in which visiting social scientists may play a useful role. Advances made by government agencies in these situations require careful evaluation since they may derive from unattainable expectations or may simply be a way of exploiting modern scientific techniques for propaganda purposes.

Research Topics and Methods

As was stated at the beginning, the outcome of cross-national research is an interaction between the particular research setting and the general goals and specific techniques brought by the researcher. Having outlined the different cultural situations, we should now examine those distinctions in topic and plan of investigation that affect a project's chances of success. At the level of research topic, the important distinction is that between subjects that are sensitive and those that are not. At the level of research design, the main difference lies between obtrusive and unobtrusive procedures.

Sensitive topics may be defined as internal matters of restricted circulation whose investigation by U.S. scholars is suspected of transcending the limits of purely scientific interest. Clearly, the definition of a sensitive topic varies from country to country. Yet the assumption that foreign countries can be employed as passive research settings has resulted in the selection of topics on the basis of theoretical considerations without regard for the ways in which those topics are defined by the country and specific population involved. The obvious alternative is to consult with local scholars and institutions prior to making a final commitment to a particular project. This step may even entail an exploratory visit to the country or countries in question, a procedure recently recommended by the Latin American Studies Association (1969).

The area of study that comes closest to being universally sensitive is politics. People in many countries are reluctant to voice political opinions. Further, studies of political parties, legislative bodies, and executive government agencies invariably raise doubts about the appropriateness of making restricted or confidential information available to foreign investigators. A clear indication of this condition is provided by Schaedel's (1969) survey of U.S. social science in Chile. While economists were generally favorably received, obtained institutional affiliation, and were aided by local research centers with their projects, political scientists appeared to enjoy the lowest reputation. Their work was the object of much suspicion and their efforts to obtain institutional affiliation were, more often than not, rejected.

Paradoxically, though, political issues are among the most popular topics in cross-national research. Interest in these problems is not limited to political scientists; a large number of other investigators have also made political research their chief area of cross-national study. While many political investigations are of undeniable value, comparative researchers in this field must be aware of the extraordinary difficulties presented by this work and the high cost that it may exact in suspicion, harassment, and challenge to a professional self-image.

Classification of research designs into obtrusive and unobtrusive is not meant to imply that one set of procedures is necessarily superior to another. Although a different terminology might be more adequate, the present one is adopted for its current popularity (Webb et al, 1966; Denzin, 1970).[4] Obtrusive measures are characterized by (1) a fairly complicated research machinery involving bureaucratic organization of hired personnel for the collection, organization, and analysis of data and (2) high time costs to the researched population whose cooperation is required, either in the form of intensive interviews from a few informants or of limited information from a large number of respondents.

Unobtrusive designs, by contrast, usually employ a few informally organized collaborators. These procedures place the burden of data collection on the observational powers of the researcher. While data collected unobtrusively may often lack the detail, systematic organization, and representativeness of conventional methods, unobtrusive designs enable the collection of information without exhausting a limited reservoir of patience. They also confront researchers with the challenge of employing their ingenuity in new ways rather than relying on routine questionnaire techniques.

Nonsensitive subjects studied in favorable social situations make the choice of research design largely dependent on technical considerations. The key feature of sensitive topics, though, is that they add a significant political dimension to the technical aspects of research. While the sensitive nature of a subject need not prevent its empirical study, its sensitivity certainly limits the range of feasible research methods. In general, unobtrusive techniques recommend themselves for this type of situation.

Conclusion

An inverse correlation seems to exist between the number of past U.S. research projects in a given country and the country's receptivity to new ones. As was noted above, the main cause of this trend seems to be a consistent absence of reciprocity between the researcher and the country or population involved. Reciprocity requires some sort of balance between the costs of an activity and the returns derived from it. More often than not, U.S. institutions have been allowed to implement their definition of foreign countries as passive research settings. This situation has carried the implication that local groups will be sufficiently rewarded by the privilege of having been chosen for study by members of an advanced scientific community and by the monetary compensation paid to local collaborators. The purpose of this final section is to summarize specific reasons for the growing foreign discontent with U.S. sociological research in Latin America (as has been noted, though, this situation does not seem restricted to Latin America; see Clinard and Elder, 1965).

A significant imbalance between costs and returns for countries involved in U.S. cross-national research has been vividly documented by surveys in several countries and the accounts of concerned social scientists (Blair, 1969; Schaedel, 1969; Whyte, 1969; Graciarena, 1965; Canton et al., 1965). Their conclusions can be summarized as follows:

1. Topics are selected with little regard for the concerns and sensitivities of countries involved.

2. Little time and effort is spent in familiarizing local students with advanced theories and methods. Whatever is conveyed is for the sole purpose of facilitating successful completion of the researcher's project.

3. Data collected in a country are almost always shipped back to the United States without depositing copies with local institutions. Hence, no one in the country involved can use the results.

4. Findings, when published, appear in English. Occasionally they have been translated, but the process has taken so many years as to render the results obsolete. Very few U.S researchers bother to write at least a preliminary report before leaving a country.

5. The role of local social scientists is usually limited to implementing unilateral directives. Cross-national relationships are seldom a true partnership but rather develop into a subordinate-superordinate situation with the U.S. personnel invariably on top.

6. U.S.-sponsored research as a whole projects an image of chaotic inefficiency. Because researchers come from numerous autonomous institutions, considerable duplication occurs. Informants in "strategic" positions become exasperated by the flow of researchers asking for valuable time in order to formulate identical questions.

The third point is a frequent complaint from Latin American students who, after taking part in U.S.-sponsored research projects, attempt unsuccessfully to obtain a copy of the data for their own work. Subordination of local personnel to foreign interests and the transfer of data to the United States without opportunity for domestic study were major causes for the public resignation of several Colombian sociologists from American University's Project Simpatico (Selser, 1966). Excessive duplication and an abusive use of informants figured at the top of the list of complaints voiced by Guatemalan scholars in Blair's (1969) survey.

There is a growing realization in foreign countries that high receptivity and cooperation with U.S. researchers have been of great use to the latter but of little relevance to the understanding of local social problems. The costs have been too high for the returns. While no detailed solutions can be offered here, the general list of issues presented above may serve as a point of departure for sensitizing foreign-bound sociologists to the importance of those being studied and to some of the specific concerns they may have.

Notes

1.　See, for example, the collection of papers presented to the Seminar on Comparative Research and Training of the Institute for Comparative Sociology, Bloomington, Indiana, 1966.

2. Through international press coverage, the effects of Camelot have extended to, and are currently felt in, other Latin American countries; see Adams (1969), Whyte (1969), and Selser (1966).

3. "Unfavorable attitudes" in this case means suspicion rather than definite hostility. Settings unfamiliar with empirical research could be alternatively characterized as expressively neutral rather than unfavorable. To do so, however, would require additional elaboration of the present scheme (Table 5.1). Further discussion does not seem warranted at this point since the purpose of the diagram is less to provide refined description than to sensitize researchers to the major cultural alternatives encountered in comparative research.

4. Unobtrusive measures as defined in psychology by Webb and his associates (1966) seem to contain an element of secretiveness, which, as the above discussion makes clear, is to be avoided in the application of any research methodology to cross-national, sociological research.

References

Adams, Richard N.

> 1969   Introduction. In Richard N. Adams (Ed.), *Responsibilities of the Foreign Scholar to the Local Scholarly Community*. New York: Education and World Affairs Publication. Pp. 5-8.

Amaro, Nelson.

> 1968   *Encuesta Sobre el Condicionamiento Socio-Cultural de la Fecundidad en Areas Marginales Urbanas-Metropolitanas, Ladino-Rurales e Indigenas Tradicionales.* Guatemala: ICAPF/IDESAC.

Blair, Calvin P.

> 1969   The nature of U.S. interest and involvement in Guatemala: an American view. In Richard N. Adams (Ed.), *Responsibilities of the Foreign Scholar to the Local Scholarly Community*. New York: Education and World Affairs Publication. Pp. 15-43.

Canton, Dario, Oscar Cornblitt, Alejandro Dehollain, Torcuato S. Di Tella, Ezequiel Gallo, Johann Galtung, Jorge Garcia-Bouza, Jorge Graciarena, Francis Korn, Manuel Mora y Araujo, Silvia Sigal, Francisco Suarez, and Eliseo Veron.

> 1965   Carta al Director: el Proyecto Camelot. *Revista Latino-Americana de Sociologia*, 2(July):251-253.

Clinard, Marshall B., and Joseph W. Elder.

> 1965   Sociology in India. *American Sociological Review*, 30(August): 581-587.

Denzin, Norman K.

1970   *The Research Act.* Chicago: Aldine.

Galtung, Johann.

1966   Letter to the Ministry of Interior of Chile. In Gregorio Selser, *Espionaje en America Latina.* Buenos Aires: Ediciones Iguazu. Pp. 134-145.

Graciarena, Jorge.

1965   Algunas consideraciones sobre la cooperacion internacional y el desarrollo reciente de la investigacion sociologica. *Revista Latino-Americana de Sociologia,* 2(July):231-242.

Horowitz, Irving L. (Comp.).

1967   *The Rise and Fall of Project Camelot.* Cambridge, Mass.: MIT Press.

Latin American Studies Association (LASA) and Education and World Affairs Council

1969   Recommendations. In Richard N. Adams (Ed.), *Responsibilities of the Foreign Scholar to the Local Scholarly Community.* New York: Education and World Affairs Publication. Pp. 8-10.

Roy, Prodipto, and Frederick C. Fliegel.

1970   The conduct of collaborative research in developing nations: The insiders and the outsiders. *International Social Science Journal,* 22, No. 3:505-523.

Schaedel, Richard P.

1969   The extent and effect of U.S.-based research in Chile: 1960-1968. In Richard N. Adams (Ed.), *Responsibilities of the Foreign Scholar to the Local Scholarly Community.* New York: Education and World Affairs Publication. Pp. 47-80.

Selser, Gregorio.

1966   *Espionaje en America Latina.* Buenos Aires: Ediciones Iguazu.

Tiempo, El.

1966   Investigadores del Plan Simpatico dicen que no hay espionaje en el pais. *El Tiempo* (Bogota), February 6, P. 1.

Timasheff, Nicholas S.

1961 *La Teoria Sociologica.* Mexico City: Fondo de Cultura Economica.

Webb, Eugene J., Donald T. Campbell, Richard D. Schwartz, and Lee Sechrest.

1966 *Unobtrusive Measures: Nonreactive Research in the Social Sciences.* Chicago: Rand McNally.

Whyte, William F.

1969 The role of the U.S. professor in developing countries. *American Sociologist,* 4(February):19-28.

Discussion

Mr. Gould. Portes, like Form, raises questions that are more than just procedural, technical, or programmatic, because they are at the same time generally epistemological; what they do, and very interestingly, forcefully, and creatively, is to inquire systematically *how* the fact of who we are has affected what we know as social scientists.

American social science was erected on a foundation of dedicated empiricism and touchingly naive faith in man's willingness to accept the bona fides of research pursued in the name of objective and dispassionate inquiry. When we were graduate students, years ago, there was widespread agreement that sociological findings carry no moral implications in themselves and that, consequently, our findings should be made available to men of any political persuasion, regardless of what they proposed to do with them—that science would somehow save us by the force of its inner objective truth. Today we are less sure.

Portes observes that an underlying assumption of American social science research has been that the milieu to be investigated is essentially passive: It doesn't talk back; it asks nothing in return for its cooperation; it adopts the role of the well-trained and well-paid prostitute in the professional bawdy house. Now, however, things have changed, at least in the context of international sociological research. What is learned can affect one's destiny, and the various interests who get studied are now aware of this fact. American social scientists consequently find acceptance of themselves and their research endeavors increasingly problematic both to foreign populations and certain segments of their own.

Sociology and anthropology were more parochial than they realized until World War II wiped away the illusory images of the world fashioned for us by imperialism. Each discipline had emphasized study of one type of society: anthropology studied the primitive isolate; sociology, Western industrial society. Each had generalized about the world on the basis of its limited perśpective. Then, in the postwar years, both anthropology and sociology began to build new scientific identities in the emerging milieu of formerly colonial countries. Anthropologists discovered cities and then state systems (and initially viewed them conceptually as if they were primitive isolates). Sociologists simultaneously discovered the non-Western world (and initially viewed it conceptually as if it were like Western industrial society).

In both cases, the objects of research had been "artless natives," I would argue, passive because unaware of social science and because subordinated to political orders where obedience and subservience ordinarily could be taken for granted. This attitude was probably true even of early sociology in the United States, both because the American population was largely passive and because social scientists treated politically motivated revolutionary situations, suffering, and cruelty as not within the legitimate province of an "objective" social science [Henry, 1963]. Social science methodologies systematically eliminated values and "self" from any consideration, or at least tried to. Kurt Wolff's pleas in the late 1940s and 1950s to integrate the old-fashioned *verstehen* injunction—"Know thyself"—into social science methodologies fell largely on deaf ears.

In recent years, however, we have been forced to become more aware of the necessity for just such self-knowledge. It may be that the populations we treated so casually in the past have always hated our arrogance and selfishness. The difference now is that they have the political resources to tell us so, to deny us access, to demand responsibility from us. Now, instead of simply diagraming subjects' interactional routines in plant, household, and village, we must also spend time trying to understand our own failures in gaining acceptance and cooperation from those we wish to study. In the process we are learning something about ourselves and our science that we may have half suspected heretofore but which only scholars like Wolff and Henry had integrated into their research. Social upheavals have rearranged social relationships in a truly revolutionary way. The new social relationships must be considered as we plan out research. Portes's paper helps to organize this new reality and can be of great help in that planning.

Each of us can document the validity of Portes's observation that (1) research topics chosen by visiting social scientists are infrequently congruent with local needs and priorities, and (2) members of most societies do not value scientific knowledge as an active approach to reality as much as Americans do.

Some of us will find Portes' distinction between unobtrusive and other kinds of research somewhat more problematic. In brief, "unobtrusiveness" varies across cultures and, within cultures, over time.

Mr. Portes. I am not claiming any particular novelty for my paper; much of what I have said is simply a systematization of things that have become obvious to anyone involved in cross-national research. I do, however, think that some of what I say suggests that some of our colleagues have been too easily persuaded that they can now do *no* viable comparative research, and I take issue with this new isolationism and its implications.

I have more than once heard the argument that deterioration of the social science image in many countries is the outcome of (1) broader international processes of growing tensions between countries (including negative reactions to U.S. imperialism) and (2) the polarization of classes, aggregation of conflicts, and new militant ideologies in many countries over which we, as sociologists, have no control. The argument continues by stating that these processes of international and national politics have resulted in rational hostilities in some countries toward U.S. research and researchers who have *not* correctly assessed rewards and costs to the host countries. Thus cooperation with U.S. social researchers may cost more than the rewards to a local population.

This argument provides us with a very comfortable rationalization. We can simply shrug our shoulders and say, "What can we do in the face of the inevitable? This is not our responsibility. It is part of a broader scheme." This rationalization may, in part, be true, but not totally. I believe that substantial responsibility for this deteriorating trend lies with research practices over which sociologists and other social scientists *do* have control. We have no right to shrug our shoulders until we have directly confronted that part of the responsibility which belongs to us. Moreover, such direct confrontation can result in theoretical and methodological benefits as well as increased mutual respect and goodwill.

Finally, I should note that I fully agree with Gould in his observation that many "unobtrusive" measures are no longer unobtrusive.

Mr. Chaplin. How can we learn from past failures? What, for example, can we tell students who want to go to Chile—or to some other site where researchers must face residual hostility, or elite distrust, or unrealistically high expectations?

Mr. Portes. Since the research climate varies from country to country, there is no single answer to these questions. There are, however, two general principles. First, since current situations reflect past experiences, it is unreasonable to expect trust—to expect that your claims about your project will be accepted at face value. Second, we must act with "discretion"—meaning here minimization of costs to research populations whose resources of patience are nearly depleted. More concretely, we should undertake to guarantee availability of results (and data) written up in the local language. Licensing by our own professional societies has also been suggested, but it would probably generate more problems than it would resolve.

I don't believe we can establish standard procedures. Nor do I believe that we should stop research in a foreign country the first time that we—or those working on other projects—are accused of being CIA agents. I do believe we must self-consciously acknowledge the difficulties and train our students as well as sensitize established foreign-bound scholars in such a way as to minimize unhappy encounters.

There is a point at which continuation of research carries risks for the population studied which are simply too high to sustain. This is true in domestic as well as in comparative research. As social research improves—and as social research findings are increasingly taken seriously by control-oriented groups—we must be careful not to pass that point.

Mr. Stryker.   I find it interesting, in a perverse sort of way, that the concern expressed in Portes's paper and by Gould in his discussion can also be taken as testimony of the current and maybe even growing significance of sociological research. Earlier we could perhaps not really consider the serious implications of what we said and did because what we said and did had no serious implications in that, by and large, nobody was listening. It appears to be the case at this point that somebody *is* listening, and it *does* make a difference. We should not, however, overestimate the impact of what any given sociologist or anthropologist does. Fools there are, but our way of work—many researchers working from disparate points of view—may yet save us from the fallability, the ignorance, the venality of one of us alone as an individual researcher.

Having made this observation and not being a comparativist, I should like to address a question to those of you who are. To what degree is what is being said peculiar in its relevance to developing societies? Would it pertain equally well in European societies? Would offering collaboration to a colleague in Europe, for example, have the same positive impact Portes suggests would result in Latin America? It seems to me that some of the European sociologists that I know, given the degree of their self-confidence, the degree of their conviction that they are better sociologists than the Americans they know, would find this discussion insultingly condescending. I raise, then, the question as to whether what has been said is equally applicable to societies generally or rather peculiar to a certain class of societies.

Mr. Friday.   Doing research in Europe is quite different from doing research in underdeveloped countries. There is no question, for example, but that Sweden, as a modern industrialized society, provides us with a good setting in which to test theories developed in work in the U.S. However, the problem of access remains, and governments must still be convinced of a researcher's legitimacy before they will open up their records. An important difference, on the other hand, can be found with regard to relations with local scholars. In contrast to what I understand as the problem in Latin America, in Sweden I found the situation more one of competition. The Swedes' response could be summed up as: Here is an American sociologist who is coming to do research in my country, research that I probably should have done but never thought to do. And if I cooperate with him and help him get the data, then he is going to get the jump on me in publications, and so on. That wouldn't look too good.

Mr. Karsh.   I find it rather dismaying that professional sociologists are sitting around here, proclaiming a sudden discovery that social relations are somehow reciprocal. I thought that was the point from which we began in introductory sociology. I learned a long time ago that it takes some doing when you ask a person, "How old are you?" There has to be some *quid* for the *quo*. A respondent can legitimately ask, "Why do you want to know? Why is it your damn business?"

If this situation holds when you are sampling around your own neighborhood, why shouldn't it be true also in India or Chile or Japan? Why does it come as a surprise that you must leave some research there, that you must have some payoffs ready and available for the people that you are going to ask questions of? Hell, the anthropologists walk around all the time with gifts. That is part of the direct payoff for informants.

Mr. Stryker.   The question isn't one of reciprocal relationships but rather of the terms of exchange.

Mr. Karsh.   How do you know that? This gets to something said earlier. If you can work out a paradigm for the cost-benefit ratios before you begin, it seems to me that there is no need to go, because you have all the answers to start with. But if you assume with Form that sociology is a process which can be understood, but only as a process, you would become increasingly more committed as you moved into your data. I don't know how you work out a priori cost-benefit ratios. At what point do you say, "The next item of data is too costly. I am going to cut it out. I don't want it"?

In a sense we do it all the time, but we do it in different ways. We say, "I have $14,000." That defines it. "I have 18 months." That defines it. Or, "I have nine months' sabbatical leave." That defines it. But those are easy definitions. The much more difficult definition is, "What are the payoffs?" At what point am I going to say, "I have enough. I don't need him anymore. The hell with his demands on me. I don't have to leave anything. I am copping out anyway"? Or, "Are my students coming back here two years from now? I must leave something for the students." That is a different proposition.

Mr. Schnaiberg.   You are now invoking a very explicit time dimension, which I think is critical. An implicit conclusion of all that has been said is that today nobody in his right mind would go to Chile, do a study, not leave any data, and then expect to go back after two years and be welcome.

Mr. Form.   If we are talking about the problem of access in comparative research, there are some dimensions that we ought to be very clear about. We need to look beyond the simple concern about what happens when you go to country X and you get a Y kind of response. One dimension is how the question you want to research is affected by its context—the social organization you want to study. Another dimension is what kinds of techniques can be used in this context. Finally, are there certain kinds of cultural impediments or facilities specific to this particular context? We need to go further than just to identify the kinds of experiences, the kinds of resistances we are going to have in foreign countries. Comparative research, comparative design requires isolating the kinds of variables one is concerned with and making some kind of prediction about how those variables are going to affect the research process.

Mr. Gould.   To return to my original comment, I don't think there is such a thing as value-free social science. We can hold values in abeyance and allow ourselves to be led by the "facts," etc., but all we are doing in this process is withholding or suspending our judgement on values as we understand them. We can be aware of these things. We can continually examine ourselves and our concepts, etc. But we can never free ourselves from our particular kind of orientation to reality.

Mr. Schnaiberg.   We are being myopic. First, we are talking about the value freedom of the sociologist, while forgetting that our subject matter is not inert. Whether *we* have a value position or not, part of the question must be *who* is defining a particular situation.

Second, we talk as if we are value consistent. My personal experience in this is that people who may be political and economic radicals in the United States become ethnocentric, status quo, laissez faire, nineteenth-century liberals when they go to an underdeveloped area. *That* is value inconsistency, and we have not discussed it. Finally, it seems to me that part of our problem is that we disregard the differences among Americans who work abroad. Not only are we all defined as Americans; we accept that label in an undifferentiated manner. This acceptance has its own set of consequences.

Reference

Henry, Jules.

1963 *Culture Against Man.* New York: Random House.

PART TWO

Design Strategies in Comparative Research

CHAPTER SIX

Standardized Case Comparison: Observations on Method in Comparative Sociology

JOHN WALTON

Northwestern University

"It is surprising, for all that is said about the value of comparison, that a rigorous comparative methodology has not emerged. The reason for this lack may be the great difficulties that a rigorous comparative methology would impose" (Porter, 1970:144).

Introduction

John Porter's observation on the methodological status of comparative sociology provides a fitting introduction to this paper since it suggests the paucity of *systematic and distinctively comparative* strategies for research in the field. This paper assesses the veracity of the point, finds it well taken, and offers one approach that may suggest alternatives to the present situation. Although focusing chiefly on methodological problems, the discussion should not be construed as a slight to substantive issues in the field. Following the style of methodological approaches such as deviant case analysis, natural experiments, or analytic induction, the strategy suggested here is intended to serve, rather than detract from, substantive theory-building.

Two matters require clarification at the outset. First, "comparative sociology" conveys a variety of meanings. Often it refers to broad comparisons between total societies. An equally common usage concerns intersocietal comparisons of subunits—regions, cities, institutions, organizations, groups, social movements, or whatever. A third usage is for *intra*societal comparisons at any one of the foregoing levels. Less common, although of growing importance, is the notion of an interspecies comparative sociology aimed at discovering the rudiments of social structure in the societies of men and other animals. Certainly a fifth legitimate usage is longitudinal comparison on one or more societies or subunits. This discussion deals primarily with the first and second kinds of comparative sociology and, to a lesser extent, with the third. Within this frame of reference, the thrust of the argument will be that comparative sociology exhibits very little by way of distinctive and rigorous methods.

We must also clarify the specific, conventional methodological strategies in comparative sociology that allegedly lack the features alluded to above. One approach that sometimes assumes the mantle of comparative sociology is the gathering together of disparate essays or studies in one volume, which may or may not seek to integrate the separate contributions (see, for example, Almond and Coleman, 1960; La Palombara, 1963). Useful as such collections may be, they do not constitute comparative research.

The Methods of Comparative Sociology

For present purposes, comparative research methods may be classified under three headings: comparative case studies (both historical and firsthand), comparative analysis of archival data, and original comparative studies employing standardized (usually survey) methods. Some comments on the strengths and weaknesses of each of these approaches illuminate Porter's point.

Although the classification and criticisms apply more broadly, the methods and applications of primary concern here come from the literature on developing areas. The literature on development is employed as a vehicle for presenting the argument largely because many of the contemporary issues in comparative sociology have been occasioned by growing research interest in less-developed societies. No implication is intended that the problems or suggestions cited here apply only to developing areas or that comparative studies of more advanced societies are not important and necessary. As occasional references will suggest, I believe, the same arguments could be made vis-à-vis comparative studies of American urban politics.

The typology suggested above does some violence to the actual complexity of research strategies, but for present purposes (i.e., for the applicability of comments on advantages and disadvantages) it is useful. It may be asked, for example, how this typology would deal with the dimensions of case study versus multiple case studies, archival data versus secondary analysis of data from original sources stored in data banks, or standard surveys versus nonstandardized interviewing. The typology copes readily with these seemingly distinct dimensions. In the first instance, since the focus is on *comparative* studies, all relevant inclusions would be multiple (i.e., two or more); second, archival data refers generally to official statistics (census data, economic data, public expenditures, etc.), while secondary analysis of material from an original survey would be included in the third category of method; finally, nonstandardized interviewing would be included under the first (case-study) approach. Obviously the utility of any typology depends upon the uses to which it is put.

Comparative Case Studies

The comparative case-study category of methods includes the more or less unsystematic comparative strategies that rely on an admixture of techniques such as historical studies, selective interviewing, observation, and the casual use of archival data. In detectivelike fashion, comparative case studies probe here and there, assembling as many pieces of information as are available into a general picture. Usually these studies are unsystematic out of necessity, and this characterization is not intended as disparaging. Indeed, certain exceptional works (e.g., Bendix, 1964; and Nash, 1957, 1959) illustrate this approach.

Advantages

1. The most obvious virtue of this approach is that it provides detail and depth, thus maximizing the *validity* of results.

2. In the hands of the skilled analyst, these results provide a rich fund of material for *generating theory*.

3. Whether or not the particular researcher chooses to build theory from his material, he will always provide information for *subsequent synthesis.*

Disadvantages

1. Again, the most obvious point is the limitation that intensive case studies impose on *sample size, representativeness,* and *generalizability.*

2. A related but distinct problem concerns the fact that the method allows for, or at least does not guard against, *selection of cases that will prove some preconceived point* (Hagen, 1962, seems to engage in this practice).

3. Somewhat conversely, the approach does not explicitly allow for *control of relevant variables* in the selection of cases as in sampling or field experiments. It should be added, however, that researchers often attempt to do this.

4. Generally, the specific procedures employed are incompletely disclosed, unsystematic, and *difficult to replicate.*

5. Precisely because of the intensiveness and detail, *key explanatory factors* may be seen in low relief. The degree to which this factor is a disadvantage depends very much on the perceptiveness of the researcher.

Comparative Analysis of Archival Data

The archival data-analysis method entails large sample or universe comparisons of readily available data on societies, nations, cities, and organizations, generally to account for some outcome such as level of economic development or program implementation by reference to a set of structural predictor variables. In the study of developing countries the works of Cutright (1963, 1965), Lipset (1959), and Olsen (1968) are notable illustrations. Aiken and Alford (1970) and Hawley (1963) have studied American cities in the same style.

Advantages

1. Such studies require considerable effort; nevertheless, relative to other approaches, the necessary *data are readily available.*

2. Large sample sizes and quantitative data allow for *sophisticated statistical analyses.*

3. Once culled from the archives, the data are available for· *reanalysis* and *verification* with different procedures or controls (e.g., Marsh and Parish, 1965; and Straits, 1965).

4. All of the above may lead to *firm generalizations.*

Disadvantages

1. Stating the obvious once more, the advantages imply the disadvantages. Perhaps the most evident drawback in this approach is that the investigator must take what is available despite his apprehensions. Specifically, the *categories* in which official statistics are recorded are not those of social science and may, at best, be only *roughly equivalent* to the *concepts* under examination.[1]

2. The *units of observation* may be *inappropriate* or *misleading.* Such is the case when comparing nations (say, on economic development) that have regional or sectoral patterns substantially different from each other.

3. Archival and official data sources usually reflect considerable bias. Such biases may be deliberate and self-serving, as in the case of self-reported national figures on economic development, or they may result from poor data-gathering procedures. Morgenstern (1963) has demonstrated that such biases characterize the supposedly rigorous economic measurement in the United States, and they are probably more severe in developing nations. Researchers often dismiss this problem, under the assumption that biases are apt to be systematic and directional (i.e., portraying the reporting unit in the best light) and therefore not a source of error in correlational analyses. But such facile assumptions are seldom supported and may easily be untenable depending on (1) the magnitudes of the individual biased estimates lumped together, even if they are unidirectional, and (2) the possibility that different motives of reporting units may produce different directions of bias. (For example, one reporting unit might want to look good for political purposes and another bad, in the hope of obtaining assistance. A familiar case in point is the double bookkeeping of law enforcement agencies that can produce figures showing either their efficiency at

controlling crime or an alarming increase in crime requiring greater budgetary support. For an excellent discussion of organizational record keeping, see Kitsuse and Cicourel, 1963.) Two provisos should be entered here. First, as researchers recognize, unsystematic bias will tend to reduce associations and thus minimize (type I) errors of propagating falsities. Second, "data quality control" procedures are available for eliminating the effects of bias, although, to date, their application has been generally limited to ethnographic data (see Naroll, 1962; Gilbert, 1967; Walton, 1970a).

4. Archival data, particularly for comparative accounts of organizational or governmental structure, reflect only the *formal structural* arrangements, not actual *processes* (such is the case with Banks and Textor, 1963). For example, a nation may be classified as having a multiparty system because legally it has more than one political party, despite the fact that a single party may dominate all elections (cf. Taiwan).

5. Archival data are *static* and *ahistorical.* This problem is particularly acute when economically advanced democracies are compared with poor and newly established states with the artifactual result that an association is found between economic development and democracy. Such comparisons neglect the significance of a nation's *point* in historical change as well as its *rate* of change economically or otherwise.

6. With special reference to cross-national studies of development, the *units* (nations) are not being compared according to data gathered through *independent observations.* Colonialism, international economic stratification, and "most favored nation" policies render spurious the comparison or correlation of internal political and economic conditions across nations. Who would compare Puerto Rico and Angola to determine whether or not their internal political arrangements were conducive to economic development? If that seems a rhetorical question, it is nevertheless the case that comparative researchers would be well advised to think about the relationship between the United States and Canada or, indeed, about international patterns of influence generally.[2]

7. The recent emphasis on international data banks clearly has merit but may lead to a situation in which such data are *overemphasized* and *overworked* to the *detriment of generating new data.*[3] Furthermore, some data are not worth retaining in any bank.

8. Finally, archival comparisons typically are *not conducive to theory generation,*[4] this problem is especially acute in comparative sociology, which has a notable dearth of useful and discriminating theory.[5]

Original Standardized Comparative Methods

Clearly the category of original standardized comparative methods is more diffuse than the foregoing ones. It is intended to embody all those comparative studies that generate new data through the use of reproducible, systematic, or standardized techniques. The large majority of studies in this tradition are surveys that employ comparable sampling procedures and interview schedules across societies, cities, or other units. Well-known illustrations include the work of Almond and Verba (1963) and Lerner (1958). Less common, although equally appropriate here, are intersocietal studies of purposive samples (e.g., elites; see Moskos, 1967). Also, within the American context, there is a growing number of standardized comparisons of cities, particularly with respect to local politics and decision-making (see, e.g., Agger et al., 1964; Crain, 1969; Rossi and Berk, 1970; Clark, 1968).

Advantages

1. With this last category in mind, Porter (1970:151) has observed that "comparative studies of newly collected data are likely to be much more useful. Specifically, such studies are useful because they *produce new data* that are tailored to the *conceptual interests* of the social scientist."

2. Potentially this approach can achieve the *validity* of case studies in a *reproducible context.*

3. It allows for simultaneous attention to *generating and testing theory.*

Disadvantages

1. The method is generally *time-consuming, difficult, and costly.*

2. For practical purposes, although not in principle, *sample sizes* are likely to be *small.*

3. Most of the available examples of this approach are not distinctively comparative. They typically involve simply doing the same thing in a variety of locations, regardless of the appropriateness of the procedures to the phenomena under examination. In comparative sociology this problem is discussed in terms of the *equivalence* of procedures, categories, and meanings across units compared. In the present context this disadvantage can be illustrated by the comparative meaningfulness of a political opinion poll administered, with all due attention to translation, sampling, and so on, in both the People's Republic of China and the United States. Clearly "political opinion"–not to mention "poll"–does not have the same meaning in the two settings; comparison is thus rendered ambiguous, if not futile. The example is not bizarre, as is evidenced by the Almond and Verba (1963) study that compares the political attitudes of Mexicans with those of North Americans, Britons, and others. The results indicate that, by comparison, Mexicans are apathetic and "acquiescent" despite other evidence of high political participation. The problem results from comparing very different political systems on only one dimension. Mexico's one-party government enjoys such wide acceptance and popularity that lower levels of participation may be less a matter of apathy than a positive sign of approval of the official party's conduct of affairs.[6] Distinctively *comparative*

strategies should involve, beyond doing the same thing in a variety of locations, taking precautions to ensure that the units studied and the subsequent results are *meaningfully comparable.*[7]

Standardized Case Comparison

In addition to providing a framework for the suggestions that follow, the above discussion generally supports Porter's claim about the absence of a rigorous comparative methodology. More precisely, it attests to the relative paucity of methodological strategies that are at once rigorous or systematic *and* distinctively comparative. Of the three types of methods characterized here, the first is not rigorous, and the second and, to a large extent, the third are not distinctively comparative in the sense of employing standards in the selection of cases that will ensure or promote meaningful comparisons and results. To be sure, there are exceptions, particularly among studies whose purpose is either intrasocietal comparison (e.g., of community decision-making) or comparison, by purposive sampling, of comparable groups across comparable societies.

The balance of this paper elaborates an alternative to the present situation. Claiming no particular originality, the notion of standardized case comparison may resolve some of the dilemmas already mentioned and systematically suggest a practical and meaningful strategy. As its title suggests, this method's purpose is to collect original data through systematic and reproducible procedures across cases that are meaningfully comparable. In a critique of public opinion polls some years ago Herbert Blumer suggested that their validity would be enhanced if they sampled "organic units," "publics" or collections of individuals that actually had some opinion on the matter under consideration. The first feature of the method proposed here tries to capture the sense of Blumer's (1948:548) suggestion through *theoretical sampling,* the selection of cases according to a stratified set of relevant independent variables. For example, comparative studies of economic development might select for research cases that vary along dimensions such as level of development; extent of industrialization; economic base of the society or region; demographic considerations such as population size and labor-force distribution; and political organization, in all cases seeking to explicate similarities and differences among the cases and to rule out extraneous circumstances. If "stratified sampling" of cases is too elegant a phrase for this process, the sense in which Glaser and Strauss (1967:55) discuss "comparison groups" may be instructive:

"Why does the researcher's comparison of groups make the content of the data more theoretically relevant than when he merely selects and compares data? The answer is threefold. Comparison groups provide, as just noted, control over the two scales of generality: first, conceptual level, and second, population scope. Third, comparison groups also provide simultaneous maximization or minimization of both the differences and the similarities of data that bear on the categories being studied. *This control over similarities and differences is vital* for discovering categories, and for developing and relating their theoretical properties, all necessary for the further development of an emergent theory. By maximizing and minimizing differences among comparative groups, the sociologist can control the theoretical relevance of his data collection."

Given this attention to the selection of cases for comparison, the second feature of the method involves the use of *standardized data-collection procedures* such as surveys or standard interviews with individuals selected by reproducible purposive sampling (e.g., nominational or "snowball" samples). These procedures, of course, are merely illustrations and do not rule out similarly standardized analyses of organizations, groups, or whatever units are to be studied. The key element is simply that *original data* are generated through *systematic procedures.*

A third feature of this method is that it allows for, and indeed is enhanced by, the judicious *incorporation of archival data.* Fieldwork and firsthand knowledge of the situations being compared enable the researcher to draw *selectively* on official data, the validity of which can be assessed by reference to additional information. To illustrate, official data on unemployment by city in Mexico uniformly underestimate its incidence and are contradicted by local-level surveys, which show substantial variation by city. Comparative analysis of the archival data would thus be misleading. Conversely, official data on electoral competition indicate local variation that is consistent with observable differences in political-party activity in several cities and is therefore more trustworthy for incorporation in a comparative study. The general point, of course, is that comparative case studies are necessary to determine which sorts of archival data are valid.

A fourth feature of the standardized case-comparison method is that it allows collection of a *broad range* of data. We have already noted that selected archival material can be integrated with original, perhaps survey or interview, data. Beyond that integration, the investigator may find it useful to incorporate historical material, the results of auxiliary studies, local documents, or whatever other data may be available across cases.

A final and most important feature of this method, alluded to above, is its potential for maximizing *theory generation.* It offers this potential by (1) providing the necessary in-depth, detailed, and original evidence and (2) emphasizing systematic comparison where the hypotheses generated can be tested and refined by reference to contrasting cases. It is worth reiterating that this advantage is particularly compelling in the field of comparative sociology, where theoretical underdevelopment is the rule.

There are, undoubtedly, numerous pieces of research that imply a method similar to what is more formally described here as standardized case comparison.

Two general illustrations come to mind. Presthus (1964) compared the power structure of two small towns in New York State; he departed from much of the literature on this topic by carefully selecting cases that had in common size, regional location, organizational membership, and certain economic characteristics but differed with respect to ethnic composition, occupational distribution, income, political characteristics, and economic viability. The original research involved systematic identification and interviewing of local leaders, case studies of public issues, a community-wide survey, comparison of census and state-government data on the two towns, analysis of local organizations, and so on. In an absorbing theoretical conclusion, Presthus brings together all of these elements, arguing that the community with a more equalitarian class structure and greater prosperity reflected a less centralized power structure. For present purposes the significance of the study lies in that it was designed to allow a thorough comparative evaluation of theoretical issues raised in earlier research.

The second general illustration is the work of Moskos (1967) on political independence and nation-founding. This study also involved a multistage procedure for the identification and interviewing of leaders, here top national leaders in six West Indian polities as they moved from being British colonies to new states. The method incorporated systematic interviewing and use of a variety of national accounts and historical and political data. Comparing the six states (all of which, at the time, were subject to similar influences from independence movements), Moskos developed theoretical ideas on the conditions under which independence is sought.

A more specific and detailed illustration, explicitly based on the considerations noted above, is discussed in Walton (1970b; 1971; 1971-1972). Essentially, this research was a comparative study of political power and economic development in four Latin American urban regions. The regional units (i.e., the cities and their surrounding areas of economic influence) were selected for their manageability in original research and because of broad intranational differences in economic development. The theoretical framework (derived in part from the works of Frank, 1967a; Geertz, 1963; Hirschman, 1958; Horowitz, 1972; Jacobs, 1970; and Nash, 1959) focused on the role of elites in the economic decision-making process; that is, it followed the theoretical tradition that emphasizes power and social structure rather than resource endowments, social psychological attitudes, or cultural values as explanations of economic development.

In order to locate cases (urban regions) that could be fairly compared despite differences in their level of development, attention was focused on the middle and the upper ends of the development continuum. Further differences in national political systems, a key theoretical consideration, were sought. The two countries finally selected were Mexico (a fairly developed Third World country with a one-party authoritatian state) and Colombia (a less-developed, although progressing, two-party competitive state).

On the local level, urban areas of similar size were desired. Further, because the theoretical literature places much importance on when and under what circumstances development begins, it was essential that the chosen cities differ historically with respect to early industrialization versus a transitional economy. Fortunately this goal could be attained within the previously mentioned parameters. Table 6.1 reflects the theoretical sampling considerations for the specific cities chosen.

Table 6.1   Sampled Cities (by National Economic and Political Differences)

Economic Development History	One-Party, Consensual, More Developed (Mexico)	Two-Party, Conflictual, Less Developed (Colombia)
Early industrialization	Monterrey (1,200,000)[a]	Medellin (1,000,000)
Transitional	Guadalajara (1,300,000)	Cali (900,000)

[a] 1968 population estimate.

The data-gathering procedures were as follows. An initial, positionally defined sample of leaders in the public and private sectors of each city were interviewed. Among other items of information sought, these people were asked to nominate top leaders, organizations, and important development projects. The second stage involved interviewing top leaders. Third, case studies of participation, influence, and the outcomes of development projects were conducted, using knowledgeable informants and local records. Finally, historical, archival, and local research data were collected in order to obtain an overall view of development achievement.

Findings of the research are reported elsewhere. Suffice it to say that differential results in economic development progress were explicitly linked to local autonomy, organizational collaboration, and elite structure (results and theoretical interpretations are reported in Walton, 1970b; 1971; 1971-1972).

Conclusion

There are probably other good illustrations of the kind of strategy suggested here. Nevertheless, it appears that most work in comparative sociology lacks rigor and distinctive comparativeness. The suggestions put forth in this paper outline some of the ways in which a truly comparative sociological method may be developed. These observations are not intended as an appeal for any type of formalism or artificially contrived rigor that would sacrifice the substantive concerns of the researcher. Imaginative work has a way of winning out somewhat apart from its procedural strengths or weaknesses. It is hoped that these observations will sensitize researchers to some of the dimensions of comparative imagination that can aid the design of inquiry.

Notes

1. Many illustrations of the loose fit between data and concepts may be found in the status-crystallization literature. For a recent discussion of this difficulty, see Broom and Jones (1970).
2. These patterns are taken as the principal cause of development or underdevelopment by writers such as Frank (1967a).
3. This trend is illustrated by studies focusing on the Banks and Textor (1963) data and the numerous reanalyses of Almond and Verba's (1963) survey data.
4. The Aiken and Alford (1963) study mentioned earlier is a notable exception to this statement and, indeed, a brilliant example of theory building.
5. Illustrative of the theoretical underdevelopment in the field are Parsons's very abstract work in societies (1963) and the many analyses that depend heavily on his work (e.g., Almond and Powell, 1966). For excellent critiques of this theoretical literature, see Frank (1967b) and Groth (1970).
6. These observations are supported in a study of Mexican voting by Walton and Sween (1971). The data indicate a roughly 66 percent turnout rate of registered voters for all elections as well as a positive correlation between turnout and support for the official party, an indication that when the "apathetic" do turn out, they exhibit a preference for the present system.
7. Perhaps the principal merit of the literature on community power is its methodological effort at broader comparison; see, for example, Clark (Ed., 1968) and Aiken and Mott (1970).

References

Agger, Robert E., Daniel Goldrich, and Bert E. Swanson.

    1964   *The Rulers and the Ruled: Power and Impotence in American Cities.* New York: Wiley.

Aiken, Michael, and Robert R. Alford.

    1970   Community structure and innovation: the case of urban renewal. *American Sociological Review,* 35 (August): 650-665.

Aiken, Michael, and Paul E. Mott (Eds.).

    1970   *The Structure of Community Power.* New York: Random House.

Almond, Gabriel A., and James S. Coleman (Eds.).

1960   *The Politics of the Developing Areas.* Princeton, N. J.: Princeton University Press.

Almond, Gabriel A., and G. Bingham Powell.

1966   *Comparative Politics: A Developmental Approach.* Boston: Little, Brown.

Almond, Gabriel A., and Sidney Verba.

1963   *The Civic Culture: Political Attitudes and Democracy in Five Nations.* Princeton, N.J.: Princeton University Press.

Banks, Arthur S., and Robert B. Textor.

1963   *A Cross Polity Survey.* Cambridge, Mass.: MIT Press.

Bendix, Reinhard.

1964   *Nation-Building and Citizenship: Studies of Our Changing Social Order.* New York: Wiley.

Blumer, Herbert.

1948   Public opinion and public opinion polling. *American Sociological Review,* 13 (October):542-554.

Broom, Leonard, and F. Lancaster Jones.

1970   Status consistency and political preference: the Australian case. *American Sociological Review,* 35 (December): 989-1001.

Clark, Terry N.

1968   Community structure, decision making, budget expenditures, and urban renewal in 51 American communities. *American Sociological Review,* 33 (August):576-593.

Clark, Terry N. (Ed.).

1968   *Community Structure and Decision Making: Comparative Analyses.* San Francisco: Chandler.

Crain, Robert L., with Morton Inger, Gerald F. McWorter, and James J. Vanecko.

1969   *The Politics of School Desegregation: Comparative Case Studies of Community Structure and Policy-Making.* New York: Anchor.

Cutright, Phillips.

1963   National political development: measurement and analysis. *American Sociological Review,* 28 (April): 253-264.

1965   Political structure, economic development and national social security programs. *American Journal of Sociology,* 70 (March): 537-550.

Forcese, Dennis P., and Stephen Richer (Eds.).

1970   *Stages of Social Research: Contemporary Perspectives.* Englewood Cliffs, N.J.: Prentice-Hall.

Frank, Andre Gunder.

1967a   *Capitalism and Underdevelopment in Latin America: Historical Studies of Chile and Brazil.* New York: Monthly Review.

1967b   Sociology of development and underdevelopment of sociology. *Catalyst,* 5 (Summer): 20-73.

Geertz, Clifford.

1963   *Peddlars and Princes: Social Development and Economic Change in Two Indonesian Towns.* Chicago: University of Chicago Press.

Gilbert, Claire.

1967   Some trends in community politics: a secondary analysis of power structure data from 166 communities. *Southwestern Social Science Quarterly,* 48 (December): 373-381.

Glaser, Barney G., and Anselm L. Strauss.

1967   *The Discovery of Grounded Theory: Strategies for Qualitative Research.* Chicago: Aldine.

Groth, Alexander J.

1970   Structural functionalism and political development: three problems. *Western Political Quarterly,* 23 (September): 485-499.

Hagen, Everett.

1962   *On the Theory of Social Change.* Homewood, Ill.: Dorsey.

Hawley, Amos.

1963   Community power and urban renewal success. *American Journal of Sociology,* 68 (January): 422-431.

Hirschman, Albert.

  1958   *The Strategy of Economic Development.* New Haven, Conn.: Yale
           University Press.

Horowitz, Irving L.

  1972   *Three Worlds of Development: The Theory and Practice of
           International Stratification.* 2nd ed. New York: Oxford University
           Press.

Jacobs, Jane.

  1970   *The Economy of Cities.* New York: Vintage.

Kitsuse, John I., and Aaron V. Cicourel.

  1963   A note on the uses of official statistics. *Social Problems,* 11
           (Summer): 131-139.

La Palombara, Joseph.

  1963   *Bureaucracy and Political Development.* Princeton, N.J.: Prince-
           ton University Press.

Lerner, Daniel.

  1958   *The Passing of Traditional Society: Modernizing the Middle East.*
           Glencoe, Ill.: Free Press.

Lipset, Seymour Martin.

  1959   Some social requisites of democracy, economic development and
           political legitimacy. *American Political Science Review,* 53
           (March): 69-105.

Marsh, Robert M., and William L. Parish.

  1965   Modernization and Communism: a re-test of Lipset's hypothesis.
           American Sociological Review, 30 (December): 934-942.

Morgenstern, Oskar.

  1963   *On the Accuracy of Economic Observations.* 2nd ed. Princeton,
           N.J.: Princeton University Press.

Moskos, Jr., Charles C.

  1967   *The Sociology of Political Independence: A Study of Nationalist
           Attitudes Among West Indian Leaders.* Cambridge, Mass.: Schenk-
           man.

Naroll, Raoul.

1962   *Data Quality Control: A New Research Technique.* New York: Free Press.

Nash, Manning.

1957   The multiple society in economic development: Mexico and Guatamala. *American Anthropologist,* 59 (October): 825-833.

1959   Some social and cultural aspects of economic development. *Economic Development and Cultural Change,* 71 (January): 137-150.

Olsen, Marvin E.

1968   Multivariate analysis of national political development. *American Sociological Review,* 33 (October): 699-712.

Parsons, Talcott.

1963   *Societies: Evolutionary and Contemporary Perspectives.* Englewood Cliffs, N.J.: Prentice-Hall.

Porter, John.

1970   Some observations on comparative studies. *International Institute for Labor Studies: Bulletin,* no. 3 (November 1967): 82-104. Reprinted in Dennis P. Forcese and Stephen Richer (Eds.), *Stages of Social Research: Contemporary Perspectives.* Englewood Cliffs, N.J.: Prentice-Hall. Pp. 141-154.

Presthus, Robert.

1964   *Men at the Top: A Study in Community Power.* New York: Oxford University Press.

Rossi, Peter H., and Richard A. Berk.

1970   Local political leadership and popular discontent in the ghetto. *The Annals,* 391 (September): 111-127.

Straits, Bruce C.

1965   Community adoption and implementation of urban renewal. *American Journal of Sociology,* 71 (July): 77-82.

Walton, John.

1970a   A systematic survey of community power research. In Michael Aiken and Paul E. Mott (Eds.), *The Structure of Community Power.* New York: Random House. Pp. 443-464.

1970b   Development decision making: a comparative study in Latin America. *American Journal of Sociology,* 75 (March): 825-851.

1971   A methodology for the comparative study of power: some conceptual and procedural applications. *Social Science Quarterly,* 52 (June): 39-60.

1971-   Political development and economic development: a regional
1972   assessment of contemporary theory. *Studies in Comparative International Development,* 7 (Spring): 39-63.

Walton, John, and Joyce A. Sween.

1971   Urbanization, industrialization and voting in Mexico: a longitudinal analysis of official and opposition party support. *Social Science Quarterly,* 52 (December): 721-745.

Discussion

Mr. Chaplin.   Walton's paper is well organized, succinct and scholarly. It systemizes the various types of comparative research—case studies, comparative studies of archival data, and cross-national surveys—and argues that none have an explicit comparative methodology. They tend to be simply studies in different societies without a well-thought-out theory of comparative research.

While he does a thorough job of criticizing, as well as showing the virtues of, each approach, Walton is particularly critical of secondary comparative analysis of archival data, almost characterizing it as factor analysis of the year-end demographic yearbook. This criticism of secondary analysis implies a healthy dislike of a common failure to do adequate homework on indicators. He is also critical of those who suspend or ignore the usual assumptions involved in the use of sophisticated statistical procedures. The general rule seems to be: The larger the number of countries one includes in any multinational study, the poorer and skimpier the data can be, the less comparable the units, and the less likely it is that indicators will be properly validated.

Walton's criticism of secondary analysis may be particularly relevant to papers like Johnson and Cutright's, Finsterbusch's, and Schwirian's [see Part 5]. Some years ago Blalock, in a talk at Wisconsin, noted a particular need today for more theory and better data, stating that statistical procedures were way ahead of data quality. Walton underlines the same point in another way; we now need specific studies of the sort he calls for. Walton's answer to the problems of comparative work is standardized case comparison. He believes that validation problems can be resolved only through long-time familiarity with a society. For example, he criticizes Almond and Verba's study, which concludes that Mexicans are relatively apathetic politically. Walton doesn't feel that Mexicans are apathetic politically and believes that this error would not have been made if Almond and Verba had known the society better.

Mr. Walton. I suppose, for those who haven't seen the piece, that it would profit us to repeat the illustration, since it deals with a fundamental problem in comparative sociological research—the problem of equivalence of acts cross-culturally. The idea behind the Almond-Verba study of democracy and participation in five nations compares—and here it gets to my biases, so I react strongly—the meaning of levels of voting and other kinds of political activity in five countries (the United States, Britain, Germany, Italy, and Mexico). Almond and Verba conclude, on the basis of how many people participate in electoral politics, that Mexico has a rather apathetic, what they call acquiescent, political culture.

The problem is that their data are not really comparative. They used voting as a cross-cultural index of the *variable* of political participation. I believe, though, that in Mexico a great deal of the "acquiescence" and lack of participation reflects rather an acceptance and, indeed, approbation of the system. In a longitudinal analysis I did of voting patterns in another place, the data show that the higher the turnout in any given election, the higher the vote for the official party. This finding suggests that those who would be labeled apathetic in the Almond-Verba scheme would turn out to be system supporters if they *did* vote.

Another problem with Almond and Verba's findings is that smaller communities are more subject to social control because people know each other; thus the official political party can be a lot more effective. In larger cities, particularly more industrialized areas, the opposition vote increases strongly, an indication that the official party's control has broken down. This finding suggests not that urbanization or industrialization per se are concomitants of political opposition but rather that the more complex the reporting unit (in this case a city or *municipio*), the less effective the political party's controls. The result is a higher opposition vote in such centers.

The larger point, of course, is that to assume the generality of Mexico's urban political culture across all of Mexico and then to compare that political culture with political culture in the United States or Great Britain or someplace like that is to lose all meaning of the sense of political action in the two places. So my argument is for a theoretical sampling of units that can be compared meaningfully, cross-culturally, for whatever dependent variables are desired.

Mr. Chaplin.   Could you pursue that argument specifically with respect to your problem? You say that voting isn't a proper manifestation of citizenship participation in Mexico. In Lima, the proper indicator would be joining the neighborhood association and fighting for property titles and city services. Elsewhere it might be involvement in rural cooperatives or in labor unions. What would be the functional counterpart, in Mexico, of voting in the United States—as a behavioral manifestation of citizenship participation?

Mr. Walton.   I don't think that there is a specific Mexican counterpart to voting in the United States. I think the closest thing might be work, since most occupations are organized by political party unions. If you are a cab driver, you are a member of a union. That union is one appendage of the official party's organization. Similarly, farmers and civil service employees, small manufacturers, and people in middle-class industrial occupations are all members of one institution or another, all of which are part of the official political party apparatus. So I suppose that the most political thing you can do in Mexico is to go to work in the morning because your job is very much tied in with the political-party apparatus.

Mr. Form.   I think Walton is right. The significant behavior which is most parallel to voting is whether the person in the occupational context engages in whatever political dimension is inserted in that occupation. In fact, work behavior may even be more significant than voting. I think the relevance of voting in the United States has been overplayed. I would say that in the United States the political contributions of time and money are more significant than the vote itself. Yet we continue to insist that voting is the significant political act.

Mr. Jones.   One very interesting aspect of Walton's paper is his concern with explanation. He claims that one virtue of his strategy is that it helps to generate theory. Comparativists must develop general propositions on the basis of particular instances and use those as models. The next step is to determine the extent to which those models are confirmed, disconfirmed, or modified by specific cases.

I think Walton's kind of strategy is congenial to this approach. If we are to have a methodological concern with comparative research because it *is* a type of methodology, we must emphasize real methodological questions, not data-gathering as such, but concern about the rules of inference, etc. And if we are to be concerned with history, what kinds of inferences can be drawn from historical data?

Viewed from this perspective, historical data [see Turk discussion, pp. 301 ff., and 307 f.] is no different than contemporary data. The problem for either is how much data we need to confirm or disconfirm propositions which have been developed.

No one can disagree that you have to have a historical perspective. The question is how we take that perspective.

References

Almond, Gabriel A., and Sidney Verba.

1963   *The Civic Culture: Political Attitudes and Democracy in Five Nations.* Princeton, N.J.: Princeton University Press.

Blalock, Hubert M., Jr.

1965   Lecture given at University of Wisconsin Department of Sociology, Madison.

CHAPTER SEVEN

Design Strategies for Comparative International Studies of Community Power

DELBERT C. MILLER

Indiana University

Introduction

Comparative international power research reintroduces and intensifies the problem of research design and method with which the researcher is confronted in comparative studies within the United States. Research in the United States presents many models of design (Swanson, 1962; Aiken and Alford, 1970:85-87; Field, 1970; Friedman, 1970). In contrast, comparative international research is very limited (for useful models, see D'Antonio and Form, 1965; Walton, 1970 and 1971a; a bibliography of research is included in Rabinovitz et al., 1967). The researcher must rely heavily on what he has learned in his own country. There are no more methodologies or instruments of measurement available to the researcher simply because he has expanded the number of communities in his research universe either at home or abroad. Yet comparative research that requires fieldwork invites a greater expenditure of time, money, and manpower, and the problem of determining what knowledge is of most worth to a growing scientific base is becoming more important. The social scientist is pledged to a search for those aspects of social structure that are relatively stable and exhibit recurring regularities or patterns. In community-power phenomena much of the data are ephemeral: the current issues, the political party in power, the current leaders and interpersonal relations between them, and sometimes even the economic and social composition of the community itself are in rapid flux. Of what value is this transitory data to a scientific commitment that seeks to build a base of knowledge characterized by persistence in time and wide scope in social space? There is very little value unless the collection of data is guided by concepts, models, patterns, or processes that may be compared and related (Kadushin, 1968; Lehman, 1969; Perrucci and Pilisuk, 1970; Bonjean, 1971; Walton, 1971b).

The comparative researcher knows that he must have a design that enables comparison among his international communities. Once undertaken, the central core of his design must be frozen. If he chooses cross-sectional analysis, then he must ask himself whether he or other researchers will be able to use his concepts and methods for future longitudinal study. Beyond that concern, he must anticipate whether he and future researchers can utilize his findings in the task of accumulating research knowledge. Walton (1966a), Gilbert (1967), and Aiken (1970), who independently have made strenuous efforts to compare large numbers of community-power studies, can attest to the difficulty of classifying previous work. Such an apparently simple task as the classification of a community as monolithic or pluralistic on the basis of data reported by different observers can bedevil the most careful research compilation. Currently we have two opposing statements, each carefully documented regarding the influence of the method employed. Walton (1966b), in a review of research on 61 communities, suggests that the type of method employed (reputational or decisional) influences a researcher's ultimate decision on whether a community is monolithic or pluralistic. Aiken (1970:492), working with an overlapping sample of 57 communities, concurs. Clark and his co-workers (1968:214-217), though, with a sample of 146 communities, say that the method bears no statistical correlation of significance. Meanwhile analysis of 14 recent comparative studies shows at least six major subjects about which data are being collected: demographic composition, economic structure, political organization, power structure, leadership values, and community public opinion (Clark, Ed., 1968:467-474).

Studies vary greatly in the number of communities included in the study sample and the kind of data employed. Some studies utilize only aggregate data from documentary sources (Hawley, 1963);[1] others combine aggregate data with interview data drawn from the field sites (Clark, 1968), and still others rely solely on interview data (D'Antonio and Form, 1965; Gamson, 1966). Money, time, and manpower requirements have a wide range, depending on design and methodology.

In field research further variation results from the widespread use of three methodologies: the decisional (or issue), the reputational, and the positional. These methods identify various structural and decision-making elements in community power. In ascertaining power relationships, many researchers have insisted that current research can no longer seek simply to describe the structure of decision-making processes but must specify as precisely as possible the types of community structures and varying conditions that give rise to different patterns of decision-making. Further, research must show how these patterns, in turn, influence the actual outcomes of community decisions (see conclusions of Adrian, Bonjean, Clark, Hunter, Scoble, Stephens, Walton, and Wirt, in Wirt, 1971:201-224). Power as a structure with a potential for action and influence as a pattern of social action are each capable of scientific treatment, but appropriate concepts and designs must be applied. Comparative study is a research adventure committed to the comparison of data not only between the cases studied but with all other relevant research.

The central questions that social scientists must answer are: What *generalizations* may be drawn about power structures and influence systems within different types of social and political structures? What is the *significance of the differences* within each of the various sociopolitical systems for power structures and influence systems? If a systematic body of knowledge about community power is to be developed, these considerations must be primary.

A number of problems must be confronted in order to insure accumulative findings. These include:

1. Selection of fruitful hypotheses and propositions for test. These should fit into whatever happens to be the current state of research development. A great deal of the current inadequacy of comparative study can be traced to an initial failure to formulate hypotheses that are meaningful for comparative purposes.

2. Construction of cross-sectional designs, concepts, and methods such that the researcher or others can use his data for longitudinal study at a later time. This requirement is vital for replication and for the study of changes.

3. Selection of communities appropriate for the design. This demand requires a classification technique that is sufficient to test independent variables rigorously and to control variables that must be held constant.

4. A standardization of methodology to include some combination of the decisional, reputational, and positional approaches to the identification of powerful leaders and organizations.

5. A complementary standardization of power-structure models so that such ambiguous concepts as monolithic and polylithic power are reduced to a quantitative measure of the relative fluidity or rigidity of power.

These problems are illustrated by the writer's original research experiences in Seattle, Washington; Bristol, England; Córdoba, Argentina; and Lima, Peru (Miller, 1970:205-208).

Selection of Fruitful Hypotheses and Propositions for Test

Clark (Ed., 1968) has formulated some 38 propositions as fruitful hypotheses for testing. Some are partially verified with consistent empirical support; for others there is little support. They relate structural variables, leadership characteristics, decision-making structures, and community outputs. These propositions complement such summaries of current continuities in community-power theory and research as have been submitted by D'Antonio and associates (1961), Presthus (1964:405-433), Danzger (1964), Walton (1966a), and Gilbert (1968).

The field is so new and there is so much to be known that research tasks may literally outrun and overwhelm the researcher. It is very important to begin, therefore, by reflecting carefully on current findings. One conclusion can be quickly drawn. The research is culture-bound; it is based largely on American communities. It is not surprising that a common generalization can be drawn from the many different studies (possibly in excess of 200).

Martin and associates (1961:10-11) write:

"The common feature in all the variations [of community power] lies in the fact that the controlling group is drawn from the business community. No study of community power, at least among those based upon urban communities within the United States, has failed to show active political participation by businessmen disproportionate to their numbers in the whole population. In consequence the only distinction that can, in fact, be observed among the community power structures is that between systems in which only the business community exercises significant power and systems in which the business community shares power with other social groups. . . . Most commonly the other groups that have offered challenges to the dominance of the business community have been the leaders of the *political parties, professional public officials* (the two are not necessarily identical), and *organized labor*" (emphasis added).

Presthus (1964:406; see also Rossi, 1961:302; and Dahl, 1961:9-86) makes a succinct distinction between economic and political leaders:

"Economic leaders, in sum, tend to dominate essentially private types of decisions that entail the use of non-governmental resources. Political leaders generally control what we have called 'public' issues; i.e., those requiring the expenditure of public funds, legitimation in the form of referenda, negotiations with politicians at higher levels of government, and meeting the conditions prescribed by the centers of power and largesse."

These summaries point clearly to the institutional power structure that is, at minimum, the modal pattern in American life. Further study of American community power structures will probably reveal relationships within known patterns. Progress, however, requires breaking out of this culture boundary. For this reason I have chosen the institutional approach to comparative power research as the starting point for the generation of hypotheses.

The essence of the institutional approach is found in its emphasis on the national and community institutional power profile as the base from which to view the relationships among other community power phenomena. Determination of the relative distribution of power in the institutional sectors invites careful probing for norms, culture patterns, values, and historic belief systems and ideologies. Subsequent steps should include study of the contemporary social structure with its economic and social base as it relates to the identity of influential organizations and leaders. Finally, interpersonal relationships among influential leaders should be examined in the light of prevailing institutional and social structure in the community and nation. The Community Power System Model was developed by Form and Miller in 1960 for comparative research purposes (Form and Miller, 1960:437-452).

The community power structure is a pattern of five component parts defined as follows:

1. The *institutional power structure of the society* refers to the relative distribution of power among societal institutions.

2. The *institutional power structure of the community* refers to the relative distribution of power among local institutions.

3. The *community power complex* is a power arrangement among temporary or permanent organizations, special-interest associations, and informal groups emerging in specific issues and projects.

4. The *top influentials* are those persons who are reputed to exert the most influence and power in community decision-making.

5. The *key influentials* are acknowledged leaders among the top influentials.

Each part is believed interrelated with, and influenced by, the nature of each successive part. This means that the entire structure is greatly influenced by the nature of the society's institutional power structure. Institutional dominance may vary among such sectors as business and finance, government, labor, military, religion, society and wealth, independent professions, education, mass communications, recreation, social welfare, and cultural and artistic institutions. In general, the power pattern of the society puts its stamp on the institutional power structure within the community. In turn, organizations and leaders draw their power and influence from the institutional power structure of the community.

This approach anchors hypothesis testing firmly to a structural base. It enables the testing of relationships that rise from institutional variations. Such tests promise to reveal important relationships and to provide information for comparative analysis (Miller, 1970:205-227).

Other major approaches applied to comparative community research in the United States have been based on typologies centering on issues; economy; social structure (demographic and political); community power system; value orientations; and community output. Only a brief treatment of these approaches can be illustrated within the scope of this paper. However, each merits careful consideration.

Typology of Issues

Barth and Johnson (1959:29-32) have suggested a typology of issues, with the aim of finding identifiable patterns of influence and communication associated with each type of issue. The design is expected to locate specific types of community structures that are regularly involved in the decision-making process for the different types of issues. A number of researchers (e.g., Gamson, 1966) have utilized this approach in various ways. Some have studied one issue, such as fluoridation, in a number of different communities (Rosenthal and Crain, 1966); others have analyzed a few salient issues (Dahl, 1961); and still others have examined a large number of issues (Freeman, 1968; Martin et al., 1961).

Typology of the Economy

The significance of local versus absentee ownership has been examined in a number of research studies and significant effects on community power have been reported. The degree of industrialization has been shown to be correlated with the concentration of power in a community (Aiken, 1970; Gilbert, 1968; Walton, 1966a). Communities with adequate economic resources differ from communities with inadequate resources; more pluralistic community power structures are assoicated with communities of adequate resources (Aiken, 1970; Gilbert, 1968; Walton, 1968).

Typology of Community Social Structure

Independent cities (central cities of metropolitan areas and independent manufacturing, commercial, or agricultural centers) are shown to be more often pyramidal, while satellite cities (suburbs or towns dominated by a nearby city) are factional, coalitional, or amorphous in power structure. Party competition is also an associated factor. The existence of two or more local parties that regularly contend for public office produces a fluid power structure. In contrast, one-party towns induce a pyramidal structure (Walton, 1968:445).

These contrasts in typology, drawn from research in the United States, suggest useful international designs.

Typology of Community Power Structures

A typology of community power structures is of paramount importance because the attempt to build a body of relationships requires a typing of the community or, as explained later, a scaling of community power structures on a single continuum.

The earliest classifications were loosely defined as monolithic and pluralistic (or polylithic). Later, more elaborate typologies were introduced by Form and Miller (1960:538-543), Rossi (1960), and Dahl (1961:184-189). Each recognized a number of patterns ranging from extreme monolithic power to extreme pluralism. Form and Miller have five classifications that they define as pyramidal (autocratic), pyramidal (aristocratic), stratified pyramid, ring or cone, and segmented power pyramids. Dahl also recognized five classifications: convert integration by economic notables, the executive-centered coalition, the coalition of chieftans, independent sovereignties, and rival sovereignties. Rossi has a list of four types: pyramidal, caucus rule, polylithic, and amorphous. When Walton (1966a:433) summarized research findings, he elected to use the following typology: pyramidal, factional, coalitional, and amorphous. Aiken (1970:522), in his examination of previous research, uses the same classification but suggests a renaming of the above as structural centralistic, structural factionalist, structural coalitional, and unstructured. He believes that these categories truly represent a scaled continuum.

Gilbert's (1968:143) quantitative examination of previous community-power research included a number of power-structure variables. When dealing with the shape of a structure, she classified studies as either "most pluralistic" or "least pluralistic." "Most pluralistic" was defined as "fluid group alliances" or "variable according to issues" (number of communities = 55). "Least pluralistic" included pyramid, multipyramid, permanent factions, or other ($N = 101$).

Value Orientations of Principal Actors and Mobilization of Bias

Bachrach and Baratz (1962:947-952) have argued that power has "two faces" — one manifest in the outcome of the overt decision-making process, the other manifest in the capacity of individuals and groups to prevent the occurrence of issues or contests that could threaten their interests. They point to the non-decision-making process as equally or more important than the decision-making process. The mobilization of bias is defined as the assertion of dominant values and the political myths, rituals, and institutions that tend to favor the vested interests of one or more groups relative to the others. Any challenge to the predominant values would constitute a salient issue; all others become unimportant no matter how much public debate and visibility might be present.

Stone's (1962:69-70) study of "Service City" documents how the operation of the "social free enterprise" doctrine sets the relative power position of the three spokesman groups: the Chamber of Commerce, the school board, and the city government. Almond and Verba (1963) have demonstrated the significance of values in the national patterns of Italy, Germany, Mexico, Britain, and the United States as those values affect the political culture of these nations. Miller (1970:228-256), in contrasting Anglo-American and Latin American cultures, has described the role of values as they affect community power structures and decision-making. One important piece of research on value orientations, the International Studies of Values in Politics (1971), involved more than 100 researchers from India, Poland, Yugoslavia, and the United States.

The importance of all this work for international community-power study lies in the possibility of locating the "two faces of power" and thus making more accurate predictions and interpretations of community decision-making under varying value distributions of power. The probing for an oligopoly of power interests involves determining the mobilization of bias, especially when, as in Latin America, powerful institutional sectors appear to operate independently of each other. Knowledge of values is equally important in understanding the nature of decision-making processes and how they function in different cultures. For example, confidence in the trust and honesty of persons, especially government officials, can be a very crucial indicator of decision-making patterns.

Typologies of Community Outputs Related to Structural Variables and Intervening Processes

An increasing number of scholars in sociology and political science wish to relate community outputs to both community power structure and decision-making processes. There is high agreement that a basic question is: Who has power, and what difference does that possession mean for the lives of men? Simpson (1967:287-291) has phrased this question in these terms: How adequately, and in what ways, do varying group interests find representation in differing power arrangements? Aiken and Alford (1970:85-87) stress that the crucial relationships are those that relate consequences to intervening decision-making processes and structural variables of the community. Martin and associates (1961:14) say that if political conflict finds a single focus, it will be upon the capital budget of the city government. Other researchers have been drawn to such common controversial issues as fluoridation, urban renewal, public housing, school desegregation, poverty programming, and allocation of resources. For such community outputs, Clark (Ed., 1968:17-23) sets out nine fundamental sets of variables, including inputs to the community, national societal characteristics, demographic characteristics of the community, economic characteristics of the community, legal-political characteristics of the community, cultural characteristics of the community, political parties and voluntary characteristics, intra-community variations in leadership characteristics, and decision-making structure of the community.

The diversity in design options is testimony to the ferment of this new and effervescent field of study. The newness and complexity of the field has driven each researcher to independent decisions about what knowledge is most valuable and what design most fruitful for his purpose. In international comparative study he must make decisions based on the hypothesized nature of community power in the host countries and upon the barriers to data collection. These concerns lead to another major consideration.

Construction of Cross-Sectional Designs, Methods, and Concepts

The methodological problems of comparative field research arise at each stage of the research process, beginning with the initial research design, continuing through construction and administration of the research instrument, and ending with final analysis and interpretation. If the institutional approach is utilized, the researcher will seek a design that will enable him to contrast major institutional variations while holding constant as many structural variables as possible. For the purposes of generalization the communities studied should be as different as possible in institutional power distributions.

This writer's research was begun in Seattle (1953-1954 and 1955-1957) and extended to Bristol, England (1954-1955); Córdoba, Argentina (1963-1964); and Lima, Peru (1965-1966). These four cities were selected for similarity in population size, degree of industrialization, and economic base. It was important that each city be of sufficient size to have fully structured institutional sectors in all areas of social life and to reveal issues common to modern industrialized cities. Cities in the 500,000 to 2 million population range fulfilled this requirement and could be studied by then-available techniques. To assure that each was an industrial city, a requirement was imposed that 20 percent or more of the labor force be engaged in manufacturing. Further, true of mature industrial cities, these had diversified economic bases with a balanced distribution of manufacturing, wholesaling, and retailing. Generally, in such a community no single economic firm can dominate decision-making.

Seattle and Bristol were first compared because they represented the traditions of Western culture. They shared a common heritage of democracy, language, industrial technology, and similar social customs. These two cities were carefully selected in order to hold constant as many social and economic factors as possible. Just as important, though, they differed in institutional power distributions. At the time of the study, Seattle was governed by a Republican mayor and a city council with a Republican majority. Their philosophy was to keep the city government out of any activity that private enterprise could and would undertake. Their goal was a tight budget on public spending for services except those that could be justified as absolutely necessary for the health and safety of the city. They pledged to support the growth and development of private industry.

By contrast, Bristol was dominated by the Labor Party, with a socialist philosophy. The Labor Party emerged as the largest political party in the city in 1918, and it has dominated the city council and its important committees continuously since 1926. The Labor Party platform has repeatedly called for nationalization of many basic industries, including steel, transport, and utilities. Party leaders have worked for a growing range of services, including national health services. The heart of the Labor Party's strength derives from the trade unions, which are powerful and well organized. Many Labor Party leaders are trade-union leaders. All affirm that they adhere to democratic socialism.

It has been repeatedly asserted that businessmen—manufacturers, bankers, merchants, investment brokers, and real estate holders—exert predominant influence in community decision-making. This was the central hypothesis brought to test within these contrasting institutional power distributions.

The research was designed so that the system model of community power structure might be applied. Special attention was given to the corollary hypothesis that top influentials in a community influence policy-making by acting in concert through cliques. We made the operating assumption that all types of power—decisional (issue), reputational, and positional—were important in delineating a community power structure. Leadership concepts appropriate to the various power levels were applied in order to delineate both the latent and the manifest exercise of power, to provide basic information for mapping the total influence pattern and decision-making processes, and to predict the resolution of community issues.

Córdoba and Lima were brought into the design in order to provide some unique institutional differences. When studied in 1963, Córdoba had been under the control of a military government for more than a year. The city's mayor-council system had been abolished and a civilian interventor was governing by appointment of the national military junta. The dominance of military power provided an important new independent factor.

The opportunity to study Lima during 1965-1966 offered the possibility of comparing two important Latin American cities. Both Córdoba and Lima are excellent urban examples of Latin American civilization. Both trace their origins back to the sixteenth century, when South America came under Spanish rule. They share a common language, religion, and extended family system. In Lima, democracy was operating within a highly divisive political-party system. Yet the similarities between the two cities make them easily recognizable products of a Latin American civilization and of industrializing influences. Each has nurtured a large landholding group, become a commercial center, gained independence from Spanish rule, oriented itself toward democratic goals, and become an industrial center. Both cities have lived in political atmospheres that are precariously balanced between democracy and dictatorship. The military junta is always an imminent force. Today, both cities are governed by the military. The unique power distribution in these two cities suggested a fruitful hypothesis.

The test hypothesis for Córdoba and Lima stated that the community power structure was a social system with business, military, religious, and political leaders dominating as key influentials at the apex of the structure. The hypothesis grew out of observations made by Latin American scholars and writers. Most of these observers had stressed that those in power were the military, the landowners, and the Roman Catholic church, plus some political and governmental leaders. Others named industrialists, bankers, and newspaper publishers. A few believed that foreign capitalists held the true reins of economic and political power. Still others said the U.S. government leaders were the real influentials in the policies carried out in Latin America as prices, loans, and investment decisions were made between governments. These observations were seldom buttressed by a body of verifiable scientific evidence. The scientific study of national and community power structures in Latin America was almost unknown. Yet there seemed to be a high degree of agreement that concentrated and conservative power was shared by the military, business, and landholding groups, the Roman Catholic church, and the political leaders. There was fairly high agreement that government was subservient to all the conservative forces. Others felt that the military and the church were also subordinate, but to the large landowners. The challenge to discover the truth about these power contentions was compelling; any analysis of the community power structure would have to search for the prevailing power forces even though the difficulties in the Latin American situation were myriad. The focus on a city rather than a nation, however, promised to make the research manageable. Certainly the test hypothesis was commonly held to be fact. But was it?

In sum, the four-city design provided for comparison of two cities within the traditions of Western culture with a contrast between strong business dominance in one and strong labor dominance in the other. Private-enterprise ideology in Seattle contrasted with democratic socialism in Bristol. The comparison of Córdoba and Lima brought the Latin American tradition into focus and provided a contrast between military and democratic governments as they shaped community power structures. Finally, the four cities were compared to each other in order to discover whether the Miller-Form System Model and its interrelated propositions would hold under the different institutional power distributions. Some major generalizations have been summarized in Miller (1970:223-225).

The experiences with this design have raised many questions relative to design strategy as a problem in comparative international community-power research. Some of the central questions are: How does one select cities that offer maximum opportunity for fruitful comparison? How does one choose a method that will provide for replication and longitudinal analysis? How can such ambiguous, dichotomous concepts as monolithic and polylithic power be reduced to a quantitative measure of the relative fluidity or rigidity of power? All of these questions are central to the designing of comparative research, especially if research results are to be accumulative and relationships ascertained under controlled conditions. The remainder of this paper will deal with these problems.

Selection of Communities Appropriate for the Design

The assumption that the institutional power structure of a society (nation) is the most important independent variable influencing community power directs attention to the differing power distributions of nations. There is growing evidence that the assumption is soundly based. Henry Teune (1970:3) reports that his findings from the International Studies of Values in Politics point to one general fact: "The fact is that what is happening at the local level in a country reflects some of the major macro-social and political processes of that country. In order to determine what these forces are, it is necessary to have a comparative, cross-national data base." Teune (1970:3) offers nation-specific explanations for the activeness of local governments in four countries:

"In India, with its emphasis on an ideology of economic development, it was the national orientation, willingness to tolerate conflict for change, and aspirations for industrialization of the local leaders at the local level. In Poland, there was almost no local governmental variation which explained [political] activeness: differences were regional, reflecting national development policies. In the United States, the socio-economic base of municipalities, particularly the economic wealth of the citizenry, dominated the explanation: blue collar, industrial cities were inactive; those with a wealthy, often meaning a "middle class" population, were active. In Yugoslavia, undergoing rapid social development largely through urbanization, the wealth and urban level of the commune best predicted its activeness—those socio-economic and political forces which are moving or changing the nation also move or change the local units with some differential effect."

These national-local linkages were verified in this writer's studies. The relationship between the institutional power structure of the nation and the institutionalized power structure of the community has been determined. Spearman rank-order correlation coefficients have been calculated for each of the cities comparing the relative power and influence of the 13 institutional sectors in the nation with their relative power in the community. The rankings have been derived in each case from expert judges or top influentials. The rank coefficients for the four cities are Seattle, .87; Bristol, .90; Córdoba, .84; and Lima, .93. These coefficients indicate a high relationship and affirm the postulate of the interrelationship of institutional structures in the nation with those in the community (Miller, 1970:217-222).

These findings stress the importance of determining significant national characteristics before selecting specific cities for cross-system study. The institutional approach stresses knowledge of the institutional power distribution of the nation. Detailed knowledge is not easily gained, although first approximations are fairly easily made. The strength of private enterprise strongly influences the character and growth of social institutions in the United States;

the Labor Party exercises a firm socialist ideology in Great Britain; the Roman Catholic church is an ideological center in Spain, Italy, and France; multiparty political systems ranging from extreme right to extreme left are found in France and Italy. Totalitarian regimes, which dictate to all social institutions, are found in the Soviet Union, the People's Republic of China, Spain, and Portugal. Military governments are present in Argentina and Peru. Ideally, the researcher would like to find societies in which totally new power distributions might be found. A nation or city whose educational institution dominated in asserting its values would provide an exciting challenge. Equal challenges could be provided by institutions such as culture and art, recreation, or social welfare. The technocratic society (under control of engineers) has been envisioned but has never materialized. A city dominated by architects and city planners would provide new and important data. Planned cities exist, but no study of their power structure is yet in the literature.

A few books exist that can help the researcher select the cities he may wish to incorporate into his design. An excellent summary of data series for comparative purposes is set forth in Russett and associates (1964:5-10); another valuable source is Taylor (1965).

An unhappy note is introduced by researchers when they report that "the most difficult variables to obtain data on, or frequently even to conceptualize in operational terms, have been the explicitly political ones like political stability—most of our intellectual predecessors too have had least success with the political variables" (Russett et al.,1964:10). One of the most ambitious attempts to secure important political variables is Banks and Textor's (1963) study. This effort represents a rating of 115 separate political entities on 57 different political and social characteristics and offers tables showing the degree of association between variables (see, for example, p. 48).

In many ways what is needed most are political variables not only for nation-states but specifically for cities. If the researcher knew in advance the type of community power structure existing in the cities selected, he could proceed without delay to test relationships. Nothing exists at this moment, but the National Opinion Research Center plans eventually to establish a permanent community sample of 200 American communities. Rossi and Crain (1968a, 1968b) set out a plan in which contact would be established with an academic informant in each of 200 selected communities. In each community a local social scientist would be appointed who could be instructed to collect information. His work would be supplemented by professional interviewers who would come to the community at various intervals. The data from these community samples would be stored for the use of all social scientists wishing to make comparative studies. This ideal has not been fully achieved, but researchers have employed smaller NORC sampling frames for comparative studies (Clark,

1968; Crain and Vanecko, 1968; Vanecko, 1969). If such a program could be developed on an international basis, cross-cultural research could be advanced markedly. Prior knowledge of community power structure would provide a ready base for the test of relationships between variables.

A Standardized Combination of the Decisional, Reputational, and Positional Approaches

There has been growing agreement that power manifests itself in many different ways and that many pyramids of power may be present in a community. Communities themselves can be seen to vary with community power structures ranging from monolithic to pluralistic in character. Research has shown that different methods tend to reveal different facets of power. The result has been almost complete agreement that more than one method should be used. The three principal methods, decisional (issue), reputational, and positional, have different capacities for exploring power as *social action* within the general normative framework of a community. Clearly, a combination of methods is good strategy if a complete community picture is desired; further, a combination provides for maximum replication and accumulation of research findings.

Community power may be defined as the network of influences that bear upon all decisions having a general effect upon the community. Community decisions of general importance occur around issues and projects; around status and power allocations in voluntary, political, and governmental organizations; in work organizations; and in everyday decisions regarding land use. The decisional, reputational, and positional techniques have specific capabilities. Figure 7.1 depicts the relationship of these techniques to the appropriate facts of community power. It shows the overlapping that develops. Note, however, that each technique is specially related to different facets.

The controversies regarding overt and covert power, public versus private, and monolithic versus pluralistic may be resolved by accepting the principle of complementarity. *Complementarity* resolves the contradiction by recognizing that the two concepts may be employed *separately* to describe aspects of the world that can be realized separately, even though the realization of one concept may preclude the immediate realization of the other. The world is subtler than man's understanding, and the contradictions that the scientist uncovers in studying nature lie not in nature itself but simply in man's own inadequate concepts. In the search for an understanding of power structures we are enjoined to look for evidence that utilizes our knowledge of both the covert monolithic theory and the overt pluralistic theory. In approaching the study of community power structures, we must be prepared for a great variety of leadership and group structures, some stable and some ephemeral. Many methods are needed. Floyd Hunter (1959:xiv-xvi), who has become identified with the reputational

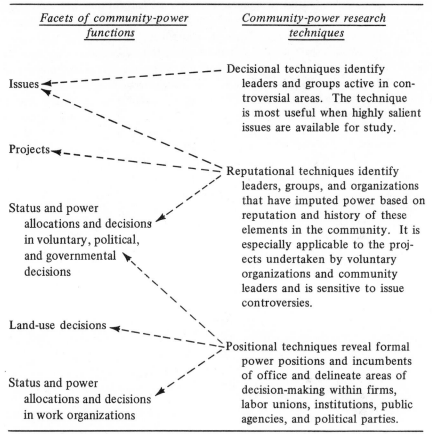

Figure 7.1 Depiction of decisional areas of community power and the technical capability of decisional (issue), reputational, and positional methods.

method, actually employed 22 different methods and techniques in his research studies (see also Hunter, 1952, for additional methods). The search for knowledge should not restrict the number of methods employed, but comparative research would be forwarded if some combination of the decisional, reputational, and positional methods were employed as a *minimal* requirement.

A Complementary Standardization of Power-Structure Models

Current research reveals the presence of many models, ranging from one-man rule to situations featuring extensive fragmentation of power, with no single person or group in control of community decisions. This continuum ranges from a monolithic pole to a pluralistic pole. Bonjean (1971:23-24) has described the polar types as *covert elitism* and *legitimate pluralism.*

An operational scale of the monolithic-polylithic continuum can now be achieved. Three factors are essential to such a determination: representation of institutional sectors by key influentials, solidary character of top influentials, and strength of political parties. Each factor is believed to bear a strong relationship to the fluidity of the power structure and to be susceptible to operational measurement. The number of institutional sectors represented by key influentials is a crude, but useful, index of a structure's institutional fluidity. The solidary character of top leaders can be classified into four types (after Walton, 1966a) according to degree of fluidity. The most fluid is an amorphous type lacking any persistent pattern of leadership; a coalitional type refers to a fluid coalition of leaders varying with issues; a factional type is identified as containing at least two durable factions; and a high solidary type with a single concentrated leadership group represents the most rigid classification. Political parties can be observed in three significant combinations: both parties strong, one strong and one weak, or both weak. Two strong, opposing parties reflect the operation of countervailing power and suggest that strong labor and government segments are represented in the community power structure. Issue outcome is often indeterminate, and a fluid condition is maintained. With a strong and a weak party or two weak parties, a more rigid character for the community power structure is indicated. It is postulated that these three factors, institutional representation, solidary character of top influentials, and strength of political parties, are highly predictive of the degree of fluidity within the total power structure.

A 24-point scale specifying high fluidity at one pole and high rigidity at the other has been developed from the combination of these three factors (see Figure 7.2). Power structures can be identified by classifying them, first, according to their representation of institutional sectors (broad, medium, or narrow); then, by the character of top influentials (amorphous, coalitional, factional, or solidary); and finally by political-party strength or weakness. The final classification places each power structure in its proper position on the scale.

Obviously the scale requires considerable refinement. When refinement has been achieved, much of the controversy over the character of pluralism can be reduced and, it is hoped, terms like monolithic and pluralistic can be discarded as too crude for research purposes. Clark (1968:580) has shifted to an index of centralization based on the number of major actors in each of three issue areas and the overlap of actors from one issue area to the next. He has found that his index scores range from 3.25 to 9.13 in his 51-community sample. A more precise grading of power structures opens up the possibility of working with quantitative variables when studying most relationships. This possibility is one of

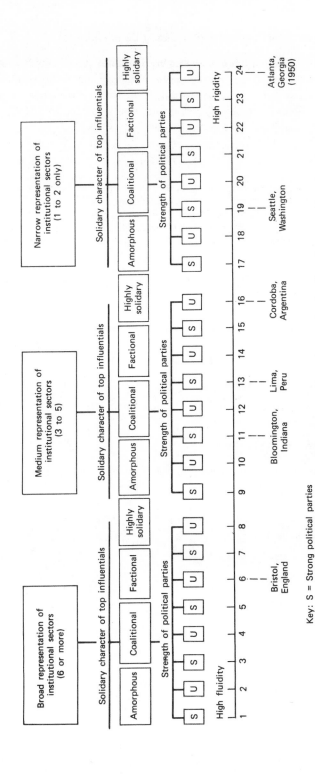

Figure 7.2 Schema for quantification of fluidity in community power structures. (*Source.* Adapted From Miller (1970:278).

the goals toward which research is now moving. Until now, a community power structure has been perceived simply as a single complex of qualitative characteristics derived after laborious research. This structure must now become a quantitative variable, more quickly determined and amenable to quantitative manipulation. The goal is not near, but it is visible.

Note

1. The Inter-University Consortium for Political Research at the University of Michigan has transferred onto magnetic tape enormous quantities of data relating to communities in the United States. Robert R. Alford and Harry M. Scoble have also collated large amounts of demographic and political data for all cities of the United States with a population over 25,000. For further information, see Clark (Ed., 1968).

References

Aiken, Michael.

   1970   The distribution of community power: structural bases and social consequences. In M. Aiken and P. Mott (Eds.), *The Structure of Community Power.* New York: Random House. Pp. 487-525.

Aiken, Michael, and Robert R. Alford.

   1970   Comparative urban research and community decision-making. *Atlantis,* 1 (Winter):85-87.

Almond, Gabriel A., and Sidney Verba.

   1963   *The Civic Culture.* Princeton, N.J.: Princeton University Press.

Bachrach, Peter, and Morton Baratz.

   1962   The two faces of power. *American Political Science Review,* 47 (December):947-952.

Banks, Arthur S., and Robert B. Textor.

   1963   *A Cross-Polity Survey.* Cambridge, Mass.: MIT Press.

Barth, Ernest A. T., and Stuart D. Johnson.

   1959   Community power and a typology of social issues. *Social Forces,* 38 (October):29-32.

Bonjean, Charles M.

   1971   Dimensions of power structure: some problems in conceptualization and measurement. In F. M. Wirt (Ed.), *Future Directions in*

Community Power Research: A Colloquium. Berkeley, Calif.: Institute of Governmental Studies. Pp. 21-37.

Clark, Terry N.

1968 Community structure, decision-making, budget expenditures and urban renewal in 51 American communities. *American Sociological Review,* 33 (August):576-593.

Clark, Terry N. (Ed.).

1968 *Community Structure and Decision-Making: Comparative Analyses.* San Francisco: Chandler.

Clark, Terry N., Willam Kornblum, Harold Bloom, and Susan Tobias.

1968 Discipline, method, community structure, and decision-making: the role and limitations of the sociology of knowledge. *American Sociologist,* 3 (August):214-217.

Crain, Robert L., and James J. Vanecko.

1968 Elite influence in school desegregation. In James Q. Wilson (Ed.), *City Politics and Public Policy.* New York: Wiley. Pp. 127-148.

Dahl, Robert A.

1961 *Who Governs?* New Haven, Conn.: Yale University Press.

D'Antonio, William V., and William H. Form.

1965 *Influentials in Two Border Cities.* Notre Dame, Ind.: Notre Dame University Press.

D'Antonio, William V., William H. Form, Charles P. Loomis, and Eugene C Erickson.

1961 Institutional and occupational representations in eleven community influence systems. *American Sociological Review,* 26 (June):440-446.

Danzger, Herbert.

1964 Community power structure: problems and continuities. *American Sociological Review,* 24 (October):707-717.

Field, Arthur J. (Ed.).

1970 *Urban Power Structures: Problems in Theory and Research.* Cambridge, Mass.: Schenkman.

Form, William H., and Delbert C. Miller.

1960 *Industry, Labor, and Community.* New York: Harper.

Freeman, Linton.

1968 *Patterns of Local Community Leadership.* Indianapolis, Ind.: Bobbs-Merrill.

Friedman, Peter.

1970 Community decision making in the United States: a review of past research. *Atlantis,* 1 (Winter):133-142.

Gamson, William A.

1966 Reputation and resources in community politics. *American Sociological Review,* 31 (February):121-131.

Gilbert, Claire W.

1967 Some trends in community politics: a scondary analysis of power structure data from 166 communities. *Southwestern Social Science Quarterly,* 48 (December):373-381.

1968 Community power and decision-making: a quantitative examination of previous research. In Terry N. Clark (Ed.), *Community Structure and Decision-Making: Comparative Analyses.* San Francisco: Chandler. Pp. 139-155.

Hawley, Amos H.

1963 Community power structure and urban renewal success. *American Journal of Sociology,* 68 (January):422-432.

Hunter, Floyd.

1952 *Community Power Structure.* Chapel Hill: University of North Carolina Press.

1959 *Top Leadership, U.S.A.* Chapel Hill: University of North Carolina Press.

International Studies of Values in Politics.

1971 *Values and the Active Community.* New York: Free Press.

Kadushin, Charles.

1968 Power, influence, and social circles: a new methodology for studying opinion makers. *American Sociological Review,* 33 (October):685-699.

Lehman, Edward W.

    1969   Toward a macrosociology of power. *American Sociological Review,* 34 (August):453-465.

Martin, Roscoe, Frank J. Munger, Guthrie S. Birkhead, Harold Herman, Lewis P. Welch, Herbert M. Kagi, Clyde J. Wingfield, and Jesse Burkhead.

    1961   *Decisions in Syracuse.* Bloomington, Ind.: Indiana University Press.

Miller, Delbert C.

    1970   *International Community Power Structures: Comparative Studies of Four World Cities.* Bloomington, Ind.: Indiana University Press.

Perrucci, Robert, and Mark Pilisuk.

    1970   Leaders and ruling elites: the interorganizational bases of community power. *American Sociological Review,* 35 (December):1040-1057.

Presthus, Robert.

    1964   *Men at the Top.* Oxford: Oxford University Press.

Rabinovitz, Francine F., Felicity M. Trueblood, and Charles J. Savio.

    1967   *Latin American Political Systems in an Urban Setting: A Preliminary Bibliography.* Gainesville: Center for Latin American Studies, University of Florida.

Rosenthal, Donald B., and Robert L. Crain.

    1966   Structure and values in local political systems: the case of fluoridation systems. *Journal of Politics,* 28 (February):169-196.

Rossi, Peter H.

    1960   Theory, research, and practice in community organization. In Charles R. Adrian (Ed.), *Social Science and Community Action.* East Lansing: Michigan State University Press. Also in Oliver Williams and Charles Press (Eds.), *Democracy in Urban America.* Chicago: Rand McNally, 1961. Pp. 382-394.

    1961   The organizational structure of an American community. In Amitai Etzioni (Ed.), *Complex Organizations, A Sociological Reader.* New York: Holt, Rinehart, and Winston. Pp. 301-311.

Rossi, Peter H., and Robert L. Crain.

    1968a   The NORC permanent community sample. *Public Opinion Quarterly,* 32 (Summer):261-272.

    1968b   Comparative community studies with large n's. *Proceedings of the American Statistical Association,* Social Statistics Section:72-80.

Russett, Bruce M., Hayward R. Alker, Jr., Karl W. Deutsch, and Harold D. Lasswell.

    1964   *World Handbook of Political and Social Indicators.* New Haven, Conn.: Yale University Press.

Simpson, Richard L.

    1967   Comment by a sociologist. *Southwestern Social Science Quarterly,* 8 (December):287-291.

Stone, Robert C.

    1962   Power and values in trans-community relations. In Bert E. Swanson (Ed.), *Current Trends in Comparative Community Studies.* Kansas City, Mo.: Community Studies, Inc. Pp. 69-70.

Swanson, Bert E. (Ed.).

    1962   *Current Trends in Comparative Community Studies.* Kansas City, Mo.: Community Studies, Inc.

Taylor, C.R. (Ed.).

    1965   *Aggregate Data Analysis: Political and Social Indicators in Cross-National Research.* The Hague: Mouton.

Teune, Henry.

    1970   Cross-level analysis: national and local systems. Paper read to the Southwestern Sociological Association, Dallas, Texas (March).

Vanecko, James J.

    1969   Community mobilization and institutional change: the influence of community action programs in large cities. *Social Science Quarterly,* 50 (December):609-630.

Walton, John.

    1966a   Substance and artifact: the current status of research on community power structure. *American Journal of Sociology,* 71 (January):430-438.

1966b Discipline, method and community power: a note on the sociology of knowledge. *American Sociological Review,* 31 (October):684-699.

1968 Differential patterns of community power structure: an explanation based on interdependence. In Terry N. Clark (Ed.), *Community Structure and Decision Making: Comparative Analyses.* San Francisco: Chandler. Pp. 441-459.

1970 Development decision making: A comparative study in Latin America. *American Journal of Sociology,* 75 (March):828-851.

1971a An exploratory study of decision making and development in a Mexican city. In F.M. Wirt (Ed.), *Future Directions in Community Power Research: A Colloquium.* Berkeley, Calif.: Institute of Governmental Studies. Pp. 169-192.

1971b A methodology for the comparative study of power: some conceptual and procedural applications. *Social Science Quarterly,* 51 (June):39-60.

Wirt, F.M. (Ed.).

1971 *Future Directions in Community Power Research: A Colloquium.* Berkeley, Calif.: Institute of Governmental Studies.

Discussion

Mr. Gould: Inherent in Miller's paper is that continuing conflict in anthropology between the structuralist and the culturalist: At what point does structuralization become meaningless because it produces an obvious truism? How much specialized cultural context can we introduce without giving up our search for universals?

Miller has attempted to introduce quantification to the cross-cultural study of power. However, when one concludes that "the power pattern of the society puts its stamp on the institutional power structure within the community" [p. 197 above], I think we must respond that we all know this; it is terribly obvious. Critics will respond to such statements in this way unless their author has some very creative ways of demonstrating that he has stated more than just a truism. We must ask if Miller has done so. I hasten to add that I find the same problem in the work of some of my most distinguished anthropologist colleagues.

Mr. Miller. What you find platitudinous was certainly not so when community-power analysis was first being undertaken. Indeed, it is apparently not so today; there are many researchers who believe that a sociometrically identified list of community leaders is a blueprint of community power structure in which power analysis is based. In brief, I am *not* simply stating that the world is round.

I agree with Walton in his advocacy of the standardized case-comparison method. My own use of that method has shown me several things—you may want to keep some of them in mind as you judge whether my conclusions are truisms and when you design your own future research.

I started by studying Seattle, Washington, 15 years ago. I soon learned that I had no confidence in analysis of a community power structure which took less than a year (I spent five years on that first study). I also became convinced that comparative study was necessary for validation of my conclusions on the institutionally structured—as contrasted to individually controlled—nature of community power.

In my subsequent studies, I have attempted, I believe with some success, to hold several contextual variables constant. I believe I have validated the claim that power is institutionally sited, whether it be in business (Seattle), a political party (Bristol), foreign industry and indigenous military (Córdoba), or several different institutions (in Peru: large landowners, the Church, and the military).

PART THREE

Approaches to
Conceptual Clarification

CHAPTER EIGHT

Aspects of the Measurement
of Class Consciousness [1]

LAWRENCE E. HAZELRIGG

Indiana University

Introduction

This paper discusses a concept—class consciousness—that some consider completely useless to our understanding of advanced industrial societies. In an earlier period of sociohistorical investigation, the social science and belletristic literatures, as well as the social commentaries and political tracts dispensed by street-corner vendors, union organizers, and the like, were copiously supplied with references to the concept. Very often it was the focus of sustained, emotionally intense debate. Certainly after Marx, a good many social scientists and historians felt constrained to do more than merely nod to the concept, and with the growth of socialist movements during the late nineteenth century, the "cultured sections" of North Atlantic societies revealed their own peculiar sensitivities to the whole notion of a militant self-conscious "underclass" by well-nigh banishing such "disreputable" words as "class" and "class consciousness" from polite conversation (Tawney, 1931:66). But later times brought forth different circumstances and different ideas, and the concept of class consciousness fell into relative disuse—more so in the U.S. literature, less so in the European, especially the Continental, literature. Indeed, today one *can* find scattered through the literature various proclamations that this concept is virtually useless for our efforts to fathom the complexities of advanced industrial society.

This paper argues that such proclamations are founded (in part, at least) on misapprehensions and misuses of the concept that have resulted from the neglect of specific conceptual and empirical measurement problems. As often as the concept has appeared in the literature, it has seldom received anything beyond a loose and typically ambiguous description. A concept that is inadequately defined can be related only ambiguously to real-world events, which are the subject of empirical measurement. This paper examines some of these problems, especially those affecting measurement in a comparative setting. The first section discusses major components in the conceptualization of class consciousness; the second, a general framework for the measurement of class consciousness; and the third, some semantic issues raised by the measurement requirements.

The paper presupposes agreement that there *are* such things in society as classes and that the concept of class is *not* "largely obsolete" or useless "so far as the bulk of Western society is concerned, and especially the United States" (Nisbet, 1959, 1970:204-206; also Dahrendorf, 1967; Wrong, 1969). Without engaging in a lengthy discussion of the sociological meanings of "class" (the literature documents a confusing array of definitions; for useful reviews of these definitional variations, see Bottomore, 1965; Gurvitch, 1965; Aron, 1964; and Ossowski, 1963, as well as the pertinent essays in the *International Encyclopaedia of the Social Sciences*), this paper has utilized the following definition: "Class" is a de facto structural property of a societal population, the fundamental dimension of which is the hierarchy of dominance or control over the processes of resource production in society (Hazelrigg, 1972, discusses aspects of this meaning). Questions regarding the symbolic culture of class, of class consciousness, and of similar matters are analytically separable and do not enter into the definition. A particular class need not be class-conscious, need not exhibit a certain set of beliefs, need not reveal a density of endogenous interactions, and so forth; whether and to what extent it does manifest such additional characteristics is an empirical question. Further, we shall eschew the view that treats "class" as a synthesis of the individual's locations in various more-or-less interrelated status hierarchies such as occupation, educational attainment, income, and consumption style or style of life—although we will consider instances in which this view has been taken. Any one of these latter status hierarchies may, in a given spatiotemporal case, be highly correlated with class structure and, if so, employed thereby as an indicator of class. But the status hierarchy does not constitute, either wholly or partially, the *definition* of class. In principle a person who uniformly ranks low in occupational prestige, formal education, annual income, and the like could be a member of a dominant class, and vice versa. (It may well be that in industrial societies over the past century, the correlation between occupational-status structure and class structure has changed appreciably in its internal characteristics if not in magnitude.)

Finally, this paper assumes what has yet to be given an adequate empirical test—and indeed cannot be until certain problems of conceptualization and measurement of class consciousness are solved—namely, that the class consciousness of a population is an important variable in propositions linking definitive characteristics of its objective class structure to its behavioral characteristics (e.g., political behaviors). In a comparative context this possibility suggests that cross-societal differences in the empirical outcomes of tests of such propositions may be accounted for at least partially by differences among the populations of those societies in degree of class consciousness.

Major Components of Conceptualization

Any consideration of the concept of class consciousness should begin with the relevant formulations of Karl Marx. While our attention must be brief for reasons of space, we shall do likewise.

Marx admitted that he was not altogether clear about the complex processes included under the label of "class consciousness." He warned explicitly (1936:145), for example, that he "only indicated a few phases" of the struggle by which "this mass," the *Klasse an sich,* "unites and forms itself into a class for itself." Marx did, however, note a series of structural conditions that facilitate the development of class consciousness (e.g., in Marx and Engels, 1959), and he sometimes stressed the essential dialectic role of the *haute bourgeoisie* in the transvaluation of proletarian identity, discussed phenomena of social and geographic mobility, and so forth. But the process of transformation entails social psychological considerations as well, and of such things Marx said very little. For the most part he treated the *Klasse für sich* analytically as a fait accompli; he noted certain historical conditions regarding its origin and its consequences but lent very little ink to the details of how it came to be. Class consciousness is approached as a full-fledged social fact: a politically concerted, communal consciousness-as-organizational-form (Lopreato and Hazelrigg, 1972, Chaps. 1 and 6).

Embryonic though it is, Marx's conceptual discussion contains much that is valuable. But *because* embryonic, it is also rather open to misuse, especially the misuse of accepting it as *other than* embryonic. To limit the utility of the class-consciousness concept to the brief hermeneutical treatment given explicitly in Marx's writing, as is sometimes done, is not very helpful. In assessing the explanatory power of the concept, we can easily expect too much of it—much more than we are inclined to expect of other species of cleavage-group identity or consciousness (e.g., those grounded in cleavages of race, ethnicity, nation, religion, or tribe). The notion of a self-conscious class tends to bring forth romantic images of "hayfork revolution"—of newly awakened masses "struggling out of the grime of oppression with a messianic vision of history glinting in their communal eye." In short, the search for evidence of class consciousness may become a search for something truly spectacular and even a bit mystical.

Such expectations—greatly overloaded for the general case and resulting in spurious rejections of the hypothesis that there is *any* class consciousness to be found in spatiotemporally specific cases—reflect a categorical conceptualization. A class either *is* class-conscious, by which is meant a usually highly stylized version of Marx's brief description, or it is *not* (which is sometimes taken to mean also the nonexistence of class, as Nisbet, 1959, 1970, seems to do). Moreover, unidirectionality is often assumed in these expectations of how class consciousness should appear empirically—that is, as a singular, persistent movement from an original to a terminal state, with the interstice conceived of in terms of chaos, anomie, and so on, and the terminal state defined as "the moment of revolution." Except for the revolution, according to this view, class consciousness is of no consequence to human affairs; indeed, it does not exist.

Many variations of the foregoing theme have been written. The point to be stressed, however, is the worth of substituting for the categorical conception a populational perspective that views class consciousness as a variable process (as Marx, 1936;173ff. did, although in an adumbrated way, in his discussion of the stages of proletarian consciousness). Rather than treating the self-conscious class as one type of class reality and the non-self-conscious class as another, as in the oft-used distinction between subjective and objective class, class consciousness may be conceptualized as a variable property of the population of a class. Intermediate levels of cleavage-group consciousness *may* have profound consequences in human affairs. And each level should be seen as problematic; it may or may not issue in a higher level.

A necessary first step toward a fully worked out populational conceptualization is decomposition of the categorical notion of class consciousness: What logical components may be delineated within it? The remaining comments in this section are intended as one accounting of such components (for other efforts, see Morris and Murphy, 1966; Miliband, 1971; and Lopreato and Hazelrigg, 1972, pt. 2). If it is incomplete—and it undoubtedly is, because of inattention to the logical connections among the several components and probably also because of nonexhaustiveness as even a simple inventory—it will nonetheless serve as a beginning.

Decomposition might begin with the social psychological processes of enlightenment. Some recognition of these, although abbreviated and somewhat ambiguous, can be discerned in Marx, and Lukács later presented his own more elaborate analysis. For Marx, clearly, the revolutionary self-conscious proletariat *is* revolutionary only insofar as it has acquired fundamental insight into the equivalence of man and the human world, into the creative, projective relationship between man and the rest of nature, into the basic workings of human society. Understanding alone cannot change the world; still, the *Aufhebung* can be achieved only by those who perform that peculiar blend of action with understanding that is designated the "revolutionary praxis." In

Lukács's (1923:62, 78ff.) version, the objective possibility of certain actions in any class situation assumes the actors' complete understanding of the dynamics of that situation, including the societal-contextual. For any class to attain full self-awareness and politicized communal identity, it must first acquire an accurate knowledge of the structure and the workings of society in toto. Thus enlightened, the class member possesses not only full comprehension of the dynamics of what are regarded as intended or anticipated outcomes of purposive action; he also fully comprehends the processes whereby purposive actions have what otherwise prove retrospectively to be *un*intended and *un*anticipated outcomes. Only when armed with such sociological omniscience can man effectively surmount the constraints of existing structures, move toward purely and appropriately intended goals, and fully control his own destiny.

Even though we must back away from the specifics of this unrealistic juncture of man and knowledge, the notion of enlightenment processes does contain some fruitful elements. Certainly an elementary component in the formation of class consciousness is an awareness that societal organization includes class relationships (whether or not they be formulated in exactly those terms) and some knowledge of their structure. The degree of awareness or understanding may range theoretically from none (the totally insentient person) to a full and complete knowledge (the sociologically omniscient person). Other decompositions of this component are possible, but this paper will examine it as a whole and ignore internal differentiations such as result from considering historical versus ahistorical views of class structure, factors determinative of class membership, and the like.

Awareness of class structure refers to the particular and ultimately unique class map that a person has in mind (from what source is presently of no concern). A second component of class consciousness is the person's assessment of his own location within that class map: To which of the classes in his conception of social structure does he belong, by his own reckoning? He may belong to none, of course, either because he does not conceive of the class structure as exhaustive of the societal population or because of "errors of logic" in his imagination (cf. Lopreato and Hazelrigg, 1972:205-209, 226ff., for examples).

But self-location in perceived class structure involves more than the question of which label(s) a person articulates as designator(s) of his place in the scheme of things. Perhaps a more suitable term for this component of class consciousness would be "self-identification," for one question of great significance is the degree to which a person's self-identity has been constructed in terms of, and anchored in, his perceived location in the class structure. One may define a particular location of self and then interpret that fact as either a largely incidental description that says nothing important about one's self or as a social fact representative of the very core of one's self-meaning. Both cases, and the great range of intermediate cases, can be covered (and thus hidden) by simple declarative statements of the general form "I am a member of X class." Again, further decompositions may be possible, but this will suffice as a beginning.

A third component of class consciousness is class interest. The possible outcomes of action affecting the control of resource production in society represent the range of alternative interests. Those outcomes that constitute advantages for a particular class are that class's interests, and those that constitute advantages *only* for that class are that class's distinctive interests. Thus, this component taps a person's awareness of the interests of the several classes in his map of class structure, particularly those of the class in (or with, or by) which he identifies himself. Conceivably a person could have constructed a fairly detailed class map, have located himself within it, and even have attained some degree of self-meaning in terms of "his" class, yet possess very little understanding of the calculus of advantages and costs to his class (and thus to himself) that result from a given set of actions. We should also separate specific awareness of one's class interests from the inclination to do anything about them. As Miliband (1971:23) depicted it recently, a worker can formulate "a clear perception of his class, and of its interests," but all the while "lack the will . . . to do anything in order to advance these interests," perhaps because of his "desire to escape from that class." And closely related to this factor, which Miliband calls "will," is the particular perception of what *must* be done if specific interests are to be advanced. In the Marxian perspective, that particular perception involves nothing less than a theory of history.

Finally, a fourth component is the class-relevant behavior of the class member—the *doing* of what must be done. This component speaks to Marx's emphasis on the test of action: class consciousness is neither the sum nor the average of what this or that individual class member thinks or feels at a given time, Marx argued, but consists in certain actions in class situations. Specifically, from the standpoint of the working class, it is action to abolish capitalist society. The general implication, then, is that the appropriate test of full or mature class consciousness is the degree to which class members act in a manner that pursues that class's interests.

As previously stated, this inventory of components of the class-consciousness concept is likely incomplete, and the logical connections among these components have not been discussed. Despite these and other shortcomings, however, this conceptual accounting provides a necessary point of departure for examining aspects of the task of *measuring* class consciousness.

A General Measurement Framework

In general format, the problem of measuring class consciousness may be interpreted as the determination of empirical correspondence between two data records, the logical components of each being determined by the conceptualization of class consciousness (see Figure 8.1). One data record is the scientist-observer's; the other, the participant's. This discussion describes some features of the two records, then examines the problem of estimating empirically the degree of inter-record correspondence, and, finally, addresses measurement problems within the context of comparative research.

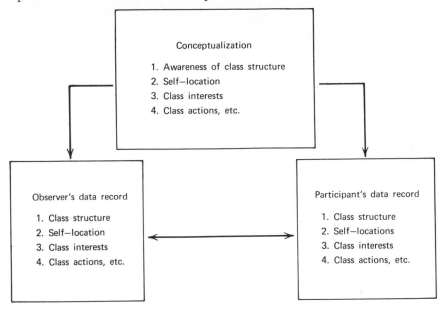

Figure 8.1 Conceptualization and measurement of class consciousness.

Descriptive Characteristics

The Observer's Data Record. The initial step in measurement is construction of the observer's data record. For the conceptualization discussed above, this step requires empirical readings on (1) the objective class structure of the given society, (2) the objective location of the population members within that structure, (3) the rationally appropriate interests, both shared and distinctive, of each class with respect to resource production and the allocation of values, and (4) those actions relevant to, including those required by, the attainment of each class's interests. These empirical readings must be founded in historically informed observations of the societal structure in question, particularly its organization of resource production and arrangements of social aggregates with respect to degrees of control over production. This is no small task, and it may be argued that the most pronounced characteristic of most recent empirical investigations of class consciousness has been their marked inadequacy in that regard. In some instances, the observer record is neglected entirely; that is, the investigator relies completely on participant readings of class structure, self-placement, and the like as empirical estimations of class consciousness.

Of the several aspects to this initial step, the matter of rationally appropriate interests poses some of the greatest difficulties (cf. Child, 1941, 1944, for one treatment). Necessarily, the concept must have a real-world counterpart—that is, in principle, at least, be empirically accessible to both the observer-analyst *and* the participant; a common error has been to build into the concept spuriously elevated expectations of the participant. By what criterion, then, can one legitimately determine the interests that are rationally appropriate to a particular class? Lukác's's answer was, in effect, "the ideology of the proletariat," but that answer is tautological, since he determined the content of the ideology according to what was rationally appropriate for the proletariat. Furthermore, to the extent that we construe ideology as a fairly elaborate and systematic mode and content of thought, Lukác's's position established an unrealistically demanding criterion for the nonruling classes, the members of which, in the nature of the case, suffer handicaps of limited (or repressive) communication codes (cf. Mueller, 1970; also Converse, 1964, and Thompson, 1963:713). Such a criterion thus contains an artifactitious bias against the discovery of ranges of participant-level awareness of class interests.

The criterion of interest must be stipulated vis-a-vis the control of resource production—to the point of either equality or dominance, depending on whether a Marxian or a Paretian governing assumption is adopted. But an "either-or" definition and measurement of "appropriate interests" must be avoided in order that variably complex conceptions of interest are not disallowed the participant. The solution lies in the fact that the objectively defined general interest may be decomposed into several more specific interests in particular action-situations. Stated differently, a class's general interest—gaining or maintaining control over resource production—may be translated into a number of specific decisions and actions with regard to issues in particular concrete situations. Class members may have a thoroughly articulated awareness of the entire range of specific interests, each related to every other through a conception of the general interest; alternatively, they (or some section of them) may have only limited awareness.

These partial understandings, even though at a lower level of consciousness vis-a-vis the class interest component, could very well include significantly consequential social facts. Thus, measurement should be suitably discriminative; the observer record must contain empirical readings for a range of specific interest-issue areas that relate to distribution of the societal population through the hierarchy of control over resource production. We shall return to this matter below.

Moving now to the fourth component of the class-consciousness concept, we must measure class-relevant action in terms of theoretically expected actions. Members are expected to act in ways that pursue the interests of the class to which they belong by observer readings, and measurement must be based on those expectations. Actual actions, of course, will diverge variably from expectations. But the interpretive context for measuring actual actions as entries in the observer record must be the answer to the question: What, given the existent class structure and its historical circumstances, must a class do in order to gain (maintain) control (greater control) over resource production? (This theoretical benchmark does not deny the relevance of other phenomena of control or dominance, such as those pertaining to the distribution of authority or the allocation of material resources; it *does*, however, assert the primacy of control over resource *production* as the fundamental reality of class.) If at a given point in the development of class structure it is in the interest of the working class, say, to gain advantages X, Y, and Z, then to what extent do members of that class engage in actions that result in X, Y, and Z?

In introducing this section, we noted that the problem of measuring class consciousness may be formulated generally as determining the degree of correspondence between the components of two data records. What, however, does "correspondence" have to do with "class action," since the observer record contains measures of the participant's "actual" actions? How can the two records differ? The answer (already suggested by the use of quotation marks around the word "actual") is that with the observer measurement entries we can only *assume* that particular expectationally interpreted actions occurred as class-motivated actions—that is, as the product of both the objective conditions of class *and* the participant's knowledge of class. A person's objectively described behavior may appear thoroughly appropriate in the sense that it results in the objectively specified advantage. And yet in terms of the logic of his own motive structures, that advantage can be gained for entirely the "wrong" reasons: *his* action was not formulated out of regard to a class-anchored self-identity and definition of goal; the *class*-advantage outcome was, from his perspective, purely accidental. Thus, correspondence at this level is a matter of *meaning*—action as meaningful behavior—which makes correspondence quite problematical. (The last section of this paper is devoted to problems of semantic structure in the construction of the data records.)

Before shifting to empirical entries in the participant's data record, we should briefly consider a practical question about the observer's measures of class action: What specific actions should we seek to examine? The obvious answer afforded by the (often highly vulgarized) Marxian view is active revolution. But that view, as it is typically formulated, is inadequate. For one reason, the formulations seldom attend carefully to the definitional problems inherent in the notion of revolution as a type of change. Precisely what *is* "revolutionary change"? To the extent that the term is taken to mean a sudden, abrupt, radical fracture in social structure, such that what comes "after" is totally unlike what was "before," the definition is historically naive and conducive to a categorical conception of class consciousness: The members of a class are class-conscious (in a state of revolution) or they are not class-conscious (in other than a state of revolution); and the transition from one state to the other is allegedly instantaneous and quite impervious to quantitative, continuous measurement. So defined, "revolution" can be only a state of mind without a material-world counterpart, so to speak—at least until the sociologically omniscient actor comes along.

Recent literature has suggested the use of "party-preference" forms of data as one set of measures for the concept of class-relevant action, sometimes with the assumption that such data may reveal support for the idea of revolutionary action (usually defined as the overthrow of a regime).[2] Relying on observations of programmatic alignment between certain political parties and specific classes, the observer assumes that a vote, an act of campaign assistance, or some other behavioral support for the "appropriate" party is indicative of class consciousness—more likely indicative, anyway, than the same act for an "inappropriate" party. Thus, the worker who votes for the Communist, Socialist, or (U.S.) Democratic Party is allegedly more likely class-conscious—or class-conscious to a greater degree—than is his fellow worker who votes for the Conservative or (U.S.) Republican Party. In practice, this approach tends to be marred by oversimplifications, gross categorizations, and even outright historical inaccuracies. For example, the confounding influences of political parties (or factionalizations, such as "Tory radicalism") that make a point of recruiting adherents from across class lines are typically ignored or understated. Categories of parties—leftist, socialist, liberal, and so on—are treated as more nearly homogeneous than they ever are. A party is assumed to be equally "left" or "right" on all manner of issues: economic, social, and political. Such is seldom the case, and many allegedly discrete, unified parties are found, on close inspection, to be *federations* of parties, each holding different views along the entire range of debated and undebated issues. Then, too, this approach sometimes rests on considerations of class-party alignment that were once true, are no longer, but persist as mythical evidence of the character of party or class, and not unusually of both.

More important, the use of party-preference data as the sole or primary measure of class action is weak in principle. It paints a picture of the political actor that says at once too much and too little of him: too much, because it overlooks the element of habituation; too little, because it tends to make of him an automaton who reacts simply to the surface expressions of party platforms. The reasons that people vote for, work for, and otherwise express positive sentiments toward a political party are many, and only some are immediately class-based. Others are indirectly class-based but become enveiled and modified. Still others are only remotely linked to matters of class.[3]

Nevertheless, data on such phenomena as voting behavior may have limited value. In addition to careful scrutiny of alleged class-party (or class-union, etc.) alignments, for example, the selection of a number of specific interest-issue areas as the focus of measurement should facilitate the employment of such data. Specifications like Lockwood's (1958:195-196) distinctions among immediate, instrumental, and ideological interests, although extended beyond the realm of workplace and labor-union issues, might prove to be useful in that regard.

The Participant's Data Record. The construction of this data record requires investigation of what Bateson (1936) called the social *eidos* of a society, on the presumption that participant "interpretations of class structure are social facts which constitute a response to the emergence or persistance of certain types of human relationships" (Ossowski, 1963: 172; cf. also Wirth, 1946: xxv). A common investigative technique, especially in those studies of class conscious-ness conducted during the past two decades, is to elicit, via conventional survey-interview instruments, the participant's image of class structure—for example, his response to such questions as: "What are the social classes in this country?" and (a follow-up question of self-placement) "To which of these classes do you (does your family) belong?" Alternative, but less often used, techniques include the content analysis of recorded interview protocols and written essays on "the structure of your society" (or some aspect thereof) solicited from everyday-world participants. Since the salience of class is undoubtedly variable in any population, which variation itself should be treated as a datum relevant to the participant record (e.g., Lewis, 1965), the participant's reading of class structure ought to be explored initially by the use of nondirective techniques regarding the existence of a class imagery. Otherwise, *petitio principii* fallacies may occur when the data are interpreted. Unfortunately, this initial exploration is seldom attempted; the usual practice is to commence data collection with, at best, a question such as: "Are their social classes in this country?"

The participant data record contains measures of the same component set included in the observer record; the difference is that these attempt to display the meanings of the everyday-world participant. The final section below contains an extended discussion of one major difficulty encountered in constructing the participant data record—namely, the problem of meaning imputation and equivalence. However, a related issue, especially apparent in attempts to measure the self-defined meaning of a particular course of action undertaken by the participant, ought to be examined now.

Discovery of a participant's motives for a particular action requires more than merely learning his *stated* reasons for executing that action. Equally involved, and more important to the resolution of imputation problems, is the elucidation of those conditions of knowledge that made his action sensible to the participant, that *enabled* him to state an intelligible reason or explanation (cf. Schutz, 1962; Peters, 1958; Blum and McHugh, 1971). In the present context the crucial questions are whether that knowledge includes knowledge of class, and to what degree class vis-a-vis other contents is important in creating the sensibility. (As a practical matter of research activity, this discovery process presupposes that the observer himself has an adequate understanding of the existent grammar of motives and the underlying "mapping rules" for the particular social structure in question.) Thus, we must consider the participant's conceptions of class structure, self, and class interests, all of which are germane in two major respects. First, the notion of correspondence between comparable entries in the data records logically includes the possibility that participant actions may be described variably on a continuum of "false" or "effective" consciousness. His actions may acquire their sensibility (to him) from a highly elaborate and detailed conception of class structure, self-location, and interests; and yet to the extent that this conception, in whole or in part, does not agree with objective measures, the participant may be characterized as identifying with, and acting according to, interests "not his own" (or his class's). It should be clear, certainly, that the mere labeling of participant conceptions or actions as indicative of false consciousness falls very far short of a proper termination of measurement and analysis, as Geiger (1949: 124-125) so strongly emphasized. Whatever the degree of correspondence between participant and observer readings—it will never be perfect and, therefore, will always indicate *some* degree of falseness—the participant's conceptions and actions are social facts and possibly highly significant social facts in their consequences (which may vary significantly according to the degree of correspondence).

Second, whether a participant's conception of class structure, self-location, and class interests is more or less correspondent with observer measures and whether it is formulated in sharp detail or blurred imagery, we must also consider the analytically separable questions of (1) the centrality of that conception to his personal identity and, thus, (2) its role in establishing the sensibility of his class-relevant actions. Conceivably a person can have constructed a very intricate image of class structure and interests and have located himself within it—all of which correspond quite well with entries in the observer's data record—and can effectively communicate this awareness to others; yet that image may have only a peripheral significance in the construction of his self-identity. The image may represent a sort of intellectual exercise, effectively compartmentalized from both the common and the fiercely personal meanings of his life in the everyday world. Stated differently, that image is not a significant part of the knowledge that makes *his* actions in the everyday world, including his class-relevant actions, meaningful to him.

Inter-record Correspondence

Given the construction of these two conceptually linked data records—one containing the observer's measures of variables related to the conceptual components and the other, the participant's readings of those counterparts as apprehended by the observer—the question of correspondence concerns the extent to which the two sets of measures duplicate each other. Logically, this correspondence holds the possibility of quantifying Marx's notions of false and effective consciousness, although these are better conceived as variable degrees of correspondence than as categorical "types" of consciousness.[4] Empirically, it should lend itself to a reliability interpretation—similar to the conventional test-retest or split-halves formulation, but in this case involving unusually complex data records.

In principle, the degree of correspondence between two records could be summarized by a single composite index. That possibility, of course, presupposes that all logical relationships among the conceptual components have been worked out. Short of that accomplishment, each matched set of record entries can be contrasted singly to yield a number of separate indices. This latter possibility may be illustrated with respect to record entries on self-location in class structure by adapting some of the cleavage indices proposed recently by Rae and Taylor (1970) to the task of determining inter-record correspondence. For a given population, the pertinent entries in the two data records will be represented as alternative descriptions of the (class) cleavage structure of that population (or, as two different cleavage structures), and "degree of correspondence" may be translated thereby as "degree of cleavage reinforcement."

Assume that, for societal population S, it has been determined that N people possess a conception of class structure—but not necessarily of their own self-locations—that corresponds highly with the readings of the observer record.[5] The N self-locations in class structure are then contrasted with observer readings of the locations of those N people; this contrast results in the possibility of varying degrees of correspondence at one level of class awareness. (Properly speaking, such cross-tabulations reveal only the *possibility* of degrees of effective consciousness, for at this point the question of correspondence is addressed only to the mapping of the participant's class conceptions; determinations of the extent to which those conceptions are central to his personal identity and centrally or peripherally involved in the conditions of knowledge that make his class-relevant actions sensible to him remain to be made.) The contrast between the two sets of data may be displayed in the standard contingency format, as in Table 8.1 (hypothetical data).

At this juncture an index of correspondence (R_S) may be computed, utilizing the interpretation of the two data sets as two versions of the cleavage structure

Table 8.1   Correspondence of Participant and Observer Measures of
Participant's Location in Class Structure [a]

Participant-Measured Class Location	Observer-Measured Class Location				
	Class A	Class B	Class C	Class D	Total
Class A	261	111	18	0	390
Class B	47	483	184	17	731
Class C	11	114	546	121	792
Class D	2	23	208	354	587
Total	321	731	956	492	2500

[a]Hypothetical data; index of correspondence: $(R_S) = .63$.

(or two different structures) of the N people. Let x_{ij} denote the frequency at the intersect of row i and column j of the table, $x_{i.}$ the marginal frequency of row i, and $x_{.j}$ the marginal frequency of column j. The number of *pairs* of the N people who are located in the same class by participant readings but in different classes by observer measurement (i.e., matched by one but mixed by the other) is

$$\tfrac{1}{2}\sum_i\sum_j x_{ij}(x_{i.} - x_{ij}) \tag{1}$$

Conversely, the number of pairs of the N people who are located in different classes by participant readings but in the same class by observer measurement (i.e., mixed by the first but matched by the second) is

$$\tfrac{1}{2}\sum_i\sum_j x_{ij}(x_{.j} - x_{ij}) \tag{2}$$

The total number of pairs of the N people whose two members are located identically by one of the data records but not by both (i.e., the sum of equations 1 and 2) is

$$\tfrac{1}{2}\left(\sum_i\sum_j x_{ij}x_{i.} + \sum_i\sum_j x_{ij}x_{.j} - 2\sum_i\sum_j x_{ij}^2\right) \tag{3}$$

Since the total number of all possible pairs of the N people is $\tfrac{1}{2}N(N - 1)$, the *proportion* of the pairs whose members are located identically by one but not both of the data records is

$$\frac{\sum_i x_{i.}^2 + \sum_j x_{.j}^2 - 2\sum_i\sum_j x_{ij}^2}{N(N-1)} \tag{4}$$

Equation 4 may be interpreted as the degree to which participant measures of self-location in class structure *diverge* from the readings given in the observer record. This equation's minimum value is zero—in which case the two sets of data are in complete agreement—but its maximum value is dependent on the number of categories in the data records. Since this maximum value is given by

$$\frac{N_{max}}{N-1} \left[1 - \frac{1}{n_p} \quad , \quad 1 - \frac{1}{n_O} \right] \tag{5}$$

where n_p is the number of categories in the participant record and n_O is the number in the observer record, we can set equation 4 in ratio to equation 5 and subtract the quotient from unity in order to obtain a readily interpretable index of correspondence (R_S) that will assume values from zero to unity.

It is useful to compute the index in this indirect and otherwise inefficient way because the first two terms of equation 4 are themselves interpretable as properties of the data records (cf. Rae and Taylor, 1970:99-103). Thus,

$$1 - \frac{\sum_i x_i.^2}{N(N-1)} \quad \text{and} \quad 1 - \frac{\sum_j x._j^2}{N(N-1)}$$

give measures of the degrees to which the N people are "fragmented" by, respectively, the participant-measured (F_p) and the observer-measured (F_O) class memberships. Individually and in ratio to each other, these indices provide additional summary descriptions of the component of class consciousness considered here in illustration.

Comparative Contexts

The measurement of class consciousness for any single society makes complex demands of the observer-analyst. Among other things, it demands a combination of historiographic sophistication, linguistic knowledge, skills in populationist research technologies, and sheer scholarly persistence that only rarely exists in sociologists today. But if the demands are great for the case of any one society, they are enormously greater for multisociety investigations. The requirements of knowledge of history and present conditions of social structure must be met for two or more societies. Multilingual abilities are usually necessary. Indeed, the investigator ought to be substantially *multicultural.*

At the level of determining inter-record correspondence per se, however, the increments contributed by each additional society in a comparative study are "only" additive. The comparisons are of the final products of the individual, necessarily society-specific researches. In each case, the task is, first, to construct adequate observer and participant data records for the particular society and, second, to determine the various empirical correspondences between the two records. Cross-societal comparisons must be of measures of correspondence between data records that are adequately sensitive to the structural and meaning characteristics of the specific societies. Obviously we cannot tear participant concepts, attitudes, and actions from their cultural contexts and expect to acquire an accurate understanding of them. But once we have gained an understanding of what Popper (1964:174ff.; cf. also Jarvie, 1964) calls the situational logic of phenomena, cross-culturally generalized statements are appropriately derivable—assuming that the several societies can be empirically located within a common framework of society-level variables. The necessities of special theory do not preclude the construction of general theory; they only make the latter more abstract, often to the level of a theoretical idealization (cf. Nagel, 1961:462; Przeworski and Teune, 1970).

The greatest difficulties inherent in cross-societal investigations of class consciousness—or of the social consciousness aspect of any cleavage structure—are found at lower levels of measurement and analysis. These difficulties must be resolved in the construction of data records; otherwise inter-record correspondence cannot be estimated. The observer's record of direct measures for a given society may harbor a variety of errors, not the least of which are those resulting from the intrusion of biased preconceptions, often well-charged ideologically, of the societal structures under examination. The disparate images of Tepoztlan conveyed by Redfield and by Lewis exemplify the problem, although only partially (cf. Paddock, 1961). On the other hand, the participant's data record does not "read itself"; the observer-analyst must interpret it. In fact, one might well speak of *two* participant records: a real one, residing only within the participant, and a derived record, filtered through the observer's interpretive apparatus. It is only the second of these that is—that *can* be—compared with the observer's data record; and in that circumstance rests one of the most critical problems in social research, namely, the problem of meaning imputation and semantic equivalence (cf., e.g., Kaplan, 1964:122; Peters, 1958; Przeworski and Teune, 1970).

Semantic Equivalence and the Meanings of "Class"

We cannot assume uncritically that the meanings that we as observers attach to "class" (or to any of its related terms) are identical with, or even closely approximate, the meanings assigned by everyday-world participants. Nor can we assume uncritically that the meanings of "class" in a given social aggregation are homogeneous. Rather, questions of meaning equivalence are a proper and necessary subject of empirical investigation. Despite the apparent obvious truth in that observation, however, studies of class consciousness have typically *not* approached questions of meaning equivalence and imputation as empirical questions, with the result that their findings are at best somewhat ambiguous. This is perhaps especially true of those studies that have been conducted in the United States, because of the more frequent usage of such terms as "lower," "middle," and "upper class," which carry less intrinsic content than do *haute bourgeoisie, Kleinburgertum*, or "proletariat," for example.[6]

There is a fairly sizable literature of research in what is conventionally referred to as class identification and images of society—that is, participant conceptions of class structure, wherein the standard procedure is to ask the respondent to indicate the "social classes in this country," perhaps to define the distinguishing (usually, the "single most important") membership trait of each, and to assign himself to one of the denominated classes (cf., e.g., Centers, 1949; Gross, 1953; Oeser and Hammond, 1954; Manis and Meltzer, 1954; Mayntz, 1958; Runciman, 1966; Davies, 1967). Data generated in this manner are aggregated according to one or some combination of a number of schemes, the three most prevalent of which are illustrated in Table 8.2 (again with hypothetical data). Of course, the aggregated distributions are also sometimes cross-tabulated against various background factors, most often an observer typology of a variable or attribute taken to be indicative of actual class position (e.g., occupation).

There are several deficiencies in this procedure, the most serious being the usually unstated assumptions that (1) these data aggregations are internally homogeneous in their semantic structures and (2) the observer-interpreted entries in the participant's data record are semantically equivalent to the real-world counterparts of which they are supposed to be measures. Either or both of these assumed properties of the data record *may* be real properties. The 90 percent of the N number of people in the second section of Table 8.2 who commonly mentioned Class B in their descriptions of class structure *may* have had identical or nearly identical meanings in mind; however, the meanings *could* have been significantly different in $.9N$ ways. The assumption of meaning equivalence, while never totally other than an assumption, must nevertheless be supported by empirical evidence.

Whatever the instrumentation and procedure employed, the observer must elicit (or discover previously recorded) responses from the participant in order to construct (or reconstruct into a usable form, to be precise) the participant's data record. But, to use an illustration from a cross-societal context, what are the semantic variations that obtain between the following sets of possible responses to (presumably) compare elicitations of "the social classes in this country": *la gente ricce, classe media, operai, classe lavoratrice, contadini braccianti* versus *die Reichen, Mittelklasse, Facharbeitern, Arbeiterschaft, Bauernschaft, Tagelohnern*? "Class" is a word that is lexically common to several different languages, with only minor variations in spelling and inflection; but how similar

Table 8.2   Illustrations of Data-Aggregation Schemes Commonly Used in the Analysis of Large-Sample Survey Data on Aspects of Class Consciousness[a]

I. Number of Classes[b]		II. Class Identification[c]		III. Class Models[d]	
Number Perceived	Distribution of Total N(%)	Class Label	% Naming Specific Classes	Type of Model	Distribution of Total N(%)
0 or 1	5	A	5	1	15
2	25	B	90	2	40
3	40	C	85	3	25
4	15	D	5	4	10
5 or more	15	Other	15	5	5
		Denied	5	Denied	5

[a]Hypothetical data shown in distributions. The first scheme of aggregation is self-explanatory. The second, Class Identification, usually takes one of two forms. In one, as illustrated in the table, respondents are classified into nonexclusive categories according to the particular classes they name (e.g., "middle class," "proletariat"). The other scheme groups them into exclusive categories according to which of a number of *sets* of classes they name as constitutive of class structure (e.g., "upper-middle-working-lower," "the rich versus the poor"). In the third scheme of aggregation, Class Models, the analyst attempts to interpret participants' responses at a higher level of abstraction; that is, he tries to infer from the respondent's listing of classes the central analytic dimension of his conception of class structure and then aggregate respondents on that basis (e.g., "a two-valued power model," "a three-valued prestige model").
[b]Cf., e.g., Kahl and Davis (1955), Mayntz (1958), Davies (1967).
[c]Cf., e.g., Centers (1949), Manis and Meltzer (1954), Davies (1967), Broom, Jones, and Zubrzycki (1968).
[d]Cf., e.g., Popitz, et al. (1961), Oeser and Hammond (1954), Bott (1957), Mayntz (1958).

are the ranges of meanings given to class, *classe, Klasse,* and so on? And how do, say, *Klasse, Schichte,* and *Stand* interrelate semantically within the one language and, in turn, in comparison with the interrelationships of their lexical counterparts in other languages? How many different English translations of certain passages of Weber exist because of the word *Stand*?

Questions of the foregoing sort touch only the surface of the imputation problem, moreover, for internal to any society or linguistic grouping are undoubtedly many significant variabilities in the semantics of "class." It is a polysemic par excellence. The precise meaning of a particular usage of this word depends partly (but only partly) on the context of its usage. For example, consider these three expressions: "They're a different class of people." "There's a class of people in this town that just don't care *how* they live!" and—to quote Woodrow Wilson (cf. Cawelti, 1965:139)—". . .the originative part of America [is] the class that saves, that plans, that organizes. . . ." The intended meaning of the word "class" could range from the most general notion of "category," wherein the content includes neither more nor less than what explicitly follows the appearance of the word in the expression, to a most highly specific and intricate meaning that lies quite outside the remainder of the expression.[7]

The meanings that are of greatest interest for this paper are those that perceive class as a positional or status term, that is, a designator of locations in social structure (cf. Edmondson, 1958:6). Even in this more narrowly circumscribed set of meanings, however, "class" can be quite ambiguous. Although this is not the place to review systematically the substantive results of research into the social meanings of "class"—if it were, there would be little to review beyond Ossowski (1963)—we should illustrate briefly the range of meanings that can be discerned in "class" as a status term.

By one popular conception, the word refers to something that a person is *in*, in the sense in which one can be inside a room or a box. There is a certain emphasis on containedness, on the boundaries of class as natural limits. Sometimes this view carries remnants of the estate principle of "station in life": one is *in* a particular class, and while vertical movement within its boundaries is expectable and respectable, movement beyond one's class is not. Popular conceptions of social structure in the United States of the middle and late 1800s, for example, were often laden with a peculiar moral fusion of legitimate expectations of personal improvement, on the one hand, and sensitivities to cultural station, on the other, as Cawelti (1965) has shown recently. Horatio Alger's depiction of Luke Walton captures some of this moral quality: Walton was "not puffed up by his unexpected and remarkable success. He never fails to recognize kindly . . . the old associates of his humbler days, and never tries to conceal the fact that he was once a Chicago Newsboy" (quoted in Cawelti, 1965:101). Remants of that attitude may still exist in areas of the United States, especially the rural hinterlands, as an implicit characterization of aspects of "class": consider, for instance, the difference between an ascending young man "who, despite his success, remembers who he is and where he came from" and the equally successful ascending young man who "puts on airs."

By other conceptions "class" is rather like a suit of clothes; it may be discarded when the wearer can afford a new one. Although the conceiver may conclude that "the whole idea of class is vague" – which in turn may suggest to him that it is "hard to recognize solid classes in this country"—perhaps at least part of his conception can be represented by the ladder image. "Class" is a set of "fuzzy lines separating groups of people who work in different jobs" or "different levels that people live at . . . mostly because they don't all make the same amount of money" or "the way we group people according to their prestige and status" or "how well a man is doing [as compared with] somebody else." Relatively little emphasis is given to notions of boundaries or containedness; more is given to the sense of a gradation of levels, or ladder rungs, *on* which people can be placed and across which they move.

Variations also exist in the evaluative properties of the meanings of "class."

According to some meanings, class is not only an important social fact but also "generally a good thing"; "beneficial to our way of life"; "a necessary mainstay of society . . . and a source of security"; and so on. For others the term refers to something that is bad or "harmful to society": it "has no good purpose, but has come to have a big part in lives of people in this country"; it is "not good for people because [it] allows too much room for criticism and ridicule"; it divides "people on the basis of often meaningless things . . . people are placed in a class often against their desires and may be held in it indefinitely." The intention here, it is worth repeating, is not to survey the entire range of meanings of "class" nor to give vent to an illustrative mood but merely to show some small part of that range by way of a few examples. The profound importance of the problem of meaning imputation and equivalence has already been demonstrated convincingly by the Londons in their reexamination of the Harvard Project on the Soviet Social System (London and London, 1966). Their findings raise disturbing queries about the validity of the results of much previous social research, especially social survey research. At the same time, they reconfirm unmistakably the necessity of incorporating *two* different sets of measurements in the participant (and observer) data record. Not only must it include readings of the particular real-world counterparts designated by the components of the concept (in this paper, class consciousness); it must also contain measures of the real-world conditions under which those previously mentioned readings were made, including not least of all the semantic properties of the communicative relationship between observer and participant.

Let's again consider Table 8.1 and the measurement operations that went into its construction, but with different class labels inserted in place of the rather abstract "Class A," "Class B," and so on (cf. Table 8.3 below). The observer-measured class locations are called "high bourgeoisie," "petty bourgeoisie," "proletariat," and "peasantry"; these four classes exhaust the range of significantly demarcated classes according to the observer's reading of the social structure and, therefore, also the range of alternative locations of the *N* people. Further assume that the participant-measured self-locations are in "the rich and powerful class," "the middle class," "the working class," and "the poor class." (We may ignore, for present purposes, the odd marginal distributions associated with these labels in Table 8.3.)

Now, as a first consideration, how do we know that the meanings intended in "high bourgeoisie" (by the observer) and in "the rich and powerful class" (by the participant) are equivalent? We do not, a priori. Since we want to determine the degree of correspondence between the observer's and the participant's readings of which class the participant belongs to, some estimation of whether the two labels mean exactly the same thing, approximately the same thing, or vastly different things is required. Otherwise it will be impossible for us to determine whether the participant's self-location is "accurate" (i.e., vis-a-vis observer readings). We must therefore investigate the intended meanings of those labels.

Table 8.3   Correspondence of Participant and Observer Measures of Participant's Location in Class Structure[a]

Participant-Measured Class Location	Observer-Measured Class Location			
	High Bourgeoisie	Petty Bourgeoisie	Proletariat	Peasantry
Rich and powerful class	261	111	18	0
Middle class	47	483	184	17
Working class	11	114	546	121
Poor class	2	23	208	354
Total	321	731	956	492

[a]The body of this table duplicates the hypothetical data of Table 8.1; index of correspondence $(R_S) = .63$.

In addition, we face a further complication. It is exceedingly improbable that the participant-measured class locations reported in Table 8.3 would exhaust the entire range of expressions employed by respondents in answer to the question: To which class do you belong? Let us assume that 15 different expressions, as opposed to the 4 shown in Table 8.3, were uttered. Do we assume by that fact that the participants-in-social-structure actually perceived precisely 15 different classes in society? Or may we assume that many of the respondents really meant the same thing but used different (although, for them, semantically equivalent) words to express their conceptions of class structure? From its immediate appearance, Table 8.3 indicates that the latter was the case, that the 15 original expressions were semantically reducible to 4. As a practical matter, such reductions are possible, of course, and perhaps even likely, depending on how closely we must approximate the criterion of meaning *equivalence* in order to have valid data records and, thus, valid measures of the degree to which those records correspond to each other. However, the inescapable point is that empirical measurements of meaning structures are *entirely necessary* to the construction of interpretable data records on class consciousness. The difference between the measurement of class consciousness in which data records are constructed as just suggested and measurement as it has been conducted typically is roughly analogous (in reverse) to the difference that Winch (1967:115) described recently "between being able to formulate statistical laws about the likely occurrences of [particular] words in a language and being able to understand what was being *said*" by someone who uttered those words. "Understanding," in that situation, "is grasping the point or *meaning* of what is being done or said."

Summary

This paper has dealt with a number of problems in the conceptualization and measurement of class consciousness. The approach to these problems was designed in accordance with some major requirements of successful comparative research. Elementary among these is the formulation of a conceptualization and measurement framework that can be applied adequately and consistently to the study of class consciousness in any particular society. Without that framework the enterprise of comparative analysis is forestalled. Assume, for example, that we wish to describe and analyze potential differences in class consciousness among England, Germany, France, Italy, Greece, and the United States, either as an end in itself or as an intervening variable in some larger explanatory construction (e.g., see Lipset and Rokkan, 1967:14, for comments about intervening variables between cleavage structures and political participation). The observed differences would be interpreted in terms of the values of specific variables substituted for the "proper name" descriptions (cf. Przeworski and Teune, 1970:26-30) of the six societies. But those interpretations can be meaningful only to the extent that the observed differences are differences among societally specific meaningful values, resulting from a common frame for the conceptualization and measurement of class consciousness.

Notes

1. The author wishes to thank Reinhard Bendix, Bernard Morris, and David Sallach, who read and commented helpfully on earlier drafts on this paper.
2. For discussions of some of the issues involved in such uses of party-preference data, see Stokes (1963), Converse (1966), and Rose and Urwin (1969).
3. To take an illustrative case, in Italy many more people vote for the Communist Party (PCI) than fill its membership rolls or are convinced of the general worth of its campaign platforms and long-range goals. For many of these, that vote is an opportunity to register a generic dissent against the current government and the bumbling state bureaucracy. For some, especially male residents of the *Mezzogiorno*, voting for her archenemy is a convenient means of "slapping the face of the church." For some, it is safer simply to vote one's true convictions at election time, while avoiding the risks and obligations of formal party membership. For some, particularly in the so-called Red Belt regions of central Italy, voting for the PCI is a more-or-less habitual remembrance of the valiant efforts of many young party members who participated in the resistance movement of World War II. For still others, it is (or was) a way of keeping the *morotei* Christian Democrats and the Nenni Socialists "honest" and energetic and perhaps, too, a tactical maneuver to perpetuate *l'apertura sinistra*. In short, it would be wide of the mark to assume that a behavioral or attitudinal expression of support for the PCI by, say, an industrial worker in Milan, Turin, or Florence is necessarily indicative of his class consciousness.
4. The notion of a "false" versus a "true" consciousness poses the epistemological dilemma of determining whose knowledge is the standard, the observer's or the participant's, when the "observer" is inevitably also "participant," and vice versa; that is, ultimately, in

what sense can one assess *non*tautologically the "accuracy" or "truthfulness' of a participant's readings of social structure? As several people have noted (sometimes excessively, since Marx was not unaware of the problem), there are tautological tendencies in the Marxian conceptualization, which presumes a rigorously pure science of society wherein the observer transcends the limitations of perspective in a manner somewhat akin to Mannheim's "socially unattached intellectual" (cf. Bottomore and Rubel, 1956:24). In any case, as a problem of scientific knowledge we can only make certain enabling assumptions about the observer's data record (given that the necessary criteria for constructing that record have been met) and proceed from there, keeping clearly in mind the fact that such assumptions *have* been made and interpreting our research findings accordingly.

5. Although this illustration assumes high inter-record correspondence with regard to measures of class structure, in an actual case that assumption would very unlikely apply to all members of a societal population. Important information would be lost if we omitted from further consideration those people whose measures of class structure were significantly discordant with the observer measures.

6. Which is *not* to say that these latter, and similar, terms are *free* of the imputation problem. Further, these "spatial" terms, as the English words are sometimes designated, have not been at all unique to the United States. "Upper," "upper-middle," "lower-middle," and "lower-class" descriptions were used in England at least as early as the mid-1800s, and, according to Ossowski (1963:124), Linde's early nineteenth-century dictionary of the Polish language lists "upper, middle, lower, lowest" as examples of "class."

7. Unless otherwise identified, the quoted expressions in this and the following four paragraphs are from material collected intermittently and nonrandomly by the author via interviews and informal conversations with various persons over a period of several months. These quoted materials are presented for illustrative purposes only.

References

Aron, Raymond.

    1964   *La Lutte de classes.* Paris: Gallimard.

Bateson, Gregory.

    1936   *Naven.* 2nd ed. Palo Alto, Calif.: Stanford University Press.

Blum, Alan F., and Peter McHugh.

    1971   The social ascription of motives. *American Sociological Review,* 36 (February): 98-109.

Bott, Elizabeth.

    1957   *Family and Social Network.* London: Tavistock.

Bottomore, T.B.

    1965   *Classes in Modern Society.* London: Allen and Unwin.

Bottomore, T.B., and Maximilien Rubel (Eds.).

1956   *Karl Marx: Selected Writings in Sociology and Social Philosophy.* London: Watts.

Broom, Leonard, F. Lancaster Jones, and Jerzy Zubrzycki.

1968   Social stratification in Australia. In John Archer Jackson (Ed.), *Social Stratification.* Cambridge: Cambridge University Press. Pp. 212-233.

Cawelti, John G.

1965   *Apostles of the Self-Made Man.* Chicago: University of Chicago Press.

Centers, Richard.

1949   *The Psychology of Social Class.* Princeton, N.J.: Princeton University Press.

Child, Arthur.

1941   The problem of imputation in the sociology of knowledge. *Ethics,* 51 (January): 200-219.

1944   The problem of imputation resolved. *Ethics,* 54 (January): 96-109.

Converse, Philip E.

1964   The nature of belief systems in mass publics. In David Apter (Ed.), *Ideology and Discontent.* New York: Free Press. Pp. 206-261.

1966   The problem of party distances in models of voting change. In M. Kent Jennings and L. Harmon Zeigler (Eds.), *The Electoral Process.* Englewood Cliffs, N.J.: Prentice-Hall. Pp. 175-207.

Dahrendorf, Ralf.

1967   *Conflict After Class.* London: Longmans, Green.

Davies, A.F.

1967   *Images of Class.* Sydney: Sydney University Press.

Edmondson, Munroe S.

1958   *Status Terminology and the Social Structure of North American Indians.* Seattle: University of Washington Press.

Geiger, Theodor.

    1949   *Klassengesellschaft im Schmelztiegel.* Cologne: Kiepenheuer.

Gross, Neal.

    1953   Social class identification in the urban community. *American Sociological Review,* 18 (August): 398-404.

Gurvitch, Georges.

    1965   *Le Concept des classes sociales.* Paris: Centre de documentation universitaire.

Hazelrigg, Lawrence E.

    1972   Class, property, and authority. *Social Forces,* 50 (June): 473-487.

Jarvie, I.C.

    1964   *The Revolution in Anthropology.* London: Routledge and Kegan Paul.

Kahl, Joseph A., and James A. Davis.

    1955   A comparison of indexes of socio-economic status. *American Sociological Review,* 20 (June): 317-325.

Kaplan, Abraham.

    1964   *The Conduct of Inquiry.* San Francisco: Chandler.

Lewis, Lionel.

    1965   Class consciousness and the salience of class. *Sociology and Social Research,* 49 (Autumn): 173-182.

Lipset, Seymour M., and Stein Rokkan.

    1967   Cleavage structures, party systems and voter alignments. In Seymour M. Lipset and Stein Rokkan (Eds.), *Party Systems and Voter Alignments.* New York: Free Press. Pp. 1-64.

Lockwood, David.

    1958   *The Blackcoated Worker.* London: Allen and Unwin.

London, Ivan D., and Miriam B. London.

    1966   A research-examination of the Harvard Project on the Soviet Social System: I. The basic written questionnaire. *Psychological Reports,* Monograph Supplement No. 6.

Lopreato, Joseph, and Lawrence E. Hazelrigg.

1972   *Class, Conflict, and Mobility.* San Francisco: Chandler.

Lukàcs, Georg.

1923   *Geschichte und Klassenbewusstsein.* Berlin: Malik.

Manis, Jerome G., and Bernard N. Meltzer.

1954   Attitudes of textile workers to class structure. *American Journal of Sociology,* 60 (July): 30-35.

Marx, Karl.

1936   *The Poverty of Philosophy.* New York: International.

Marx, Karl, and Friedrich Engels.

1959   *Manifesto of the Communist Party.* In Lewis S. Feuer (Ed.), *Marx and Engels: Basic Writings on Politics and Philosophy.* Garden City, N.Y.: Anchor. Pp. 1-41.

Mayntz, Renate.

1958   *Soziale Schichtung and sozialer Wandel in einer Industriegemeinde.* Stuttgart: Ferdinand Enke.

Miliband, Ralph.

1971   Barnave: a case of bourgeois class consciousness. In Istvãn Mészãros (Ed.), *Aspects of History and Class Consciousness.* London: Routledge and Kegan Paul. Pp. 22-48.

Morris, Richard T., and Raymond S. Murphy.

1958   A paradigm for the study of class consciousness. *Sociology and Social Research,* 50 (April): 298-313.

Mueller, Claus.

1970   Notes on the repression of communicative behavior. In Hans Peter Dreitzel (Ed.), *Recent Sociology, No. 2.* New York: Macmillan. Pp. 101-113.

Nagel, Ernest.

1961   *The Structure of Science.* New York: Harcourt, Brace and World.

Nisbet, Robert A.

1959   The decline and fall of social class. *Pacific Sociological Review,* 2 (Fall): 11-17.

1970   *The Social Bond.* New York: Knopf.

Oeser, O. A., and S. B. Hammond.

1954   *Social Structure and Personality in a City.* London: Routledge and Kegan Paul.

Ossowski, Stanislaw.

1963   *Class Structure in the Social Consciousness.* London: Routledge and Kegan Paul.

Paddock, John.

1961   Oscar Lewis's Mexico. *Anthropological Quarterly,* 32 (July): 129-149.

Peters, R.S.

1958   *The Concept of Motivation.* London: Routledge and Kegan Paul.

Popitz, Heinrich, Hans P. Bahrdt, Ernst A. Jüres, and Hanno Kestig.

1961   *Das Gesellschaftsbild des Arbeiters.* 2nd ed. Tubingen: Mohr.

Popper, Karl R.

1964   *The Poverty of Historicism.* 3rd ed. New York: Harper.

Przeworski, Adam, and Henry Teune.

1970   *The Logic of Comparative Social Inquiry.* New York: Wiley.

Rae, Douglas W., and Michael Taylor.

1970   *The Analysis of Political Cleavages.* New Haven, Conn.: Yale University Press.

Rose, Richard, and Derek Urwin.

1969   Social cohesion, political parties and strains in regimes *Comparative Political Studies,* 2 (April): 7-67.

Runciman, W.G.

1966   *Relative Deprivation and Social Justice.* London: Routledge and Kegan Paul.

Schutz, Alfred.

1968   *Collected Papers: I. The Problem of Social Reality.* The Hague: Martinus Nijhoff.

Stokes, Donald.

    1963   Spatial models of party competition. *American Political Science Review,* 57 (June): 368-377.

Tawney, R.H.

    1931   *Equality.* London: Allen and Unwin.

Thompson, E.P.

    1963   *The Making of the English Working Class.* New York: Pantheon.

Winch, Peter.

    1967   *The Idea of a Social Science.* New York: Humanities Press.

Wirth, Louis.

    1946   Preface. In Karl Mannheim, *Idealogy and Utopia.* New York: Harcourt, Brace. Pp. x-xxx.

Wrong, Dennis H.

    1969   Social inequality without stratification, In Celia S. Heller (Ed.), *Structured Social Inequality.* London: Macmillan. Pp. 513-520.

Discussion

Mr. Anderson.   Let me just mention one thing about Hazelrigg's paper. I won't discuss it much since an illness in his family prevents him from being here to defend himself. The one critical comment I would make is that he could well have used actual past investigations of the things he is talking about rather than hypothetical examples and data; then we could see in more concrete form what it is he is talking about in his tables and analysis.

Mr. Stryker.   I think that Hazelrigg's paper has considerable relevance to the central problem of comparative sociological methodology. His argument is that the measurement of class and class consciousness is unique to the society in which that measurement occurs. That measurement is a function of the specific historical circumstances of that society and of sources of variability, cultural and otherwise, that enter into determining class and class consciousness in a society.

As I see it, he is addressing the following question in this paper: Given that the measurement of variables as important as class and class consciousness must be unique to a society, how can we overcome that uniqueness through concept formation that will enable us to study this phenomenon across societies? This issue is clearly central. Walton addressed it [see pp. 189ff., above] when he noted the irrelevance of voting behavior in Mexico as an index of apathy or alienation or comparable kinds of phenomena. This problem is what people are talking about when they refer to conceptual equivalence versus phenomenal identity. Hazelrigg's attack may not solve this problem, but he has raised an issue that is clearly central to comparative sociology.

CHAPTER NINE

Measuring Individual Modernity: A Near Myth[1]

MICHAEL ARMER

Indiana University

ALLAN SCHNAIBERG

Northwestern University

Introduction

A major focus of comparative social psychological research has been to identify and measure "individual modernity," or the set of individual values and beliefs that theoretically are associated with modernization and that better fit a man for life in modern society (Inkeles, 1966). Underlying most research in this area are premises that a single dimension of modernism exists along which societies can be distributed, that societies at each point along this continuum tend to share certain social and cultural patterns, and that these sociocultural patterns lead to, result from, or occur concomitantly with patterns in values, beliefs, and behaviors of individuals. It follows that there exists a single dimension of modernity along which individuals in all societies can be classified and that, in societies at higher levels of modernity, the average level of individual modernity will be higher. Further, individuals in more sectors or environments *within* societies will tend to be more modern than those in less modern sectors.

This statement is too generalized to capture the subtleties and qualifications of specific discussions on individual modernity, but it does make explicit the theoretical rationale that underlies much of the research. It should be noted that, contrary to Stephenson's (1969) criticism, this rationale clearly does not preclude cultural or individual variation; it merely emphasizes the proposition that certain common perspectives and behavior will be found among individuals who experience modern sociocultural environments, regardless of other personal

249

or collective differences in perspectives and behavior (cf. Lambert, 1964). However, this theoretical rationale and the term "modernization" imply a unilinear model of change with respect to the selected sociolcultural and individual patterns of behavior. The notion of a unidimensional continuum of societal modernization (on which analyses of individual modernity partly rest) has been subjected to considerable criticism (Bendix, 1967; Blumer, 1964; Gusfield, 1967; Illich, 1969). In addition, there have been some highly critical evaluations of the concept of individual modernity (Frank, 1967; Stephenson, 1968; Horowitz, 1970; cf. Inkeles, 1969a, 1970).

And yet few sociologists would argue that societal change is random; the process of industrialization appears to be associated logically and empirically with changes in other spheres of social organization and individual behavior (Moore, 1965). With respect to individual perspectives, clear cross-cultural similarities have been demonstrated for people belonging to similar sectors in different societies (Doob, 1960; Inkeles, 1960; Smith and Inkeles, 1966; Kahl, 1968). In short, while acknowledging the plausibility of many theoretical critiques regarding the unidimensionality of societal and individual modernization, we are struck by what appears to be extensive empirical support for the existence of individual modernity under similar sociocultural conditions. Research shows remarkably strong and consistent relationships of individual modernity to formal education, industrial experience, and urban residence (Kahl, 1968; Inkeles, 1969b; Armer and Youtz, 1971; Schnaiberg, 1971). However, there exist virtually no direct empirical evaluations of the generalizations in most of these modernity studies (cf. Feldman and Hurn, 1966; Feldman and Kendrick, 1968; Jacobson and Kendrick, 1970).

What are the value-orientations that have been used to define individual modernity across cultures? Within the past five years there have been numerous attempts to answer this question at the theoretical level, including essays by O'Connell (1965), Inkeles (1966), and Peshkin and Cohen (1967), and several studies have proposed multiple-item measures of modernity (Smith and Inkeles, 1966; Dawson, 1967; Doob, 1967; Kahl, 1968; Schnaiberg, 1970a; Armer, 1970; Armer and Youtz, 1971). Included in these measures have been components such as independence from family ties, a sense of personal efficacy, an empirical orientation toward causality, and receptivity to change.

Several features shared by these scales of individual modernity raise questions about their measurement value in comparative empirical research. First, all have been developed and tested primarily in Third World nations. We lack information on whether they provide meaningful measurement among individuals in modern, urban-industrial societies or, for that matter, in small, undeveloped primitive societies. The limitations of "pseudo cross-national" designs (Hyman, 1964) are just as applicable in constructing cross-national instruments as in testing cross-national hypotheses. Evidence is needed on the utility of these scales in discriminating modernity levels among individuals in societies with substantially higher and lower levels of socioeconomic development than are represented in Brazil, Mexico, Israel, Nigeria, Pakistan, Chile, Argentina, India, and Turkey. (Frey, 1970:202, even suggests that most of these nations are oversampled and unrepresentative of Third World nations.)

Second, although all of these scales are intended to measure the same or very similar phenomena, they reveal prima facie differences in content. This situation is not suprising in view of the vast array of values, beliefs, and behaviors that may be subsumed by the construct of individual modernity. The studies differ to some degree in their definitions of the domain of content as well as in the techniques used to sample and measure items included in scales of modernity. Although no exact procedures can be specified for domain-sampling (Bohrnstedt, 1970; Robinson et al., 1968), the resulting item differences raise the question of whether the scales are truly equivalent. To what extent do scales of individual modernity measure a common construct rather than different "modernities" for each scale?

Third, little or no comparable information is available on the measurement properties of these scales, especially information pertaining to retest reliability and construct validity (Campbell, 1960). This lack is particularly critical because some scale components and items approximate the components and items found in measures of anomia, alienation, middle-class values, and other constructs already in use. Although correlations of modernity with these variables may be expected on theoretical grounds, the correlations should be lower than correlations between separate measures of the same construct if it is indeed a distinct construct. Therefore, evidence is needed of the discriminant validity (Campbell and Fiske, 1959)[2] of modernity scales from scales of other well-known, presumably distinct, constructs. Moreover, the modernity scales may be subject to various response biases, especially acquiescence response bias. In short, what evidence is there that modernity scales measure a distinctive trait rather than one of the more common traits or measurement factors with which they might be confounded?

These basic questions require investigation if we are to evaluate the meaningfulness and utility of modernity scales. Specifically, evidence is needed (1) that the scales differentiate respondents in a reasonable fashion in modern (and other) societies, (2) that the scales are reasonably equivalent, and (3) that they are reasonably reliable and valid. The objective of the research reported here was to investigate these matters systematically by assessing the similarities and differences among alternative measures of individual modernity in a large urban-industrial setting in the United States. Specifically, examination was made of the distributions, equivalence, internal consistency, retest reliability, and construct validity of modernity scales constructed by Smith and Inkeles (1966), Kahl (1968), Schnaiberg (1970a), and Armer (see Armer, 1970; also Armer and

Youtz, 1971). To the extent that the evidence does not meet the requirements specified above for any or all modernity scales, the utility of those scales must be called into question. If evidence is lacking for all scales, we must consider the possibility that individual modernity is a myth and not a meaningful concept.

At this point, we should comment on the significance of this study for comparative social psychological research on modernization. Existing measures of modernity are rapidly being incorporated into comparative and foreign-area research. Inkeles (1969b), for example, reports that one of his measures is being used in more than 20 pure and applied projects in developing countries. But without evidence of cross-cultural utility and of scale equivalence, it is impossible to say whether discrepancies between findings in different studies are real or an artifact of unsuspected measurement limitations or differences. Moreover, research based on unreliable or invalid indexes may actually obstruct understanding of the changes in perspectives, behavior, and needs of individuals in modernizing societies. In short, information is needed on cross-cultural utility, scale equivalence, reliability, and validity of the separate scales of modernity in order to minimize misinterpretation and to maximize the value and the cumulativeness of results from past and future comparative studies.

Data and Methods

The present paper is based on interview data collected in connection with a study of the relationship between modern values and family-planning norms and practices; the study was begun in August 1970, in the Uptown area of Chicago. The first wave consisted of a nonprobability sample of 156 white married males and was followed by second and third waves at approximately nine-week intervals. The second wave included 109 reinterviews and 22 interviews with new respondents, while the third wave included 98 reinterviews and 24 new respondents. A team of five male interviewers conducted all three waves. This paper's findings are based on completed data analysis from the first two waves.

Uptown is a low- and middle-income, ethnically heterogenous residential area about five miles north of the Loop in downtown Chicago. It was selected as the setting for the research on both practical and theoretical grounds. Among practical considerations were resource limitations that made it unfeasible to consider most alternative locations abroad or in the United States. Furthermore, locating in the United States avoided major translation problems, which hamper foreign-language research.

From a theoretical standpoint the site has distinct advantages in that it is comparable to those included in the urban portions of Smith and Inkeles's, Kahl's, Schnaiberg's, and Armer's studies. This is an important point of reference because a large majority (over 75 percent) of the respondents in all four of the original studies lived in urban areas. Further, Uptown includes a high proportion of recent low-status migrants from rural areas, a composition pattern common to urban areas in developing societies. Finally, a substantial share of the sample is in an unstable, insecure, or marginal labor force category. Their situation is thus comparable to that of persons in petty trades, traditional labor, and the like who were involved in the previous studies. Thus, although the overall composition of the sample reflected a more homogeneous and somewhat higher class distribution than previous samples, we find a high degree of equivalence between the Uptown sample and the original research samples, while still allowing considerable difference in sociocultural context. It is hoped that in the future we can offset some of the anticipated lack of variability in individual modernity in the Uptown sample by undertaking similar research in other settings.

The interview schedule included items from Smith and Inkeles's Short Form 6 Modernity Scale (OM-6), Kahl's Modernity I and II Scales, Schnaiberg's Emancipation Scale, and Armer's Individual Modernity Scale. These scales are all based on a limited number of structured questions intended to be applicable across cultures. The fact that the scales are relatively easy to administer and uncomplicated in measurement increases their attractiveness to many social scientists for use in comparative research. In addition, information was obtained on Srole's (1956) Anomia Scale, Middleton's (1963) Alienation Scale (omitting one item dealing with cultural estrangement), acquiescent response bias, socioeconomic status, and personal-background factors.

The modernity scales were included in all three waves, and the anomia and alienation scales were included respectively in the first and second waves. Acquiescence was measured by discrepancies in responses to a set of eight reversed items corresponding to the eight polychotomous items in Kahl's Modernity II Scale. Those respondents whose average code on the eight reversed items was discrepant with the average code on the original items by less than 1.00 were identified as nonacquiescent. Socioeconomic status was a composite index based on a summation of dichotomized responses to three items measuring educational level (less than four years of high school versus four years or more), occupational prestige (blue-collar versus white-collar), and family income (less than $7500 versus $7500 or more). The scales of anomia, alienation, and modernity were constructed using scoring procedures and weights identical with those employed in the original sources. (Item weights for Kahl's scales are averages of those reported for his Mexican and Brazilian samples.)

Results

Three major questions are involved in the analysis and comparison of the individual modernity scales. The first is whether the obtained scores from respondents living in a modern, urban-industrial society are reasonable. Do the several scales differentiate and distribute Uptown respondents with respect to individual modernity in a way that appears sensible when compared with the results for respondents in the original research in non-Western, nonindustrial societies? Second, are the several scales equivalent? Do they all measure a relatively unitary construct of modernity or do they appear to be measures of different constructs? Third, what are the absolute and relative merits of the modernity scales in terms of standard measurement criteria? To what extent are the scales internally consistent, stable, and valid? In particular, is there clear differentiation of modernity from other well-known constructs or from measurement artifacts such as acquiescent response bias?

Modernity Distribution in Uptown

Item-selection, scoring, and weighting procedures varied considerably in the studies by Smith and Inkeles, Kahl, Schnaiberg, and Armer; thus a comparison of means and standard deviations in their original units of analysis would be ambiguous. In order to facilitate comparison, all four distributions have been transformed by setting the theoretical minimum modernity score equal to 0 and then dividing by the theoretical maximum modernity score $[X_i = (X_i - X_{min}) / (X_{max} - X_{min})$, where X_i is the transformed score for the ith case], which gives a new range from 0 to 1. Thus, if an individual gave the most modern response possible to each of the 14 items in Smith and Inkeles's scale or to each of the 22 items in Kahl's Modernity I Scale, his modernity score would equal 1.00 for each of these scales. The means and standard deviations of the Uptown distributions on each scale are reported in Table 9.1.

One major difference in scoring techniques employed in the original studies should be noted. Smith and Inkeles, and Schnaiberg, dichotomized items into modern and traditional responses at the median of each response distribution, while Kahl and Armer maintained fixed, largely polychotomous response codes. Dichotomization at the median sets the mean of each item and of the total scale as close to .50 as possible, given the particular response distributions. This technique has the effect of maximizing the variance of items and scales, which in turn contributes to the internal consistency reliability and to the maximum possible correlation with other variables. On the other hand, this scoring procedure makes the comparison of absolute modernity in two or more societies difficult, if not impossible, because the scoring of items is not equivalent across samples. These scales, then, have a greatly reduced value for comparative research. One can still compare "relatively modern" or "relatively traditional" individuals across societies, but levels of absolute modernity may differ greatly between these individuals in different societies. In short, this procedure tends to produce a culture-specific measure of modernity even though items and dimensions remain the same across cultures. (See Inkeles, 1969a, for a critique of culture-specific measures.)

Table 9.1 Transformed Means and Standard Deviations of Selected Individual Modernity Scales

Scale	Number of items	Uptown Sample (Wave I)		Original Source		
		Mean	s.d.	Mean	s.d.	N
Smith and Inkeles's OM-6	14	.66	.19	unreported[c]	–	
Kahl's Modernity I	22[a]	.63[b]	.14	unreported	–	
Schnaiberg	24	.57	.14	.45	.23	803
Armer	22	.61	.11	.39	.14	591
		(N = 156)				

[a]Kahl's 22 items are only those constituting the multiple-item themes which in turn constitute "core" values in both the Mexican and Brazilian data.
[b]Kahl's scale has been reversed to be consistent with the other scales in which a high score means "more modern."
[c]Smith and Inkeles (1966:362) do not report the mean score for the OM-6 Scale. They do report the mean score for their Long Form Overall Modernity (OM) Scale in all six nations to be "about 1.54," which is equivalent to .54 on our transformed scale.

Leaving this difficulty aside for the time being, it would seem reasonable to find differences in the degree and distribution of modernity scores in Uptown by contrast with distributions obtained in the original sources. Unfortunately information on means, standard deviations, and other distribution properties is generally absent in the original studies. However, Inkeles (1966) reports that his scale has been successfully used in the United States, and Kahl (1968:50) reports a distribution of Modernity III scores for housewives in the United States that appears to compare well with the distributions in his data from Brazil and Mexico. Thus there was preliminary indication that the modernity scales were applicable to modern industrial societies as well as to developing societies.

A more detailed comparison can be made in the case of Schnaiberg's and Armer's scales because the original data from Turkey and Nigeria are available. The Turkish data are limited to the Ankara portion, which is most comparable with Uptown data; it consists of a probability area sample of 803 married women. Armer's sample consisted of 591 young men residing in Kano City, which is part of the larger Kano metropolitan area of 125,000 in northern Nigeria. Individual modernity distributions for these two samples have been transformed in the same fashion as the Uptown distributions and the means and standard deviations are also reported in Table 9.1 in the "original source" columns.

It is clear from examination of the means of scales for the Uptown sample that all are above the scale midpoint (.50), indicating central tendencies toward the modern end of the continuum. Smith and Inkeles's distribution is furthest from the midpoint, which is suprising in view of their scoring procedure, and it also has the highest standard deviation (.19) in the Uptown data. Detailed examination of the data reveals that the high mean score is caused by extremely skewed distributions on many of Smith and Inkeles's items. Skewed distributions also occurred to a smaller degree on the other three scales and help to account for the means above .50. The higher standard deviation reflects in part the smaller number of items constituting Smith and Inkeles's OM-6 compared to the other scales.

Comparisons of the original Turkish and Nigerian data with the Uptown data show modernity scores closer to the traditional pole and below the scale midpoint. It is also apparent from the standard deviations that the Uptown sample is more generally homogeneous on Schnaiberg's and Armer's scales than were the original Turkish and Nigerian samples. In general, these findings are all reasonable and consistent with expectations of higher levels of modernity for comparable cross-national populations in a modern, industrial society like the United States, by contrast with Turkey, Nigeria, or other less-developed nations. Furthermore, the lower variation in modernity scores for the Uptown sample when compared to the original samples is understandable in terms of (1) the more restricted range of variation in social status and other factors in Uptown, compared to that in Turkey and Nigeria, and (2) the general absence of extremely traditional individuals in an urban-industrial center of an industrialized society. Modernizing influences in modern society are extremely pervasive; virtually all residents of Uptown are exposed to the mass media, urban life styles, education, contact with modern individuals, and other modernizing influences (Inkeles, 1966). On the other hand, these influences are differentially experienced and therefore result in variation in individual modernity, as observed in the Uptown data.

In sum, the modernity scores behave in ways that are consistent with theoretical expectations, and they appear sufficiently differentiated to warrant further analysis of scale equivalence, reliability, and validity.

Equivalence of Scales

Alternative survey research approaches to measuring modern values are well illustrated by the Smith and Inkeles, Kahl, Schnaiberg, and Armer scales. Smith and Inkeles began with a list of 33 themes reflected in 119 items that were reduced through a combination of item-selection procedures to a "final distillate" of 14 items known as the OM-6 scale. This scale consists of 10 dichotomized attitudinal items and 4 dichotomized behavioral and informational items. Kahl began with 58 items, tapping 14 themes, that were reduced through factor analytic techniques to a 22-item scale that included subscales of activism, low integration with relatives, preference for urban life, low perceived community stratification, mass-media participation, and low perceived stratification of life chances. All were attitudinal measures except for the mass-media items. Armer also used a factor analytic approach and concluded with 22 attitudinal items measuring dimensions of mastery (efficacy and activism), tolerance of other groups, belief in empirical causality, orientation to the future, independence from family ties, and receptivity to change. Schnaiberg's scale consisted of 24 dichotomized items tapping nuclear-family role structure, mass-media participation, and environmental orientation; all were selected by factor analysis from a pool of 46 items. One of the items asking about "wife's leisure activities" was omitted as inappropriate for the present analysis.

Despite these differences in dimensions, items, and procedures, all four of the scales are intended to identify a set of attitudes, values, and ways of acting that are associated with a modern society. It is assumed that the items and subscales are intercorrelated and form a general value syndrome of modernism. "On the average, a man who is high on some will also be high on the others, although there is room for variation" (Kahl, 1968:21). None of the authors differentiates types of modernity, and all suggest that their conceptions are relevant to the central values distinguishing modern from traditional societies. Thus individuals who are identified as relatively modern on one scale should also be identified as relatively modern on the others. In short, to the extent that the scales are reliable and valid, they should intercorrelate highly even if they emphasize different components of the general value system of modernity.

Assessment of the degree of equivalence in scale scores can be made from scale intercorrelations reported in Table 9.2. Values in the diagonal are internal-consistency reliability coefficients (Cronbach's coefficient alpha), and values below the diagonal are correlations corrected for attenuation due to less than perfect reliability. Intercorrelations above the diagonal range from $r = .40$ to $r = .64$ and thus represent an average explained variance among the scales of approximately 25 percent. None of the scales correlate perfectly or even near perfectly with the others, although all are associated positively at moderate levels. In short, the scales are interrelated with each other but are not equivalent indicators of individual modernity. While each scale measures a portion of some common phenomenon, each also includes measurements of parts of reality that are not measured by other scales.

The extent to which this lack of equivalence is caused by random fluctuations in the measurement operation (i.e., measurement error) rather than by systematic differences in what is measured can be estimated by correcting the correlations for attenuation. Of course, this "correction" does not negate the fact that measurement error interferes with accurate estimation of individual modernity, but it facilitates evaluation of whether the "true" scores are reasonably equivalent, even if observed scores are not.

The corrected correlations below the diagonal in Table 9.2 are substantially higher than the uncorrected correlations above the diagonal, especially the

Table 9.2 Intercorrelations of Modernity Scales (With Scale Reliabilities in Parentheses and Corrections for Attenuation Below the Diagonal)

Modernity Scale (Uptown, wave I)	Smith and Inkeles's OM-6	Kahl's Modernity I	Schnaiberg's Scale	Armer's Scale	Average Correlation	
					Uncorrected	Corrected[c]
Smith and Inkeles's OM-6	(.64)[a]	.54	.45	.57	.52	.79
Kahl's Modernity I	.77[b]	(.76)	.40	.64	.53	.77
Schnaiberg's Scale	.64	.57	(.64)	.41	.42	.63
Armer's Scale	.95	.97	.68	(.56)	.54	.87

[a]Cronbach's alpha = $(n/n\text{-}1) / (1 - \Sigma \sigma_i^2 / \sigma_x^2)$. This is a generalization of Kuder and Richardson's KR20 internal-consistency reliability formula. Because each scale is seen as a general syndrome of modernity comprised of subscales or items that are correlated, but substantively independent of each other (as with most scales of socioeconomic status, intelligence, etc.), the alpha coefficient of reliability may be interpreted as a lower bound estimate (Bohrnstedt, 1970).

[b]Correlations below the diagonal are corrected for attenuation due to unreliability: $r_{T_x T_y} = (r_{yx} / \sqrt{r_{xx'} r_{yy'}})$, where r_{xy} is the uncorrected sample correlation and $r_{xx'}$ is the reliability of x.

[c]Corrected for attenuation due to unreliability.

intercorrelations of Armer's, Kahl's, and Smith and Inkeles's scales. The corrected intercorrelations of these three scales range from .77 to .97, an indication that about three-fourths of the variance can be accounted for. This result is far from perfect equivalence but suggests a high degree of covariation among "true" scores.

Reliability of the Scales

Having determined that the scales are measuring largely the same phenomenon and that the scores appear consistent with expectations of individual modernity, we now proceed with an estimate of whether scale reliabilities and validities meet minimal standards. Also, since the preceding evidence suggests that the scales are not highly equivalent, it becomes more important to determine which scales have the highest reliability and validity. It should be noted that these questions regarding the absolute and relative merits of scales can only be answered with respect to particular populations; that is, the reliability of a scale refers to reliability for a given sample and may vary for other samples.

Two major types of measurement reliability can be estimated in this study: internal consistency and test-retest reliability. Internal consistency reliability is an estimate of the extent to which a scale is free from random variation among items, or "measurement error." The assumption is made that a scale is intended to be homogeneous or unidimensional and thus items should tend to covary. To the extent that the scale produces a high ratio of random variation (instead of covariation) to total variation, reliability estimates are lowered.

For the modernity scales, it follows that reliability is decreased in those scales that were constructed by intentionally selecting items that best measure the separate components of modernity rather than those that best measure the central tendency or general concept. For example, Kahl and Armer selected items to measure a multidimensional concept of modernity consisting of several components; this selection tends to reduce correlations between items in different scales, which in turn reduces reliability. This effect is offset to some extent by Kahl's and Armer's selection of subscales that cohere. In the case of Schnaiberg's scale, no item-analysis was involved on theoretical grounds and all items and subscales were retained in his factor analyses leading to a measure of general modernity. This procedure also allows low internal consistency. In short, internal-consistency reliability has limitations as an estimate of reliability for heterogeneous scales such as the modernity measures in this study. Reliability testing assumptions of nearly equal item difficulty and intercorrelation are not met, especially for scales that select items to represent the separate components rather than overall modernity.

An alternative and perhaps more appropriate estimate of reliability is test-retest correlations. However, interpretation of retest reliability coefficients is not without its own complications caused by change in "true" scores, recall of previous answers, and other contaminating factors.

Internal-consistency and test-retest reliabilities are reported in Table 9.3 for each of the modernity scales. No attempt has been made to standardize coefficients for the effects of different test length and scale variance. The internal-consistency reliability coefficients for wave I range from .56 to .76 and for wave II from .54 to .80. These are not exceptionally high, but they are comparable to reliabilities computed with the Uptown data for Srole's well-known Anomia Scale (.67) and for Middleton's Alienation Scale (.59).

Table 9.3   Internal Consistency and Test-Retest Reliability of Modernity Scales in Uptown Sample

| | Cronbach's Alpha | | |
Scale	Wave I	Wave II	Test-Retest
Smith and Inkeles's OM-6	.64	.54	.81
Kahl's Modernity I	.76	.80	.80
Schnaiberg's Modernity	.64	.55	.74
Armer's Modernity	.56	.57	.66
Srole's Anomia	.67	–	–
Middleton's Alienation	–	.59	–
Socioeconomic Status	.54	.56	.87
N	(156)	(109)	(109)

Comparison of wave I with wave II reliability coefficients reveals an interesting anomaly: Reliability coefficients for Kahl's and Armer's scales remain constant or become slightly higher, while the coefficients for Smith and Inkeles's and Schnaiberg's scales drop substantially. This irregular finding illustrates the variability across samples of reliability estimates for a given measure. For some reason, the 109 people who were reinterviewed in wave II appear to be less internally consistent in their responses to Smith and Inkeles's and Schnaiberg's items than the 47 people who were not reinterviewed, or perhaps they became less consistent between wave I and wave II. But why did that inconsistency affect these two scales and not all four?

One possible interpretation is that both the Smith and Inkeles and Schnaiberg scales were based on items dichotomized on the basis of the wave I distributions: because of selective sample attrition of more traditional respondents between wave I and wave II, the resulting scales suffered a greater reduction in "true score" variance than was true of the two remaining polychotomous scales (Kahl and Armer). This truncation of variation served to reduce the correlations between items in these dichotomous scales and thus reduced the internal-consistency reliability measures. An examination of the decline in normalized standard deviations from wave I to wave II for the four scales confirms this possibility: the wave II normalized standard deviations declined by 16 percent of the wave I standard deviations for Smith and Inkeles's scale and by 12 percent for Schnaiberg's scale, by contrast with only 4 percent for Armer's scale and an increase of 1 percent for Kahl's scale.

The test-retest reliability coefficient reported in Table 9.3 for the four modernity scales ranges from .66 to .81 and indicates the consistency of scores across administration waves. The correlations are highest for Smith and Inkeles's and Kahl's scales, which may reflect in part the inclusion in these scales of some behavioral and information items that are more objective and less likely to vary across waves. Consistent with this explanation is the high retest reliability of the socioeconomic-status (SES) measure (.87), which comprises three objective indicators (annual income, occupational class, and education level).

In any event, a comparison of modernity scales on reliability estimates indicates that Kahl's scale is generally superior to the others in our Uptown sample and that Armer's scale tends to have the lowest reliabilities. All of these scales meet minimum conventional standards with the possible exception of Armer's scale on wave I and all but Kahl's scale on wave II.

Validity of the Scales

There are no independent, error-free criteria of individual modernity against which to validate the modernity scales in this study, but we may investigate their convergent and discriminant validity. "When a construct is proposed," according to Campbell and Fiske (1959:84), "the proponent invariably has in mind distinctions between the new dimension and other constructs already in use. One cannot define without implying distinctions, and the verification of these distinctions is an important part of the validational process." Campbell and Fiske point out that validation requires (1) evidence of relative convergence of scale scores of tests designed to measure the same construct (convergent validation) and (2) evidence of relative independence or lower correlations with tests designed to measure other constructs (discriminant validation). It is important to emphasize that validation requires not only that scales purporting to measure a construct be positively correlated with each other but they be correlated *more highly* with each other than they are with scales purporting to measure distinct constructs already in use.

Several of the more plausible constructs with which modernity may be confused are anomia, alienation, and middle-class values. Anomia as measured by Srole's scale involves a general orientation of despair, which seems to characterize some of the modernity items negatively, especially in Kahl's scale. Alienation, involving components of powerlessness, normlessness, isolation, and meaninglessness, seems to be inversely reflected in modernity items dealing with personal efficacy, individualism, nonempirical casuality, stratification of life chances, and so forth, although the similarity is unrecognized or unacknowledged by the modernity-scale authors. Finally, the possible overlap between middle-class values and modern values leads us to include a measure of socioeconomic status in the schedule. This enables us to explore the possibility that the term "modern values" might simply be an alternative label for middle/class values to which most Western social scientists subscribe. In sum, the question is: Are modernity scales indistinguishable from measures of the well-established constructs of anomia, alienation, and socioeconomic status, or are they valid measures of a distinct construct?

Intercorrelations of modernity scales with measures of anomia, general alienation, and socioeconomic status are reported in Table 9.4, along with the average correlation of each modernity scale with the remaining three modernity scales. The anomia correlations are based on wave I data and the alienation correlations on wave II, while socioeconomic-status correlations are reported for both waves I and II. Evidence of the modernity scales' construct validity is provided to the extent that average convergent correlations between modernity scales are high relative to the discriminant correlations with other scales.

Table 9.4   Convergent and Discriminant Validity Coefficients of Modernity
Scales in Uptown Sample

Modernity Scale	Wave I			Wave II		
	Convergence	Discriminance		Convergence	Discriminance	
	Average *r*	Anomia	SES	Average *r*	Alienation	SES
	($\bar{r}$)	(*r*)	(*r*)	($\bar{r}$)	(*r*)	(*r*)
Smith and Inkeles	.52	-.44	.48	.45	-.49	.38
Kahl	.53	-.60	.34	.47	-.62	.31
Schnaiberg	.42	-.43	.36	.36	-.44	.35
Armer	.54	-.52	.39	.40	-.39	.30
N	(156)	(156)	(156)	(109)	(109)	(109)

Comparison of the convergent coefficients with the discriminant coefficients for anomia and socioeconomic status in wave I shows higher discriminant than convergent coefficients for Kahl's and Schnaiberg's scales with anomia (-.60 and -.43) and almost as high discriminant as convergent coefficients for Armer's scale with anomia (-.52) and for Smith and Inkeles's scale with SES (.48). In wave II, all of the modernity-score correlations with alienation were essentially equal to, or higher than, the convergence of modernity scales, and Schnaiberg's scale also had a relatively high correlation with SES.

In short, the evidence suggests rather low discriminant validity in both waves for the four modernity scales, especially with respect to scales of anomia and alienation. In other words, the modernity scales tend to predict scores on anomia, alienation, and, to a lesser extent, socioeconomic status about as well as they predict the other scales of modernity. Conversely, measures of anomia and alienation appear to predict modernity scores almost as well as do the modernity measures. These findings cast serious doubt on the discriminant validity of modernity scales.

Interpretations

Before drawing conclusions about the conceptual or measurement inadequacies of the modernity scales, several alternative interpretations should be considered. Among these are two methodological interpretations involving the possibility of (1) differential attenuation and (2) acquiescent response effects, and two theoretical interpretations involving conceptions of anomia and alienation (1) as components of modernity or (2) as natural concomitants of minority or deviant value-orientations (traditionalism).

Differential-Attenuation Interpretation

The first alternative interpretation is that correlations of modernity scales with anomia, alienation, or SES that are equal to, or higher than, modernity-scale intercorrelations may be a statistical artifact of the higher measurement reliability of these "extraneous" variables. Since the maximum possible observed correlations between any two measures (r_{xy}) is equal to their "true" correlation multiplied by the square root of the product of their reliabilities (i.e., $r_{xy} = r_{T_x T_y}\sqrt{r_{xx}\cdot r_{yy}}$, where the "true" correlation is $r_{T_x T_y}$), the lower reliabilities of modernity scales may attenuate their "true" intercorrelations more than their correlations with anomia and alienation. According to this interpretation, correcting for attenuation due to unreliability of the measures should reveal higher "true" correlations between modernity scales than between modernity and other scales.

The corrected correlations are reported in Table 9.5. Contrary to this possible interpretation, we find essentially the same pattern of correlations as was observed in the uncorrected data in Table 9.4. The changes that do occur tend to indicate even less discriminant validity than in the uncorrected data. For example, Smith and Inkeles's and Schnaiberg's scales show less discrimination from SES, and all of the modernity scales show less discrimination from alienation than was observed in the uncorrected correlations. In short, the differential attenuation interpretation is not supported by the available evidence.

Acquiescent-Response Interpretation

The fact that anomia and alienation show such high correlations with modernity, especially with Kahl's Modernity Scale, suggests an acquiescent response

Table 9.5   Convergent and Discriminant Validity Coefficients of Modernity
Scales in Uptown Sample (Corrected for Attenuation)

Modernity Scale	Wave I			Wave II		
	Convergence	Discriminance		Convergence	Discriminance	
	Average *r*	Anomia	SES	Average *r*	Alienation	SES
	(*r̄*)	(*r*)	(*r*)	(*r̄*)	(*r*)	(*r*)
Smith and Inkeles	.79	-.67	.81	.78	-.86	.69
Kahl	.77	-.85	.53	.71	-.90	.46
Schnaiberg	.63	-.65	.61	.62	-.77	.63
Armer	.87	-.84	.71	.66	-.67	.53
N	(156)	(156)	(156)	(109)	(109)	(109)

interpretation. Each of the scales, and especially Kahl's, included items with agree-disagree, yes-no, and similar response alternatives, and it is well known that such items are particularly susceptible to acquiescent response bias. In addition, the direction in which the items are worded is nearly constant in Kahl's scale and in the anomia and alienation scales. Thus, the relatively high discriminant correlations could result in part from an acquiescent response effect. The need to test for response-set effects in the validation of scales has been frequently emphasized (e.g., Campbell, 1960).

In order to test this interpretation, a measure of acquiescent response pattern was constructed on the basis of discrepancies between responses to forward and reversed statements of the eight items in Kahl's Modernity II Scale. Those respondents identified as having acquiescent response patterns were eliminated, and the correlations between modernity scales and the other constructs were subsequently reexamined for the subsample of nonacquiescent respondents (see Table 9.6).

The evidence in Table 9.6 indicates that the pattern and approximate magnitude of correlations for the total sample persists for the nonacquiescent subsample. The major change is a decrease between .04 to .09 points in the convergent correlations of wave II modernity scales. This decrease has the effect of increasing the evidence of low construct validity for wave II data. The results clearly do not support an explanation of the lack of discriminance between scales of modernity and other constructs by attributing it to acquiescent response patterns.

Components-of-Modernity Interpretation

A third possible interpretation of the relatively high correlations of modernity with anomia, alienation, and SES is that these constructs should rightfully be considered as additional components of the general construct of modernity. Modernity is perhaps a broader construct than was conceived in earlier research and should include these constructs as an integral part.

Table 9.6   Convergent and Discriminant Validity Coefficients of Modernity
Scales in Uptown Sample (Nonacquiescent Subsample)

Modernity Scale	Wave I			Wave II		
	Convergence	Discriminance		Convergence	Discriminance	
	Average *r*	Anomia	SES	Average *r*	Alienation	SES
	$(\bar{r})$	(r)	(r)	$(\bar{r})$	(r)	$(\bar{r})$
Smith and Inkeles	.51	-.44	.48	.40	-.49	.32
Kahl	.51	-.60	.33	.43	-.63	.31
Schnaiberg	.40	-.40	.36	.28	-.41	.30
Armer	.51	-.47	.39	.31	-.32	.25
N	(141)	(141)	(141)	(101)	101)	(101)

If this interpretation is viable, we would expect these new components to behave like the modernity components explicitly recognized in the literature—that is, to correlate with general modernity at about the same level as do other components. In Table 9.7, Kahl's Modernity I Scale is correlated with each of Kahl's component subscales and with the anomia and alienation scales. The results show that Kahl's subscale-to-scale corrected correlations (.20 to .65) are generally lower than the correlations of anomia and alienation with the total scale (-.60 and -.62, respectively). Thus, anomia and alienation tend to correlate *higher* with general modernity than do the subscales of modernity themselves.

Table 9.7 also reports the modernity subscale correlations with anomia, alienation, and socioeconomic status. Surprisingly, the modernity subscales (with the exception of "community stratification" and "urban preference") tend to correlate as highly with the constructs of anomia (-.22 to -.51) and alienation (-.30 to -.50) as they do with the construct of general modernity.

The results are repeated in the case of Armer's scales and subscales (wave I subscale-to-scale *r*'s = .05 to .36, wave II subscale-to-scale *r*'s = .10 to .44, subscale-to-anomia *r*'s = -.11 to -.55, and subscale-to-alienation *r*'s = -.09 to -.38). The subscale-to-scale correlation analysis is not repeated for Smith and Inkeles's scale or for Schnaiberg's scale because item-selection on the basis of subscale measurement was not employed in constructing these scales. However, it is possible to examine Smith and Inkeles's average *item*-to-scale correlations (corrected for part-whole effects) for wave I (.28) and for wave II (.22), compared to average correlations of their modernity items to the anomia scale

(-.22) and to the alienation scale (-.23). For Schnaiberg's scale the average item-to-scale correlation (corrected) is .22 for both wave I and II, compared to average correlations of his modernity items to the anomia scale of -.18 and to the alienation scale of -.17.

Table 9.7   Correlation of Subscales with Kahl's Modernity I, Anomia, Alienation, and Socioeconomic Status (Corrected for Part-Whole Effects).

Subscale	Wave I			Wave II		
	Modernity I	Anomia	SES	Modernity I	Alienation	SES
Mass-media participation	.20	-.25	.21	.28	-.41	.22
Activism	.46	-.51	.24	.55	-.50	.18
Stratification of life chances	.46	-.50	.35	.56	-.45	.30
Community stratification	.53	-.41	.16	.65	-.45	.25
Urban preference	.48	-.26	.22	.58	-.34	.28
Independence from family	.30	-.22	.00	.28	-.30	.04
Anomia	-.60					
Alienation				-.62		
N	(156)	(156)	(156)	(109)	(109)	(109)

Clearly, anomia and alienation do not "behave" like other modernity components, and some of the components and items of the modernity scales appear more closely associated with anomia or alienation than with modernity. The evidence does not support the argument that low discriminant validity results from the fact that anomia and alienation are components of modernity.

Traditionalism-as-Deviance Interpretation

A fourth possible interpretation is very similar to that made by Harrington (1962): To be traditional (poor) in a society where most people are traditional (poor) is very different than being traditional (poor) in a society where most people are modern (rich). In terms of our study, it could be argued that the relatively high correlations of alienation and anomia with traditionalism are a function of the fact that the "traditional man" in contemporary America is a social deviant and is therefore more likely to be both alienated and anomic. This interpretation focuses on the distribution of modernity (and related social and economic characteristics) within the society and might be termed the "compositional effect of societal complexity," or the "distributional effect." It presupposes that we would *not* find such high correlations with anomia and alienation in the original studies, or if we did, they would have occurred because there were modernizing trends and aspirations in these transitional societies strong enough for a high proportion of the traditional population to be already anomic and alienated (see, e.g., Kardiner's discussion, 1967:184, and Armer's, 1970, interpretation of psychological malaise among less-educated Nigerian youth).

Unfortunately this problem is often defined away in modernity studies through devices like the use of variable cutting points (for dichotomization of items into "modern" and "traditional" poles) from one society or sample to another (Smith and Inkeles, 1966). Or the issue is simply ignored or sidestepped by failure to examine the consequences of drawing nonprobability and very unrepresentative samples (vis-à-vis the total population of the society), consequences that are both substantive *and* statistical (Schnaiberg, 1968:Chap. 4, and 1970b). Research designs themselves may be restricting the field of interpretation in that all studies have consistently undersampled rural and traditional populations and thus failed to consider that a high proportion of the *society* studied is traditional (if divided using the same cutting points as for the sample).

The principal limitation of this interpretation for our present purposes is that it does not adequately explain why the several modernity scales tend to correlate *higher* with alienation and anomia than with each other (i.e., why they show low discriminant validity). Even if we accept the argument that being traditional in a society where most people are modern contributes to individual anomia and alienation, the correlation between separate measures of the *same* general construct (modernity) should be higher than their correlations with scales of other, presumably distinct constructs (anomia and alienation). This situation is obviously not the case in the present data, and the findings cannot be accounted for solely in terms of compositional or distributional effects, although replication is needed in other settings.

Discussion and Conclusions

The evidence and interpretation presented above pose serious problems for those engaged in research on individual modernity. What are we to conclude? Is individual modernity a meaningful concept or a myth? In this connection, it is worth remembering that all of the scales have undergone extensive pretesting, refinement, and research use. They are among the least complicated, most widely applicable scales of individual modernity proposed in the literature. Why should a set of measurements emerging from such careful and systematic statistical and theoretical screening raise the specter of invalidity?

Some may protest that the *real* myth is in the adequacy of the present analysis. It may be argued that the present findings are artifactual—a product of our research site in an urban-industrial society or of our measures and techniques of analysis. Let us consider these matters.

As to the site of the research, both Smith and Inkeles (1966) and Kahl (1968) indicate that their measures would be appropriate for use in industrial societies, and Kahl has so used his measure (Kahl, 1968:50). Indeed, the distributions for our replicated measures in Uptown are fairly similar to those in the original studies; we do have somewhat more "modern" response patterns overall, as would be expected in a Western urban-industrial area, but the gradation of scores is quite comparable to the gradations in the original studies. What we clearly do *not* find is that "individual modernity," whatever it may be, is a quality that is "required of the citizens of modern societies" (Inkeles, 1966:150).

With respect to our measures of modernity, we have attempted to replicate the original modernity scales as closely as possible and have omitted only items that did not appear viable across cultures. For example, those items that failed to appear significant in *both* Kahl's Mexican and Brazilian studies were dropped, as were some of the culturally specific "production-consumption" and "religiosity" items of Schnaiberg's scale. Furthermore, we have used the same scale-construction techniques as in the original research, even to the point of replicating factor loadings or weights in appropriate scales. In addition to these efforts toward faithful replication, we have considered extraneous, but contaminating, factors such as acquiescence bias, something that few of the original studies attempted to examine or control.

Thus, we feel confident that the measures and techniques are almost as close a replication of the original methods as, for example, each of the six studies of Smith and Inkeles's project represent vis-à-vis each other or, alternatively, as close as Kahl's Brazil and Mexico studies. To the best of our knowledge, then, while acknowledging the incompleteness of our data and preliminary analysis, we do not find the "myth" of modernity in our research setting or replication methods.

Where does the problem lie, then? What is "modernity"—a construct with inadequate empirical delineation; a social psychological chimera; part of a broad, important, but as yet ill-defined, set of orientations; or what? It is important to repeat that this paper is primarily concerned with the adequacy of scales as measures of the modernity construct, not with the adequacy of the construct of modernity as determined by the confirmation of theoretically predicted correlations with measures of other constructs. Discriminant validity requires that "measures of the same trait should correlate higher with each other than they do with measures of different traits" (Campbell and Fiske, 1959:104). Clearly, all four modernity scales in their present form fail to provide statistically valid measures of individual modernity among Uptown residents, and hence the universal value of the scales is questionable.[3] It may be possible to improve the scales through various operations, but this possibility does not change the fact that the scales are not demonstrably valid measures in the form in which they have been proposed. At best, the *concept* of individual modernity may be meaningful as a distinct concept, but the *measurement* of modernity has apparently been unsuccessful. At worst, the notion of individual modernity as a distinct set of orientations may be a myth, at least for some populations. It should be noted that the findings do not necessarily indicate that modernity scales are universally invalid, just as the previous studies do not show them to be universally valid. Clearly what is needed is further evaluation of the modernity scales in other settings in order to specify and refine them insofar as possible, which is the goal of validity assessment.

Thus, we are left with the final conclusion in doubt: either "modernity" *does* have a distinct empirical reality, which present measures have *not* adequately captured, or there is *no* distinctive universal concept of modernity that exists, save in the minds of social scientists. Regardless of which position one takes, the notion that social science has been able to develop a universally valid measure of modernity appears to be false.

Notes

1. The research reported in this paper is supported by grants from the U.S. Public Health Service (HD 04977), CENFINN, Indiana University, and the Center for Urban Affairs, Northwestern University.

2. There have been several recent reformulations of the Campbell and Fiske approach (Jackson, 1969; Jöreskog, 1968, 1969), but these are generally variations in statistical manipulation rather than changes in the basic structure of the initial argument. The only sociological applications of the model that we are aware of are Summers and associates (1970) and Althauser and associates (1971).

3. A recent fundamental critique of the Campbell and Fiske model (Althauser and Heberlein, 1970; Althauser et al., 1971) poses some troublesome questions about interpretation of the discriminant and convergent validity coefficients. The central issue is that of correlated error, or common "methods effects" across scales that are being evaluated. In terms of our findings, however, there appears to be less ambiguity, since the critique appears most applicable to cases in which the measures *do* indeed show construct validity; that is, Althauser and associates (1971) are more concerned that the initial model *over*estimates construct validity. Furthermore, in testing for the effects of acquiescence, as we do, we have in fact incorporated some of the recent critique, treating acquiescence as just such a common "methods factor" and separating out its effects from the evaluation of the scale validities. Interestingly enough, our results are in the direction indicated by the Althauser and Heberlein critique, since the modernity scales' lack of construct validity is even more apparent when we analyze the nonacquiescent subsample.

References

Althauser, Robert P., and T. A. Heberlein.

1970   Validity and the multitrait-multimethod matrix. In E. F. Borgatta and G. W. Bohrnstedt (Eds.), *Sociological Methodology 1970.* San Francisco: Jossey-Bass. Pp. 151-169.

Althauser, R. P., T. A. Heberlein, and R. A. Scott.

1971 A causal assessment of validity: the augmented multitrait-multimethod matrix. In H. M. Blalock, Jr. (Ed.), *Causal Models in the Social Sciences.* Chicago: Aldine. Pp. 374-399.

Armer, Michael.

1970 Formal education and psychological malaise in an African society. *Sociology of Education,* 43 (Spring):143-158.

Armer, Michael, and Robert Youtz.

1971 Formal education and individual modernity in an African society. *American Journal of Sociology,* 74 (January):604-626.

Bendix, Reinhard.

1967 Tradition and modernity reconsidered. *Comparative Studies in Society and History,* 9, no. 3:292-346.

Blumer, Herbert.

1964 Industrialization and the traditional order. *Sociology and Social Research,* 48 (October):129-138.

Bohrnstedt, George.

1970 Reliability and validity assessment in attitude measurement. In G. Summers (Ed.), *Attitude Measurement.* Chicago: Rand McNally. Pp. 80-99.

Campbell, Donald T.

1960 Recommendations for APA test standards regarding construct, trait or discriminant validity. *American Psychologist,* 15 (August):546-553.

Campbell, Donald T., and D. W. Fiske.

1959 Convergent and discriminant validation by the multitrait-multimethod matrix. *Psychological Bulletin,* 56 (March):81-105.

Dawson, J. L. M.

1967 Traditional versus Western attitudes in Africa: the construction, validation and application of a measuring device. *British Journal of Social and Clinical Psychology,* 6, no. 2:81-96.

Doob, Leonard.

    1960   *Becoming More Civilized.* New Haven, Conn.: Yale University Press.

    1967   Scales for assaying psychological modernization in Africa. *Public Opinion Quarterly,* 31 (Fall):414-421.

Feldman, Arnold S., and Christopher Hurn.

    1966   The experience of modernization. *Sociometry,* 29 (December):378-395.

Feldman, Arnold S., and John Kendrick.

    1968   The experience of change in Puerto Rico. *Howard Law Journal,* 15 (Fall):28-46.

Frank, Andre G.

    1967   Sociology of development and underdevelopment of sociology. *Catalyst,* No. 5 (Summer):20-73.

Frey, Frederick W.

    1970   Cross-cultural survey research in political science. In R. Holt and J. Turner (Eds.), *The Methodology of Comparative Research.* New York: Free Press. Pp. 173-294.

Gusfield, Joseph.

    1967   Tradition and modernity: misplaced polarities in the study of social change. *American Journal of Sociology,* 72 (January):351-362.

Harrington, Michael.

    1962   *The Other America: Poverty in the United States.* New York: Macmillan.

Horowitz, Irving L.

    1970   Personality and structural dimensions in comparative international development. *Social Science Quarterly,* 51 (December):494-513.

Hyman, Herbert H.

    1964   Research design. In Robert E. Ward (Ed.), *Studying Politics Abroad: Field Research in the Developing Areas.* Boston: Little, Brown. Pp. 153-188.

Illich, Ivan.

1969   Outwitting the "developed" countries. *New York Review of Books*, November 6, pp. 20-24.

Inkeles, Alex.

1960   Industrial man: the relation of status to experience, perception, and value. *American Journal of Sociology*, 66 (July):1-31.

1966   The modernization of man. In M. Weiner (Ed.), *Modernization*. New York: Basic Books. Pp. 138-150.

1969a   A commentary on "Is everyone going modern?" *American Journal of Sociology*, 75 (July):146-151.

1969b   Making men modern. *American Journal of Sociology*, 75 (September):208-225.

1970   Reply. *American Political Science Review*, 64 (June):593.

Jackson, Douglas N.

1969   Multimethod factor analysis in the evaluation of convergent and discriminant validity. *Psychological Bulletin*, 72 (July):30-49.

Jacobson, Barbara, and John Kendrick.

1970   Education: social fact or social process? *American Behavioral Scientist*, 14 (December):255-272.

Jöreskog, K. G.

1968   Statistical models for congeneric test scores. In *Proceedings*, 76th Convention, American Psychological Association. Washington, D.C.: APA. Pp. 213-214.

1969   A general method for analysis of covariance structures with applications. *Research Bulletin 69-47*. Princeton, N.J.:Educational Testing Service.

Kahl, Joseph A.

1968   *The Measurement of Modernism: A Study of Values in Brazil and Mexico*. Austin: University of Texas.

Kardiner, Abram.

1967   Models for the study of collapse of social homeostasis in a society. In S. Z. Klausner (Ed.), *The Study of Total Societies*. Garden City: Anchor. Pp. 177-190.

Lambert, Richard D.

 1964 Comment: comparativists and uniquists. In William T. de Bary and Ainslie T. Embree (Eds.), *Approaches to Asian Civilizations.* New York: Columbia University Press. Pp. 240-245.

Middleton, Russell.

 1963 Alienation, race and education. *American Sociological Review,* 28 (December):973-977.

Moore, Wilbert.

 1965 *The Impact of Industry.* Englewood Cliffs, N.J.: Prentice-Hall.

O'Connell, James.

 1965 The concept of modernization. *South Atlantic Quarterly,* 64 (Autumn): 549-564.

Peshkin, Alan, and Ronald Cohen.

 1967 The values of modernization. *Journal of Developing Areas,* 2 (October):7-22.

Robinson, John P., J. G. Rusk, and Kendra Head.

 1968 *Measures of Political Attitudes.* Ann Arbor, Mich.: Institute for Social Research, The University of Michigan.

Schnaiberg, Allan.

 1968 Some determinants and consequences of modernism in Turkey. Unpublished Ph.D. dissertation, University of Michigan.

 1970a Rural-urban residence and modernism: a study of Ankara Province, Turkey. *Demography,* 7 (1):71-85.

 1970b Measuring modernism: theoretical and empirical explorations. *American Journal of Sociology,* 76 (November):399-425.

 1971 The modernizing impact of urbanization: a causal analysis. *Economic Development and Cultural Change,* 20 (October):80-104.

Smith, David H., and Alex Inkeles.

 1966 The OM Scale: a comparative socio-psychological measure of individual modernity. *Sociometry,* 29 (December):353-377.

Srole, Leo.

    1956   Social integration and certain corollaries: an exploratory study. *American Sociological Review,* 21 (December):709-716.

Stephenson, John B.

    1968   Is everyone going modern? A critique and a suggestion for measuring modernism. *American Journal of Sociology,* 74 (November):265-275.

Summers, Gene F., L. H. Seiler, and G. Wiley.

    1970   Validation of reputational leadership by the multitrait-multi-method matrix. In E. F. Borgatta and G. W. Bohrnstedt (Eds.), *Sociological Methodology,* 1970. San Francisco: Jossey-Bass. Pp. 170-181.

Discussion

Mr. Waisanen. The Armer and Schnaiberg paper as it grapples with conceptual analysis is good and important, but like all such papers in this fledgling stage of behavioral science, it produces some discontent. Many of us are interested in "modernity" as a state and in modernization as a process at either the individual or social structural levels. But there are many also who are puzzled, wary, and disenchanted with the term.

My own doubts have been strong enough to produce occasional thoughts that the concept may be so fuzzy and culture-bound as to be beyond reclamation. But so far I have continued, perhaps unwisely, to shove such thoughts aside. For I perceive in the literature of sociology and social psychology other concepts, like intelligence, stratification, integration, identification, and power, with similar conceptual fuzziness.

While Armer and Schnaiberg give us reasons to question the modernity concept, we should also note that they give us some reason to see promise in it. First, the interscale correlations among the four scales that were used [in Table 9.2], when corrected for attenuation, range from .57 to .97. Second, the test-retest reliability coefficients [Table 9.3] range from .66 to .81. Third, there is reason to assume some predictive power in the variable. The correlation coefficients between the several scales and the amonia and alienation measures [Table 9.5] range from -.65 to -.90. Of course, we can always ask questions about correlation values of this kind, but within the traditional mode of assessing a concept's viability, the measures of interscale association, reliability, and predictive power are strong.

The interesting question asked by Armer and Schnaiberg points to the negative relationship between modernity and alienation. One of the most significant subdimensions of alienation, according to Seeman [1959] and to a large amount of research that has been done on alienation, is the dimension of powerlessness. The modernity-alienation relationship may be telling us that there is, indeed, a relationship between these various modernity scales and a condition of self-perceived purpose or influence which is the other side of the alienation concept and is consistent with the negative correlations. In that case, self-perceived influence *is* a part of that behavioral configuration, that cognitive style which is modernity.

Mr. Armer. Let me briefly review the objectives of our paper and its relationship to Waisanen's comments. Essentially, its purpose was to assess the utility of a particular variable which is frequently found in comparative research—namely, individual modernity. The strategy we followed was, first, to examine the performance of various measures of that variable in the U.S. in comparison with use of the same measures in earlier studies in developing areas of the world. In addition, we attempted to assess the measurement reliability of the modernity scales plus their convergent and discriminant validity. The assessment of discriminant validity is based on the assumption that, for a variable to be viable or useful, it should measure whatever construct it was intended to measure better than it measures ostensibly different constructs. There is a fundamental notion here, which has been well presented by Campbell [1960; also Campbell and Fiske, 1959] in his papers on convergent and discriminant validity, that a measure of a construct should show higher correlations with other measures of the *same* construct than with measures of presumably distinct constructs already in use.

In our paper, as Fred Waisanen has accurately indicated, the scales of modernity do indeed show reasonably high coefficients of reliability, reasonably high coefficients of convergence with other measures of modernity, and reasonably high coefficients of correlation with other constructs such as anomia, alienation, and SES. But the critical point is that the correlations with these last three supposedly distinct constructs were approximately as high, if not higher, than were the intercorrelations among the modernity scales themselves.

He is absolutely correct in suggesting that, and I think I quote him here correctly, "within the traditional mode of assessing" the utility of measures, these measures of modernity perform quite well. I would suggest, though, that the "traditional mode" does not provide a very adequate test of the utility of these measures and that what needs to be done and what we have attempted to do is to test the extent to which measures of modernity discriminate themselves from measures of other variables. We find the modernity measures lacking in this regard and, therefore, lacking as measures of the concepts they are intended to measure.

Our conclusion from this finding is not that there is no such thing as modernity; we allow for the possibility that there may be something called modernity but argue that it hasn't yet been adequately measured. That's why we (lispingly) call the measurement results a "near myth." The evidence we have found should *not* lead one to gain confidence in the measurement of modernity; indeed, the evidence is quite to the contrary and, at least for Schnaiberg and myself, quite devastating. All of the scales performed in such a way as to *undermine* confidence in these measures of this particular construct.

Now with regard to the association of these measures with alienation, Waisanen pointed out the similarity between the powerlessness dimension of alienation and the notion of low self-perceived influence or lack of personal efficacy which is frequently involved in modernity scales. Indeed, it was that very similarity which we noted and which led us to suspect that there might be some confusion between these variables.

One would think, if anomia or alienation were really components of the modernity construct, that they would perform much like the other components. However Table 9.7 shows anomia and alienation correlated with Kahl's Modernity I Scale at approximately .6, while the stated components of modernity all have much *lower* correlations with Kahl's modernity scale. Indeed, these subscales of Kahl's Modernity I Scale correlate *higher* with anomia and alienation than they do with the Modernity I Scale itself when corrected for part-whole effects.

These findings suggest that alienation is *not* a component of modernity. Indeed, it appears as if the components of modernity really predict alienation scores better than they measure modernity. Perhaps these modernity scales are simply alternative measures of alienation or of other constructs.

The conclusion which we reach in the paper is that the presently available measures, which are being rapidly introduced into comparative research, are measures about which one should have some very strong reservations pending further evidence of their worth. And that goes for our own as well as for the other scales.

Mr. Schnaiberg. I am interested in the reluctance of many social scientists to view the concept of modernity critically. It seems to me that this reluctance is part of what Andre Gunder Frank [1967] talks about at great length in his attempt to point out the simplistic evolutionist and/or diffusionist approaches underlying the study of social and economic development, etc. It is widely assumed that there is an evolutionary sequence leading to ultimate convergence and that the resulting convergence will be modern man and modern institutions. Moreover, often by our behavior as social scientists and/or technical advisors to underdeveloped areas, we act as if it is inevitable that modernity will result as an end state and that modernity is a desirable goal which we should facilitate.

Mr. Portes.   I have reactions to the Armer and Schnaiberg paper. First, their findings of very high correlations between modernity and alienation and anomia are suggestive for the sociology of knowledge. All of these scales for measuring different theoretical concepts have been constructed by American, or at least Western, social scientists, and implicit in all of them is a good pole and a bad pole: It is better to be nonalienated than alienated, nonanomic than anomic, and modern rather than traditional.

This goodness of one pole and badness of another may well account for the similarities. I suggest, as an interpretation of the high corelation found by Armer and Schnaiberg, that perhaps what all of these scales are measuring at a more general level is some aspects of our own minds.

The second point is that individual modernity is perceived as a facilitator or concomitant of social-economic development at the societal level. This relationship seems to be the ultimate reason for our concern with the issue of modernity. We assume that a change in the way men think and behave will have some sort of bearing on the likelihood of their becoming incorporated into the affairs of the world: The greater the modernity of a population, the greater the development of its society. Thus the more similarly people in a nation think and act to people in Western societies, the greater is the likelihood that that nation will become a member of the First or Second World in an economic sense. The relationships between modernity at the individual level and at the collective level, between population and development, though, are problematic. It is quite possible that a compartmentalization or a mixture of tradition and modernity would facilitate development more efficiently than pure modernity.

Mr. Schnaiberg.   To use Herbert Hyman's [1964] terms, I think we often engage in pseudocomparative analysis when we contrast underdeveloped societies with developed societies like our own. We talk as if we were ignorant of all the problems in our own developed society, as if there were perfect integration of all the institutional sectors in our own society. For example, we talk about education without mentioning the pervasive class biases in present-day American education. One way or another we are all aware of these biases, yet we don't consider them in our comparative research. We suddenly forget our theories of integration and rationality when we switch to analysis of underdeveloped areas. They get our cast-off theories and methods and our cast-off ideal-typical approach to the analysis of social development. I think that situation is very much in error.

Mr. Form.   The criticism I have of all discussion of modernism really boils down to the assertion that this concept is value-laden; the developed world is trying to impose something on the Third World. And yet there is economic change occurring all over the world. Something is going on that social scientists are trying to describe and explain. Somebody calls it "modernism." Now you may not like that term because it is kind of an imperialistic concept, yet the kind of change that is going on needs to be labeled something. I'd like to see the discussion move from the ideological tag on a particular kind of concept to analysis of what is really going on. If you think there is imperialistic development, a movement of rising class consciousness, or something else that seems to be happening universally in these countries, let's get at it. Let's get some measures and start working on those kinds of things.

Mr. Armer.   I am concerned with the direction that this discussion has taken. We're starting to discuss substantive issues rather than sticking with methodological problems in comparative research. Modernity happens to be a fairly popular variable and has been measured with some degree of sophistication in comparative research. But our paper could have dealt with any variable. I think the important point for this conference is that we social scientists may be using many concepts in comparative research which have similar kinds of methodological problems. These concepts may be confused on a conceptual level, or there may be measurement problems such as those that we have begun to illustrate in connection with the concept of modernity.

Another point that this paper illustrates is that many measures like modernity have been developed or tested largely in non-Western, nonindustrial nations. The modernity variable, for example, has really not had a chance to be examined in a truly comparative perspective. Except in the few instances mentioned in the paper, it hasn't been tested in nations at greatly different levels of socioeconomic development.

This situation reminds me of Herbert Hyman's [1964] critique of the pseudocomparativist methodology. In much of our comparative research we go to other countries, examine the structural characteristics there at either a sociocultural level or psychological level, and make pseudo-comparisons with what we "know" to be the case, or think we know to be the case, in more advanced or urban industrial societies. These comparisons are nothing more than pseudocomparisons, and they may often be invalid.

What this paper represents is an attempt to come back to an urban industrial society and try out these measures, which presumably have cross-cultural utility but which have been developed from a restricted set of societies. Before any clear-cut statements can be made about the utility of these and other scales, we should repeat this kind of research in other nations at different levels of development or in different types of nations.

Mr. Haller. I would like to take advantage of the opening that Armer has just given us and look at psychological modernity and similar kinds of concepts from the other end of the spectrum. It happens that there are almost no test-retest checks on these key, sociopsychological constructs for genuinely illiterate, rural, isolated populations.

Two or three years ago, a couple of us did a survey in such an isolated area of rural Brazil that 50 percent of the population had not been in any kind of school at all. The highest level of education within our sample of 500 or so randomly selected household heads was five years. Within that group, we ran test-retest checks on our various indices. Some were objective indices, loosely speaking, and some were subjective. We had some indices which you would expect to be relatively durable and some that people familiar with the local culture would normally expect to change very rapidly.

The long and short of it is that the subjective sociopsychological constructs of anomia, psychological modernity, alienation, and even aspiration for children had test-retest correlations which were abominably low. They were so low that we concluded that these variabilities were completely indefensible in this kind of situation. This indefensibility is attributable neither to sloppy data-gathering procedure nor to a general lack of test-retest reliability in the variables taken as a total set. The more objective types of indices ran up test-retest reliability as high as 1.0, usually in the area of .90.

Mr. Schnaiberg. Would you perceive that if a factory of some kind were opened tomorrow, members of that community would be able to participate effectively, punch their clocks and maintain a viable economic enterprise, given a relatively short, one or two-month, training period in the skills required to participate?

Mr. Haller. I wouldn't be surprised. I don't know for certain, obviously, but probably they could.

Mr. Stryker. I am interested in Schnaiberg's question regarding whether the people could handle the introduction of a factory. That question and others have been raised as part of an approach to studying this phenomenon of modernity at the general population level. But what is important from the viewpoint of the social psychology of modernization is not what the general population may be like on this dimension but rather what potentially key personnel are going to be like. Who are the people who will manage the factories? Who are the political elites in these societies? Who are the potential decision-makers? What are *they* like?

It seems to me that there is a tendency to ignore what we know about the social structure in which these people exist and within which the social psychological variables presumably must operate.

Mr. Haller.   One of the underlying notions in this whole debate over psychological modernity is whether a potential large-scale labor force *can respond* to the elite leadership that might be provided through factories and bureaucracies and what not.

Mr. Miller.   Armer and Schnaiberg have been willing to say that modernity does not show validity on the ground that the modernity measures tend to predict scores on anomia, alienation, and, to a lesser extent, socio-economic status about as well as they predict other measures of modernity. They claim that these findings cast serious doubt on the validity of the modernity scale.

But have they used a hard variable? I suspect they would answer, "Yes, we used socioeconomic status." But one wonders, and I hope they agonize over the question of whether they really used validating criteria such that we could conclude that a sound knockdown of modernity had occurred. What about behavioral characteristics? Why don't we have some hard data on behavior that represents the modernity concept? I am not ready to jettison a concept whose invalidity has not yet been demonstrated to me.

Mr. Schnaiberg.   Miller has raised an issue about the use of behavioral measures of modernity. I don't know exactly what you are talking about, but let me call to your attention that my measure, based on Turkish data, is largely a behavorial measure, and both Kahl's and Smith and Inkeles's scales include behavioral items.

Mr. Waisanen.   As a clarification of some of my observations on the Armer-Schnaiberg paper, I do not want to be associated with a position which defines this effort as an effort to knock down the *concept* of modernity. They have quite correctly, and better than any other source I know, questioned the adequacy of the *scales* that are presently available and commonly used.

Clearly their purpose is an important one. It does not knock down the notion of some kind of individual change associated with societal change, whether this change be labeled modernity or something else, but it does charge us to look now at the concept's theoretical underpinning and to reexamine the appropriate indicators for that concept. Without that kind of work, the concept is not viable. With that kind of work, though, it may be.

References

Campbell, Donald T.

1960   Recommendations for APA test standards regarding construct, trait or discriminant validity. *American Psychologist,* 15 (August):546-553.

Campbell, Donald T., and D. W. Fiske.

1959   Convergent and discriminant validation by the multitrait-multi-method matrix. *Psychological Bulletin,* 56 (March):81-105.

Frank, Andre G.

1967   Sociology of development and underdevelopment of sociology. *Catalyst,* No. 5 (Summer):20-73.

Hyman, Herbert H.

1964   Research design. In Robert E. Ward (Ed.), *Studying Politics Abroad: Field Research in the Developing Areas.* Boston: Little, Brown. Pp. 153-188.

Seeman, Melvin.

1959   On the meaning of alienation. *American Sociological Review,* 24 (December):783-791.

PART FOUR

Comparative Applications of Qualitative Methods

The Sociological Relevance of History: A Footnote to Research on Legal Control in South Africa

AUSTIN T. TURK

Indiana University

Introduction

In all legal systems the terms of legal discourse and the forms of legal organization are characterized by a heavy emphasis upon their antiquity, or at least their derivation from, and compatibility with, the conceptual and organizational models used when the foundations of social order were poured. Thus, the theoretical-methodological relevance of history is a problem soon and frequently met in the sociology of law; and considerable energy has been spent in efforts to solve that problem or to demonstrate that there is no problem to be solved. Sociologists have long tended to emphasize the "dependency" of law *in* social context (Stone, 1966: 470-545), to view legal conceptions, organizations, and processes as subordinate, correlative, or even epiphenomenal aspects of social reality. In recent years there has been a renewed interest in law *as* social context, capable of determining or affecting other social phenomena—whether by its special efficacy in the regulation and facilitation of social interaction (Selznick, 1968,1969; Schwartz and Skolnick, 1970) or by its special qualities as a weapon in social conflict (Dahrendorf, 1967, 1968; Turk, 1969, 1970, 1972). To the extent that law is considered a dependent phenomenon, the historicity of law appears to be taken pretty much for granted—either respectfully as intrinsic to the definition of law (majestic institutions and noble traditions) or disrespectfully as merely part of the camouflage hiding the realities of power and domination. Emphasis upon the causal significance of law leads to a more direct confrontation with its historicity—its real and its putative historical dimensions—as perhaps a contributor to its causal impact. Evan (1965:289), for instance, has suggested that a necessary condition for legal change to promote social change is that "the rationale of a new law clarify its continuity and compatibility with existing institutionalized values."

One way to treat the problem of assessing the causal significance of law's historicity is to investigate the functions of legal symbolism, as Thurman Arnold (1935) has done. Law's historicity is narrowly construed as imagery, serving to promote acceptance of the current realities of legal control by giving them the appearance (never fully the truth) of enduring, reliable guarantors that the exigencies and contingencies of social relationships are under control. The elderly trappings of law are viewed as among the necessary fictions that help the law to accomplish its dual task of minimizing and regulating social conflict while encouraging and facilitating social integration.

Arnold's approach, although highly useful, obviously stops short of the problem of determining the causal significance of law's factual historicity as distinct from its putative historicity. Indeed, it can be difficult to distinguish between the real and the putative history of a legal system. Legal historians have not always been able to achieve highly objective accounts, whether because of technical limitations or political constraints, nor have they always wished to be objective. While the emphasis upon law's historicity is often explicable as propaganda, I have encountered more complex interpretive problems in attempting to assess the present significance of the past for the sociological analysis of legal control in South Africa (Turk, 1970). For example, Arnold's emphasis upon law as symbolism encourages too facile an analysis of legal discourse and reasoning as merely hypocritical, even Machiavellian, devices without subjective import for those who have legal authority. As a methodological footnote to the South Africa study, this paper aims to clarify and amplify the working solutions that were sketched and illustrated in my earlier effort.[1]

Few sociologists will deny the importance of historical scholarship; but the relative lack of professional investment (e.g., degrees, doctoral minors, listed special interests, research publications) in the study and use of historical materials indicates that few have developed more specific understandings of how and why history is relevant and usable in sociological work. A more specific understanding is sought in the following comments on historical explanation and on the sociological relevance and use of historical materials.

Historical Explanation as Scientific Theory

One of the least sensible of the metatheoretical discussions that enliven sociological shoptalk is the apparently eternal debate over the relative importance of descriptive, detailed, specific knowledge (read "research") and analytical, abstracted, general knowledge (read "theory"). Clearly, the process by which scientific knowledge is produced involves the creation of both *reality models*—sets of assumptions (expressed as "data") constituting a picture of what some piece of reality may look like and how it may be expected to work—and *theories*—statements specifying at least the conditions associated with the emergence, persistence, and dissipation of such realities and ideally also the (causal) forces bringing about those conditions. Neither aspect of this process can be sloughed; it is not getting the job done either to assert airily that "good description *is* theory" or to proclaim that a division of labor between researchers and theorists is somehow fundamental. The tough chores of explication and specification have to be done *both* ways. Nevertheless, the old argument persists in many forms, one of them being the opposition of caricatures of history to caricatures of sociology.

The historically inclined among sociologists (e.g., Nisbet, 1968:91-104; 1969:251- 304) seem prone to argue that the literature of historical scholarship is richer and more real, concrete, meaningful, informative, and so on than are the products of mid-twentieth-century sociological inquiries, especially those employing quantitative research techniques. The historically inclined sociologists' natural enemies are those generally unscholarly, but highly scientific, colleagues who attempt to set and maintain rigorous methodological standards and tend to ignore historical literature, including that of their own discipline, as prescientific and nonscientific junk. Most sociologists, however, take neither a pro-history nor an anti-history position but politely leave history to the historians, while they themselves get on with sociology. All three positions—positive, negative, and indifferent toward history—help to perpetuate the notion that historical and sociological knowledge are somehow basically different—that historical knowledge is specific, or descriptive, and sociological knowledge more general, or theoretical. This notion, a heritage from old and continuing wars between academic establishments and academic entrepreneurs, has motivated efforts to find essential demarcation lines between history and sociology, history and historical sociology, historical and other sociology, and historical and other kinds of explanation. Such attempts have, from a scientist's perspective, left historical inquiry in a limbo between chronicling and amateur, although stylish, theorizing, on the one hand, and sociological inquiry stunted by the neglect of essential data sources, on the other.

Historians and their philosphical analysts have long sought to pin down what it is that makes historians more than chroniclers. Whether emphasizing artistic, scientific, or political criteria, seemingly all agree that historians selectively organize material. I am unconcerned here with the view that the historian's distinctive reason and aim is artistic expression—a view that Hofstadter (1968:3-19) finds to be a creature of amateurism and aristocracy and a victim of academicism and democracy. I am similarly unconcerned with the view that the historian's proper goal is to achieve political effects, whether on behalf of establishments or of revolutions (Zinn, 1970). I *am* concerned with the view that historians differ from chroniclers in that historiography implies a search for *explanations* as at least ultimate objectives (White, 1965; Lipset and Hofstadter, 1968) and with the scientific nature or relevance of historical explanation.

By now it is clear that the *logic* of "historical" explanation is indistiguishable from that of "scientific" explanation (Nagel, 1961:548-575; Hempel, 1965:231-243; cf. Leff, 1971:66-90). Empirical regularities are demonstrated by controlled observation of human actors and events, by the authentication and content analysis of documents and other artifacts, and by appeals to the opinions and conclusions of conventionally recognized experts and authorities. Having established agreed-upon facts, the seeker of explanations moves on to the task of finding and showing temporal/spatial and/or mathematical (logical) connections among his empirical regularities. Although the demonstration of connections among facts is an extremely difficult and necessary job, such a demonstration of concomitant variation, temporal sequencing, similar mathematical properties, or other associations yields a primitive explanation roughly equivalent to pointing one's finger at a plug in a wall socket, a connecting cord, and an operating switch in order to explain why an electric fan is running. This "actuarial" approach explains empirical regularities by showing connections among them and explaining those connections by showing ever more complex patterns of association (Leff, 1971, seems to believe this kind of explanation to be distinctively historical). Because actuarial explanation does not account for the origin, persistence, and dissolution of the demonstrated association patterns, those who desire or require "better" explanations—who respond to every "how" with a "why"—look for explanatory principles beyond that of association. Invariably, it appears, the principle chosen involves some notion of *causation,* expressed in some language of forces, agencies, processes, or whatever by which things are produced, preserved, altered, destroyed.

Given that in explanation both historians and scientists do essentially the same things—establish empirical regularities, find and demonstrate associations among such regularities, and propose causal explanations of their findings—there is still the relatively uniquist focus of the historian's data collection and analysis coupled with his relatively vague conceptualizations of historical causation. Where the scientist is impatient to get on with the categorization of empirical regularities and emphasizes parsimonious methods for gathering and processing such raw material, the historian relishes the gathering and processing of raw material and emphasizes authenticity rather than parsimony. Where the scientist generates and employs explicit reality models and causal theories, the historian asserts what he has found and what caused what, without much explicit attention to his causal theory beyond perhaps some metatheoretical comments about philosophies of history. Obviously, both historians and scientists vary between these polar stereotypes, and there is overlapping between the two.

Nonetheless, assuming that the modal historian and the modal scientist behave approximately as I have stereotyped them, the view that such behavioral differences are attributable to past and ongoing competitive professionalization and academic politics is still far more defensible than the view (at best a graceful acceptance of the academic status quo) that historians and historical inquiry *must* be different from scientists and scientific inquiry because they have *been* and usually *are* different.

Regardless of whether it is produced by scientists or by historians (according to their credentials, identities, or departmental affiliations), an explanation is the application of a general notion about association/causation to a specific set of facts turned up by an investigator as he tried out his reality model. Either scientists or historians may attempt anything from the exceedingly specific and detailed explanation of a highly specific set of data to the exceedingly general and abstract explanation of a highly refined set of empirical generalizations. And either may by necessity or ignorance wind up confronting very sloppy and ambiguous data with a primitive and unconvincing explanation. In either case, the product should be evaluated with reference to whether the investigator did the best possible job of getting, analyzing (selectively organizing), and explaining his data. Methodological necessity is a legitimate excuse for methodological inadequacies, just as the lack of a pool of explanatory ideas—a history of theorizing about such data as that at hand—is an acceptable excuse for theoretical weaknesses. However, ignorance of available methodological tools developed to overcome the data problems with which the investigator is faced is unacceptable, as is ignorance of relevant explanatory efforts and of logical aids in concept formation and theory construction. All have sinned in some manner and degree, scientists (certainly sociologists) and historians alike; but while both have sinned often out of necessity, the historian has, probably more than the scientist, sinned out of ignorance.

The kind of ignorance I have in mind is the ignorancee of *scientific* methodology, theory construction, and substantive theoretical and empirical literatures. It is this ignorance, produced by the professional and organizational bifurcation of history and science, which has left those historians attempting the determination and explanation of empirical regularities so often vulnerable to the methodological criticisms brought together in Popper's devastating essay on the "poverty of historicism" (Popper, 1957). The "theodicy" and "all-pervasive mysticism"—in addition to the unfamiliarity with relevant literature—lamented by Howard Becker in his appreciative examination of Toynbee's mighty attempt at historical sociology (Becker, 1950:149–154) are indicative of the vague, grandiose, value-loaded, and dogmatic kind of theorizing that has generally been identified as historical explanation, insofar as explanation beyond the actuarial level has been attempted. Recognizing that some historians and scientists have been trying (albeit tactfully) to reduce the scientific ignorance of historians

(Lipset and Hofstadter, 1968; Small, 1970; Landes and Tilly, 1971), I believe that the work of historians will, for the time being, prove more useful to sociologists as a source of data than as a source of explanations. (Contrary to the prejudices of many sociologists, it is not the data of historians that is so highly suspect but rather what historians do with their data.)

Although historians' explanations sometimes provide the germ or even the rough sketch of a scientific explanation, they require an inordinate winnowing relative to their yield. Theoretical, especially causal, explanation is an occupationally hazardous venture for the historian, whose professionalization encourages him to "mistake interpretations for theories" (Popper, 1957) and "unilluminating metaphors" for causal propositions (White, 1965). The historian's professional handicap is that he is not trained to think in terms of *variables*—to perceive specific empirical regularities in terms of how they fit into the categories (the "conceptual variables") of a reality model and how they may thus be made to serve in testing theories addressed to the reality model.[2] Historians are not trained to see that small facts must be promoted into indicators and measures of variables and big ideas broken down into propositions about variables before the theoretical explanatory worth of either the facts or the ideas can be determined. Having concluded that most historians are not yet equipped to make scientific use of their materials, I want now to consider why sociologists in particular need to bother with history and how we can make historical materials usable.

History as Sociological Data

We sociologists need historical data for the same reasons we need comparative social-structural and cross-cultural data: to determine the range of applicability of our reality models and the explanatory power of our theories. Single-society and short-time research resulting in timeless functional tracings of how things are connected have constituted an improvement over vague evolutionist speculations (cf. Barnes, 1948) and archival ethnography and sociography. However, such functionalism has been (and I think clearly is) unable either to generate an adequate scheme for categorizing data from different societies or to proceed from associational to causal explanations. Consideration of the first problem is beyond the scope of this paper (although certainly not of this conference); I will only suggest in passing that Marsh's (1967) commendable attempt to provide a scheme for comparative analysis was not entirely successful, for it demonstrates the functionalist's ability to compare structures relative to his inability to compare processes or even to furnish the kind of studies needed for such comparisons.

Functionalism's inability to handle processes satisfactorily is linked to its inability to produce causal explanations; both weaknesses result from the failure to incorporate historical data systematically into the analysis of contemporary data. The return to evolutionism (Marsh, 1967:322-327; Parsons, 1966) evidences the theoretical bankruptcy of functionalism—looking to the old enemy for help with the problems of movement and change![3] Even the social anthropologists, aware of the same difficulties, seem to be resisting evolutionism in favor of exploring—of course, rather gingerly—alternatives such as conflict theory (Lewis, 1968). Lewis, trying hard to preserve the amenities, at least senses what adding history does to functionalism:

"[The] great value of history for anthropology is that by its very nature and on account of the factual material which it reveals it becomes impossible to sustain any longer the old view of institutions as existing only to maintain the identity of particular structures. Function has meaning and utility less in its *status quo* maintenance aspects than in referring to the actual engagement and interests of people in different roles and positions" (Lewis, 1968:xxiv).

"[To] understand how a given structure works, or rather how it is worked, it seems more profitable to pose our questions in terms of the extent to which the individual's commitment to a given pattern, or set of social relations and obligations serves his interests in a fashion which, in the circumstances, he regards as most advantageous" (Lewis, 1968:xxii).

"[To] understand social change properly, both historically and in its modern setting, and to exploit its theoretical implications, we need to look at institutions less in terms of their contributions to social solidarity at a particular point in time, than in terms of the extent to which they cater for the personal and property security needs of the individual occupants of status positions and of social categories" (Lewis, 1968:xxi).

In effect, Lewis is saying that functional analysis is virtually impossible when historical data are introduced because history points up the struggles of real "people in different roles and positions" to insure the satisfaction of their "personal and property security needs" by what they perceive as the "most advantageous" structuring of "social relations and obligations." Not only is causal analysis impossible without historical data, but the introduction of historical data into the analysis of current empirical regularities (i.e., as "now" instead of "prior stage" data) makes it impossible to avoid causal analysis.

It is, of course, not enough merely to assert that historical data is sociologically necessary because causal analysis is impossible without, and functional analysis impossible with, such data. Many sociologists remain officially unconvinced that causal analysis is either necessary or feasible; some even continue to pretend that there is no such thing as causation. They have the right to demand exposure to a more specific argument for the necessary and causal use of history in sociological analysis. In response, I offer the following propositions as *empirical* generalizations about sociological research:

1. Sociological research establishes *social* regularities and connections among them, *cultural* regularities and connections among them, and connections between the *social* and the *cultural*. The social-cultural distinction is one way of indicating that sociologists study both regularities in human action and interaction and regularities in the symbol-creating and-using concomitant with such action and interaction. Patterns of social behavior, interaction, and interdependence are connected to one another and to patterns of cultural perception and belief, valuation, norming, communication, and affective expression, which are also connected to one another. *Associational* explanations in sociology consist of tracing (mapping) social-social, cultural-cultural, and social-cultural connections.

2. Sociological research asserts explicitly or assumes implicitly the constraining effects upon human behavior of both social and cultural facts. The notion of "constraining effects" is logically equivalent to that of causation, implying that the operation of $a, b, c, \ldots, i$ upon $d, e, f, \ldots, j$ produces $x, y, z, \ldots, k$.

3. *Causal* explanations in sociology consist of statements specifying *how* social and cultural facts constrain, and therefore, produce human behavior. Such statements may emphasize either social or cultural facts as the more fundamental and may then either use the less highly regarded kind of facts as intervening variables or try to ignore them altogether. To the extent that sociological explanations are of human behavior defined in personal and interpersonal terms, sociology offers social (and/or cultural) psychologies alternative or supplementary to other psychologies. To the extent that human behavior is defined in organizational, institutional, societal, or other larger-collectivity terms, sociology offers social sciences alternative or supplementary to other social sciences. Whether the focus is social psychological or social scientific, however, specifications of how social and cultural facts constrain human behavior eventually introduce a *learning* mechanism (socialization, social learning, conditioning, acculturation, enculturation, etc.) by which direct or vicarious exposures to social and cultural facts contribute to behavior patterning.

4. *Learning* is a causal conception of how the operation of prior regularities helps to produce subsequent ones. Whether sociologists are explaining individual, group, or larger-collectivity behavior, some conception of learning—more or less precisely formulated—is used to refer to the causal process that transforms individual, group, or larger-collectivity history into a part of present behavioral reality.

It is unfortunate that the concept of learning is, despite some vague notions about cultural transmission, so closely associated with the study of individual behavior, while history is associated with the study of what goes on within and among larger collectivities, especially polities. "History" is simply the available data on the socialization, learning experiences, social background, reinforcement schedules, and such of larger collectivities, whose defining regularities are the cummulative results of the socialization of many past and contemporary individuals. Regardless of the focus of analysis—individual, group, or larger collectivity—one must know what has been learned in order to explain current, and to predict future, patterns of behavior. Since sociologists conceptualize behavior patterns *as* social and cultural regularities, it turns out that *learning* is the primary causal process by which independent are related to dependent social and cultural regularities.

With varying recognition of an individual's varying capacity to initiate and select as well as receive experiences, we can explain the social and cultural regularities of his behavior as largely, if not entirely, the products of what he has learned—for better or worse—in exposure to, and interaction with, the prior regularities of society and culture. The regularities of a collectivity's behavior are similarly explicable as the products of what the collectivity has learned, if we recognize that collectivity learning is the vector sum of many individuals' learning experiences, perhaps over several generations. Moreover, for collectivities as for individuals, the results of earlier learning become highly significant parts of later learning environments. Individuals singly and collectively define current environmental realities within cultural patterns and behave adaptively or maladaptively vis-a-vis those realities in terms of the social patterns learned in interaction with past realities. Therefore, historical data are essential if we are to explain why people as individuals and as collectivities currently think and act as they do and why—so far as their past behavior has affected their external natural and social environments—their current "ecological" and "foreign relations" (Turk, 1972) environmental realities are what they are. Furthermore, it is only by assuming the continuation of learning that we have a basis for predicting that specific behavior changes, adaptive or maladaptive, will be associated with specified changes in the realities with which people must contend. In conclusion, without historical data there can be no causal *theory* of either social order or social change.

Given that it is necessary to use historical data, there are indeed difficult problems in trying to do so. The methodological problems involved in transforming historical materials into sociological data are, however, neither greater than, nor qualitatively different from, those confronted by sociologists in transforming any set of materials into data. If our reality models and theories demand particular data, we plan the collection of materials to maximize our chances of being able to organize what is collected in terms of the variables required. Always we either do the work ourselves, getting as close as possible to direct observation of the social and cultural phenomena of interest, use what others have done, or wind up doing both.

Actually, *most* of the material we turn into sociological data is not primary data in any strict sense. We rarely make our own observations of individuals (especially the powerful, the strategic decision-makers of collectivities) acting and reacting in reference to specified social and cultural facts. We mostly "make do" with individuals' own observations of both their behavior and the social and cultural facts associated with it; or we make do with secondary analysis of material collected (and often organized as other than the precise data we need) by ourselves or our hirelings on other occasions and generally for different purposes; or we use material collected (and usually organized as other than the specific data needed) by others interested for all kinds of reasons in finding out something about human behavior. These others whose material and data we use are more often nonscientists than scientists, and their standards of reliability and validity typically range from barely admissible to virtually nonexistent. In contrast to the credentials of other data collectors, including the subjects and respondents upon whose observations we rely so heavily, the credentials and skills of modern historians—particularly those committed to science rather than art or politics—as collectors of authentic facts and as analysts sensitive to the need to avoid distorting facts in the course of interpreting them are hardly to be challenged by sociologists. By our customary standards, as distinguished from our ideals, the historical data provided by today's historians constitute a windfall. In any case, until we sociologists add historiographic techniques to our methodological toolkit, we shall have to continue relying upon historians and, at the minimum, become familiar enough with their work to discriminate among indispensable, good, usable, and hopeless sources—as we must in using other secondary sources.

Rather than finding usable material our problem is more likely to be deciding what to leave out. Becker's rule-of-thumb was to ignore whatever is not relevant for "the purpose at hand," and his effort to communicate what he meant by "culture case study" via "constructive typology" adds up to the guiding principle that material, including the historical, should be arrayed in descriptive terms amenable to, and suggestive of, sociological explanatory propositions (Becker, 1950:214-216). Like most of us, Becker talked a better game than he played; but we can hardly improve upon his statement. Clearly, one can never be certain of making no mistakes; nonetheless, *specification* (1) of expected empirical regularities and the connections among them in terms of the variables of an explicit reality model and—ideally—(2) of the causal paths implied by an explicit theory reduces the risks of including irrelevant and excluding relevant materials. Whether our purpose at hand involves a problem specifiable in terms of "microvariables" or one specifiable in terms of "macrovariables" (the distinction is Lazarsfeld's, in Small, 1970:52), specification of the kinds of data we think we need appears to be the best general prescription available for avoiding the problems of too much, too little, and the wrong kinds of material.

Conclusion

It follows from the preceding argument that the history of a legal order becomes sociologically usable only if those authoritative statements of empirical regularities (events, occurrences) and—especially temporal—connections between regularities that historians provide are selectively analyzed, translated, reconstituted, and (of course) torn out of context to fit some more general explanatory scheme built around social and cultural variables. The sociological paradigm outlined above emphasizes the prime significance of learning through social interaction. This significance is both *social*—in that the consequences of earlier interactions and learning are found in the structural, institutional, and organizational constraints and boundary conditions of later individual and collectivity behavior—and *cultural*—in that what people *think* happened can be as important a set of constraints and conditions as what actually did happen. History thus provides the materials of which present social, including some crucial environmental, realities are constituted, as well as the constituents of present cultural realities, including the realities of the lessons that men believe to have been taught by historical experience and that they try to apply to their contemporary realities. Whether they seek to confirm or to deny those realities, to prevent or to accomplish change, and whether they repeat old patterns or create new ones, men are forced to contend with, and to use, the social and cultural residua of past efforts undertaken in response to the real and perceived social and cultural realities of the past.

To speak of a legal order is to focus upon structures, both social and cultural, both adaptive and maladaptive, that men have both inadvertently and deliberately created in trying to eliminate the contingencies of social interaction so as to increase their survival chances and enhance their opportunities for more gratifying lives. The more frequently men are constrained (by economic interdependence, sexual attraction, natural barriers, common enemies, or whatever) to interact, the more frequent and salient are the instances of reciprocity—punishing and rewarding—by which they jointly learn to reduce unpredictability. As more and more social relationships, including authority relationships (Turk, 1969:30-52), are formed in this reciprocating process of collective learning and as the human capacity for symbolizing produces cultural structures purporting to describe, explain, and justify the social structures, the structuring that has been achieved comes itself to be valued and assigned extraordinary significance, expressed in terms ranging from the most underdeveloped cosmologies to the most highly developed theories of natural law.

The process of reducing uncertainty becomes increasingly complex and difficult as nature, technology, population growth, and encounters with other societies and cultures combine to produce increasing social differentiation, necessarily accompanied by cultural differentiation. The crucial points in social interaction are identified, largely through "trouble cases" (Hoebel, 1954), and the authorities of the collectivity involved are driven to respond by creating laws (typically in the guise of affirming familiar cultural norms) and a more explicit organization of social control. Relatively implicit patterns of individual deviance control come to be supplemented and overlaid by quite explicit structures of legal control aimed increasingly at social categories, recalcitrant or subversive organizations, and subpopulations. The assumption that there are generally understood and accepted interaction patterns, that there is a normative structure, becomes increasingly untenable; and the authorities, insofar as they are committed to preserving the collectivity without radical structural changes, search most sincerely and diligently for ways to restore or create normative structure. Their definitions and understandings (and misunderstandings) of legal control problems and of the alternatives available for dealing with those problems are derived primarily from historical experiences with control problems as these experiences are reflected in the legal system of the collectivity.

Since a legal system includes both a cultural structure and a social structure, both an agglutination of conceptualizations and thoughtways and a network of social relationships and behavior patterns, one begins to determine the causal significance of the system's historicity by investigating (1) the extent of similarity and continuity between the legal cultural premises of past and present authorities—including accepted substantive, organizational, and procedural models as well as more abstract conceptions of the nature and province of law—and (2) the extent to which innovation is prevented or hindered by the structuring of social interaction within the organization of control and between the organization and the other components of the society.

Very briefly, analysis of South African history indicates that South Africa's authorities are relying heavily upon legal cultural premises originating in seventeenth-and eighteenth-century Dutch law and hardened by the experiences and remembrances of Dutch colonial administration, British imperialism, and the conflicts subsequent to the 1910 unification of South Africa (Turk, 1970). Explicit authoritarianism; strict legalism in the making, interpreting, and enforcing of laws; stern moral rejection of deviants and outsiders; and a readiness to punish severely those who resist the ruthless exercise of legal authority—these are the salient characteristics of South Africa's legal culture, and increasingly so as the de-anglicization of South African law proceeds.

Furthermore, it appears that the organization of control in South Africa inhibits adaptive organizational and procedural changes and thereby contributes to the problems of legal ordering (Turk, 1972). The institutional inability of the judiciary to prevent or effectively ameliorate parliamentary irresponsibilities and decisively limit executive discretion; the de facto and largely de jure insulation of the police and corrections agencies from effective monitoring and serious challenge; the highly militarized, top-down organization of the police; and the heavy commitment of enforcement resources to secret and political policing—these are only some of the most important social products of South Africa's legal history.

The translation of South African legal history into the language of sociological variables has barely begun. Nevertheless, enough work has been done to make it clear that the theoretical—the causal—explanation of the South African legal system must encompass the history of that system. Just as clearly, neither social theorists nor those who seek a more secure and a more humane world including South Africa are helped by the dismaying notion that history is a unique happening from which can be learned nothing of explanatory significance for other times and other societies. Fortunately for both theory and action, men plainly do learn and therefore generalize from their experiences; and the cultural and social products, including legal systems, of their learning experiences become constraints, whether fetters or guides, upon their subsequent responses to subsequent experiences.

Notes

1. Those interested in the substantive research are referred to the indicated references and to other works in progress on various aspects of a comparative study of legal control in South Africa and the United States. Copies of published and unpublished papers will be furnished upon request.

2. While the historian may be content to analyze his materials in terms of the specific relationships among unique entities and occurrences, the scientist cannot, by the nature of his task, accept the recognition of uniqueness as the stopping point for analysis. In the construction of scientific theories—which is the effort to surpass the limitations of uniquist explanations—the *variable* is the most fruitful kind of conceptual entity so far invented. Thinking in terms of variables has enabled scientists to express ideas of relationship and causation in a form eminently susceptible to reality testing yet flexible enough in application to leave room for revolutionary innovations both in "normal" theory and research technology and in the reality models underlying the knowledge-producing enterprise (Kuhn, 1962).

3. It may well be that the functionalism-evolutionism issue has never been as real as it seemed. Stinchombe (1968:104) argues cogently that a functional causal structure generally implies what he calls a historicist structure when applied to explaining the persistence of tradition in specific cases.

References

Arnold, Thurman.

    1935   *The Symbols of Government.* New Haven, Conn.: Yale University Press.

Barnes, Harry Elmer.

    1948   *Historical Sociology: Its Origins and Development.* New York: Philosophical Library.

Becker, Howard.

    1950   *Through Values to Social Interpretation.* Durham, N.C.: Duke University Press.

Dahrendorf, Ralf.

    1967   *Society and Democracy in Germany.* New York: Doubleday.

    1968   *Essays in the Theory of Society.* Stanford, Calif.: Stanford University Press. Esp. pp. 129-214.

Evan, William M.

    1965   Law as an instrument of social change. In Alvin Gouldner and S. M. Miller (Eds.), *Applied Sociology.* New York: Free Press. Pp. 285-293.

Hempel, Carl G.

    1965   *Aspects of Scientific Explanation and Other Essays in the Philosophy of Science.* New York: Free Press.

Hoebel, E. Adamson.

    1954   *The Law of Primitive Man: A Study in Comparative Legal Dynamics.* Cambridge, Mass.: Harvard University Press.

Hofstadter, Richard.

    1968   History and sociology in the United States. In Seymour Martin Lipset and Richard Hofstadter (Eds.), *Sociology and History: Methods.* New York: Basic Books. Pp. 3-19.

Kuhn, Thomas S.

    1962   *The Structure of Scientific Revolutions.* Chicago: University of Chicago Press.

Landes, David S., and Charles Tilly (Eds.).

    1971   *History as Social Science.* Englewood Cliffs, N.J.: Prentice-Hall.

Lazarsfeld, Paul F.

    1970   A sociologist looks at historians. In Melvin Small (Ed.), *Public Opinion and Historians: Interdisciplinary Perspectives.* Detroit, Mich.: Wayne State University Press. Pp. 39-59.

Leff, Gordon.

    1971   *History and Social Theory.* New York: Anchor. Originally published in 1969.

Lewis, I. M. (Ed.).

    1968   *History and Social Anthropology.* London: Tavistock.

Lipset, Seymour Martin, and Richard Hofstadter (Eds.).

    1968   *Sociology and History: Methods.* New York: Basic Books.

Marsh, Robert M.

    1967   *Comparative Sociology: A Codification of Cross-Societal Analysis.* New York: Harcourt, Brace and World.

Nagel, Ernest R.

    1961   *The Structure of Science: Problems in the Logic of Scientific Explanation.* New York: Harcourt, Brace and World.

Nisbet, Robert A.

    1968   *Tradition and Revolt: Historical and Sociological Essays.* New York: Random House.

    1969   *Social Change and History: Aspects of the Western Theory of Development.* New York: Oxford University Press.

Parsons, Talcott.

    1966   *Societies: Evolutionary and Comparative Perspectives.* Englewood Cliffs, N.J.: Prentice-Hall.

Popper, Karl.

    1957   *The Poverty of Historicism.* London: Routledge and Kegan Paul.

Schwartz, Richard D., and Jerome H. Skolnick (Eds.).

    1970   *Society and the Legal Order.* New York: Basic Books.

Selznick, Philip.

    1968   The sociology of law. In *International Encyclopedia of the Social Sciences,* vol. IX. New York: Macmillan-Free Press. Pp. 50-59.

    1969   *Law, Society, and Industrial Justice.* New York: Russell Sage Foundation.

Small, Melvin (Ed.).

   1970   *Public Opinion and Historians: Interdisciplinary Perspectives.*
           Detroit, Mich.: Wayne State University Press.

Stinchcombe, Arthur L.

   1968   *Constructing Social Theories.* New York: Harcourt, Brace and
           World.

Stone, Julius,

   1966   *Social Dimensions of Law and Justice.* Stanford, Calif.: Stanford
           University Press.

Turk, Austin T.

   1969   *Criminality and Legal Order.* Chicago: Rand McNally.

   1970   Legal control in South Africa: the present significance of the
           past. Paper read at annual meeting of the Rural Sociological
           Society, Washington, D. C. (August 29).

   1972   The limits of coercive legalism in conflict regulation: South
           Africa. In Ernest Q. Campbell (Ed.), *Racial Tensions and National
           Identity.* Nashville, Tenn.: Vanderbilt University Press. Pp.
           171-198.

White, Morton.

   1965   *Foundations of Historical Knowledge.* New York: Harper & Row.

Zinn, Howard.

   1970   *The Politics of History.* Boston: Beacon.

Discussion

Mr. Chaplin.   Sociology has generally been ahistorical, although it didn't begin
that way. We are all aware that Weber and Durkheim, particularly Weber,
started sociology off in a comparative and historical framework. One
reason for the current growth of historical sociology is that it tends to be
cheaper and more feasible than overseas, "make your own data" research.
A better reason for doing historical research is that the area of social
change, both at the theoretical and the methodological levels (in terms of
statistical techniques), has been the weakest in sociology. Whatever
problem one is studying, one should see it in historical context as well as

with respect to what is happening at the present time.

At least two well-known sociologists have made very different use of historical material. Smelser (1959), in studying the British textile industry, reworked probably the most heavily studied period and topic in British history by imposing a sociological perspective on it. Tilly (1964) took a very different approach in his French research. He collected his "own" data directly from archives but at the same time remained a sociologist by imposing a generalizing perspective on what he was doing.

Mr. Schnaiberg.   I suspect, from my own experience with younger historians, that many are sociologists in form and action rather than historians and that we should be very cautious about treating them as an independent arm of social science in general rather than as substantially similar to ourselves. That possibility may pose problems, though. It seems to me that there is a very clear relationship regarding who we find it easiest to talk to and work with. It has certainly been my experience in dealing with people outside of history—for example, in economics—that I find it easiest to work with people who are most like me. Homophilia is a basis of interaction in professional as well as nonprofessional areas. But if we choose to work with scholars who are like us rather than different, we may miss something very important.

If we are going to be honest comparativists, we should think about sociology in the same way we are thinking about history. For example, why do sociological data clearly lag behind certain areas of sociological methodology? How do sociological data compare in this regard with historical data? One intriguing point is that we all have data, particularly contemporary data, from comparative research which we have not used, probably will not use, and which will likely never be used unless we release it. Yet most of us are terribly cautious about releasing such data. Why this situation exists is related to the social organization of research and to fundamental, methodological questions. In historical research, any scholar can pick up another's data, replicate the work, and validate the historical sources at least to the same level as a historian. It has been my experience, though, using contemporary sociological microdata, that this situation certainly does not hold for the sociological data we have gathered.

We are incredibly inefficient in using such data. Consequently, gathering it is among the costliest forms of research. Further, we are far more cavalier with those $100,000 projects than with $2500 worth of xeroxing of historical research material which in in the public domain to a much greater extent than our sociological data. By working in this way we miss one of the great merits of historical documents, which is that they don't have the same pattern of political reactivity that our contemporary data gathering has.

Mr. Hill.   How can you judge the reactivity of an historian after the data-gathering has been completed? I think the argument can be made that historical data is every bit as reactive as any other kind of data, depending on the way one samples; perhaps even more so.

Mr. Manning.   This historical data we have is almost totally limited to people in the upper classes and people in power. That fact poses still another question of validity.

Mr. Hill.   Many of us admire historians because they are so much more concerned about the problems of validation than the average sociologist grinding his material through a factor analytic design. My specific concern is with the logical process by which one validates something many years after the fact. I am not so much concerned with whether Rembrandt actually did a particular painting as about the validity of the *report* that he did. Now, we can analyze the quality of the paper, the quality of the ink, and the signature of a particular historian, but how do we validate the report? When you consider, as Turk has done, the function of history for a particular social-control system, at what point can you trust the validity of a particular historian's report in the sense that you trust the validity of a contemporary subject's report?

Mr. Chaplin.   When you say "validate the historian's report," I assume you include what I mean by the historian's problem of validity. Was a document really written by its purported author? Did Shakespeare write Shakespeare, or did Bacon? A report as a whole should include discussion of authorship as well as of the objectivity and completeness of the report itself. Also one should realize that each generation of historians doesn't accept the validity of the previous generation's interpretation of history. In that sense, historians lack a common definition of validity, and that is our main criticism of them. Historians have the idea that each generation has to rework the same data and come up with different conclusions. So we don't deal with history at that level. We are more interested in history as a data source. At that level, historians do know their stuff.

Mr. Schnaiberg.   We are talking about validity, but that term is used at a variety of levels in research terminology. I think Hill is concerned with the validation of measures, *not* the interpretation, *not* the external validity of the report, but rather with starting at the beginning and questioning the validity of the data, the elemental portions of the research.

Mr. Chaplin. We may decide that the data used and evaluated by an historian are irrelevant to an hypothesis because they are not a good indicator of the phenomenon in question. To go back to Tilly, he examined the French counterrevolution and threw out the French's historical interpretations of it. Then, beginning with their data on the number of riots, which was validated up to a point, he obtained information on the personal characteristics of the people in the mobs. This additional data greatly increased our understanding of this social movement. There was little question about the number of disturbances, but the historians hadn't proceeded to the next level of data analysis, which we sociologists consider more relevant: the social characteristics of the participants. Instead of challenging the validity of data on number of riots or how many people were in them, he simply said that these data were not sufficient indicators to explain social revolution.

Mr. Hill. Let's take an example: 150 years from now an historian is relying on Vietnamese "body-counts". He knows that we today were suspicious of those body-counts. How does he preserve that suspicion?

Mr. Turk. If he is doing his job right, he will be exploring the minutia in the newspapers currently available, all the political hassle in the U. S. over the question of body-counts and their validity. He will be getting into the military records of U. S. officers in Saigon and the questionings in press conferences.

Mr. Hill. Do you have that kind of data for the beginnings of the legal institutions in South Africa?

Mr. Turk. As a matter of fact, yes, a pretty good report. With Teutonic thoroughness they have kept it.

Mr. Chaplin. If the historian keeps adding the numbers up, he'll likely find that the number of bodies adds up to more than the number of armed forces that were there. He will conclude, therefore, that the military must have been killing civilians. Historians do that kind of work.

Mr. Grimshaw. It strikes me that Tilly and others are developing a descending series for validity. If you are interested in, say, violence, the *report* of an event of violence is probably the most valid kind of data, probably more accurate than what is said about dates, which is probably more accurate than what is said about the number of deaths, which is probably more accurate than what is said about the number of injuries and arrests, etc. Sociologists need to sort out these kinds of descending or ascending orders of reliability and validity.

Mr. Tien.   I am not a defender of the body-count practice, but I was disturbed both by what I heard from Dave Chaplin and by Hill's question. Both imply that a good historian and/or sociologist should verify whether or not *counts* are accurate. That implication misses an important feature of the body-count practice. As an historical fact, that practice has had an impact on society *and* on individual behavior. Whether or not the counts are accurate, they have sustained a war for quite some period of time and produced massacres of various scopes. Thus a good historian must go beyond the validity of a particular count and consider the effect that that count has had.

Mr. Gould.   It strikes me that good historians and good social scientists do roughly the same things but with different emphases. What good history does one read that doesn't make creative use of a lot of the concepts and a lot of the kinds of data that we use in the social sciences, and vice versa? I think that the difference between good history and good social science is perhaps the kind of emphasis that you give in the questions you ask. Nadel (1951) once argued that one difference between the anthropologist and the historian was that the anthropologist attempts to discern the general by looking at the unique. The historian, by contrast, brings the general to bear on the unique.

It seems to me that, when doing a piece of empirical research in sociology or anthropology, when working in the ethnographic present or its equivalent in sociology, there comes a point at which one begins to ask certain kinds of questions which can only be answered by resorting to history. For example, for years the concept of paternalism in Japanese factories had been attributed, by numerous non-historically oriented anthropologists, to a continuation of the traditional paternalistic relationship that goes far back in Japanese history. Then a Japanese social historian or economic-social historian, Tominago (1967), disproved this assertion. By doing good social history, he discovered a whole period in Japanese industrial development during which not only was this paternalistic relationship not used—it was actually disowned. Only during the later stages of Japanese economic development, when labor was in short supply because Japanese industry was growing faster than Japan's population, did these paternalistic features creep into the Japanese factory as a means of retaining workers in a very, very modern economy. Without good social history, such findings can't be made.

Mr. Schnaiberg.   Historical demography has benefited tremendously from the use of historical data, not just body-counts and other conventional kinds of demographic data but rather unusual data like Johnson and Cutright have used—baptismal records, genealogical data, etc. Good research—including narrow case studies, careful historical research, and aggregated approaches—which is guided theoretically rather than by operational definitionalism, will almost always force us to move away from the conventional data sources. Really, since data often force us to revise our theories, we ought to push historical documentation and kookie data sources to the limits of their potential utility so that we find even broader sets of theoretical and pragmatic issues.

Mr. Chaplin. I want to get back to the matter of validation. I agree with Turk's admiration for the historians' more demanding standards for validation of data. Data use and validation should be a major focus of concern for us. There are sociologists who hold that, particularly in underdeveloped countries, a study based on a large amount of relatively poor data is superior to a very strong statistical study which limits itself to a very restricted period of time and very specialized problem and which concentrates very hard on validating what data is derived and putting it into its full local context. I think they are wrong.

Shifting focus, though, I feel that Turk overdoes the role of learning processes in the study of change, almost suggesting a Freudian model of history with respect to considerations of early socialization. His approach seems to suggest the possibility of aggregating the ways in which groups of individuals learn, with the ultimate goal being prediction of mass behavior changes in whole societies.

Mr. Turk. I see socialization as a continuing process. It is virtually a synonym for learning. To me learning is a causal process which we can fully comprehend only by simultaneously examining time series data for individuals *and* the rich data we can obtain from historians.

If I understand your remarks regarding the learning notion, you are implying that the principal value of invoking history is to put things into social context. Beyond mere context, I am trying to work out a more systematic way to use history as data, seeing historical context as the stairway which leads up to what we happen to be studying at the present.

The alternatives, it seems to me, are either (1) to continue playing with some kind of emergentism whereby, when we deal with societies and introduce historical data, we attempt to talk causation at a level far removed from anything that happens with real people or (2) to attempt to develop some sort of composition laws [Brodbeck, 1959] whereby we can move from explaining individual behavior in terms of individuals' historical experiences to an explanation of very complex levels of social structure by cumulating the learning experiences of many individuals through time. The important aspect of such composition laws would be to spell out how the consequences and conclusions reached by specific sets of individuals become contingencies for conclusions to be reached by later sets of individuals. At the moment, we just refer vaguely to the possibility of composition laws. We skip all the hard problems by jumping to an emergentist concept of how history becomes important for us. Just to say that history is needed for understanding social change, though, doesn't say anything.

Mr. Chaplin.   How do you propose to aggregate individual learning experiences to explain the emergent structural characteristics of specific societies? How, for instance, would you related individual learning processes to change in the class structure? The class structure change will bring about a resocialization of class manners, let's say, but how do you explain the change in class structure by learning processes, with learning as the causal variable? The causal emphasis on learning seems to suggest a microsocial-psychological level of analysis which is the hardest level to pursue both in historical and cross-cultural contexts. Haven't you opted for a way of studying history that is going to be particularly difficult as soon as you start studying non-elite groups? It may be theoretically desirable to work in this way, but in fact it is precisely the social psychologists who find the greatest problems in working abroad; their perspective is just as relevant, but they find it exceptionally difficult to design comparable measures.

Mr. Turk.   I think you suggest part of the answer when you refer to elites. We must distinguish between simple arithmetical aggregation and the necessity to discover where strategic decision-makers are located. Which individuals have the greatest effect on decisions that have later repercussions for later individuals? The goal is not simply to end up one day with social structure. We need to find those sets of real people whose decisions carry import far beyond their own immediate concerns. Clearly we need to introduce a power variable into our design when we search for the experiences of real people which have led to real decisions.

Mr. Form.   I suspect that what historians want most from sociology is a conceptual apparatus which gives them a greater sensitivity to organization and enriches their interpretation. They will not, however, use sociological terms in their own work. My own experience suggests that there are no specifically historical methods; there are simply ways in which we can cast a conceptual network over time series data.

Now let me put a broader question to this conference. How do you locate a problem which is best answered within some kind of historical framework? And having located such a problem, what kind of procedures do you then follow? It seems to me that the problem would have to include at least two historical eras and we would have to ask: What validity problems will I encounter as I attempt to compare these two (or more) periods in time, presuming some theory of social change and these particular units?

Mr. Turk. I don't know how you decide whether you have a historical problem or not. Comparative historical research requires more than just comparing the effect of one factor on another at different times. If you theorize, say, that the allocation of power resources constrains individual behavior, you must first establish the existence of some allocation of resources and then determine how individuals perceive their alternatives for action. You establish social structure in data terms and trace its implications in terms of contingencies for individual behavior.

If you then wish to explain how that allocation came to be, you have an historical problem; there's no way out of it. In order to explain *how* your particular bits and pieces of historical data relate to explaining your current class structure, you must consider—as I have argued—(1) how people in the past learned, under earlier and different sets of constraints, to perceive and act in certain ways, and (2) why certain people have wound up today in specific categories, while others have wound up in other categories. Such explanations must clearly be historical.

Mr. Chaplin. I want Mr. Form to state a general type of problem that doesn't require an historical dimension.

Mr. Form. I would suggest that no question ought to be studied either historically without any contemporary research or vice versa. Suppose you are testing an hypothesis about the kind of community-power changes that occur as you move from communities with less complex to those with more complex social organization. You may not want to start now and continue for a generation or two. So you begin instead by taking small, simple problems and some very complex kinds of problems and begin to ask questions about them. You find out what is answerable, what your problems are, what kind of data you want, etc. So far you've done good comparative research.

Then you can attack precisely the same question from an historical dimension. You might shift types of locale and ask the very same question. Now what kind of data do you confront as you move backward in time or forward to the present? In what areas are your data better or worse as you move toward the present? What kinds of questions are best answered from the historical perspective that cannot be answered from the contemporary perspective? This is what I think a comparative sociologist *should* be doing.

Mr. Gould. Wasn't it the historian Maitland [cited in Evans-Pritchard,

1962:26] who said that if anthropology isn't history, it is nothing? I think you can turn that around: If history isn't sociology, *it* is nothing. I think the two converge profoundly.

Mr. Chaplin.   So one strategy would be for the sociologist to study a modern problem that already has an historical base rather than the other way around.

References

Brodbeck, May.

  1959   Models, meaning and theories. In Llewelyn Gross (Ed.), *Symposium on Sociological Theory.* White Plains, N.Y.: Row Peterson. Pp. 373-403.

Evans-Pritchard, E.E.

  1962   Social anthropology past and present. In E.E. Evans-Pritchard, *Essays in Social Anthropology.* London: Faber and Faber.

Nadel, S.F.

  1951   *Foundations of Social Anthropology.* Glencoe, Ill.: Free Press.

Smelser, Neil J.

  1959   *Social Change in the Industrial Revolution.* Chicago: University of Chicago Press.

Tilly, Charles.

  1964   *The Vendée.* Cambridge, Mass.:   Harvard University Press.

Tominago, Ken'ichi.

  1967   Some sociological comments on the Western view of Japanese society. Unpublished manuscript. University of Illinois.

CHAPTER ELEVEN

Assessing Children's Language Using Abilities: Methodological and Cross Cultural Implications

HUGH MEHAN

University of California, San Diego

Cultural Deficiency, Cultural Difference, and School Performance

Cultural Deficiency and Cultural Difference

Lower-class native American, black, Chicano, Puerto Rican and other minority group children perform poorly in school by contrast with their middle-class contemporaries. Cazden (1970) says that the language use and school performance problems of lower-class children have been explained in one of two ways:

1. Language learning is the acquisition of a repertoire of behavior or responses, hence the interpretation that unsuccessful lower-class children have "less" language and culture. Explanatory terms like "cultural deprivation," "cultural deficit," "vacuum ideology," and "restricted code user" (see, for example, Bereiter and Englemann, 1966) all connote a nonverbal child who is not as "full" of language and ability as his socially more fortunate contemporaries. The culturally deprived child is said to be the product of an impoverished environment. Overcrowded facilities, infrequent social contact, inconsistent discipline, and few cultural artifacts among which to discriminate, it is argued, provide limited opportunities for the child to become verbally expressive and develop cooperative, perceptual, and attitudinal skills.

2. Language learning is the acquisition of a set of rules for the construction of utterances. This generative view of language (Chomsky, 1965) leads to the interpretation that all children learn language, but some children acquire a version, say, of English, that has some structural features or combinational rules

309

different from those of Standard English (SE). These structural differences produce anomolies for the Non-Standard English (NSE) speaker who is required to use SE in the classroom.

Labov (1969) and Stewart (1964), among others, have shown the systematic organization of NSE at the syntactic and phonological levels. Although Black English (BE) and SE draw phonemes from the same pool, they are combined by different rules. In BE, final and/or penultimate consonants are often deleted in conversation; instead, only the lengthened vowel is pronounced, so that word-pairs such as "God" and "guard", "bowl" and "bold", "toe" and "toll" are homophones for the BE speaker but not for the SE speaker. Consonant clusters, especially those with /t/, /s/, /d/, and /z/, are simplified in the final position of words; hence pairs like "pass" and "past", "called" and "call", "sick" and "six" are also homophones for the BE but not the SE speaker. Failing to recognize the distinctive BE phonological structure led Deutsch (1964) to conclude that black children could not discriminate sounds as well as white children, while Melmed (1971), by providing a disambiguating context for BE homonyms, was able to reject that conclusion.

There are syntactic differences in BE as well: possessives and negatives are marked differently; the copula is not obligatory; the third-person singular does not have an obligatory morphological ending; and verb agreement is different (Baratz, 1970; Mitchell-Kernan, 1969). Labov (1969) has demonstrated that these differences do not produce illogical or restricted discourse; in fact, some seemingly "restricted" passages of BE actually express thoughts and logical relations more directly than equivalent passages from "elaborated" SE.

Although the "deficit" rather than the "difference" thesis has been dominant among educators during the last two decades, the "deprived" child's "impoverished" cultural or linguistic system has not been shown to inhibit actual classroom communication or to interfere with the ongoing teaching-learning situation. Instead, the behavioral and academic difficulties of such children have been documented by the use of data gathered from formal tests conducted outside the classroom.

Performance Assessment

This research, part of a larger sociolinguistic study,[1] investigated the language-using abilities of elementary school children in contrasting educational environments and linguistic systems by videotaping and analyzing adult-child interaction in Spanish and English in the classroom, in testing encounters, and in the child's home (Mehan, 1971).

One of the Southern California schools studied used a series of psycholinguistic tests to evaluate each child's language skills. Children's results on these tests contributed to later decisions regarding placement in one of the three first-grade classrooms (Leiter, in Cicourel et al., in press). The children who scored lowest on the diagnostic tests were all placed in one classroom. Their poor test performance, coupled with their low socioeconomic status (SES)—and, often, Chicano origin—seemed to make these children prime examples of the "culturally deprived child" placed in a special classroom designed to accelerate academic progress.

One difficulty experienced by these children on the school's diagnostic tests was an inability to respond accurately to questions asking for discriminations based on prepositional phrases that express locational reference. Because the children had had difficulty with prepositions and other grammatical forms, the teacher presented them with language development lessons to teach them the requisite grammatical forms. My informal comparison of the children's responses on the fall diagnostic test with their work in early language-development lessons showed that some children gave correct responses in one situation but not the other. These differential performances prompted me to examine these two situations, to see whether the socially organized features of the interrogation procedure itself were contributing to the children's performance and the school official's evaluations of it.

Testing the Test

Assumptions Underlying Test Structures

The educational test is constructed with assumptions about (1) the nature of cognitive abilities, (2) the experiences and language of the respondent, (3) the basis of the respondent's performance, and (4) the testing situation.

1. The educational test, although not always an IQ test, incorporates assumptions about the nature of mental abilities that originated in intelligence-testing theory. Spearman (1923) proposed that each individual possesses a general intelligence factor (g). Intelligence is viewed as a fixed mental capacity "of the individual to act purposefully, to think rationally, to deal effectively with his environment" (Wechsler, 1944:3). The implication is that intelligence is an underlying mental ability. Underlying mental abilities are composed of previously learned experiences, accumulated knowledge, and skills."Simply stated, if learning opportunities and all other factors are equal, those persons who learn the most and perform the best probably have greater innate mental capacity than those who learn and perform most poorly" (Mercer, 1971:322-323). Tests measure these experiences learned in the past.

2. The tester assumes that the meaning of instructions, questions, and answers is obvious to the test-taker and is shared by the test-constructor, test-taker, and test-administrator. The test items serve as unambiguous stimuli

which tap the respondent's underlying attitudes about, or knowledge of, certain factors.

Each test item is deemed clear and unambiguous because the test-constructor assumes that persons taking the test have had experience with the test items, whether they be words, pictures, or objects, and that the test experience will be the same as the prior experiences he has had with these items. Because of this assumed similarity of experience, test-takers will interpret the items in the same way the test-constructor did when he compiled the items. Because each test item will be interpreted only in the way intended by the test-constructor, the test-taker's reasons or purposes for making certain choices or for giving certain explanations are assumed to match the purposes of the tester.

Each question asked has a correct answer, which is produced by connecting a stimulus instruction and a test item. The respondent who answers questions properly is assumed to have searched for, and found, the intended connection between questions and materials. While correct answers to questions are seen as products of correct search procedures, incorrect answers are seen as resulting from faulty reasoning or a lack of underlying ability, knowledge, or understanding.

3. The educational tester makes the same assumptions about the measurement of behavior that the experimental psychologist makes: "A psychological experiment, then, can be symbolized by *S-O-R*, which means that *E* (understood) applies a certain stimulus (or situation) to *O*'s receptors and observes *O*'s response" (Woodworth and Schlosberg, 1954:2). The test-taker, like the experimental subject, responds to the stimulus, and his response is a direct and sole result of the "stimulus acting at that moment and the factors present in the organism at that moment . . . $R = f(S,O)$" (Woodworth and Schlosberg, 1954:3).

4. The respondent's behavior is considered to be the sole result of his underlying abilities and stimulus application, because other factors and variables that might be influential are subject to standardization and control.

"Standarization implies uniformity of procedure in administering and scoring the test. . . .Such standardization extends to the exact materials employed, time limits, oral instructions to subjects, preliminary demonstrations, ways of handling queries from subjects, and every other detail of the testing situation" (Anastasi, 1968:23).

The tester (or experimenter) is supposed to present the stimulus while holding other factors in the situation constant. The tester is supposed to be standardized in his presentation of stimuli so that all respondents face the same conditions, thus permitting comparisons of performances and replications.

Briefly then, the assumptions made by the formal test include the following:

1. The abilities being tested are the products of past experience.

2. Cultural meanings are shared in common by tester and respondent.

3. The respondent's performance is an exclusive function of underlying abilities and stimulus presentation ($R = f\,[S,O]$).

4. Stimuli are presented to respondents in standardized ways, and the testing situation is controlled.

Examining the Assumptions of the Formal Test

The structure of the testing encounter was examined in two ways. First, six of the first-grade children who took the spring test were videotaped. After the tests were over, I informally interrogated the children about their perceptions and understandings of the testing materials. Second, versions of the formal test that systematically altered its features were presented to the first-grade children.

The language development tests employed by the school utilize picture-identification tasks, in which children are asked to identify the grammatical forms represented by a series of pictures. A child answers a question by pointing to a picture. Instead of using only one kind of stimulus, I used three alternative versions of the picture-identification task. I had children demonstrate their knowledge of orientational prepositions by manipulating their hands, manipulating small objects, and drawing pictures in response to the instructions I gave. I contrasted the formal testing characteristic of a strange and unfamiliar environment by presenting the "orientations tasks" to children in the less formal surroundings of the classroom and (to a few) in the familiar settings of their homes. To examine the "common culture" assumption, the general research design required that one test be presented in Spanish to those children familiar with that language and that all children's definitions and conceptions of testing materials be analyzed. Six classroom and six home testing encounters were videotaped.[2] The results of the children's performances on the two sessions of school-administered tests and on the variations appear in Tables 11.1 and 11.2.

Tables of scores like these or more general comments—for example, "Adam has command of prepositions" or "Sarah does not comprehend the negative or the orientational prepositions"—are characteristically provided to teachers after a testing session and entered into the child's school record. However, such tables or statements (1) fail to capture the child's reasoning abilities, (2) do not show the negotiated, contextually bound measurement decisions that the tester makes while scoring the child's behavior as "correct" or "incorrect," and hence (3) obscure our understanding of how well the child has grasped the task at hand.

Table 11.1   Results of Language Testing in One First Grade

Child	School Tests		Variations	
	Fall	Spring	Class	Home
1 (Jean)	73	69	93	100
2 (Clarc)	10	50	86	86
3 (Leslie)	46	76	44	65[a]
4 (Lora)	10	25	33	60[a]
5	50	61	86	
6	52	54	77	
7	75	85	75	
8	65	70	80	
9	60	75	75	
10	50	50	50	
11	15	25	37	
12	60	75	55	
13	35	70	75	
14	55	85	87	
15	35	65	67	
16	63	77	80	
17	50	54	60	85[a]
18	85	95	93	
19	56	86	55	75[a]
20	10	36	33	
21	85	95	95	
22	35	50	45	
23	75	85	85	
Total	1140	1512	1566	

[a]Tested in Spanish at home.

Table 11.2   Mean Language Test Scores for Three First Grades

Classroom	School Tests		Orientation Task I
	Fall	Spring	
1	49.5	65.7	68.0
2	73	87	
3	77	82	

The Children's Conceptions of the Test

One question on the school language test (the Basic Concept Inventory, Englemann, 1967, henceforth BCI) asks respondents to decide which child in a group is the tallest. Because the children's heads are obscured, the test-taker is supposed to reply that he can't make that judgement. However, many children examined selected one specific child in the picture as the tallest. When I interviewed the children after the spring test and asked why they had chosen that boy, they replied that he was the tallest boy because "his feet are bigger." Investigating the thread of reasoning used by the children, then, shows that they understood the *intent* of the question—to discriminate and compare—but they were not using the same criteria as the tester. Because they were not using the criteria *intended* (but never explicated), answers that indicated that one child was taller than another were marked wrong. In this case, though, a wrong answer does not index a lack of ability but rather the use of an alternative scheme of interpretation.

Another question on the BCI asks the child to decide which of two boxes a ball is in after the tester has told him (by touching it) which box the ball is *not* in. The child is expected to point to the box that the tester has not touched. The question following that on the BCI asks the child to decide which of *three* boxes a ball is in after the tester has again told the child which box does not contain the ball. The child is expected to say that the problem cannot be solved. Many children failed to answer this question correctly; they chose one, or sometimes both, of the remaining two boxes. In a follow-up interview, when asked why they chose one of the other boxes (instead of saying that the problem could not be solved) the children replied, "You said it's not in that one." I think these children find it untenable to doubt an adult's word. An adult has told the child that a state of affairs actually exists: "There is a ball in one of these three boxes." The child has been told that the ball is not in one, so he reasons, "It must be in one of the other two because the adult said so." Again, these children's answers were marked wrong, but not necessarily because they lacked the proper reasoning ability; rather, they lacked the sophistication necessary to doubt an adult's word.

Another question instructs the child to choose the "animal that can fly" from among a bird, an elephant, and a dog. The correct answer (obviously) is the bird. Many first-grade children, though, chose the elephant along with the bird as a response to that question. When I later asked them why they chose that answer they replied, "That's Dumbo." Dumbo (of course) is Walt Disney's flying elephant, well known to children who watch television and read children's books as an animal that flies.

Yet another question asks the child to "find the ones that talk" when shown pictures of a man, a boy, a dog, and a table. Children frequently include the dog along with the man and the boy in answers to this question. For those children who have learned to say that their pets "speak" or "talk", that is not an unlikely choice. Deciding that the child does not know how to use the verb "talk" correctly would, in this case, be erroneous, for that decision would have resulted from an unexamined assumption that both adult and child attribute the same characteristics to objects or are attending to them in the same way.

For another question, children are shown a picture of a medieval fortress, with moat, drawbridge, and parapets, and three initial consonants, *D*, *C*, and *G*. The child is supposed to circle the correct initial consonant. *C* for "castle" is correct, but many children chose *D*. After the test, when I asked those children what the name of the building was, they responded, "Disneyland." These children used the same line of reasoning intended by the teacher, but they arrived at the wrong substantive answer. The scoresheet showing a wrong answer does not document a child's reasoning ability or lack of it, however; it only documents that the child indicated an answer different from the one the tester expected.

These descriptions demonstrate that the child can exist simultaneously in a number of different "realities" or worlds (Schutz, 1962:207-259), that is, the "factual" world of everyday life and the world of fantasy. The child who says that animals can fly and talk is (from the adult point of view) mixing and blending the characteristics of fantasy and everyday worlds. The test, however, assumes that the child is attending to stimulus items only from the viewpoint of the everyday world in which dogs do not talk and elephants do not fly. The test assumes further that the child keeps the world of play, fantasy, and television out of the testing situation. Yet as these anecdotes demonstrate, the child of age 4-6 does not always keep his realities sequentially arranged. Because the child may be operating simultaneously in multiple realities, valid interrogations must examine why he answers questions as he does and determine what children "see" in educational materials; testers must not use answers exclusively.

The following discussion shows that different interpretations of any one child's abilities can be made, depending on which testing results are examined. For example, there is considerable variation in the bilingual children's productions when their responses to English and to Spanish instructions are compared. In response to both Spanish and English instructions to *place* her hand on a table and an object on a line, Lora placed her hand on the

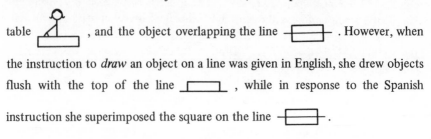

table ___, and the object overlapping the line ___ . However, when the instruction to *draw* an object on a line was given in English, she drew objects flush with the top of the line ___ , while in response to the Spanish instruction she superimposed the square on the line ___ .

Lora also responded differently to the "above" instructions. In response to the instruction "Put your hand above the table," she put her hand off to the side of the table ; she put it on top of the table, though, when the equivalent Spanish instruction, "Ponga tu mano arriba de la mesa," was given . Although pictures drawn in response to Spanish and English commands overlapped the line, objects manipulated wound up under the line .

When Lora was asked in English to put her hand under the table, she touched the underside of the table ; when responding to the Spanish equivalent "Ponga tu mano debajo de la mesa," though, her hand did not make contact with the underside of the table . This interpretation of "under" seemed to carry over to the object manipulation phase of the task. When asked in English to put a square under the line, she first lined it up flush with the underside of the line ; then she picked up the paper and placed the object under the page, so that it was sandwiched between the table and the paper. This interpretation was not rendered when the Spanish instruction, "Has un rectangulo debajo de la linea," was given. Instead, the object was placed between the line and the bottom edge of the paper.

Leslie's responses also varied when different materials were used and when the instructions were presented in different codes. While Leslie raised her hand off the table in response to the English instruction "Put your hand above the table" , she placed her hand flush on the table top when the equivalent instruction was given in Spanish. The former version was echoed in her response to the Spanish of "Put a square above the line" , while the latter version appears in the English equivalent of this instruction and in both picture-drawing exercises: . In short, Leslie's interpretations of this preposition are inconsistent within linguistic codes and across tasks; each question-answer sequence seems to produce its own unique rendition. Leslie's responses to the "under" questions in Spanish and English are replicas of Lora's responses.

It is notable that both children drew lines on their papers differently when the instructions to do so were given in different codes. Both drew diagonal lines from the top left of their pages to the bottom right when they were asked in

English to do so ▱ . Both children drew horizontal lines when

asked: "Has una linea en medio del papel" ⊟ .

In sum, a document of the children's correct and incorrect responses such as Table 11.1 does not show the variation in the children's answers across materials, tests, and languages of interrogation. Conventional testing techniques cannot determine if a child's wrong answers are caused by a lack of ability or represent his equally valid alternative interpretations.

The Test Assembly Process

The table of correct answers and the schematic representations of children's responses like those above are static displays, which do not capture the contextually bound, fluid and dynamic activities that constitute those answers.[3] As I reexamined the videotape of the testing sessions that produced Table 11.1 I found that the results were not as unequivocal as they appeared in tabular form. The testers deviated from the requirements of a mechanical, uniform presentation of instructions and stimuli to respondents. The school test required a series of pictures to be presented to respondents, each with the instruction "Look at the picture." The following variations on that introductory comment are just some of those recorded during the school-administered testing session that I videotaped (similar deviations occurred in the informal tests that I presented and may be observed in any interrogation; Friedman, 1968, documents the same phenomenon in social-psychological experiments)[4]:

1:7	Look at that picture and show, ah, find. . . .
4:17	Y'see all the things in that picture?
8:1	Let's look at that one.
11.1	Now you look at those pictures.
3:3	I want you to look at that picture and tell me what you see by looking at the picture.
1:8	Look at this picture now.
5:9	See all those pictures?
5:10	What those?
5:11	OK, now I want you to find the right ones.

Under the criteria of the formal test, test-takers are supposed to respond only to stimulus materials presented to them, but these respondents are not receiving the same stimulus instructions. Some are being told to look and find the correct pictures; others are being told just to look. No child, however, is told what constitutes a correct answer. The child is expected to operate without this information.

On reexamining the videotapes, I found that when children were asked a question, they presented many displays. If I looked at one of the other displays that the children presented rather than those originally scored, a substantially different evaluation of each child's performance would have been obtained. In cases where a child had been marked wrong, an instance of the correct display was apparent in his actions, and vice versa. If that display, rather than the one noted by the tester, had been recorded, the child's overall score would have changed.

When answering questions, the child is supposed to touch that picture or part of a picture that best answered the question asked. Often the children either did not touch any part of the objects represented in the picture or covered more of the picture than was required by the question. Because the child's response was ambiguous, the tester had to determine the boundaries of the answering gesture. Depending on where the space *between* the pictures was assigned, the tester either marked the child's answer right or marked it wrong.

When the children touched two or more pictures in succession, the tester had to decide which of the movements was intended by the child as his answer. On a number of occasions, the children began to answer before the complete question was asked. Regardless of whether or not the correct picture was touched, the tester did not count the action as an answer. It seemed that the responses had to be given *after* questions had been completely asked in order to be considered answers to questions.

Some children touched the page of pictures with both of their hands simultaneously; others laid their palms flat on the page while answering a question. In these cases, one hand touched an "incorrect" part of the page, while the other hand touched the "correct" part. To count a child's answer as correct in these cases, the tester had to assign the status of "hand indicating an answer" to one hand and not the other.

The following example is representative of the way in which the tester assigned the status of "answer" during the "orientations tasks." In the hand-manipulation phase of the orientations task, after I finished my instruction, "Put your hand below the table," Clarc placed his hand in the air:

 (1) hand raised

I repeated the substance of the instruction, "Below the table," and Clarc modified his initial response. He lowered his hand slowly until it was parallel with, and off to the side of, the table top:

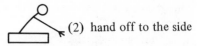

(2) hand off to the side

He paused there, and I said nothing. His hand continued in the arc he had been describing until it was as far down below the table as it would go:

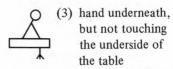

(3) hand underneath, but not touching the underside of the table

At that point, realizing that I had, in fact, influenced his behavior and thereby modified his answer, I attempted to neutralize this influence by saying, "Put it anywhere you want." Clarc left his hand in the last position (3), and I scored that "final" placement "correct". Note, however, that at least three separate displays were given in response to the question asked. The production of multiple responses was obviously influenced by the challenges I made to the child's responses. With each challenge, the child modified his behavior until his arm could literally go no further under the table. Had I recorded either of his first two displays as his "answer" rather than challenging those displays, the child would have been considered wrong on this question.

The protocol conditions of the formal testing procedures are violated in other ways. In the school tests, the child is supposed to touch the correct picture as soon as the question is read. Often more than one picture is to be touched in response to a question. Ideally, the child is supposed to touch all pictures as soon as the question is read. Often the child only touches one. When this occurs, a tester employs various practices to elicit further answers from the child. A tester may prompt the child with verbal cues like "That one?" or "Is that the only one?" These cues tell the child to continue searching for more answers in the series. A similar cue is provided nonverbally when the tester pauses after a response and does not immediately go on to the next question. The pause serves as a cue to the child to keep looking for a correct answer. When the tester either provides a commendatory comment like "Good" or "Fine" or goes immediately on to the next question, the child is prohibited from providing any more responses or changing answers he has already given.

Not only do testers contribute to respondents' productions, but respondents interrupt and thereby contribute to their interrogation. During a test, the tester is supposed to ask questions and the respondent is supposed to answer them. But if a respondent asks the tester a question instead of just answering the tester's question, the adult is forced to respond to the demand made of him by the respondent; that is, the adult/tester has to respond to the demand made of him by the child/respondent *before* the child answers the original test question.[5] The tester can ignore the child's request and repeat the original question; he can pause and say nothing; or he can provide a "neutral" comment like "Do whatever you think is best." Regardless of the tester's reaction to the child's request, though, the child gains further information that influences his interpretation of the original request made of him.

The following interchange exemplifies the manner in which a child gains supplemental information from a tester's responses to the child's questions. The child was asked to draw a circle above the line. She placed her pencil on the paper at a point slightly above the diagonal line she had drawn and asked, "Above? Right here?"

I interpreted the child's action as a request for information about the suitability of an answer that she was considering giving. She had not yet committed herself to producing a particular answer but was asking for confirmation of a possible answer in advance of its production.

The request for information required me to respond in some way. Regardless of my action, the child would learn something about the suitability of the answer she was proposing. I chose to repeat the question as a way out of the dilemma posed by her question. The child then reviewed the entire paper. Her pencil wandered all around the area of the line—both above and below it. She finally settled on this point:

While performing this act she asked, "Right here?" Perhaps exasperated, perhaps convinced that she now "knew" the answer, perhaps unable to restrain myself, I said, "OK." The child drew a circle at the second point and got the question right.

Summary

This examination of testing interaction shows that test assumptions are not met in practice. Stimulus items are not presented in standardized ways. Test materials do not always have the same meaning for tester and child. The child's performance is not just the result of his ability and the stimulus presented but is also influenced by contextually provided information. The respondent's answers are not the product of the tester's passive record-keeping; they emerge from the tester's interpretive assessment of the child's actions.

The tester is not just examining and recording the child's response. He is actively engaged in assigning the status of "answer" to certain portions of the child's behavioral presentation. The tester is according differential status to similar behavioral displays produced by the child as answers to questions, because the tester is not seeing the child's display in isolation from other aspects of the testing situation. The fingers used to point and the hand laid on the page are included in a perceptual field and seen against a constantly changing background of features that include the questions asked, the child's restlessness, his performances on previous questions, teachers' reports about him, and the tester's expectations for the child's performance on any particular question. Therefore, the "same" behavioral display, seen against different backgrounds, is interpreted differently; it obtains a different reading. In short, test-taking and test-scoring are interpretive and interactional processes and should be approached and studied as such.

Cross-Cultural and Methodological Implications

Performance in Different Interrogation Contexts

I have argued that examining only a document of a child's correct and incorrect scores makes it impossible to determine his understanding of test materials, prohibits evaluation of his interpretive abilities, and prohibits comparison of his test performance with his performance in daily experiences. When a child's abilities are assessed in different situations and with different materials, his performance is shown to vary. The results of the children's performances on two sessions of school-administered tests and on my variations of them appear in Tables 11.1 and 11.2. A review of these tables can lead to opinions about the child's language-using abilities in general and his understanding of orientation instructions in particular. Comparing the three first-grade classes, one can see that the children in the classroom under study (#1) received consistently lower scores than the children in the other two grades. Although their test scores improved on the spring test, they did not improve as much as those of children in the other two grades. Comparing the scores of children in first grade #1 shows that the children scored better on the informal tests than on the formal. While only 3 children scored at an acceptable level for the first grade on the fall test and 10 did so on the spring, 13 obtained acceptable scores on the informal tests.

The scores of children who speak both Spanish and English show that Leslie's formal-test score was slightly higher than her informal-test score (presented in English), while Rosa, Laura, and Lora scored the same on the English informal variations as on school tests. All four Spanish speaking children scored higher when questions were asked of them at home in Spanish than when questions were asked of them at school in English. If this difference in performance were shown to be systematic across all bilingual children, it could lead to the conclusion that these children understand instructions better when they are presented in their native language. This conclusion, in turn, could lead to the recommendation that bilingual children be instructed and tested in their native language (Baratz, 1970, Stewart, 1964).

These results are consistent with those of other studies that have examined the child's performance in different contexts of interrogation. Labov (1969) and Lewis (1970) have shown how black children produce more vivid, complex, and spontaneous utterances in peer-centered, unstructered situations than they do in the power relationship of teacher over child. S. Philips (1970) has documented the reluctance of Indian children from the Warmsprings Reservation to participate in classroom verbal interaction when it is competitive and adult-organized and -controlled, by contrast with the eagerness of these same children to speak out when activity is unstructured, unsupervised, and group-centered. These results suggest that the minority child's poor school performance may result from the structure of the interrogation encounter rather than from any inherent lack of ability.

Language and Meaning in Educational Testing

These results, which show variations in children's performance across tasks, situations, and language systems, inevitably lead to certain questions: Which performance represents the child's real ability? Should formal or informal tests, strange or familiar materials be used to evaluate children? Should learning be conducted in a structured or an "open" classroom? Because of the difficulties inherent in developing "culture/free" and "culture-specific" tests,[6] existing tests have commonly been modified by translation in response to the problems raised by the need to test children from different cultures (Mercer, 1971).

Darcy (1963) summarized the bilingual-testing literature. The consistent findings reported were (1) bilingual subjects received significantly lower scores than comparable monolinguals, (2) bilinguals received lower scores when tested in their language than when tested in English, (3) bilinguals scored lower on verbal tests than on nonverbal tests. The second result was explained by saying that the children were instructed in English, while their native-language training stopped, for all intents and purposes, when the children entered primary school; thus the translated versions of the formal test probably differed significantly from the native language familiar to the children.

Translating assessment materials will not solve the school problems of the lower-class or bilingual child, because the content of the entire interrogation encounter, not just the words of the test, is culture-bound. Questions, materials, and referents reflect the content of the culture in which the test was developed.

Simply translating the content of a test designed for persons socialized in one culture into the language of another does not eliminate the cultural difference. Furthermore, the respondent's performance together with the observer's evaluation of that performance constitute an interpreted and negotiated process. Although my analysis of interrogation encounters is not finely enough calibrated to indicate which particular situational features available to a child contribute to his answer on a given occasion, I have shown that much more than just the presentation of stimulus items serves as the source of the child's answer. Although the tester assumes variations in stimulus presentation, believing that his intervening activity does not contribute to a child's understanding of test materials and is unimportant in his evaluation of the respondent's performance, I have shown the child is not attending to stimulus items in isolation and that the tester is not passively recording "answers."

The questions and materials appear against a background composed of the negotiated aspects of the question-answer sequence, including verbal and nonverbal cues. The respondent has to interpret the entire interrogation setting, the translation of materials, or the substitution of one mode of interrogation for another; test-taking must be seen against a situationally provided background. Simple translation and the exclusive reliance on any single kind of instrument to evaluate competence are limited solutions, for such practices fail to recognize that each communicative encounter is self-organizing (Zimmerman and Pollner, 1970:94-100), and each question/answer sequence imposes its own perceptual demands and interpretive requirements on respondents and evaluators. In short, each encounter between interrogator and respondent has its own social organization and unique features that produce different (not necessarily better) evaluations of a respondent. Therefore, instead of searching for a single "best" test, the recommendation made here is to study the interpretive process in any interrogation and to examine a child's performance under different conditions of interrogation.

Language and Meaning in Cross-Cultural Interrogation

Sociological research is often based on a small number of closed-answer survey questions.[7] Thus, it may frequently be asked whether a researcher's question carries the same meaning for respondents that it does for the social scientist who constructed it. The equivalence-of-meaning problem is especially acute in cross-cultural research because respondents do not share the researcher's cultural background. In such situations the cross-cultural researcher faces the same problems as the educational tester in the research just described. Further, the cross-cultural researcher has dealt with the problems that language and meaning pose for research in much the same way as the educational tester: he searches for the lexical equivalence of questionnaire items (Deutscher, 1968).

The simplest approach to lexical equivalence has involved substituting dictionary definitions in the target language for terms from the original system. A slightly more sophisticated approach to cross-cultural interrogation is called back-translation.[8] These techniques attempt to achieve stimulus equivalence for the researcher, but they do not examine the conceptual equivalence of questions for the respondent. Just as a lexically equivalent test item may have different meanings for a child and a tester, a translated questionnaire item may have different meanings for respondents from different cultures. H. Phillips (1959:190), for example, reports that "He often daydreams" became "When he sleeps during the day, he dreams" when this phrase was translated into Thai for a research project. When the phrase "Genevieve suspended for prank" was translated into Japanese and back to English again, it became "Genevieve hanged for juvenile delinquency" (Kluckhohn, cited by Grimshaw, 1969a:3) If *amigo* and *Freund* were substituted for "friend" in questions about national character, one might conclude that Spanish subjects were more outgoing, and German subjects more reserved, than Americans, because of the frequency with which the subjects used the friendship term (Deutscher, 1968). However, these terms do not stand for the same referent; for the German, *Freund* is reserved for intimates, while the Spanish direct *amigo* to even the most casual acquaintance (Grimshaw, 1969b:317, discusses the use of various terms for "friend"). When the Londons (1966) examined the translation of questions used on the Harvard Soviet survey, they found marked differences in derived and intended meanings.

Intercultural researchers, like educational testers, assume that the background experiences of their subjects are sufficiently similar to have provided a common core of meanings for the terms employed in questions. When cross-cultural studies are conducted, though, the researcher cannot assume that the scales built into questions are equivalent for respondents of different cultures.[9] Suppose, for example, that a researcher is comparing the wealth of respondents cross-culturally. A person who reports owning a one-acre farm in the United States may be considered "poor" by American standards, but how should a Vietnamese who owns that same amount of land in Vietnam be categorized? A researcher who classified this Vietnamese as "poor" without determining the local standards of wealth would be unable to make valid comparisons, because a one-acre holding may not have an equivalent rank in the two economic systems.

Likewise, when respondents are asked to make subjective judgments—for example, "Are you happy?"—they are not provided the norms or standards of others within their own culture as a baseline against which to compare their responses. When such questions are asked across cultural boundaries, the possibility increases that respondents are not applying the same standards; that possibility, then, should be made an explicit aspect of the investigation. Behavioral questions such as "I attend political meetings (or church, or club meetings, etc.) regularly" or "I vote in elections" and attitudinal questions like

"I think the government is doing an adequate job" seem to be objective. However, voting and attending church or meetings may not have the same value in different cultures and may not have the same meaning even among different respondents within the same culture. Behavioral and attitudinal questions require the cross-cultural researcher to establish the similarity of norms within each culture and to determine the equivalence of question-meaning among his respondents.

Hence, translation techniques do not guarantee cross-cultural conceptual equivalence because these techniques are only concerned with the investigator's meaning of the questions asked; they do not examine respondents' interpretations. To achieve cross-cultural equivalence, the researcher must do more than translate questions; he must not rely solely on the products of interrogation when analyzing data. He must in addition treat the interpretive process as a problematic aspect of his research by examining the perceptual and definitional practices that respondents use to answer questions.

Further Suggestions for the Use of Videotape

Findings that demonstrate that respondents and researchers rely on a contextually provided background of features to interpret materials can lead to recommendations to improve or repair the interrogation encounter. Friedman (1968), for example, concluded his penetrating study of the "unintended stimulation" provided to experimental subjects with recommendations for the reform of experimental research. He suggested that experimenters and subjects be randomized and that instructions and stimuli be mechanized in order to minimize experimenter effects. Unobstrusive (Webb et al, 1966) or blind (Friedman, 1968) measures may avoid interactional "contamination," but they result in extreme behaviorism. Even if interrogation is mechanized, the respondent will still construct a background against which to interpret materials; further, the investigator will not have access to the respondent's interpretive system. If the investigator is removed from interaction with the respondent, he is forced to analyze behavior from a position of ignorance; he does not know how subjects interpreted the various stimulus items and the whole interrogation encounter. The researcher's knowledge about social behavior is dependent upon his research methods, which, in turn, are dependent upon his social knowledge (D. Phillips, 1971:53). Because the researcher must always view respondents' behavior against (usually unstated) background assumptions, the more he knows about the everyday life of his respondents, the more valid will be his observations from any one study.

In short, I am not recommending that findings about contextually based interpretations be used to try to eliminate experimenter effects, to reduce measurement error, or to improve reliability. Instead of trying to control and suppress respondents' and researchers' contextually bound interpretive work, I recommend that the negotiated aspects of data presentation and measurement be studied as interactional phenomena so that the ways in which respondents and researchers make sense of the interrogation encounter can be better understood. Videotape can be effective instrument for this purpose.

If a cross-cultural investigator is conducting survey research, he can select a subsample of subjects from each cultural group and videotape the interrogation encounter between the interviewer and the respondent, instead of just "probing" selected questions (Schuman, 1966). The videotape subsequently provides the researcher with a document that he can check in order to determine what information the respondents used to answer questions. He can check the videotape to determine how investigators coded responses or instances of behavior into data classes. The researcher can also show the videotape of an interrogation to respondents immediately after an encounter so that they can provide the thoughts and interpretations they had about the questions.[10]

Videotape can be used effectively in other aspects of cross-cultural research as well. The investigator who enters either a local or a foreign research setting is relying on his personal background of experience to interpret the setting. A videotaped record of encounters between researchers and natives will provide both the researcher and his audience with the information on which respondents relied to answer questions—in effect, the real materials upon which analysis is based. As researchers become more familiar with, or are "built into," their research settings, their preceptions of situations change. Because information gathered in later stages of the research can influence interpretations made earlier, McCall (1969) suggests that researchers compare observations made at different stages of investigations. Sequentially arranged video segments gathered at various stages of an investigation can be analyzed so that the consequences of changing interpretations for theoretical conclusions can be documented. The researcher who enters the field usually has a problem to investigate and a sense of the evidence he expects to gather in support of his guiding hypotheses. Visually available data can keep ideas and interpretations public and provide the basis for alternative interpretations of the same data.

Alternative formulations of the same situation, available through the eyes of different informants, can be formalized by using videotape as a stimulus document. Different types of informants—for example, the "naïve informant," the "old hand," the "malcontent," the "outsider" (researcher) (see Dean, cited by Cicourel, 1964:63-65)—can each be asked to "tell about" a videotaped segment of naturally occurring social activity. The structure of the varying interpretations will provide insight into the social distribution of native knowledge, perspective differences in perception, and the changing time structure of accounts.[11]

Alternative versions of the same situation, available through different research instruments, can be formalized in the same way. Some participants in videotaped interaction situations can be interrogated about their experiences by fixed-choice questions, others by open-ended questions, and so on. The interplay between the respondent's experience and the mode of inquiry will aid efforts to coordinate field research and interview techniques, thereby contributing to an "ethnography of interrogation" (Grimshaw, 1970).

In short, videotape can contribute to "objectification" (Cicourel, 1968a: 2) in social science research by making publicly available the rules of interpretation and the grounds upon which conclusions are based. Because videotape enables the researcher to document instances of his phenomena in situationally based behavioral displays, a natural history of descriptions and conclusions is available to other social scientists for comparison, criticism, and extension.

Notes

1.   The overall contrastive study of language acquisition, language use, and school performance has been assisted by a Ford Foundation Grant (Aaron V. Cicourel, Principal Investigator). The study utilized data gathered in 1969-1970 from two elementary schools in Southern California (see Cicourel et al., in press). Language-*using* abilities are contrasted with linguistic abilities per se. The generative linguist (e.g., Chomsky, 1965) constructs a set of abstract principles to account for the speaker-hearer's ability to produce and understand sentences. This research has been concerned with how the speaker-hearer *applies* his linguistic, social, and interpretive knowledge in everyday situations of language use (cf. Cicourel, 1968a; Hymes, 1968; Labov, 1970; Mehan, 1972).

2.   This research is obviously not the first critical examination of educational tests. Educators, psychologists, and sociologists have long been concerned with the accuracy and fairness of educational tests. Previous criticisms of testing, however, have dealt only with the *product* and *results* of testing (i.e., the test scores of different groups of children have been compared). When differences in test scores (interpreted as ability) have been found, attempts have been made to make tests "culture-free" (e.g., Goodenough's draw-a-man, David-Eel's games, the Raven Progressive Matrices) or to develop culture-sensitive tests (e.g., by translating tests into the respondent's native language, as has been done with the Peabody Picture Vocabulary Test, the Stanford-Binet, and the WISC). Mercer (1971) presents a concise summary of this literature. The examination of tests reported here differs from previous studies in that testing is treated as an interactional accomplishment. The meaning of the testing situation, the source of the respondent's answer, and the tester's scoring are examined from within ongoing testing situations.

3.   The way in which production procedures and practices are said to constitute socially organized settings is explained by Garfinkel (1967), Cicourel (1968b, 1969, 1970, and in press), Garfinkel and Sacks (1970), Wilson (1970), and Zimmerman and Pollner (1970).

4.   Numbers refer to the full transcript of the school-administered testing session; transcripts that are part of this study may be examined upon request.

5.   Sacks (1967-1970) and Schegloff (1968, 1971) have proposed that when one question follows another in conversation, the question asked second is answered

before the one asked first. Schegloff (1971) calls this an "embedded question" sequence (see Figure 11.1).

Turn	Speaker	Response
1	Tester	Question
2	Child	Question
3	Tester	Answer
4	Child	Answer

Figure 11.1 "Embedded question" sequence

6. From its appearance in 1926, Goodenough's draw-a-man test was considered a possible culture-free test of intelligence because it was nonverbal, presumably not subject-matter related, and the referent drawn was universal. Recent testing has shown, however, that Goodenough scores correlate highly with the presence, familiarity, and encouragement of representative art in a society, a factor that seems to be a function of a society's degree of modernization (Dennis, 1966). These kinds of findings have lead Goodenough to say:

   "The present writers would like to express the opinion that the search for a culture free test, whether of intelligence, artistic ability, personal-social characteristics, or any other measurable trait is illusory, and that the naive assumption that more freedom from verbal requirements renders a test equally suitable for all groups is no longer tenable (Goodenough and Harris, 1950:339).

7. D. Phillips (1971:3) points out that the vast majority of sociological studies (90 percent in the *American Sociological Review* between 1962 and 1969; 92 percent in the *American Journal of Sociology* and the *American Sociological Review* combined between 1965 and 1966) utilize the survey.

8. Brislin (1970) gives a comprehensive review of back-translation in comparative research. He outlines the potential sources of error in translation and suggests elaborate procedures to achieve stimulus equivalence. (These include using simple materials; eliminating metaphors, colloquialisms, pronouns, passives, and subjunctive sentence constructions from the English version; matching multiple blind translations; and probing certain answers.) His criterion for the success of translated materials is the researcher's satisfaction with results. Brislin does not, however, consider it necessary to validate the translation against the respondents' everyday experiences.

9. The same point applies for intracultural researchers as well, but that point falls outside the purpose of this paper. See instead Cicourel (1964).

10. One of my students, Nick Maroules, is employing this technique (first suggested by Cicourel, 1964:103) to validate a political survey. He is uncovering implicit questions hidden under surface questions and is finding that respondents' schemes of categorization do not match the researchers', a result that casts doubts on routinely reported research findings.

11. Cicourel (in press) has termed this process "indefinite triangulation"; it should be compared to Denzin's (1969) concept of "multiple triangulation." Whereas Denzin says that using multiple data sources and many research techniques and strategies will

aid an investigator in arriving at the "facts" of a social situation, Cicourel suggests:

"that every procedure that seeks to 'lock-in' evidence, thus to claim a level of adequacy, can itself be subjected to the same sort of analysis that will in turn produce yet another indefinite arrangement of previously established particulars in 'authoritative,' 'final,' 'formal' accounts. Indefinite triangulation attempts to make visible the practicality and inherent reflexivity of erveryday and scientific accounts."

Indefinite triangulation has been used by Boese (1971), who graphically demonstrates the varieties of interpretation that a native signer and a second-language signer place on a piece of conversation between a child and a deaf parent. Jennings and Jennings show how the analysis of a language-assessment session changes through time and varies according to the scheme of interpretation employed; Roth and MacKay are showing the contrast between teachers' and childrens' interpretations of educational materials (Cicourel et al, in press). Shumsky (1972) shows how interpretations of an encounter-group session change across time and vary with the perspective of the participant.

References

Anastasi, Anne.

    1968   *Psychological Testing.* New York: Macmillan.

Baratz, Joan C.

    1970   Teaching reading in an urban Negro school system. In Frederick Williams (Ed.), *Language and Poverty.* Boston: Markham. Pp. 11-24.

Bereiter, Carl, and Siegfried Englemann.

    1966   *Teaching Disadvantaged Children in the Preschool.* Englewood Cliffs, N.J.: Prentice-Hall.

Boese, Robert.

    1970   *Natural Sign Language and the Acquisition of Social Structure.* Ph.D. dissertation, University of California, Santa Barbara.

Brislin, Richard W.

    1970   Back-translation for cross-cultural research. *Journal of Cross-Cultural Psychology,* 1 (September): 185-216.

Cazden, Courtney.

    1970   The neglected situation in child language research and education. In Frederick Williams (Ed.), *Language and Poverty.* Boston: Markham. Pp. 81-101.

References   331

Chomsky, Noam.

1965   *Aspects of the Theory of Syntax.* Cambridge, Mass.: MIT Press.

Cicourel, Aaron V.

1964   *Method and Measurement in Sociology.* New York: Free Press.

1968a   *The Social Organization of Juvenile Justice.* New York: Wiley.

1968b   Verso una sociologia evoltiva del linguaggio e del significato.
        Rassegna Italiana di Sociologia, 9:21-258. Trans.: The acquisition
        of social structure: towards a developmental sociology of language
        and meaning. In Jack Douglas (Ed.), *Understanding Everyday Life.*
        Chicago: Aldine, 1970. Pp. 136-168.

1969   Generative semantics and the structure of social interaction. In
        International Days of Sociolinguistics. Rome: Luigi Sturzo Insti-
        tute. Pp. 173-202.

1970   Basic and normative rules in the negotiation of status and role. In
        Hans P. Drietzel (Ed.), *Recent Sociology 2: Patterns of Com-
        municative Behavior.* New York: Macmillan. Pp. 4-45.

In   Ethnomethodology. In Thomas A. Sebeok (Ed.), *Current Trends*
press. *in Linguistics,* vol. XII. The Hague: Mouton.

Cicourel, Aaron V., Kenneth Jennings, Sybillyn Jennings, Kenneth Leiter,
    Robert McKay, Hugh Mehan, and David Roth.

In   *Language Use and School Performance.* New York: Seminar
press. Press.

Darcy, Natalie T.

1963   Bilingualism and the measurement of intelligence. *Journal of
        Genetic Psychology,* 103 (December):259-282.

Dennis, Wayne T.

1966   Goodenough scores, art experience, and modernization. *Journal of
        Social Psychology,* 68 (April):211-228.

Denzin, Norman.

1969   *The Research Act.* Chicago: Aldine.

Deutsch, Cynthia.

1964   Auditory discrimination and learning: social factors. *Merrill-
        Palmer Quarterly,* 10 (July):277-296.

Deutscher, Irwin.

    1968   Asking questions cross-culturally: some problems of linguistic comparability. In Howard S. Becker, Blanche Geer, David Riesman, and Robert S. Weiss (Eds.), *Institutions and the Person: Papers Presented to Everett C. Hughes.* Chicago: Aldine.

Englemann, Siegfried.

    1967   *The Basic Concept Inventory.* Chicago: Follet.

Friedman, Neil.

    1968   *The Social Nature of Psychological Research.* New York: Basic Books.

Garfinkel, Harold.

    1967   *Studies in Ethnomethodology.* Englewood Cliffs, N.J.: Prentice-Hall.

Garfinkel, Harold, and Harvey Sacks.

    1970   The formal properties of practical actions. In John C. McKinney and Edward A. Tiryakian (Eds.), *Theoretical Sociology.* New York: Appleton-Century-Crofts. Pp. 338-366.

Goodenough, Florence, and D. Harris.

    1950   Studies in the psychology of children's drawings. *Psychological Bulletin,* 47 (September):369-433.

Grimshaw, Allen D.

    1969a   Language as obstacle and as data in sociological research. *Items,* 23 (2):17-21.

    1969b   Sociolinguistics and the sociologist. *American Sociologist,* 4 (November):312-321.

    1970   Some problematic aspects of communication in cross-cultural research in the United States. *Sociological Focus,* 3, no. 2:67-85.

Hymes, Dell H.

    1968   On the ethnography of speaking. In Joshua A. Fishman (Ed.), *The Sociology of Language.* The Hague: Mouton. Pp. 99-138.

Labov, William.

    1969   The logic of Non-Standard English. In George Alatis (Ed.),

Linguistics and Language Study, Monograph Series 22. Washington, D.C.: Georgetown University Press. Pp. 1-22, 26-31.

1970　The study of language in its social setting. *Studiuem Generale,* 23, no. 1:30-87.

Lewis, Louisa.

1970　Culture and Social Interaction in the Classroom. *Working Paper 38.* Berkeley: Language-Behavior Research Laboratory, University of California, Berkeley.

London, Ivan D., and Miriam B. London.

1966　A research-examination of the Harvard Project on the Soviet Social System. *Psychological Reports,* pt.2: 1011-1109.

McCall, George J.

1969　Data quality control in participant observation. In George J. McCall and J.L. Simmons (Eds.), *Issues in Participant Observation.* New York: Addison Wesley. Pp. 1-45.

Mehan, Hugh.

1971　*Accomplishing Understanding in Educational Settings.* Ph.D. dissertation, University of California, Santa Barbara.

1972　Language-using abilities. *Language Science,* 22 (October): 1-10.

Melmed, Paul.

1971　*Black English Phonology.* Monograph 1. Berkeley: Language-Behavior Research Laboratory, University of California, Berkeley.

Mercer, Jane R.

1971　Institutionalized Anglocentricism. In Peter Orleans and William R. Ellis, Jr. (Eds.), *Race, Change, and Urban Society.* New York: Russell Sage. Pp. 311-338.

Mitchell-Kernan, Claudia.

1969　*Language Behavior in a Black Urban Community.* Ph.D. dissertation, University of California, Berkeley. Published as *Working Paper 23,* Language-Behavior Research Laboratory, University of California, Berkeley. Also Monograph 2, Language-Behavior Research Laboratory, 1971.

Philips, Susan U.

    1970   Acquisition of rules for appropriate speech usage. In George
            Alatis (Ed.), *Linguistics and Language Study*, Monograph Series
            23. Washington, D.C.: Georgetown University Press. Pp. 77-101.

Phillips, Derek.

    1971   *Knowledge From What?* Chicago: Rand McNally.

Phillips, Herbert P.

    1959   Problems of translation and meaning in field work. *Human
            Organization*, 18 (Winter): 184-192.

Sacks, Harvey.

    1967-   Unpublished lecture notes. University of California, Los Angeles
    1970   and, Irvine.

Schegloff, Emanuel A.

    1968   Sequencing in conversational openings. *American Anthropol-
            ogist*, 70, no. 6: 1075-1095.

    1971   Notes on a conversational practice: formulating place. In David
            Sudnow (Ed.), *Studies in Social Interaction*. New York: Free
            Press. Pp. 75-124.

Schuman, Howard.

    1966   The random probe. *American Sociological Review*, 3 (April):
            218-222.

Schutz, Alfred.

    1962   *Collected Papers*, Vol. I: *The Problem of Social Reality*. The
            Hague: Martinus Nijhoff.

Shumsky, Marshall.

    1972   *Encounter Groups: A Forensic Science*. Ph.D. dissertation, Uni-
            versity of California, Santa Barbara.

Spearman, Carl.

    1923   *The Nature of Intelligence and the Purpose of Cognition*. London:
            Macmillan.

Stewart, William A.

    1964   Foreign language situations. In William A. Stewart (Ed.), *Non-*

Standard Speech and the Teaching of English. Washington, D.C.: Center for Applied Linguistics. Pp. 1-15.

Webb, Eugene J., Donald T. Campbell, Richard D. Schwartz, and Lee Sechrest.

1966   *Unobtrusive Measures.* Chicago: Rand McNally.

Wechsler, David.

1944   *The Measurement of Adult Intelligence.* Baltimore: Williams and Wilkens.

Wilson, Thomas P.

1970   Conceptions of interaction and forms of sociological explanation. *American Sociological Review,* 35 (August): 697-709.

Woodworth, Robert S., and Harold Schlosberg.

1954   *Experimental Psychology.* New York: Holt.

Zimmerman, Don H., and Melvin Pollner.

1970   The everyday would as a phenomenon. In Jack Douglas (Ed.), *Understanding Everyday Life.* Chicago: Aldine. Pp. 80-103.

Discussion*

Mr. Hill.   You have described instances in which the tester seems to provide hints and cues to the child. This leads me to ask: Do you doubt the child's answers? I ask this because there are times when a good interviewer will depart from a standard protocol on purpose in order to assess the validity of an answer. I am not as concerned with meeting standard testing procedures as I am with assessment of the variable.

Mr. Mehan.   What troubles me is the way in which results are reported. In a testing situation only the results are reported. You don't see a record of those instances in which the tester deviated or gave hints or cues. As a result, you have no way of assessing the impact of deviations from standardized procedures.

Mr. Anderson.   You indicated that you thought the saying of "Good" after a child's response tended to close off alternative choices on the part of the child. It looked to me, in one of your selections, like the child made a definite point and quite before the tester said, "Good." I didn't get the impression that there was any ambiguity.

*The Mehan discussion was quite different in structure from all others in this book. In addition to his paper, Mehan presented several videotape selections showing children's and testers' behavior .in actual test-taking situations. It is the specifics of these selections to which questioners often refer.

Mr. Mehan.   There are many times in a testing situation when the tester feels absolutely certain of a child's answer, yet a moment later the child changes his answer. After that happens a couple of times, the tester wonders about the answers that seemed so certain earlier. Then everything becomes problematic. So simply presenting test results does not allow an investigator to separate "certain" cases from "problematic" ones.

Mr. Anderson   Do you interpret silence as a probe for a correct answer or as a noncommunication?

Mr. Mehan.   In some instances, silence seems to cue the child to continue, but other times it doesn't.

Mr. Anderson.   Are you saying that the tester is doing some things she shouldn't do?

Mr. Mehan.   By providing hints and cues, she is violating testing protocol.

Mr. Anderson.   But you have also said that sometimes silence communicates a cue. How can giving cues be avoided, then?

Mr. Mehan.   Now you have my point. Communicating cues can not be avoided and so should be made an explicit part of the interrogation procedure. The testing situation contrasts sharply with the classroom situation. In the classroom hints and cues are routine; in the test, though, cues are not supposed to be present. The testing situation is bizarre, then, because the child is, in effect, told not to rely on the ways he was taught to learn in class but rather to operate in a strange and unknown way. When we find, as we have, that the test is like the classroom in that cues are operating in both situations, I recommend either not relying so heavily on test results or studying the testing encounter more thoroughly.

Mr. Straus.   If the tester had not said "Good" to some responses, her silence would have cued the child by telling him to continue searching. But if the tester had been uniform in her presentations, there would be no cueing.

Mr. Mehan.   I would like to run tests to see if testers can actually refrain from giving cues.

Mr. Straus.   That attempt would conflict with other things testers are taught—namely, to be supportive and warm.

Mr. Schnaiberg.   It seems to me that the way to do testing would be to have a standardized video presentation.

Mr. Mehan.   First of all, I don't think that standardization could be achieved. I don't think you could build a program that could handle such unplanned occurrences as the child's dropping his pencil or need to go to the bathroom or noise from the lawn mower outside obscuring the question. But let's assume you *could* standardize the stimulus presentation. That procedure would still not enable the investigator or tester to decide what the child or respondent was attending to as he made his response. Since I think the tester is interested in the child's reasoning abilities, that procedure would only obscure more deeply the topics we need to study.

Mr. Form.   Can you say that a tester helps a poor kid more than a rich kid, or something like that?

Mr. Mehan.   My data make no such implication.

Mr. Form.   Then this whole question is a psychological or clinical concern, not a sociological problem.

Mr. Hill.   Wait a minute. There isn't one of us that would send a videotape machine out on an interview.

Mr. Form.   Of course not.

Mr. Mehan.   Why not?

Mr. Hill.   Because we think we do it better, even though we don't really understand our data gathering mechanisms. And by God, if we let Mehan go out and interview, I don't care if the interviewer-interviewee reaction is a psychological problem; he is getting at the generation of data, and I want to see what happens.

Mr. Mehan.   I would be happy to go along and do this work with any of you who use surveys.

Mr. Form.   I don't care whether he stimulates one guy or another; I want to know test results: whether they go up or down or sideways.

Mr. Simpson.   I thought testing protocols were deliberately set up to settle the kid down. The tester has to relate to the kid. Thus the testing question becomes: Is a tester good with kids—lower-class kids, upper-class kids, emotional kids.

Mr. Mehan.   And in the final analysis the question becomes: In what way is the tester's ability to deal with kids reported as part of the results? When the tester is writing up results, does she say, "This child got 75 percent correct but seemed anxious; therefore, his score should be raised"? No. This doesn't happen.

Mr. Anderson.   You are presenting this research as though it were somehow new and dramatic information. I can't conceive that testers haven't been taught how to handle ambiguous cases.

Mr. Mehan.   The way the tester handles the problem of ambiguous answers is to channel the response or to mark it as incorrect. They do not routinely examine the child's reasoning to see what led to the ambiguous responses.

Mr. Anderson.   The task is to get an answer. The task is to infer, based on the respondent's response, what answer best represents his ability at that time. The task is not to infer some sort of subjective intention on the part of the respondent.

Mr. Mehan.   I am not recommending that the concept of context is particularly new; I *am* recommending that it be treated as a subject of inquiry rather than pushing it aside.

Mr. Anderson.   I can't understand what you are talking about when you say that. A great deal of effort in the training of interviewers is directed precisely *at* coping with that problem. There isn't any attempt to stick it under the rug.

Mr. Mehan.   How are coders trained in that particular problem? What are coders told to do when a respondent says, "I don't know what this question means."

Mr. Anderson.   This matter is handled in pretesting. If a word is producing different responses, that fact is reported and discussed. Sometimes another word is chosen. That is not hiding from it or putting it under the rug.

Mr. Mehan.   I am saying that treatment should go beyond seemingly questionable items to all items because you don't necessarily know in advance which items are questionable for your respondents. The matter of meaning equivalence between respondent and interviewer needs to be examined continually, especially across cultures and languages.

Mr. Finsterbusch.   I wonder what the child is interested in doing in the test. I wonder to what extent he is really motivated to give correct answers, as compared to his interest in moving on to the next question. If you confuse him, he will do anything, just like one of Skinner's pigeons, until it is the right thing.

Mr. Mehan.   If the child is trying to give you what you want rather than what the test is presumably asking, doesn't that make the testing situation strange?

Mr. Menanteau.   I think your point was made in terms of cross-cultural research. When the word is passed, among local people, that someone is testing or interviewing, immediately the local situation changes. The value orientation of the subjects to answer in a particular way is a very critical piece of knowledge to have when one is evaluating an instrument.

Mr. Mehan. What is required, then, is a judgment of the fit between what a respondent says in an interrogation with other aspects of his daily life. If a respondent says he is not prejudiced, then we must check his behavior in other situations in order to judge the validity of his response.

Mr. Strodtbeck. You continue to say that under standardized testing techniques, a child may be erroneously marked wrong when the tester influences the child's answer. But I have never seen such amateurish management of children in a test situation with so many unnecessary distractions; to use these presentations to downgrade a perfectly legitimate quasiprofession, I think is just outrageous.

Mr. Mehan. Interrogation is an interactional phenomenon in which the respondent is relying on much more information than just the stimulus being presented by the tester. We can not assume that a correspondence exists between the interrogator's world and the respondent's world. We must investigate that fit. In one of those presentations I did influence a child; if that situation had been a formal test, the kid would have been marked wrong, but not because he didn't know the answer but rather because the tester influenced his response.

Mr. Anderson. How do you find out that we *must* investigate a respondent's world? That sounds extraordinarily authoritarian.

Mr. Mehan. If you are interested in the potential validity of an instrument, I think that task is a requirement. If you are interested in the child's reasoning ability, then I think it is a requirement.

Mr. Bird. I think many of these tests are simply based on false assumptions about language and the semantic values and parameters that come into play when a child is asked a question about "over the line" and "over the table," for example. You have two things going on in some of those selections. The child is working with a piece of paper, which requires him to flip into a two-dimensional grammar. You said, "Put the circle above the line." The kid is operating in three dimensions. That circle is above the line. And when you said, "Put it below the line," his first effort was to turn the piece of paper over so that he could get the circle under the line. There is nothing illogical about that. And there is no way in which you can determine from any testing situation when the child is operating in a two- or three-dimensional space.

Mr. Mehan. That's one of the points I have been trying to make: the child's representations are indeterminate when assessed by adult models.

Mr. Bird. There are a number of other things that could be said about this paper. One regards the validity of the test described. In itself, I think the test is based on a number of false assumptions about language. First, I don't think it's clear whether you can get at what words mean through any kind of a standardized test, although you could say that a word or a sentence has an analysis in terms of its truth conditions and its truth values. A linguist, though, is not necessarily interested in the truth values of any particular sentence.

In standard English, there are two parameters that I think is important to determine when considering a world like "over" where "over" is used as a locative. There is a parameter of location; for example, let's say X is over Y. That X may be at any point touching the upper surface or at any point about the upper surface. Either may be the location parameter. The other parameter, the other presupposition, is that if X is touching the upper surface, then there is a parameter of size: X must be larger than Y so that X covers Y.

Now, I think there is good evidence to show that in certain social groups, certain subsets of society, only one of these parameters is used. In one of these subsets, I could locate my hand *over* the television by laying my hand on top of it, as I have just done, and say, "My hand is over the television." And in certain Black English dialects, this would be perfectly valid. My hand would, in that context, be over the television set. People in those societies are using only one parameter. The size parameter is not included.

If someone has not included both parameters in his analysis of "over," is he more illogical, or culturally deprived, or what? If his society lacks that parameter, what do we say about it intellectually? The conclusion that I would have to draw is that his society and we just don't speak the same language. So false assumption number 1 is that the meanings of words and sentences are discrete and determinate. That is demonstrably false.

False assumption number 2, which follows from 1, is that all speakers of a given community will normally arrive at the same grammar; that is, all speakers of the same community would assign the same meaning to the same sounds. That also is demonstrably false.

False assumption number 3 is that the way *we* behave linguistically is a logical way to behave. People who do not behave like us are, therefore, illogical or inferior. It seems to me that tests based on such assumptions are false, and their elimination is a job for a linguist and not necessarily a sociologist. If there were a corpus of data to which a researcher could return during the analytic process, the test would be greatly enhanced. It is this possibility that I consider to be the greatest advantage of this videotape material; there is a definite corpus about which you can test and make hypotheses. If the test falls down, the record is still there. That is of a great advantage.

Mr. Portes. It seems to me that the merit of these presentations has been to offer a quite interesting illustration of the limitations of measures. On the other hand, let me stress again that by no means is this a new topic and certainly not one that is scarcely discussed in methodological treatments.

If not, why the multiplicity of items when approaching measurements of mental ability or attitudes? A multiplicity of items exists precisely to maximize reliability or internal consistency by allowing a canceling out of measurement error or limitation in particular items. A multiplicity of items will work in most cases unless there is a consistent bias.

The examples of testers shown on the videotape do not seem to offer consistent biases. In one instance they are going one direction, in another instance in the other. So many items of this nature may maximize internal consistency, which should be the first consideration.

A second consideration is that of validity, which is essentially a relative question and depends on whatever it is the researcher is trying to measure. Obviously, if these measures were intended to measure intrinsic intelligence or intrinsic mental ability, they would be unjustifiable, especially if they were applied to people who are only partially familiar with the cultural assumptions on which the tests are based.

On the other hand, if the researcher wants to measure familiarity with variable categories employed in *this* society, the test may be quite valid; in that case middle-class children will score better than Chicanos, and validly so.

I think that Mr. Bird's discussion as a linguist fits within the general issue of validity. What he has said, essentially, is that these tests will not be valid if we want to measure certain things. On the other hand, though, we may be interested in issues like the relative familiarity of different groups with dominant verbal categories. In a way, then, the discussion can be placed very well within the methodological categories of reliability and validity that we have traditionally used.

Mr. Grimshaw. Yes, it is true that people have been concerned about problems in the ethnography of interrogation, but my guess is that there is less concern here with the validity of the instruments themselves than with what goes on in the encounter. If an instrument's validity is questionable, then simple extension of the number of questions from 10 to 20 only compounds and doesn't resolve the matter of validity even though some kind of spurious reliability may be attained.

Mr. Anderson.   Let me be very brief. It is my interpretation of much that has gone on here that we are substantially in agreement with the evidence that you present. When we shift from the evidence to interpretation of that evidence, though, disagreement occurs. Mehan interprets the results one way, Bird another, I still another, and somebody else in testing may have a still different interpretation.

Presumably all of us, if it is a matter of importance to us, have some obligation as responsible scholars to bring evidence to bear upon our interpretations as well as on the original subject studied. And I for one haven't heard any presentations of evidence that your interpretations are better, more accurate, more descriptive, or fits some sort of test better than anybody else's interpretation.

Mr. Grimshaw.   You say we all agree on the evidence that Mehan has shown us, that we simply disagree on interpretation. Unfortunately, there are researchers in the field who have *not* accepted evidence like Mehan's, who are satisfied with what they're doing, who feel that language translations of instruments and cross-cultural transporting of techniques is generally nonproblematic. They'll get someone whom they think is bilingual, but who may not be bicultural, and simply ask him to translate an instrument. They don't really believe there is any problem that can't be resolved by iterations of back-translations.

Mr. Schnaiberg.   Again we're missing a point. What about the social consequences of this work? We clearly understand systematic (e.g., social-class-related) error, which doesn't seem operative here except insofar as all these kids were preselected for the test. There is that kind of overriding framework. The thing we miss, though, is that there are social consequences in terms of these kids' life histories. The interpretations we put on consequences of this sort are very different, depending on whether there is some kind of systematic error, in which case we call it discrimination, and whether there is random error in an analytic sense which can be corrected. We can't correct for attentuation in a one-shot criterion for placement. The one-shot effort produces a form, if you will, of individualized inequity that functions as a inequitable social process within the school system. This is a social process even though it may be based on a kind of psychological testing.

Mr. Stryker.   There is one element in Mehan's presentation that I think has been overlooked or at least neglected, and that is this business of making deliberate use of the interrogator as part of the experimental situation.

Perhaps the point can be clarified by reference to the experimental-demand literature. All of us knew from the Department of Agriculture studies in the 1930s that interviewer characteristics made a hell of a lot of difference in subjects' responses. That fact is not new nor, for that matter, was our recent discovery of experimenter demand new. All of us who had done social psychological experiments were perfectly aware of the fact that our subjects were in the social role of subject and in that role often were trying to give us what they thought we wanted in the experimental situation. What *is* relatively new, it seems to me, is the kind of thing that some social psychologists are suggesting—that is, that we turn experimental demand to theoretical advantage by introducing it as a variable in our experiments. That, as I understand it, is part of what Mehan is saying as well when he remarks, "Let's turn the disadvantage of the interrogation situation into an advantage by making it an explicit part of the experimental situation." I think that is a perfectly sensible, reasonable point that has been overlooked in much of the discussion to this point.

PART FIVE

Comparative Applications of Quantitative Methods

CHAPTER TWELVE

Some Analytical Problems in the Comparative Test of Ecological Theories

KENT P. SCHWIRIAN

The Ohio State University

The purpose of this paper is to discuss some of the basic methodological problems encountered by ecologists as they increasingly engage in comparative tests of fundamental ecological theories and models. In addition to describing many of the problems, several sets of new data are introduced to aid in assessing the scope and gravity of many of these problems. The first section of this paper deals with a number of general problems that arise in all comparative ecological analyses. The second, third, and fourth sections focus on fundamental methodological issues in the ecological models most frequently employed in comparative studies: factorial models, distance gradient and sectorial models, and segregation models. The final section discusses the need for empirical, multivariate causal models that bring together several independent variables in explaining various aspects of ecological patterning.

Some General Problems in Comparative Ecological Analyses

Ecologists usually depend on official sources of information for their data. The problems and pitfalls of using international statistical sources have been identified by many comparative demographers (see, e.g., Carrier and Farrag, 1959). Of concern here, though, are those special problems faced in testing ecological models, which usually demand high quantities of detailed, urban-subarea data. And unfortunately for comparative ecological research, such data have not been collected for many of the world's cities, thereby precluding the possibility that their ecological structures may be identified through application of rigorous statistical procedure. However, with increasing frequency such data are now being collected, and in the next 20 years it is quite likely that some usable data will exist for many of the world's largest urban complexes.

Where data for cities in different societies do exist, there are still four major problems common to all ecological investigations: (1) the comparability of urban-subarea units across societies; (2) the variations in quality of urban-subarea data between societies; (3) alternatives in cross-sectional and longitudinal analyses; and (4) the appropriateness of various units of analysis—the city versus the metropolitan area.

The comparability of subarea units across societies is best viewed using the theoretical concept of "natural area" or neighborhood that underlies most ecological analysis. Basic ecological theory asserts that the city may be seen as a collection of differentiated natural areas that are unique to a large extent in population composition, subculture, and emergent behaviors. Ecological models attempt to describe and explain both the pattern of differentiation among the neighborhoods and their particular spatial geometry. In working with subarea data collected by official sources, two important questions emerge: (1) To what extent are the official, statistical subareas adequate operationalizations of the natural area? (2) To what extent do the subarea units of cities in one society correspond to those of other cities in the same and in other societies; for example, to what extent are the census tracts of Chicago, San Juan, and Montreal; the *shiyakhat* of Cairo and Alexandria; and the wards of Tokyo and Calcutta similar operationalizations of the cities' natural areas? Unfortunately, ecologists have given little more than passing concern to these questions since such systematic evaluations are usually beyond the resources of the individual investigator, who must all too often make do with the data on hand.

The variation between societies in quality of urban-subarea data is one of the most serious problems the comparative ecologist faces. For valid data on a massive scale to be obtained in any nation, a whole research process must be characterized by excellence all the way from research design through data collection and analysis. Unfortunately the research resources in many nations are simply inadequate, and the result is collection of dubious data, which invalidates any attempt at systematic analysis. The United Nations and other organizations are working to upgrade research skills and capabilities, but it will be some time before comparative researchers, including ecologists, can place complete trust in the statistics of many nations.

A third fundamental problem arises when the ecologist attempts to investigate theories about the operation of longitudinal process, yet his only available data are cross-sectional. Especially in developing nations, usable urban-subarea data do not extend back for more than 5, 10, or 20 years at most. While this problem is not unique to ecology, ecologists, unlike other sociologists, have generally not constructed those types of causal models that might be tested with cross-sectional data. For example, ecologists have not expressed theories as sets of recursive equations (Blalock, 1964). Were they to do so, some headway could be made in assessing the reasonableness of some ecological assertions. Ecologists, however, are still somewhat fortunate since many nations are now collecting urban-subarea data that, in 20 to 30 years, will form a solid foundation for longitudinal investigations.

Finally, in studying the ecological structure of a given community, the researcher must determine how much of the community he will include in the analysis. Should the city or the metropolitan area be the focus? For comparative research the issue becomes—the extent to which the metropolitan and city units are comparable ecological aggregates across societies. In some nations the officially defined metropolitan areas are almost totally urban, with the resident population entirely included in the urban labor force. In other nations the metropolitan areas are "over-bound" in the sense that they include large fringe agricultural populations. Thus, when comparing two such communities—a totally urban aggregate with one that mixes urban and agricultural populations and areas—the ecologist has two strictly noncomparable units. Generally there is much greater similarity among nations in what they define officially as the "city" unit than in what they define as the "metropolitan area." Unless the ecologist is certain about the comparability of two metropolitan areas from different nations, it is far safer for the investigation to be limited to city segments of the metropolises.

Some Problems in the Use of Factorial Models

Factorial ecology (Schwirian, 1971) is one of the most frequently used ecological approaches today. "Factorial ecology" refers to a series of differing approaches to urban ecological structure whose common bond is the statistical technique of factor analysis. The two major factorial approaches are *social-area analysis* and *factorial ecology* per se (Berry and Rees, 1969). The principal difference between social-area analysis and the more general factorial-ecology analysis is in the data inputs of the analysis. Social-area analysis limits the input variables to those called for in the theoretical scheme of Shevky, Bell, and Greer (Shevky and Bell, 1955; Greer, 1962), while factorial ecology includes a much wider range of variables (usually almost all of those at hand). The social-area variables generally deal with *social rank; familism* or life style, as indicated by fertility, female labor-force participation, and housing; and *ethnicity*. The social-area framework maintains that the nature of the relationships among the variables, and their corresponding factor structures, are to some extent a function of the society's degree of economic development or social scale. "Social scale" is generally taken to mean the extent of the division of labor within the society and the degree of elaboration of the integrating institutions and mechanisms.

Factorial-ecological studies have been done for many world cities (for bibliographies, see Abu-Lughod, 1969; Murdie, 1969). In the use of these models several analytical problems have surfaced. They are (1) comparability of factor structures given different data inputs (social-area variables versus the much broader number in the factorial ecology per se studies); (2) general methods of computation (factor analysis versus component analysis); (3) types of factor rotation (orthogonal versus oblique) and their differing implications for the construction of multivariate causal models; and (4) extent of the community studied and its implications for interpretation.

The comparability problem has become particularly troublesome. Since the variable inputs for factorial ecology are greater in number and of a wider variety than those of social-area analysis studies, the number of factors extracted through factorial-ecological investigations generally exceed the number through social-area analysis. Factorial ecology identifies many more dimensions of urban, social, and physical organizations. For example, in a study of Helsinki, Sweetser (1969) identified several ethnic factors, while in Boston (Sweetser, 1962) he identified a nonwhite factor separate from other ethnic factors. Pederson (1965), in a study of Copenhagen, identified, in addition to the usual gamut of factors, others dealing with population growth and mobility. In a study of Calcutta, Berry and Rees (1969) report numerous factors including literacy, high-status Muslim, and a host of specific land-use configurations.

The discovery of factors unique to the variable inputs for specific cities makes factorial-ecological studies difficult to compare in more than very gross terms. Not only are the factorial-ecological studies difficult to compare with each other; they are, as has been noted, difficult to compare with social-area analysis studies. At least social-area studies are fairly comparable with each other since their data inputs are quite similar, if not exactly the same. But, of course, what social-area studies gain in comparability, they lose in explaining total variance in the ecological structure of the particular city investigated. By limiting the variable inputs to the three categories listed above, other important general and unique local configurations in a city's development may be missed.

Factorial-ecological investigations have used a variety of computational techniques in seeking to identify aggregates of variables differentiated in urban space. Some early studies employed *cluster analysis* (Tryon, 1955) and its extension, *linkage analysis* (Sweetser, 1962). In more recent studies cluster and linkage analyses have been supplanted by *principal-components analysis* (Gittus, 1964-1965) and *factor analysis* (Carey, 1966). Despite the use of both components and factor analysis, however, there has been little systematic consideration of which model best fits the substantive problem. A basic difference between the two statistical models is that only components analysis takes the data as given and determines the dimensions of the space defining them. This method makes no assumption about the existence of common underlying factors as does factor analysis. Indeed, factor analysis necessitates some hypothesis as to the number of underlying common factors in a problem. It is certainly time for ecologists to consider seriously the efficacy of these two models for identifying major dimensions of urban structure, since their alternative application to a given set of data can produce somewhat different results (Harman, 1967; King, 1969; Rummel, 1970).

Further, ecologists should note the similarity or dissimilarity of statistical models used when comparing the structures of two or more cities. All too frequently, incautious comparisons of factor structures for different cities are made even though the structure of one city was derived by factor analysis while that of the other was calculated through components techniques.

The choice between these two computational models poses one set of problems. Another serious concern is the particular factor-rotation model employed. In almost all factorial-ecological studies in which factor rotation is calculated, the orthogonal model is selected. There has been some controversy in statistical literature, though, over the relative merits of orthogonal versus oblique factor rotation (Rummel, 1970:386). Factorial ecologists have ignored this controversy, generally relying on an uncritical selection of the orthogonal approach. The essential difference between orthogonal and oblique rotation models is that any lack of correlation among obliquely rotated factors is an *empirical* finding, while the lack of correlation among orthogonally rotated factors is *imposed* by the orthogonal model; that is, the oblique rotation provides for the possibility of correlation among factors, while the orthogonal does not. Of course, it is quite possible that an oblique rotation will yield uncorrelated factors, in which case the orthogonal solution may offer a better approximation of simple structure. However, if oblique rotation is bypassed in favor of orthogonal, which itself may be considered as a special case of oblique rotation, the researcher will never know whether there is an underlying relationship among the factors that might be of some substantive interest in itself.

Essentially, it is argued here that ecologists should opt more frequently for oblique rotation. Two reasons seem paramount. One concerns the similarity between assumptions of the oblique model and general empirical conditions; the second, which deals with the requirements for building one class of multivariate causal models, is more pragmatic.

In urban ecological research there is general consensus that social status, familism, and ethnicity are meaningful dimensions of urban organization. In urban-subarea studies, whose purpose is to identify these dimensions for a given city, it is common practice to rotate the extracted factors orthogonally. The orthogonal model demands that the dimensions be completely uncorrelated with each other. Now we know from numerous studies that the dimensions are not related. For example, we know that race *is* related to social status; that race *is* related to fertility; and that fertility *is* related to social status. Since it is empirically known that these variables are related, it seems that the more appropriate research strategy would be to recognize these interrelationships by applying an oblique rotation to the extracted factors. After the data have been rotated in this fashion, then the researcher's concern can be with both the emergent factor structure and the correlations among the factors.

At this point we might ask whether the form of factor rotation greatly affects the emergent factor structure. While we know theoretically that it does, we might ask what happens empirically to typical urban subarea data. As a partial answer to this question, data on two cities will be displayed, rotated with both orthogonal and oblique (Biquartimin) techniques. The cities are fairly representative of two major types. One, Ottawa, Canada, is a large city in a highly developed society. The other, Mayaguez, Puerto Rico, is a small city in an emerging society. Current theories about the relationship between urban structure and societal development would lead us to expect the factorial structure of Ottawa to be highly differentiated on factors corresponding to social status, familism, and ethnicity, while the factor structure of Mayaguez should be much less differentiated, with perhaps one or two factors that represent a general social-organization dimension. For the census tracts of both cities we have selected six variables that measure level of education, level of occupation, infertility, female participation in the labor force, housing in single-family units, and concentration of the foreign-born. The operationalizations of these measures have been discussed elsewhere (Schwirian and Smith, 1971; Schwirian and Matre, 1969). The data for each city were submitted to the same form of principal-components analysis; then the extracted factors were rotated orthogonally. A second analysis was subsequently performed and the factors rotated obliquely. The results appear in Table 12.1.

For Mayaguez three factors were rotated orthogonally. Factor I seems to tap a fairly general social-organization dimension, since all but the dwelling-unit variable load on it. Factor III seems also to be a social organization factor that differs from the first in that foreign/born loads high on III, low on I. In addition, infertility loads high on I and low on III. The second factor is unique in the sense that only one variable—dwelling—has a high loading on it. In the obliquely rotated factor structure, Factor I is a "stronger" social-organization factor, since all but one of the variables now correlate with it. Factor II is still the dwelling-unit factor, while Factor III is very weak and no longer potentially meaningful. The factor-congruency scores (Harman, 1967:270) show that oblique Factor I correlates very strongly with both orthogonal factors I and III. Oblique Factor II correlates strongly with orthogonal II, and oblique Factor III is generally uncorrelated with both orthogonal I and III. Thus for Mayaguez, which is a small city in a developing society, the oblique rotation gives a more parsimonious summary of the general undifferentiated nature of its urban subareas: For the residential areas of Mayaguez, social status is associated with ethnicity and both, in turn, are associated with infertility and female labor-force

Table 12.1   Orthogonal and Oblique Rotated Factors and   Factor-Congruency Scores for Mayaguez, Puerto Rico, and Ottawa, Canada.

	Orthogonal				Oblique			
	I	II	III	IV	I	II	III	IV
Mayaguez								
Occupation	.775	.189	.577		.938	.150	-.169	
Education	.702	-.053	.691		.988	-.095	-.025	
Infertility	.923	-.019	.369		.883	-.054	-.410	
Women in labor force	.572	.085	.783		.968	.042	.126	
Multiple dwelling	.026	.997	.062		.024	.998	-.028	
Foreign-born	.366	.086	.921		.939	.042	.371	
Ottawa								
Occupation	.978	-.107	-.064	.038	.983	-.010	-.050	.048
Education	.925	-.317	-.029	-.024	.909	-.230	-.003	.003
Infertility	.024	.269	.209	.939	.056	.204	.147	.913
Women in labor force	.098	.905	.190	.264	-.015	.895	.126	.168
Multiple dwelling	-.408	.855	.011	.129	-.336	.829	-.050	.031
Foreign-born	.064	.122	.971	.191	-.048	.062	.963	.115

Congruency

Mayaguez				*Ottawa*				
Orthogonal	Oblique			Orthogonal	Oblique			
	I	II	III		I	II	III	IV
I	.957		.348	I	.996			
II		.996		II		.993		
III	.968		.188	III			.995	
				IV				.995

participation; only housing-type is independent of the more general social-organization dimension.

For Ottawa, a large city in a highly developed society, we would predict marked factorial differentiation. Both the orthogonal and the oblique rotations yield very similar factor structures. For both factors, social status separates from the familism and ethnic indicators. In addition the ethnic variable separates from status and familism. Women in the labor force and dwelling units separate from status, ethnicity, and fertility. The similarity in factor structure for the two techniques is well illustrated by the factor-congruency scores, all of which are over 0.99. Thus, while there is marked factorial differentiation, the orthogonal and oblique factor rotations yield very similar factor structures. While there is very little differentiation factorially, however, the oblique rotation, which does not force factor-independence, results in a more parsimonious summary of the undifferentiated factor pattern.

The second argument for using oblique rather than orthogonal factor rotation is very pragmatic. Given that a researcher wants to build a causal model and has adopted a path-analysis form with all of its limitations and given that the number of independent variables is sufficiently large that he needs to reduce them to a more manageable number, then the requirements of the path model essentially demand that oblique rather than orthogonal rotation be employed. Orthogonal rotation results in groupings of independent variables, with no relationships among them; the only resulting model that may be tested is that depicted in Figure 12.1, in which the variables are from a study of the demographic, environmental, and social correlates of community mortality levels (Schwirian and Rico, 1971a). Such a model is fairly uninteresting from the causal standpoint and somewhat unrealistic since past studies have shown the independent variables to be related. Oblique rotation would display some relationships, thereby permitting the examination of a model that indicates relationships among the independent variables. In the cited example, an oblique rotation was performed, and the correlations among the factors appear in Table 12.2. The model derived from past studies that was actually examined with these data appears in Figure 12.2. A fuller discussion of the model and the extent to

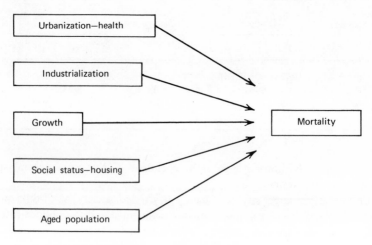

Figure 12.1   Path model with uncorrelated independent variables.

Table 12.2 Correlations Among Oblique Factors for Puerto Rican
Mortality Study (1960)

Variables	1	2	3	4	5	6
1. Urbanization-health	1.0000	.2273	.2569	.3462	-.1010	.0950
2. Industrialization		1.0000	.0734	.3499	-.0297	.1140
3. Population growth			1.0000	.3178	-.2006	.3712
4. Social status-housing				1.0000	.1442	.1291
5. Aged population					1.0000	.0389
6. Mortality						1.0000

which it fits the data appears later (p. 368) in this paper. To reiterate the point made earlier, then, the uncritical selection of orthogonal factor rotation eliminates any statistical possibility for analyzing relationships among independent variables, thereby precluding the examination of any model in which the time-order of independent variables is of interest.

In the first section of this paper it was noted that one serious problem in ecological research is the extent of the community area investigated. The choice is generally between the total standard metropolitan statistical area (SMSA) or the city segment only. Sweetser (1969) argues that the subareas of a metropolis are sufficiently unique in social organization that separate factor analyses should be calculated for the different areas. If so, then, the argument is not whether to factor the data for the city's subareas or for the metropolitan subareas; *both* city and fringe areas should be separately factored and then compared. While his argument for factoring a metropolis' subareas separately is indeed worth noting, though, current practice in ecological research has been to focus on either the city or the metropolitan area exclusively.

In the case that a given metropolitan area's boundaries are "true-bound" in the sense that the statistical area corresponds to the expanse of urban functional integration, then the whole metropolitan area is the appropriate choice. In the case of metropolitan areas that are over-bound and therefore have included in their official statistics values describing not only the urban population but the surrounding functionally differentiated fringe population as well, the city is the more appropriate choice for analysis.

If alternative factor analyses were calculated for the metropolitan expanse of a community and then for the city segment only, different factor structures would result if (1) the fringe segment of the metropolitan area were so different ecologically from the city portion that there was a significant difference between the correlation *matrix* for the city and the correlation *matrix* for the fringe, and (2) the number of subarea units in the fringe was large by contrast with the number for the central city.

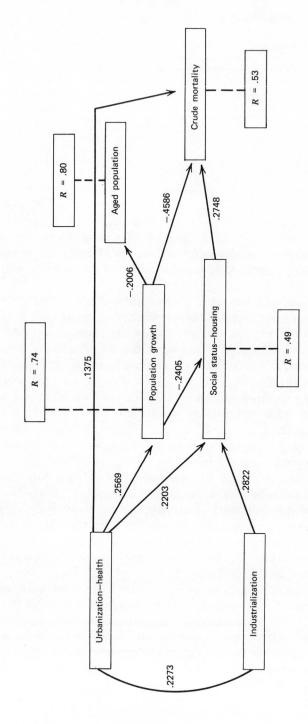

Figure 12.2 Path model with correlated independent variables.

Some relevant data on this problem are shown in Table 12.3. They are census tract data for San Juan, Puerto Rico, and we have alternatively factored the city data and the data for the total SMSA. The city analysis is based upon 86 tracts. The metropolitan analysis is based upon 137 tracts (51 tracts are located outside the city in the fringe). The fringe segment of the San Juan metropolitan area has a larger concentration of agricultural workers than does the city, and the fringe population has a lower social status, as indicated by education, income, and occupation (Schwirian and Rico, 1971b). The variables analyzed are those typical of social-area analysis, and they were factored and rotated through the Oblimin Oblique Technique. From Table 12.3 it may be noted that the factors correspond to the following dimensions: social rank (with female labor-force participation), housing, fertility, and foreign-born. The factor-congruency scores between the matching factors of the city and of the metropolitan area are all over 0.98. Thus, even though the fringe segment of the San Juan metropolitan area is somewhat differentiated ecologically from the city, the emergent factor structures are very similar. In interpreting these data, though, one caveat is needed: This researcher's experience in Puerto Rico suggests that the San Juan metropolitan area is fairly true-bound.

Table 12.3   Oblique Rotated Factors for San Juan, Puerto Rico, City and
SMSA (1960)

Variables	City				SMSA			
	I	II	III	IV	I	II	III	IV
Occupation	.878	.063	.015	.195	.831	.090	.018	.233
Education	.908	-.091	-.008	.142	.904	-.030	.001	.171
Infertility	.254	.100	.830	.123	.398	.162	.719	.101
Women in labor force	.822	-.144	.271	-.147	.938	-.068	.121	-.089
Dwellings	-.079	.990	.050	.022	-.026	.993	.044	.022
Foreign-born	.349	.107	-.144	.762	.304	.076	.069	.810

Factor Congruency Scores

City	SMSA			
	I	II	III	IV
I	.992			
II		.993		
III			.955	
IV				.989

Distance Gradient and Sector Models

Studies of the spatial ecology of cities generally take as a starting point the geometric aspects of the Burgess (Park, Burgess, and McKenzie, 1925) theories. According to the Burgess model, there is a direct relationship between neighborhood social status and distance from the center of the city. Thus, the concentric-zone scheme associated with Burgess envisions a city whose inner core is made up of low-status populations and whose outer fringe is populated by those of higher social status.

The main alternative to Burgess's model is the sector model associated with Hoyt (1939). Having studied a large number of American cities, Hoyt argued that the status differences between subareas were distributed more by sector than by distance gradient. A number of studies have provided support for this proposition (see Anderson and Egeland, 1961; Schwirian and Matre, 1969; and Schwirian and Smith, 1971). These studies have not served to invalidate the concentric-zone approach but have rather produced a picture of the metropolis in which status is distributed by sector, while familism, particularly housing, is distributed more by distance gradient.

One major criticism of studies examining either or both models concerns the methodology employed in delineating urban sectors and zones. In applying the concentric-zone scheme, investigators generally mark off arbitrary distances from the center of the city that yield a regular spatial pattern of concentric circles, usually one mile apart. In applying the sector model it has been common for investigators to lay off sectors at a set degree of angle from a north-south orientation at the city's core. Usually the sector are 30 degrees wide, but some studies have identified sectors of less, while others have identified sectors of wider angles—sometimes even 90 degrees. The essential point here is that in empirical practice, ecologists have used fairly arbitrary measures of sectors and concentric zones in the partitioning of urban subareas (e.g., see Murdie, 1969).

In using these arbitrary delineations ecologists have assumed that their arbitrary urban geometrics are adequate operationalizations of the classic schemes. There is danger in such assumptions. James Quinn (1940) pointed out that a crucial test of the basic models can be made only if *ecological,* and not just arbitrary spatial, delineations are followed. Thus, in laying off the distances gradients within a city, a time-cost function should be employed rather than a set mileage factor. And in laying off sectors, angle delineation should be abandoned in favor of sectors that follow ecological barriers, including main routes of transportation, railroad lines, bodies of water, and major topographical distortions. Ecologists have opted for the more arbitrary approach, no doubt, because of limited time and funds. However, it is certainly time that we determine the analytical implications of the arbitrary techniques we so frequently use.

To assess the effect of arbitrary versus ecological delineation of urban subareas, I have taken the census tract data for the Columbus, Ohio, SMSA and have applied two schemes to the delineation of the subareas. The first is arbitrary and fairly representative of common practice today. First, distance zones were laid off at one-mile distances from each other starting at the center of the city (the intersection of Broad and High streets). Three mileage zones were identified. Then eight sectors were laid off at 45-degree angles to each other with the initial orientation being north-south and the orientation mode being the main intersection. The census tracts at the 24 intersections of distance and sector demarcation were selected for analysis.

The second scheme is more in keeping with the ecological *assumptions* of the zone and sector models. To establish travel-time zones from the center of the city, we determined the average travel time in morning traffic between the central intersection and outlying points using the main arteries from the city's center to the periphery. Then zones were marked off at 5-minute intervals. As might be expected, the resulting isochronal zones were not geometrically circular. They reflected distortions generated by density variations in housing and shopping and arterial confluence. Eight sectors were laid off that followed the city's rivers, main streets, and rail lines. At the intersection of each of the 3 isochronal zones and 8 sectors, a tract was selected for analysis. Thus this scheme yielded 24 tracts as did the more arbitrary approach.

The question to be answered here is: Do we reach the same conclusion about the distribution of subarea characteristics regardless of the scheme used for subarea delineation? We investigated two variables that in past studies had been found to vary by distance and sector. One was the median school years of the adult population of the tract; the other was the percent of dwellings in the area that contained only one unit. The data were from the 1960 population census. To aid in assessing the relative importance of distance and sector effects, two-way analysis of variance (ANOVA) was calculated even though the tracts are a population and not a strict random sample. Two ANOVA's were performed, one for the data classified arbitrarily and one for the data classified ecologically. The results are in Table 12.4.

For the education variable, both approaches lead us to reject the null hypothesis regarding the distance effect; we cannot, however, reject the null hypothesis on the sector effect. With both schemes we find that the distribution of education level in the Columbus SMSA is a function of distance gradient and not sector location. Approximately 41 percent of the total sum of squares of education level is explained by distance in the arbitrary scheme, while approximately 30 percent is explained by distance in the ecological classification.

For the housing variable in both schemes we must reject the null hypothesis regarding distance effect, but we cannot reject it regarding the sector effect.

With both schemes, then, we conclude that the distribution of single-unit housing in Columbus is a function of distance gradient and not sector. About 77 percent of the sum of squares of housing is explained by distance on the arbitrary scheme and about 56 percent by distance on the ecological scheme.

Table 12.4   Two-Way ANOVA for Education and Housing Variables for Columbus, Ohio, 1960 SMSA Tracts Classified by Arbitrary and Ecological Sectors and Distance.

	Education		Housing	
Source	Arbitrary	Ecological	Arbitrary	Ecological
	F	F	F	F
Distance	8.91^a	4.67^a	47.60^a	17.47^a
Sector	1.72	1.06	2.12	1.97

[a]Indicates the F ratio is statistically significant beyond the .05 confidence level.

These data indicate that both the arbitrary and the ecological approach lead to the same conclusion about the distance and sector effects on the two variables. Thus we tentatively conclude that if the arbitrary schemes are *detailed enough*, they probably do little violence to our conclusions about the ecological distribution of phenomena in a city. Still further explorations of additional variables in other cities need to be made, though, before any firm conclusions can be reached.

Segregation Models

The measurement of residential segregation in cities has been the subject of several discourses. The issues generally revolve around (1) the criteria that a segregation index should satisfy, (2) the appropriateness of alternative units of observation, and (3) the conceptual and empirical similarity of existing indexes. This paper will not review the various discussions, because they have been so ably treated in other sources (see, e.g., Taeuber and Taeuber, 1965). The focus of this discussion is on measurement of the clustering aspect of segregation, which is generally ignored by most segregation indexes. The essential point is that for most of the segregation indexes used in ecological research today, any number of spatial patterns in ghetto distribution will yield the same segregation index value. For example, Figure 12.3 shows two cities divided into a number of city blocks. The shaded blocks are assumed to be totally black in population, while the unshaded areas are assumed to be totally white. If the *index of*

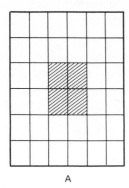 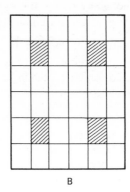

A   B

Figure 12.3 Distribution of totally white (unshaded) and totally Black (shaded) blocks in two cities.

dissimilarity, one of the most frequently used value is 100 in both cases. For the city on the left, the blacks are highly ghettoized into four adjacent black blocks. For the city on the right, though, the black blocks are scattered throughout the city such that each black block is adjacent only to totally white blocks. While the blacks of both cities are totally segregated according to the index of dissimilarity, they are still much less concentrated in city *A* than in city *B*. These figures suggest that the total degree of segregation and extent of clustering are separate independent variables that will have different behavioral consequences for both white and black urban populations.

Given that clustering is different from segregation, then, ecologists should be more concerned about measuring the clustering aspect of ethnic residential distributions. One attempt to handle this problem has been made by Virginia Sharp (1970a, 1970b). Through discussion of the Sharp Index of Segregation we illustrate one attempt to measure residential segregation by focusing on the clustering problem. The Sharp index is

$$S = 1.00 - \frac{\displaystyle\sum_{i=1}^{K} \left(\frac{\displaystyle\sum_{j=1}^{m} P_j}{m} \right)}{K}$$

where

K = the total number of areas for the city—in most cases census tracts or enumeration districts

m = the total number of blocks within tract *i* with the percentage

of nonwhite occupied housing units greater than the city
average of percent nonwhite occupied households

P_j = percent of blocks adjacent to block j (where bock j contains
greater than the city average percent nonwhite occupied
housing units) containing less than the city average percent of
nonwhite occupied housing units

Applying this index to the examples in the figure we find the S for city A to
be 38.5 percent, while the S for city B is 0.0. Thus, for a black block in city A,
an average of 38.5 percent of the surrounding blocks will also be black blocks.
For city B, on the average, none of the surrounding blocks will be black. The
higher the index, the greater the percentage of adjacent blocks that will be black.

The index satisfies a number of criteria for "good" segregation indexes:

1.   Its base is a nonnegative function of the proportions black in the tracts
and in the tract population.
2.   The index value ranges from 0 to 100, with 0 equaling no concentration and 100 complete concentration.
3.   The intermediate index values may cover the possible intermediate
score values.
4.   The index is independent of the size of the total population and
the percent black of the city.
5.   The index is applicable across cities where block data are available.

The only major defect in ease of hand-computation. With computers,
however, calculations may be done quickly and easily. Even though this index is
more difficult to calculate than the more standard measures used today, it
permits determination of the clustering aspect of residential location and
segregation. It is hoped that this discussion of the Sharp index will stimulate
some interest, concern, and future work by ecologists along this line and,
perhaps, provide a newer focus for segregation methodologies.

Some Multivariate Ecological Models

Most ecological investigations to date have been either very detailed studies of
one city's ecological structure or descriptions of some ecological patterns across
several cities. What has been lacking in the literature to date are systematic
attempts to explain differences in ecological structures in terms of some
multivariate framework. In this section, two multivariate ecological models are
discussed. It is hoped that ecologists will find the substantive results of some
interest and that the approaches used in the models may stimulate interest in
further analyses.

First Example

The first example is from Schwirian and Smith (1971). They argue that the factorial ecology of cities is a function of two independent variables: city size and level of economic development of the society in which the city is located. Thus;

factorial differentiation = f (city size, level of societal development)

The effects of the independent variables are not additive. It is argued that in societies low on the economic-development continuum, there is little societal differentiation in social status, familism, and ethnicity; therefore, in urban residential space, regardless of city size, there is little ecological differentiation of the three dimensions. In highly developed societies just the reverse is true; societies with marked societal differentiation of status, familism, and ethnicity across the whole society show community residential patterns that are highly differentiated in terms of these three dimensions, regardless of the city size. Thus, in both very developed and very underdeveloped societies, city size is not a factor in urban ecological differentiation.

For a society undergoing economic development, the rates of social change are not uniform across the whole society. Change proceeds at a much faster pace in the region of the primate city, the portal for economic development. Change comes first to the primate city and then diffuses throughout the rest of the society. Since there are differences in the rate of change, there is a bifurcation in life styles and social organization between the primate region and the other, more isolated sections of the country. The primate city is the first to take on a changing ecological patterning. In effect, in the midst of the development process the primate city becomes ecologically very much like cities in highly developed societies. The more isolated cities maintain their traditional ecological patterns for a much longer time period. Thus, a cross-sectional investigation of urban ecological patterns in a developing society should show considerable difference in structure between the largest or primate city and the secondary or smaller ones. In sum, then, city size is a factor in urban ecological differentiation in the developing society but not in either highly developed or generally underdeveloped societies. In the developing society, city size is a rough indicator of a city's place in the urban system through which change will diffuse.

To examine this theory, Schwirian and Smith (1971) pointed out that the studies of large cities in low-scale societies such as Cairo (Abu-Lughod, 1969) and Alexandria (Latif, 1970) show little factorial differentiation. With such studies as a background for their analysis, they wanted to determine whether there were ecological differences by city size in developed (by contrast with developing) societies. The developed society selected for investigation was Canada; the developing, Puerto Rico. A large- a medium-, and a small-sized city

Table 12.5 Oblique Rotated Factors for Canadian (1961) and Puerto Rican (1960) Cities

Variable	Factors			
	I	II	III	IV
Ottawa				
Occupation	-.010	.983	.050	-.048
Education	-.230	.909	.000	-.003
Infertility	.204	.056	-.147	-.913
Women in labor force	.895	-.015	-.126	-.169
Dwellings	.829	-.336	.050	-.051
Foreign-born	.062	-.048	-.963	-.115
Windsor				
Occupation	.117	-.930	.070	.131
Education	-.300	-.910	.125	.047
Infertility	.173	-.593	-.690	.062
Women in labor force	.207	-.187	-.036	.864
Dwellings	.908	.110	-.077	.204
Foreign-born	.009	.277	-.928	.012
Kingston				
Occupation	-.183	-.674	-.556	-.119
Education	.154	-.948	-.000	-.072
Infertility	.069	-.040	-.986	.024
Women in labor force	.943	-.219	.007	.005
Dwellings	.925	.141	-.054	-.215
Foreign-born	.319	-.165	-.015	-.839

within each were selected for investigation. The three Canadian cities are Ottawa, Windsor, and Kingston. The three Puerto Rican cities are San Juan (the primate city); Ponce (the second city), which is connected to San Juan on the principal, cross-island transportation link (which other research has shown to be growth-producing; see Matre and Schwirian, 1970); and Mayaguez, the smallest major city and the most isolated. The population figures for the Canadian cities were for 1961, while the figures for the Puerto Rican cities were for 1960. The matches were San Juan (432,377) and Ottawa (268,206); Ponce (114,286) and Windsor (114,376); and Mayaguez (50,147) and Kingston (53,526). The size matches for the medium and smallest cities were very good. The difference between San Juan and Ottawa was permitted, since, in function, both are societal capitals and administrative centers and both perform similar control functions within their societies.

The data for the factorial structure of the six communities are in Table 12.5. In the table it may be noted that all three Canadian cities are highly differentiated regardless of city size. All three cities show social status separating

Table 12.5 — continued

Variable	Factors			
	I	II	III	IV
San Juan				
Occupation	-.878	-.063	-.015	-.195
Education	-.908	.091	.008	-.142
Infertility	-.254	-.100	-.830	-.123
Women in labor force	-.822	.144	-.271	.147
Dwellings	.079	.990	-.050	-.022
Foreign-born	-.349	-.107	.144	-.762
Ponce				
Occupation	-.930	-.020	-.048	.086
Education	-.883	-.035	-.099	.126
Infertility	-.335	-.037	-.805	.046
Women in labor force	-.968	-.037	-.078	-.060
Dwellings	.046	.990	.012	-.003
Foreign-born	-.497	-.034	-.121	.663
Mayaguez				
Occupation	-.938	-.150	.169	
Education	-.988	.095	.025	
Infertility	-.883	.054	.410	
Women in labor force	-.968	-.042	-.126	
Dwellings	-.024	-.998	.026	
Foreign-born	-.939	-.042	-.371	

from ethnicity and familism. Likewise, ethnicity separates generally from social rank and familism (with the exception of the moderate correlation of fertility with foreign-born in Windsor). Also in both the largest and the smallest Canadian cities, female labor-force participation and housing separate from infertility, while in Windsor all three familism variables separate from each other. Thus, in accord with the theory, the Canadian cities fail to show ecological differentiation by city size.

For the three Puerto Rican cities, factorial differentiation does seem related to city size. The factorial structure for San Juan is much like that of cities in a developed society in that status, familism, and ethnicity separate in factor space. The exception is San Juan's female labor-force participation, which correlates much more strongly with social rank than is true of those factors in Canadian cities. This finding is not particularly suprising, given the traditional definition of the upper-class female's role in Latin society: If the upper strata of society is the first to modernize, then we would naturally expect the definition of the female role to change first at that social level. The factorial structure of Ponce is generally differentiated, except that both female role and foreign-born are more correlated with social rank than they are in either San Juan or in the cities of Canada. The factorial structure of Mayaguez is highly undifferentiated. Factor I shows high correlations of all variables except housing, which separates itself completely. Thus, for the Puerto Rican cities, factorial patterning does seem to be a function of city size and position in the development network; San Juan and Ponce are more like their counterparts in Canada than they are like Mayaguez.

Another way of examining the effect of city size and societal development upon ecological differentiation is in terms of the correlation between education level and infertility. Table 12.6 shows correlations between education and infertility for the six cities by city size and level of societal development. The lowest correlation between the two variables is for the largest city in the developed society: $r = 0.016$ for Ottawa. The highest is for the smallest city in developing society: $r = 0.908$ for Mayaguez. At each city-size level the correlation between education level and infertility for the developing society is larger than the corresponding correlation for the city in the developed society.

Table 12.6   Correlations Between Occupation and Infertility for Canadian and Puerto Rican Cities, Classified by City Size and Level of Societal Development

| | Level of Societal Development | |
City Size	Moderate	High
Large	San Juan: $r = .626$	Ottawa: $r = .016$
Medium	Ponce: $r = .686$	Windsor: $r = .585$
Small	Mayaguez: $r = .908$	Kingston: $r = .682$

Both the factor structures and the pattern of correlations between education and infertility strongly support the central proposition of the study, which is that the city's ecological structure is to some extent a function of both city size and level of societal development. The model is summarized in Figure 12.4.

Second Example

The second multivariate example is from a paper by Schwirian and Rico (1971a). The dependent variable is community aggregate mortality level as indexed by the crude death rate. The study takes as its starting point the vast body of literature dealing with aggregate correlates of community death rates. The independent variables of past studies may be grouped as *demographic* (e.g., age structure), *social organizational* (e.g., education level and the elaboration of health-care services), and *environmental* (e.g., housing quality and the pervasiveness of sanitary waste facilities). The purpose of this study was to examine the

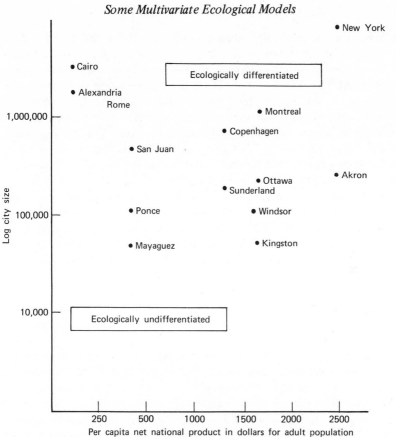

Figure 12.4 World cities by population size and scale of parent society.

relationships both between mortality level and the demographic, social organizational, and environmental variables and among the independent variables themselves. In the study it was suggested that the correlations of both the independent variables with the dependent variable and of the independent variables with each other are a function of the society's level of development. The empirical segment of the paper focused on community mortality in a developing society, Puerto Rico. The unit of analysis was the *municipio*. The mortality rates for Puerto Rico's *municipios* were calculated from vital-statistic reports. Most of the independent variables were from the 1960 U.S. census for Puerto Rico. Health statistics were from reports of Puerto Rico's Department of Health.

The study initially included 23 variables whose purpose was to tap different aspects of demographic structure, social organization, and environmental conditions. The variables were than factored and subjected to an oblique rotation, the resulting factors being urbanization and health care, industrialization, rate of population and economic growths social status and housing quality, and aged population. The factor scores for the *municipios* on there five factors were treated as the independent-variable values with mortality rates, the dependent variable. The independent variables were then ordered into an assumed causal pattern on the basis of existing literature. The resultant model appears in Figure 12.2 (see p. 356). The model hypothesized that urbanization-health has both a direct effect upon mortality and an indirect effect through rate of population growth and status-housing. The effect of industrialization is indirect, through the status-housing dimension. Population growth and status-housing are seen as having direct effects upon mortality. Aged population was originally hypothesized to have a direct effect upon mortality, but analysis led to the elimination of its causal link. Growth apparently affects both the aged concentration and mortality, and when growth is controlled, the association between aged population and mortality becomes statistically insignificant.

The model was examined through path-analytic techniques; the path coefficients (standardized partial-regression coefficients) appear in Figure 12.2. To test the adequacy of the model, the path coefficients were used to predict a correlation matrix. The predicted matrix was then compared to the original matrix. The predicted and original matrices appear in Table 12.7. They are very similar; in fact, a test of the significance of differences between the two matrices failed to reject the null hypothesis. Only two of the predicted correlations show any difference from the observed corresponding values: The model predicts an r of -0.05 between urbanization-health and aged population, while the observed r is -0.10; the model also predicts an r of 0.06 between aged and status-housing, while the observed r is 0.14. In both cases, though, the observed and the predicted r's are low in absolute value. The model explains 22 percent of the variance in community mortality level and seems to fit the empirical data fairly well.

Table 12.7   Observed (Above Diagonal) and Predicted (Below Diagonal) Correlations from the Path Analysis

Variable	1	2	3	4	5	6
1. Urbanization-health	1.0000	.2273	.2569	.3462	-.1010	.0950
2. Industrialization	.2273	1.0000	.0734	.3499	-.0297	.1140
3. Population growth	.2569	.0584	1.0000	.3178	-.2006	-.3712
4. Social status-housing	.3462	.3463	.3136	1.0000	.1442	.1291
5. Aged population	-.0515	-.0117	-.2006	.0629	1.0000	.0389
6. Mortality	.0950	.0843	-.3722	.1311	.0746	1.0000

The two ecological models discussed in this section illustrate the type of direction open to ecologists. It is high time that we moved from the level of simply describing ecological patterns to more sophisticated analyses incorporating several independent variables within a multivariate framework whose purpose is to explain ecological phenomena.

Summary

Cross-cultural researchers have long been aware of the problems inherent in collecting valid, reliable, and comparable data. And certainly these problems are no less so for the comparative ecologist, who must all too frequently depend upon official sources for community indicators. Among the most important problems that must be faced are (1) the comparability of urban-subarea units across different societies, (2) the variations in data quality between societies, (3) the alternatives in cross-sectional and longitudinal analysis, and (4) the appropriateness of city versus metropolitan area as units of analysis.

Beyond the data-collection problems are those related to analytical procedures and techniques. It has been suggested here that among the more pressing for the ecologist are the following:

1. Comparability problems (between studies of urban-subarea characteristics employing factor-analytic techniques) that arise from:
   A. differences in the scope of data inputs and in specific variables
   B. differences in computational models (factor analysis versus component analysis)
   C. differences in factor rotation models (orthogonal versus oblique)
   D. differences in the comparability of the community area (cities versus metropolitan areas)
2. The procedures used in delineating ecological zones and sectors
3. The preoccupation with measuring residential differentiation to the exclusion of the clustering or ghettoization dimension
4. The tendency for ecological studies to ignore potential multivariate analyses for the simpler case-study descriptive approach.

It is beyond the scope of this paper to deal exhaustively with each of these problems and their solution, but the data presented suggest that these problems are well worth consideration by comparative ecologists. Indeed, the goal of this paper has been to serve as an open invitation and a call for more rigorous, comprehensive, and creative methodological examination of problems in comparative ecological research.

References

Abu-Lughod, Janet L.

1969   Testing the theory of social area analysis: the ecology of Cairo, Egypt. *American Sociological Review,* 34 (April): 198-211.

Anderson, Theodore, and Janice Egeland.

1961   Spatial aspects of social area analysis. *American Sociological Review,* 26 (June):392-399.

Berry, Brian, and Philip H. Rees.

1969   The factorial ecology of Calcutta. *American Journal of Sociology,* 74 (March):445-491.

Blalock, Hubert M., Jr.

1964   *Casual Inferences in Nonexperimental Research.* Chapel Hill: University of North Carolina Press.

Carey, G. W.

1966   The regional interpretation of Manhattan population and housing patterns through factor analysis. *Geographical Review,* 56:551-569.

Carrier, N. H., and A. M. Farrag.

1959   The reduction of errors in census population for statistically under-developed countries. *Population Studies,* 12 (March):240-285.

Gittus, Elizabeth.

1964-   An experiment in the definition of urban subareas. *Transactions*
1965   *of the Bartlett Society,* 2:107-120.

Greer, Scott.

1962   *The Emerging City.* New York: Free Press.

Harman, Harry H.

1967   *Modern Factor Analysis.* Chicago: University of Chicago Press.

Hoyt, Homer.

1939   *The Structure and Growth of Residential Neighborhoods in the United States.* Washington, D.C.: Federal Housing Administration.

King, Leslie J.

  1969   *Statistical Analysis in Geography.* Englewood Cliffs, N.J.: Prentice-Hall.

Latif, Abdel-Hamid.

  1970   *The Ecological and Social Structure of Alexandria, Egypt: An Examination of Urban Subarea Data, 1947 and 1960.* Ph.D. dissertation, Ohio State University.

Matre, Marc D., and Kent P. Schwirian.

  1970   Highway development and community population growth in Puerto Rico, 1898-1960. Paper presented at the 1970 Annual Meeting of the Population Association of American, Atlanta, Georgia.

Murdie, Robert A.

  1969   *Factorial Ecology of Metropolitan Toronto, 1951-1961.* Department of Geography, Research Paper no. 116. Chicago: University of Chicago.

Park, Robert, E. W. Burgess, and R. D. McKenzie.

  1925   *The City.* Chicago: University of Chicago Press.

Pederson, P. O.

  1965   An empirical model of urban population structure: a factor analytic study of the population structure in Copenhagen. Mimeographed. Copenhagen: The Technical University of Denmark.

Quinn, James.

  1940   The Burgess zonal hypothesis and its critics. *American Sociological Review,* 5 (April):210-218.

Rummel, R. J.

  1970   *Applied Factor Analysis.* Evanston, Ill.: Northwestern University Press.

Schwirian, Kent P.

  1971   Analytical convergence in ecological research: Factorial analysis, gradient, and sector models. In David Sweet (Ed.), *Models of Urban Structure.* Lexington, Mass: Heath. Pp. 135-159.

Schwirian, Kent P., and Marc D. Matre.

   1969   The ecological structure of Canadian cities. Research paper. Columbus: Department of Sociology, Ohio State University.

Schwirian, Kent P., and Jesus Rico-Velasco.

   1971a   An ecological analysis of mortality in Puerto Rico. Working paper, Mershon Caribbean Project. Columbus: Ohio State University.

   1971b   The residential distribution of status groups in Puerto Rico's metropolitan areas. *Demography,* 8 (February):81-90.

Schwirian, Kent P., and Ruth K. Smith.

   1971   Primacy, modernization, and urban structure: the ecology of Puerto Rican cities. Paper presented at the 1971 meetings of the American Sociological Association, Denver, Colorado.

Sharp, Virginia.

   1970a   Changes in spatial residential segregation through time: a case study. Columbus: Department of Geography, Ohio State University.

   1970b   Toward a quantitative measure of spatial segregation. Columbus: Department of Geography, Ohio State University.

Shevky, Eshref, and Wendell Bell.

   1955   *Social Area Analysis, Illustrative Application and Computational Procedures.* Stanford University Series in Sociology, No. 1. Stanford, Calif.: Stanford University Press.

Sweetser, Frank L.

   1962   *The Social Ecology of Metropolitan Boston: 1960.* Boston: Massachusetts Department of Mental Health.

   1969   Ecological factors in metropolitan zones and sectors. In Mattei Dogan and Stein Rokkan (Eds.), *Quantitative Ecological Analysis in the Social Sciences.* Cambridge, Mass.: MIT. Press. Pp. 413-456.

Taeuber, Karl E., and Alma F. Taeuber.

   1965   *Negroes in Cities.* Chicago: Aldine.

Tryon, Robert C.

   1955   *Identification of Social Areas by Cluster Analysis.* Berkeley and Los Angeles: University of California Press.

Discussion

Mr. Anderson:　　The principal question I would like to raise in connection with Schwirian's paper is, What are the advantages of aggregating data? When is it appropriate to aggregate and when not so appropriate?

In terms of systems analysis, there are two situations in which one should aggregate information. First, if one is dealing with a system which has relatively decoupled subsystems (that is, technically decoupled or only weakly coupled), then it is appropriate to aggregate into those subsystems. In practice this operation means that, if in fact transfers of information or material goods or whatever occur between subsystems in the form of aggregates, then those subsystems constitute a meaningful unit of aggregation. Decoupling tends to occur, in systems-analysis terms, whenever the internal processes in some subunits are subject to control at the aggregate level. In fact, one of the primary functions of the control units is to shift the interaction from an individual basis to an aggregate basis.

Second, aggregation is also appropriate whenever the time constants in the processes *within* the subsystems are much shorter than the time constants in the processes *between* the subsystems. For example, a local community is a meaningful unit of aggregation because daily activities tend to occur within it whereas only occasional (for example, monthly, yearly) activities tend to occur between communities. The difference in the time constants, within certain time periods, generally indicates decoupling. We can treat systems as decoupled within certain time periods even though, within much longer time periods, couplings of these systems must be considered. These are the two primary conditions under which aggregation is a meaningful phenomenon.

I cannot find either condition met by Schwirian's paper. It doesn't seem to me that census tracts or the equivalents of census tracts are meaningful aggregates either in the sense of serving as units of local control or in the sense that interactions within tracts have different time characteristics than interactions between tracts. Hence, I find it rather hard to defend basing an entire system of multivariate analysis upon aggregation at the tract level. Schwirian does discuss this matter to some extent, although not quite in that phraseology.

Mr. Schwirian:　　Let me respond to the issue you raise from a systems approach to aggregate data regarding the meaningfulness of urban subareas, whether they be census tracts or blocks. Let's focus on the tracts in our cities or the wards in Tokyo or comparable units. I wonder if there isn't a kind of decay process across societies in terms of how well those units meet your two conditions for aggregation. You are essentially correct that in the

United States or Canada, census tracts aren't satisfactory because behavior patterns cut across tract boundaries, control functions are absent, etc. In highly traditional societies, though, cities have more of a ward pattern, and there is greater "ghettoization" of the urban population. In these cases, census tracts or other subunits might be quite appropriate. The problem is, of course, if we accept your conditions and also the possibility that there might well be a decay process across societies in meeting these conditions, then statistical comparison between societies becomes exceedingly difficult. This is the first problem I would like to point out.

My second point really doesn't bear on Anderson's comments. It deals with a larger question faced by those working in modern ecology, namely: Can we do cross-cultural or comparative research without ever leaving Bloomington, Indiana, or Columbus, Ohio? The increasing availability of large quantities of census data from many developing nations has made it quite possible to stay in the United States, pump data through our computers, and come out with some generalizations. You can study migration streams, the correlation of fertility or mortality with other social variables, and other problems without taking any field trips abroad. For ecological research, though, the absence of fieldwork would be exceedingly dangerous. Many of you have on occasion played around with census-tract data for cities, and you know you can only go so far in looking at the regressions or the indexes that you build on the basis of census tracts. Beyond that point you must go to the field and investigate the anomalies that show up; adequate explanation requires this.

What is insidious about this problem is that with the cutback in money for research projects abroad, I can conceive of us training international comparative sociologists in the future who never leave the Midwest. I don't know what the implications will be for our disciplines, but from my perspective, it is certainly very undesirable.

Mr. Johnson: In the discussion of Walton's paper [p. 190] the point was made that comparative study has everything it needs methodologically, while lacking theory to guide us in the proper use of the methods. Schwirian's paper considers this issue in the specific context of ecological analysis of urban areas, but his points are applicable in a broader area as well.

I would like specifically to talk about his discussion of factor analysis as a method of *creating* variables useful in ecological studies. His point is well made that in the past you could dump a lot of variables into the computer and get out a factor analysis. You can let the machine do things for you, but very often you don't know what it is doing, and the method limits the theory you can apply. You generally apply the theory *after* you have done your work. If you look at the models underlying these methods, you see that essentially they are underidentified. That is, the general factor-analytic model has more unknowns than knowns, and certain statistical, mathematical restrictions must be imposed so that a solution can be developed. The most common restriction imposed is that the factors are orthogonal, or uncorrelated with each other. A model can be easily solved if you require that the factors be orthogonal.

Now, you don't necessarily solve issues of underidentity by allowing oblique (that is, correlated) factors, because oblique models require more restrictive assumptions than you have in the orthogonal situation. These models are not related to your theoretical perspective on the underlying variables or to how you think the variables may be related. You just hope the results will come out right.

What I want to say is that we don't have to operate that way any more. There are factor-analytic methods which allow you to play around with these things yet within the context of the theoretical models you propose. You can specify the kinds of restrictions you want in your model, then hypothesize about the variables being measured and relate them to the underlying indicators. You can then test how these components and variables correlate. In short, you make your own theoretical assumptions which you fit into a factor model, and then you test whether the results fit your theory or not. Finally, you can apply the same model to several populations or to different sets of data; then you can have comparability, which I think is what Schwirian wanted.

Mr. Form:　But these models are limited by the available data. That is the horrible thing. No matter what kind of theoretical perspective you have, you only have certain kinds of data for Mayaguez. So my question is: Did Schwirian ever visit Mayaguez to see whether the actual ecological structure differed from that reflected by his data? I've been there, and it struck me that it did have a clear ecological structure, but his data don't show it. Why? Because he didn't have the kind of data necessary to put into his model?

You can talk from now to doomsday about it, but if a census doesn't include the kind of data your theoretical model demands, then you can't really test your theory.

Mr. Johnson:　O.K., but that failure isn't made explicit unless you have a theory to test. When you just use all the measures you have and let the factors come out as they may, you often unwittingly have some influence over the outcome because of the kind of implicit factor models you are using. These kinds of influences are recognized as important if you start with an explicit theory, which I don't think most users do.

CHAPTER THIRTEEN

Problems in the Analysis
of Latin American Illegitimacy [1]

DAVID R. JOHNSON

University of Nebraska

PHILLIPS CUTRIGHT

Indiana University

Introduction and Background

Many of the papers presented at this conference have focused primarily on conceptual and methodological problems and used substantive material only to illustrate. Such treatment is entirely appropriate for important single concerns that in and of themselves can destroy or substantially modify a given research project. Form's discussion (Chapter 3) of distrust exemplifies this kind of problem. The problems we have faced in our study of Latin American illegitimacy have not fallen into one or two clear-cut categories. Instead, with each step in our research, new difficulties have appeared. Therefore, in order to illustrate these problems and their resolution, we have written a basically substantive paper. The various conceptual and methodological difficulties appear in the exposition of the specific substantive issues to which they are related.

The 17 Latin American nations included in this study (see Table 13.1 below) are in many ways indistinguishable from other less-developed populations on various measures of fertility, mortality, and socioeconomic development. But they are very different from most other less-developed nations in their level of illegitimacy. Hartley (1970: Chart 1) finds that 12 of the 66 nations reporting illegitimacy ratios to the United Nations around 1965 had ratios of 400 per 1000 births or higher. All 12 were in either the Latin American or Caribbean area. The mean illegitimacy ratio around 1960 of the 17 Latin nations in this study was about 431, with a standard deviation of 185, while the mean illegitimacy rate per 1000 women aged 15 to 49, not legally married, was 136 with a standard deviation of 56. Both the ratio and the rate for these 17 Latin nations are 8 to 9 times larger than the ratio or rate for developed nations (Cutright, 1971b: Appendix I).

One advantage of confining an analysis of illegitimacy in less-developed regions to Latin America is that most Latin nations share a common history of conquest by Iberians, a common language, and a common religious faith. In the interests of comparability we have excluded those Latin populations lacking self-government and those whose colonial rulers were not Iberian. Bolivia and Brazil were also omitted because their legal definitions of illegitimacy and marriage were not comparable with the basically similar definitions used by governments of the 17 other Latin countries chosen for this study. The result of these selections was that we were able to study the effects of different levels of social, demographic, and economic development on illegitimacy rates in a set of nations with a common, and perhaps unique, history.

Two problems that we confronted in our research were statistical adequacy and comparability. As is true in many less-developed nations, Latin vital statistics often understate births. Statistical analysis can only proceed, therefore, after data on births have been adjusted for reporting errors. However, as we demonstrate, deficiencies in the birth data have not been sufficiently serious to block meaningful analysis. (Given limited information demographers have developed procedures to correct for large errors in vital statistics.) Similarly, data on the literacy, urbanization, and ethnic composition of Latin populations are not exactly comparable among nations. Indeed, the question for any researcher wishing to use reported information on such variables is not simply whether perfect comparability exists; rather it is whether the *degree* of error is such that use of the data will lead to faulty conclusions. We demonstrate that the relationships among these variables indicate a tolerable level of cross-national comparability.

In our view technical problems inherent in the measurement of fertility rates and the indicators of development used in this paper are less important than the problems of conceptualization and analysis. Proper conceptualization involves careful study of Latin history and mating-marriage patterns as well as an understanding of how socioeconomic measures relate to the analysis of illegitimacy. An adequate interpretation of measures of association among variables depends not only on a researcher's knowledge of a given statistical technique but also his knowledge of the meaning of variables selected for analysis. The following pages illustrate our reasons for interpreting variables as we do, some pitfalls to be avoided in cross-sectional analysis, and some problems encountered when inappropriate measures of illegitimacy are used.

A major feature that distinguishes Latin populations from those in other less-developed countries is their mating and marriage patterns. In Latin countries a large proportion of households are composed of a man and a woman (and their children) living together in a conjugal relationship without benefit of a legally recognized marriage contract. These unions, variously referred to as consensual, free marital, or common-law unions, are an important source of illegitimate births. Recent censuses of Latin countries have enumerated the consensual type of sexual union. Such relationships are normally defined as de facto unions, without the appropriate civil (or legally recognized) contracts that "possess a certain character of permanence" (Mortara, 1964:73). The evidence available from several Latin American populations (Arriaga, 1968; Stycos, 1968: Chap. 13) suggests that consensual unions are less stable than legal unions.

In addition to consensual and legal marriages, a third form of regular sexual union—which might be termed the "extraresidential" union—is often found in Latin American and Caribbean populations. This union exists when a male maintains a sexual relationship with a woman who is neither legally married to him nor lives in the same household (Smith, 1962). This pattern has been described for the Caribbean region by Goode (1960), Smith (1962), and Stycos (1955: Chap. 5; 1968: Chaps. 12 and 13). Azevedo (1965) and Hutchinson (1957) discuss this pattern in Brazil, while Service and Service (1954) and Reh (1946) comment on Paraguay. Adams (1957, 1960) has found both the consensual and the extraresidential patterns in Guatemala, El Salvador, Nicaragua, and Costa Rica.

Research such as ours is hampered by the fact that the extraresidential union has not been enumerated in the censuses of most Latin nations; female members of such unions are classified as single. Births to single women, especially the higher-order births, have been used (Mortara, 1964) to estimate the prevalence of such unions in some nations.

Both extraresidential and consensual unions are more common among lower-class than middle- or upper-class women (Stycos, 1968:244). It may be that, lacking effective bargaining power from their kin groups (Goode, 1960), lower-class women risk illegitimate children through extraresidential or consensual unions in a mating process that may eventually result in a legal marital union. This sequence of events is accepted, but not preferred, by women (Rodman, 1966). Whether an extraresidential or consensual union actually hastens the date of a legal union is unknown. What is known is that this mating pattern results in the birth of many illegitimate children.

There have been several efforts to explain the origins, prevalence, and variation in these patterns and the related variation in illegitimate births among Latin populations. The most widely known and best developed theory is discussed below.

Goode's Theory: National Integration and Illegitimacy

Using data from Africa and the New World south of the Mason-Dixon line, William Goode (1960, 1961, 1967) has attempted to demonstrate a relationship between community and national integration and levels of illegitimacy. Goode proceeds from the principle originally advanced by Malinowski (1930): In all societies legitimacy is rewarded and illegitimacy condemned. The illegitimacy level therefore indicates, to Goode, the degree to which a community is able to obtain compliance with the norm of legitimacy. Communities unable to obtain compliance have high illegitimacy levels because they lack the appropriate mechanisms for social control. These controls operate through the manipulation of status rewards and social position. Goode argued theoretically that high illegitimacy levels should be found in those areas lacking a coherent social and cultural system. The destruction of a coherent system will reduce social controls and lead to high illegitimacy because the constraints to enter legal marriages are weakened. Without reintegration, a phase occurs in which the old ways have been discarded, but new customs and social patterns of control have not yet been adopted. This phase, referred to as a state of anomie or normlessness, is conducive to high illegitimacy levels. In support of his hypothesis Goode argued empirically that the high illegitimacy levels for Negroes in the United States, for immigrants to the cities of Africa, and in many Latin American and Caribbean countries are caused by low integration and normlessness.

The conquest of the New World by the Iberians was marked by extensive physical destruction of the Indian population as well as of Indian social and cultural traditions. According to Goode, the early Iberians did not, as did the Spanish in the Philippines and the British in India, leave the customs and culture of the indigenous population intact. Instead, deliberate efforts were made to induce or force the Indian population to accept Iberian ways of life. Missionaries were zealous proselytizers for the Roman Catholic faith. Western customs were introduced to replace Indian customs. Populations were relocated on large landholdings to facilitate their conversion to Catholicism and provide a convenient, cheap labor pool. After nearly 500 years of contact with Western culture, the major result has been an almost complete disappearance of pre-Columbian social and cultural organization.

Goode maintains that while the vast majority of Latin American people speak an Iberian language and claim Catholicism as their religious faith, nonwhites have not been integrated into the dominant social, economic, and cultural system. Caste relations between whites and Indians and mestizos block occupational mobility. The Roman Catholic Church, while encouraging acceptance of the faith by the Indians, gave them few roles in the administrative and social functions of the Church. Particularly important to the study of illegitimacy has been the fact that financial obstacles were placed in the way of Church weddings. Marriage in the Church had little to attract the poor in a subsistence caste society, and the ruling hierarchy had little interest in enforcing legal marriage among the lower classes. As a result, high levels of consensual union without the sanction of either Church or state became characteristic of many segments of Latin American societies.

In his analysis of Latin American illegitimacy ratios, Goode sets out to demonstrate that (1) the early destruction of Indian cultures and the subsequent lack of community and societal integration caused present-day Latin mating and marriage patterns, and (2) *national* differences in illegitimacy ratios are inversely related to national levels of sociocultural integration. Further, higher rural than urban illegitimacy ratios *within* specific Latin populations are caused by a lower rural than urban level of community integration.

In testing the first hypothesis, Goode notes that the Iberian conquest of the New World differed from other colonial situations in the extent to which the indigenous cultures were penetrated and destroyed. We would argue, however, that while cultural destruction in Latin America *may* indeed be responsible for the alleged early high illegitimacy rate among Indians, rigorous comparative study using historical and cross-national data for other populations with histories of conquest, colonialism, and cultural destruction is required before this hypothesis can be confirmed or rejected.

Further, the presence of other historical conditions directly relevant to mating patterns and consensual unions in Latin America suggests that factors other than cultural destruction may possibly account for Latin mating and marriage patterns. For example, the original colonizers from Spain and Portugal were often married men who left their legal wives at home and established extramarital mating relationships with Indians or slaves (Morner, 1967:21-31); this pattern has continued. Certainly the number of original colonizers who mated in this way and produced racially mixed (mestizo or mulatto) offspring was initially small compared to the size of the indigenous population. Nevertheless, as a result of the Indian populations' rapid decimation from disease and maltreatment plus the continued in-migration of Europeans and interracial matings (the vast majority extralegal), by 1800 more than one-fourth of Latin America's population was of mixed racial and illegitimate origins (Morner, 1967:98-99). Clearly, then, one may question Goode's hypothesis that present-day mating and marriage patterns were caused by the destruction of Indian culture.[2]

Rather, one may argue that the behavior of the Iberian males was adopted by their illegitimate mestizo offspring, who grew in number over the years. The white ruling elite continued to exploit the subordinated and helpless female population, and mestizo males gradually accepted this pattern as legitimate. The increase in sexual exploitation eventually included much of the subordinate female population but was perhaps *moderated* by the growth of the consensual marriage pattern, which was probably preferred by women to the extra-residential pattern. Since males wishing to avoid legal marriage as a condition for copulation often stood at the higher reaches of social status and power, there was little the women they chose as sexual partners could do to resist. From this perspective, today's Latin mating-marriage patterns can be seen as the rather unique product of a series of historical circumstances that allowed upper-status men to exploit, with impunity, a subordinate female population. The illegitimate children that result from such patterns are the unintended consequence of sexual exploitation; they provide no evidence either that the norm of legitimacy had been abandoned or that the primary cause of the new patterns was the destruction of Indian cultures. This view does not deny the destruction of Indian cultures. It does, however, provide an alternative hypothesis to the cultural-destruction theory as the cause of mating and marriage patterns that have resulted in high illegitimacy.[3]

Goode's empirical analysis of recent illegitimacy ratios in Latin countries first examines differences within each nation. He suggests that urban populations are more assimilated (or integrated) than rural populations; therefore, consensual marriages, and hence illegitimacy, should be lower in urban than rural areas because of higher compliance with norms regarding legal marriage. Comparison of urban and rural illegitimacy ratios (Goode, 1961: Table 2) shows the expected lower ratios in urban areas; Goode then concludes that the lower urban ratios occur because urban populations are more integrated. We would argue, however, that urban populations differ in many ways from rural populations, and it may be the other differences (discussed below) rather than the degree of integration that produce the observed differences between urban and rural illegitimacy ratios.

Although differences in illegitimacy ratios within nations were related to urban or rural residence, Goode found that the correlation of these ratios with a measure of national urbanization across nations was only .50. From this "low" correlation he concluded that illegitimacy differences across nations could not be understood with objective measures of socioeconomic and demographic development; rather, such national differences could best be assessed with a measure of national integration.

Goode's measure of national integration for politically independent nations was based on qualitative assessments of five "integration" dimensions, which were then combined to yield a single rank for each country (except the four that were not classified because of lack of information). The five dimensions were (1) maintenance of caste barriers, (2) extent of ethnic homogeneity, (3) national programs for education and economic development, (4) the size of "pockets" of geographically and socially isolated people, and (5) judgments regarding "native" participation in national political affairs, and labor exploitation (Goode, 1961: Table 4, n.). Correlation of the national integration ranks with illegitimacy ratios was over .90—a finding that appears to validate empirically the national-integration explanation of illegitimacy. However, the reliability and validity of Goode's ranks are unknown. Moreover, examination of the characteristics used to determine national integration suggests that certain conventional, objective measures of economic, social, and demographic factors might also explain the variation in national illegitimacy ratios without invoking the concept of national integration.

The national-integration theory also has other weaknesses. It focuses attention on mating and marriage patterns alone, neglecting the possible impact of varying levels of birth control on illegitimacy rates. Further, Goode's choice of an empirical measure, the illegitimacy *ratio* (illegitimate births per 1000 total births), was unfortunate since the ratio is powerfully influenced by the level of marital fertility and the proportion of women legally married. The illegitimacy *rate* (illegitimate births per 1000 women 15—49 years old, not legally married) is the preferred analytical statistic because it measures the probability of an illegitimate birth in the population of unmarried women and is not biased by factors that raise or lower the number of legitimate births (Kumar, 1969; Cutright, 1972b: Appendix).

When one analyzes variations in national illegitimacy rates, both the degree of fertility control and the mating-marriage pattern must be considered. The importance of fertility control can be illustrated with the following hypothetical examples. Assume (1) annual general fertility rates of 300, 200, or 100 per 1000 legally or consensually married women 15-49; (2) equal fertility rates to women in each kind of marriage; (3) zero illegitimate births to unmarried women not living in consensual unions; and (4) different proportions of women not legally married who are in consensual unions. For a population in which half of the unmarried women are in consensual unions, the illegitimacy rates per 1000 women not in legal unions will vary from 150 to 50, depending solely on the level of fertility control. If only 30 percent of the unmarried are in consensual unions, the illegitimacy rates will be 90, 60, or 30. So long as the level of fertility control is allowed to vary, the illegitimacy rate will differ even though the percent in consensual unions remains constant. Clearly, then, the analysis of illegitimacy rates must consider those factors that affect fertility control as well as those that affect marital status.

National Differences in the Immediate Causes of Illegitimacy

The immediate causes of an illegitimacy rate are (1) sexual activity, including age at entry into a sexual union, the proportion of unmarried women in such unions, and frequency of intercourse; (2) voluntary control over conception through contraceptive practices, including sterilization; (3) voluntary control over gestation by induced abortion; (4) involuntary controls over conception, because of sterility; (5) involuntary control over gestation, measured by spontaneous fetal-loss and stillbirth; (6) marriage prior to the delivery of a child conceived outside legal marriage; and (7) valid and complete registration of illegitimate births (Cutright, 1971a:27).

We have already noted that exclusive emphasis on mating-marriage patterns implicitly restricts one's attention to only the first of the seven possible immediate causes. Both direct and indirect evidence, however, indicates that Latin populations vary in their use of contraception and induced abortion as well as in their respective percents of unmarried women engaged in nonlegal sexual unions. Less well understood is the variation among populations with regard to involuntary controls over conception and gestation. It *should* be the case that malnutrition, disease, and postpartum amenorrhoea cause the poorest Latin populations to show relatively higher levels of spontaneous fetal-loss and involuntary sterility[4] than the populations of Latin nations at higher levels of development. Such differences would tend to *reduce* the variation in illegitimacy rates related to measures of socioeconomic development. Nothing is known about variation among nations regarding the probability that an out-of-wedlock conception will be legitimated by the time of birth. It seems likely that variation on this probability is small, and even if this conjecture is not true, the independent causal impact of this factor (as opposed to an effect that could be shown arithmetically) is doubtful (Cutright, 1971a; 1972b). Analysis of U.S. data indicates little reason to suspect much invalid reporting of illegitimate births among whites in the United States (Cutright, 1972b:Appendix). One would therefore suppose that variation among Latin nations in false registration related to social stigma would likewise be a minor source of error. After adjustment for underregistration of births, one can be reasonably confident that the actual count of illegitimate births is as accurate as is the count of legitimate births. Since data are available only on the first three factors, they alone are discussed below.

Sexual Activity

A fairly direct indicator of sexual activity by the unmarried population (and the one used in our analysis of illegitimacy rates) is the percent of unmarried women living in consensual unions. Although this statistic neglects extraresidential unions (thus hampering perfect measurement of sexual activity among single women), it does capture a major source of national differences in sexual behavior that should be related to varying illegitimacy rates.

Contraception and Abortion

In nations outside Latin America, the use of contraception is positively related to the educational level of the woman. Recent studies in large urban areas of seven Latin American nations indicate that use there also increases with education (Jones and Nortman, 1968:16). Between 65 and 83 percent of the legally or consensually married women who had completed secondary school had tried some method; among similar women with no schooling, the comparable statistic ranged from only 12 to 43 percent.

Within the same nation, rural women are less likely than comparably educated urban women to attempt to control pregnancy; the percentage of women using some type of contraception is 30 to 40 percent lower in rural than in urban areas. One would, therefore, predict greater fertility among rural women (Jones and Nortman, 1968:15-16; rural-urban comparisons are for Colombia, Mexico, and Costa Rica).

An analysis of urban populations in seven Latin nations (Requena, 1968:790) considered the effectiveness of contraceptive methods used, abortion use, pregnancy rates, and number of children born. The data show a large difference between the percentage of women using effective methods and the percent using some method. The pregnancy *rate* per 1000 woman years decreases with increasing levels of effective contraceptive use. The abortion *rate* per 1000 woman-years is lowest in Argentina (which also shows the most effective use of contraception) and highest in Mexico (which shows the least effective use of contraception). Finally, the abortion *ratio* per 1000 pregnancies is highest in Argentina (246) and lowest in Colombia (117). Since Argentinian women report the highest use of effective contraceptive methods and are more likely than women in most other Latin populations to abort unwanted pregnancies when they occur, they have smaller families. Fertility rates in Argentina are much lower than those of most other Latin populations.

Studies of hospital records around 1960-1965 in nine nations provide an independent source of data to supplement the survey data measuring abortion use by Latin American women (Jones and Nortman, 1968:17-18). There are sharp differences among the nine nations. For example, Venezuela reports 196 while Panama reports 348 abortions per 1000 births. A study from Uruguay estimates an abortion ratio of 750. These statistics gain credibility when we contrast these figures with the observed birthrates (see Table 13.4, below) of these nations around 1960. The only nation (Chile) with longitudinal data shows a pattern of increasing abortion use from 1937 to 1960 accompanied by a drop in the birthrate.

Some interview data on abortion use by marital status were gathered by Requena (1968:795). He reports induced abortion rates per 1000 married and single women around ages 15-49 in Santiago, Chile, and in Costa Rica. The induced abortion *rate* per 1000 legally and consensually married women 15-49 was 49 in Santiago and 26 in Costa Rica. The abortion *rate* per 1000 single women was 19 in Santiago and 11 in Costa Rica ("Costa Rica" probably refers to the San Jose urban area). Abortion *ratios* per 1000 pregnancies of single women are also reported. This measure of abortion use shows that in Santiago (25 percent), Colombia (14 percent), and Costa Rica (9 percent), single women are somewhat more likely than consensually or legally married women to abort a pregnancy.

Interpreting the Meaning of Variables in Cross-Sectional Analysis

Although we have now documented (1) substantial differences among Latin nations in the use of voluntary means for controlling fertility and (2) the relationship of literacy and urban location to birth control within nations, the way in which one interprets correlations between variables such as percent white, literacy, or urbanization with illegitimacy rates depends on some understanding of historical trends. How did it come to pass that one nation now has a higher proportion of whites than some other nation? Does a high proportion of white persons measure "ethnic homogeneity" and national integration, or is it likely to index other population characteristics that might equally well explain the lower levels of consensual marriage and illegitimacy in the white versus the mixed populations? Is it likely that *changes* in literacy or urbanization since, say, 1900 have moved Latin nations from a condition of past homogeneity to one of heterogeneity in the present? Are the observed differences in national illegitimacy levels in 1950 or 1960 likely to have been caused by *changes* in literacy or other indirect integration factors that occurred over the prior several decades? Such questions are at the heart of the causal inferences that Goode derived from his analysis of illegitimacy ratios for 1950. We argue that modern migration patterns, not socioeconomic development and national integration, is the crucial factor affecting modern Latin American illegitimacy.

In-migration and Measures of Ethnic Homogeneity

Discussions of assimilation or integration patterns within Latin American populations often assume that the distribution of a given population into white, mestizo, mulatto, and Indian and Negro categories is the outcome of differential patterns of intermarriage between the indigenous and the in-migrant white (or in-migrant slave) populations. Stated differently, the current ethnic-color status of a population is the end result of 400 to 500 years of assimilation, or the absence of it. Thus, the existence of high proportions of Negroes or Indians might be taken as a measure of the persistence of caste barriers, while the proportion of mixed persons might be seen as an index of assimilation.

In Latin America, though, racial classification, particularly of Indians, Negroes, and mixed persons, depends on more than genetic origins. For example, Indians wearing Western clothing, living in cities, and speaking Spanish are classified as mixed, regardless of racial origins (Morner, 1967). The classification "white" may provide a more meaningful indicator of the ethnic and racial status of a Latin population. Table 13.1 shows the percentage distribution to white (or unmixed European), mixed, and Indian and Negro categories. Although nations high on percent Indian and Negro tend to be low on percent white, only 38 percent of the variation in either indicator is related to the other. The unexplained variation is caused by fluctuations in the size of the mixed population.

Table 13.1   Percentage Distribution to Ethnic and Color Groups (c. 1960-1965)

Nation	White	Mixed	Indian and Black
Argentina	90	9	1
Chile	30	65	5
Colombia	25	65	10[a]
Costa Rica	80	19	1
Cuba	72	15[b]	13[a]
Dominican Republic	15	70[b]	15[a]
Ecuador	10	50	40
El Salvador	5	75	20
Guatemala	2	44	54
Honduras	2	86	12
Mexico	15	55	30
Nicaragua	17	68	15[a]
Panama	10	65	25[a]
Paraguay	21	54	25
Peru	11	20	60
Uruguay	90	9	1
Venezuela	20	65	15

Sources. Guye (1967:468); Union Panamericana (1963:260); Johnson (1969: Table A); and Kurtz (1969).
[a]Populations in which blacks, rather than Indians, are heavily represented.
[b]Over half are mulattos rather than mestizos.

The historical processes that have resulted in a given ethnic-color composition in 1960 need not be considered as solely the result of differential caste or ethnic barriers within a given nation. The color homogeneity of a given nation may, for example, occur because only whites or only Negroes populated that territory and not because a caste barrier exists. To interpret properly the meaning of variation among nations in ethnic-color composition thus requires some idea of in-migration patterns. Some data on this subject are shown in Table 13.2.

The far right-hand column shows the percent white around 1960 and ranks the nations from high to low. The first column shows the proportion that is found when the total number of in-migrants from 1881 to 1930 is divided by the total population in 1930. For example, about 49 percent of the Argentinian population in 1930, compared to only 2 percent of the Mexican population, could be thought of as relatively recent white in-migrants. While it is certainly true that many migrants were dead by 1930 and some had returned to Europe, this measure does provide a rough gauge of the extent to which the nations represented in Table 13.2 had or had not received large waves of European in-migrants during later decades. (Comparable data for the United States is also shown for comparative purposes; note that both Argentina and Uruguay had a *larger* relative number of in-migrants than did the United States.)

Table 13.2   Percent of 1930 Population Represented by   1881-1930 and 1821-1932 In-migrants[a]

Nation	1881-1930	1821-1932	1960 Percent White[b]
Argentina	49	54	90
Uruguay	23	43	90
Cuba	19[c]	22	72[d]
Paraguay	na	3	21
Mexico	2[e]	na	15
United States	23	28	88

Sources. Based on W. S. Woytinsky and E. S. Woytinsky (1968:304, 309).
[a]The figures in this table tend to overstate the impact of in-migration, since the number of migrants who returned to Europe is unknown. See Thistlethwaite (1964).
[b]Percent white from Table 13.1 above.
[c]1881-1900 Cuba estimated at 50,000.
[d]The high proportion white in Cuba may be questioned.since some 43 percent of the total population around 1861 were slaves (Collver, 1965:105). The large volume of in-migration from 1905 to 1929 occurred during and just after World War I and was caused by the boom in Cuban sugar and the concurrent depression in Haitian and Jamaican sugar exports (Collver, 1965:107). A large proportion of the Cuban in-migrants during that period were, therefore, black. Given these considerations one tends to view the figure of 28 percent mulatto or black as an underestimate.
[e]1881-1910 Mexico estimated at 80,000 in-migrants.

Table 13.2 shows that Latin nations are extremely different in the degree to which they received large waves of European migrants around the turn of this century. The nations with large proportions of whites in 1960 were those that had attracted large numbers of European migrants during recent decades, while those with small proportions had not. The impact of such enormous differences in in-migration waves among Latin nations should not be underestimated (Collver, 1965:31, also emphasizes this factor).

Further, the characteristics of Europeans migrating around 1900 were radically different from those of migrants who settled Latin nations in the seventeenth and eighteenth centuries. The new in-migrants carried with them skills and values that were distinctly different from those held by earlier migrants. These skills and values pertained directly to marriage arrangements and fertility control, education, and characteristics related to socioeconomic development. One would expect, therefore, that Latin nations with a higher proportion of modern Europeans would have less illegitimacy than Latin nations with few such persons (see discussion below).

An additional point of interest in Table 13.2 is the apparent variation in timing of in-migration. For example, extending the time period back to 1821 does little to change the relative size of the in-migrant population in Argentina, Cuba, or Brazil, but it nearly doubles the number for Uruguay. For the most part, though, Table 13.2 indicates relatively little in-migration to most Latin nations between 1821 and 1881; the bulk of migrants from 1821 through 1931 arrived *after* 1881.

Some additional data (Collver, 1965:101) reveal that Costa Rica, in spite of registering 80 percent white in 1960, added only 40,000 migrants to its population from 1880 to 1930. The result is a percentage figure of 8.0 percent of the 1930 population, a figure below that of Brazil but probably higher than that of some other Latin nations. Costa Rica achieved such a high level of whites simply because the territory had very few Indians to begin with, few slaves were imported, and the mortality rate of Indians and slaves was high (Guye, 1967). Of somewhat more direct relevance for the study of fertility is the information that Costa Rica, in spite of its high percent white, apparently differs sharply from nations like Argentina in that the white population of Costa Rica has not received a large-scale in-migration of modern Europeans. Rather, like the white populations of many other Latin nations, Costa Rica's whites descended from those who settled the territory before 1800.

Table 13.2 shows only that the waves of in-migration varied from nation to nation and that such variation is one cause of the ethnic-color composition around 1960. We now turn to the evidence that Latin populations with sizable proportions of whites *should* have different marriage and fertility patterns and socioeconomic development levels than hold for populations with few such persons.

The three southern European nations (Portugal, Italy, and Spain) that contributed most heavily to the modern in-migration stream to Latin nations had adopted the European pattern of late marriage before 1900 (Hajnal, 1965:102). Second, by 1960 the late marriage pattern in these three nations was related to relatively low crude birth and gross reproduction rates (United Nations, 1965:90-92). One would expect, then, that the in-migrants to Latin America around the turn of this century carried with them attitudes and practices regarding marriage and fertility control that were common to other European nations at the time. It is unlikely that these patterns were discarded upon arrival in Latin America. Rather, one can assume that the introduction of large numbers of modern Europeans probably caused a gradual reduction of birthrates in the receiving nations.

Crude birthrate trends in southern European and Latin nations with long-run data corroborate this view (see United Nations, 1958, 1965; Leasure, 1963:271; Collver, 1965:26-28, 32, and 163; Gendell, 1967:151). In the three southern European nations, the relatively low birthrates already achieved by 1900 continued to decline. Among Latin nations, only Argentina, Uruguay, Chile, and Cuba show declining rates after 1900. The data thus show that the Latin nations with declining fertility tend to be those that have experienced large waves of modern European in-migration. These nations tend also to have a high percent white and lower fertility around 1960.

Trends in Socioeconomic Development and Illegitimacy

The national-integration theory of illegitimacy assumes that both the level of, and changes in, characteristics such as literacy and urbanization are responsible for variation in illegitimacy and consensual ratios. Goode used various measures of national integration (urbanization, caste barriers, education programs, etc.) to show that differences in illegitimacy ratios among Latin American nations reflect the extent to which slave and Indian populations had become integrated into the national social and cultural systems. The use of such measures, however, implies a time in the past when these nations had similar illegitimacy and consensual levels. Those nations in which caste carriers fell first, literacy and urbanization advanced most rapidly, and so on are assumed to have reduced their illegitimacy levels more than other nations. Goode thus inferred change from a hypothetical uniform past by using cross-sectional measures collected during the 1950s. Without *evidence* of uniform past levels of literacy and illegitimacy among nations, however, the correlation observed in 1950 cannot be interpreted as evidence of a causal impact by increasing literacy (and integration) on illegitimacy.

The problem of inferring causal relationships with cross-sectional data similar to Goode's has been discussed elsewhere (Cutright and Wiley, 1969-1970). For the moment, let us simply state that the differences in literacy and urbanization levels among Latin nations have persisted over long periods of time and that these differences were probably magnified by differential in-migration of Europeans after, say, 1840. The assumption of a uniform past level of consensual marriage, illegitimacy, or socioeconomic characteristics among Latin countries is false. This assumption, however, is at the heart of static analysis of recent national illegitimacy differences and therefore deserves further discussion.

Cutright and Wiley (1969-1970) report correlations for energy consumption and literacy of about .95 in 40 nations measured in 1930 and again in 1960. The rank order of nations on either measure scarcely alters over the three-decade period during which large absolute changes occurred. It seems likely, then, that a similar pattern of national differences on various socioeconomic-development measures has existed for many decades among Latin countries. What now can be said of differences in illegitimacy?

Measures of illegitimacy ratios are available for only 9 of the 17 nations in our study for years near the turn of the twentieth century. The completeness and reliability of these data are questionable (Collver, 1965). Still, it is possible to ascertain the degree of dependence of 1950-1960 variations in illegitimacy ratios on 1885-1910 variations among these nine nations. If much of the 1960 variation among nations is explained by differences in 1900, then socioeconomic *changes* in the last 50 years can *not* account for much of the 1960 differences among nations.

Table 13.3   Early and Late Illegitimacy Ratios for Nine Latin
American Nations

Country	Year of Measurement	Illegitimacy Ratio
Chile	1903-1905	357
	1960	*159*
Costa Rica	1883-1885	188
	1960	*231*
Cuba	1900-1905	342
	1930	*300*
Ecuador	1921-1925	315
	1960	*342*
Mexico	1895-1897	376
	1960	*250*
Panama	1912-1916	689
	1960	*635*
El Salvador	1899-1905	510
	1960	*630*
Uruguay	1896-1905	259
	1954	*211*
Venezuela	1909-1911	704
	1962-1963	*536*

Sources. Early ratios from *Encyclopedia Britannica*, vol. XII (1953:85); Arriaga (1968: 182), for Venezuela; U.N. *Demographic Yearbook* for later years.

Early and late illegitimacy ratios are shown in Table 13.3 The correlation of the ratios for these nine nations is .85. Seventy-two percent of the variation in late ratios is explained by the early ratios. Thus, less than 30 percent of the variation in the ratios of these countries around 1960 can be accounted for by socioeconomic changes in the last 50 or 60 years, by errors of birth registration, by possible changes in national definitions of illegitimacy, or by changes in marital status and marital fertility, any of which can also cause illegitimacy ratios to change. Clearly, the bulk of the variation among Latin American nations in illegitimacy ratios around 1960 can be traced back to conditions that existed before the twentieth century. Recent literacy programs, recent government policies towards Indians, land reform, and the lowering of caste barriers could not have had much relative impact on the illegitimacy levels, whatever their effects may have been on national integration.

In general, this review of the sources of change or stability in national differences among Latin populations suggests that several measures used by Goode in his national integration ranks may have been inappropriate. Further, since it is the illegitimacy rate rather than the ratio that measures the probability of an illegitimate birth to the population of unmarried women, the rate should be the dependent variable. Finally, most of the variables used in the following analysis have now been given some historical and substantive interpretation; we would now expect the percent white, literacy, and urbanization rates to affect illegitimacy, not because they constitute alternative measures of integration but because populations high on these characteristics have marriage and fertility control behaviors that depress illegitimacy.[5]

Analysis of Illegitimacy Rates

We computed two illegitimacy rates. The first simply used the number of women 15-49 as the denominator; the resulting rate can be termed the illegitimacy rate for all women. The second is more familiar. For Latin nations this rate includes consensually married, single, divorced, and widowed women 15-49 in its denominator and excludes only the legally married. Kiser and associates (1968:139) have noted that an illegitimacy rate using women in all marital statuses may be useful if the error in marital status reporting is large. The correlation between the illegitimacy rate for all women and the rate for women not in legal marriages in 17 Latin nations is .98. Therefore, we conclude that analysis of either rate would yield similar results, and we restrict our discussion to the illegitimacy rate based on women 15-49 not in legal marriages.

Illegitimate Births to Women Not in Consensual Unions

If the only illegitimate births in Latin countries were to women in consensual unions, a study of the proportion of women in such unions and their fertility rates would yield an accurate estimate of the illegitimacy rate. But women outside consensual unions also have illegitimate children. Two systematic proofs of this statement exist in addition to the evidence cited above on the extraresidential mating pattern and on abortions and births to single women (Requena, 1965:40).

First, Johnson (1969:Fig. 6.1) has plotted the consensual ratio[6] against the illegitimacy ratio for 18 Latin nations. The correlation between the two measures yields an R^2 of .96, but the regression equation has a y-intercept of 129. Thus a Latin population with *no* women in consensual unions would be expected to have an illegitimacy ratio of 129 per 1000 births. Given the high percent of the 15-49 population in legal unions (implied for our hypothetical population with zero consensual unions) and high marital fertility rates, an illegitimacy ratio of 129 would be accompanied by a high illegitimacy rate for single, widowed, and divorced women.

A second proof also exists. Table 13.4 shows, for the 15-49 age group around

Table 13.4 Actual and Expected Illegitimacy Rates for Women 15-49 Not in Legal Unions (c. 1960)[a]

Nation	Actual 15-49 Rate Unmarried[b]	Expected 15-49 Rate Unmarried[b]	Error	Actual 15-49 Legal Rate	Unmarried in Consensual Unions (%)
Argentina	43	16	27	143	11.3
Chile	48	18	30	237	7.4
Uruguay	66	14	52	121	11.3
Colombia	78	61	17	327	18.7
Mexico	100	48	52	293	16.3
Cuba	104	71	33	186	38.2
Costa Rica	106	55	51	339	16.2
Paraguay	135	64	71	282	22.7
Ecuador	137	84	53	290	28.8
Peru	167	66	101	236	28.1
Panama	168	73	95	175	41.9
Guatemala	169	116	53	221	52.4
Venezuela	188	96	92	272	35.3
El Salvador	189	97	89	258	37.6
Honduras	193	93	100	220	42.1
Nicaragua	199	101	98	260	38.7
Dominican Republic	218	123	95	253	48.5

[a]Expected 15-49 illegitimacy rate computed under the assumption that all illegitimate births are to consensually married women having a 15-49 fertility rate equal to the fertility rate to legally married women aged 15-49. Positive error indicates that the actual unmarried rate was higher than the expected rate. All errors are positive. Rates corrected for under-registration of births.

[b]"Unmarried" refers to all women 15-49 not in legal marriages.

1960, the actual and expected illegitimacy rates for women not in legal unions, the fertility rate for legally married women, and the percent of unmarried women who are in consensual unions. From these statistics one may derive the expected illegitimacy rate for women not in legal unions *if* only consensually married women were delivering illegitimate children. The expected illegitimacy rate under this assumption will be the product of the percent of the unmarried who are consensually married multiplied by the fertility rate of the legally married. Aside from measurement error, the major question is whether in fact fertility rates of the consensually and legally married are equal. The fertility of women in consensual unions may be depressed by the greater instability of consensual than legal unions, but this effect would tend to be offset by the older average age and, hence, lower fecundity of women in legal marriages. These two effects may cancel out to produce rather similar fertility rates between the two groups. For example, Stycos (1968:206) reports similar fertility, controlling age, between consensually married and legally married women in Puerto Rico and Jamaica. Arriaga (1968: Table 13) finds little difference in completed fertility of Venezuelan women, whether legally or consensually married, while Stycos (1968:211) reports similar findings for Puerto Rico.

Column 2 shows the expected illegitimacy rate under the assumption that only consensually married women deliver illegitimate children and that their fertility rate is equal to that of the legally married. Column 3 shows that in every case the expected illegitimacy rate is well below the actual illegitimacy rate; we interpret this fact as further evidence that women not in consensual unions are also having illegitimate children.

If the assumption that legal and consensual fertility are equal is invalid, is it likely that correction for this "error" would indicate that our conclusion is incorrect? Take the example of Panama. Assume that instead of a marital fertility rate of 175, we applied a rate of 250 to the consensually married. This rate of 250 would result in an expected illegitimacy rate of 105—an estimate that is still lower by 63 points than the actual rate of 168.

We emphasize that the rates in Table 13.4 are *not* the estimated illegitimacy rates to never-married, widowed, and divorced women since the consensually married are still in the denominator. When the consensually married in Panama, for example, are removed from the denominator and illegitimate births to the consensually married estimated from a fertility rate of 250 are removed from the numerator, the estimated illegitimacy rate to single, widowed, and divorced women aged 15-49 is 108 per 1000. We conclude that illegitimacy in Latin America is not solely a result of consensual marriages. Rather, substantial illegitimacy rates to women outside consensual unions exist in all nations.

The Correlates of Two Measures of Illegitimacy

Table 13.5 compares the correlates of various independent variables with two measures of illegitimacy. The final column provides a summary measure of the gain or loss of a given independent variable's relationship to illegitimacy depending on whether we use the ratio or the rate for unmarried women. For example, literacy, urbanization, and percent white explain *more* variation in the rate than in the ratio. Marital fertility rates correlate *negatively* with the ratio and *positively* with the illegitimacy rate, as one might expect.

Table 13.5   Correlations of Independent Variables with Two Measures of
            Illegitimacy: 17 Latin American Nations (c. 1960)

	Correlations		
			Gain or Loss
Independent	Illegitimacy	Illegitimacy Rate,	in Explained
Variables	Ratio	Unmarried, 15-49	Variance[a]
Percent literate (age 15+)	-.702	-.755	8
Percent urban (20,000+)	-.579	-.647	8
Percent white	-.596	-.693	12
Marital fertility rate	-.113	.193	2
Catholic institutional strength	-.847	-.652	-29
Consensual ratio	.975	.864	-20
Percent in legal marriage	-.932	-.845	-15
Percent consensual marriage	.960	.848	-20
Percent in unmarried in consensual unions	.953	.863	-16
Percent in legal or consensual unions	.431	.325	-8
Illegitimacy ratio	1.000	.883	-22

[a]Difference in square of zero-order correlation with illegitimacy ratio versus illegitimacy rate to unmarried women aged 15-49 not in legal marriage. A positive number means that the independent variable explained more variance in the rate than it did in the ratio. Marital fertility rates and marital status indicators apply to women 15-49.

The Catholic Institutional Strength (CIS) index[7] and the consensual ratio both suffer an enormous drop in their ability to account for variance in rates as compared to ratios. Of special interest is the difference in explained variance in illegitimacy depending on whether the percent of unmarried women in consensual unions is correlated with the ratio or the rate. Our interpretation of this statistic was that it measured sexual activity of unmarried women that might lead to an illegitimate birth. The decline in the correlation of this measure from .95 to .86 when the measurement of illegitimacy shifts from the ratio to the rate may indicate that factors other than sexual activity and consensual marriage are involved in determining the rate.

The correlation of .98 between the two measures of illegitimacy rates noted above (p. 392) can be contrasted with the relatively modest (.88) correlation of the ratio to the rates for unmarried women. The ratio is *not* an adequate measure of the rate for unmarried women, and one might therefore expect determinants of the illegitimacy rate to be somewhat different from the determinants of the ratio.

Path Analysis

The means, standard deviations, and correlations used in the following analyses are shown in Table 13.6. The rationale behind the use of each independent variable, with the exception of the measure of CIS, has been discussed in preceding sections. CIS was introduced because one might expect that populations with a high level of CIS would be more likely to enter legal than consensual unions because of Church pressures to marry, easier access of the population to priests, and continuing campaigns by the Church to marry those in consensual unions. Figure 13.1 shows two models that we developed to account for variation in illegitimacy rates.

Table 13.6   Means, Standard Deviations, and Correlations of Variables Used in Analysis of Illegitimacy Rates: 17 Latin American Nations[a]

Variable		1	2	3	4	5	6	7	8
Literacy	1	1.00	.80	.83	.52	-.71	-.73	-.70	-.33
Urbanization	2	–	1.00	.63	.42	-.62	-.64	-.58	-.52
Percent white	3	–	–	1.00	.33	-.58	-.61	-.60	-.39
Catholic institutional strength	4	–	–	–	1.00	-.84	-.85	-.85	.29
Unmarried in consensual unions	5	–	–	–	–	1.00	.98	.95	-.03
Consensual ratio	6	–	–	–	–	–	1.00	.97	-.03
Illegitimate ratio	7	–	–	–	–	–	–	1.00	-.11
Marital fertility rate	8	–	–	–	–	–	–	–	1.00
Mean		66.9	30.3	30.3	208.0	29.1	311.5	431.5	241.9
Standard deviation		15.2	15.2	31.3	81.3	14.0	171.1	185.3	60.1

[a]See Figure 13.1 for variable actually used. Correlations with the illegitimacy rate are shown in Table 13.5. The mean and standard deviation of illegitimacy rates for women 15-49 not in legal marriages were 135.8 and 56.1, respectively.

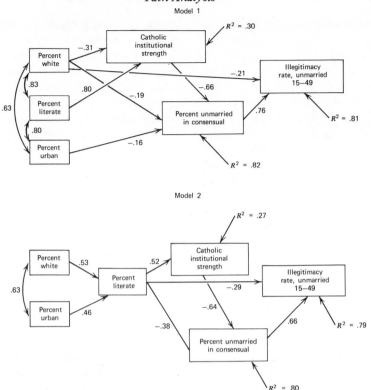

Figure 13.1 Path models to account for variance in illegitimate fertility rates in 17 Latin American countries c. 1960.
Note: Residual paths omitted and replaced by R^2. In Model 1, paths of .15 or less are not shown. In Model 2, only variables with paths shown were used in calculation of paths and explained variance.

In Model 1, percent white, literacy, and urbanization are not placed in a causal order but are treated as exogenous variables that affect CIS. Thirty percent of the variance in CIS is related to the three exogenous variables. Because of the high intercorrelations among the three exogenous variables, substantive interpretation of their paths to the CIS variable is hazardous. CIS precedes the percent of unmarried women in consensual unions—a measure of coital activity in the unmarried population. Eighty-two percent of the variation in the percent of the unmarried in consensual unions is explained by the four variables preceding it. These five independent variables are seen as determinants of the illegitimacy rate.

The five variables in Model 1 account for 81 percent of the variation in illegitimacy rates. The largest path to the illegitimacy rate is a positive path from percent unmarried consensual. The magnitude of the paths, however, is somewhat deceiving, particularly those leading from the exogenous variables—percent white, literate, and urban. The high intercorrelations among these three variables suggest that their primary influence on illegitimacy rates will be a joint influence *not* ascertainable from direct paths. Together, the three exogenous variables alone account for 59 percent of the variation in illegitimacy rates. CIS adds an additional increment of 11 percent, while the addition of percent unmarried consensual adds 11 percent more to the explained variance. This "forward" method of allocating explained variance places the greatest weight on the three exogenous variables.

Reversing the order in which we allow variables to remove explained variance (the "backward" method), we find that the percent unmarried in consensual unions explains, by itself, 74 percent of the variance; the addition of CIS adds nothing, while the remaining 7 percent explained variance is shared by the three exogenous variables. The backward solution places the greatest weight on percent unmarried in consensual unions. However, neither the forward nor the backward method captures the network of relationships among the variables in the model. The main way through which the exogenous variables affect illegitimacy rates proceeds via their direct effects on CIS as well as their direct effects on the percent unmarried in consensual unions. Although most of the impact of the exogenous variables on illegitimacy rates is indirect (through their effects on CIS and percent unmarried in consensual unions), those variables also show a direct path to the illegitimacy rate. *CIS* affects illegitimacy rates through its impact on the percent unmarried in consensual unions but has no direct effects on illegitimacy.

Interpretation of direct paths and expained variance in Model 1 is hampered by (1) the large number of independent variables applied to the small number of countries, and (2) the high degree of multicollinearity of the independent variables. Model 2 simplifies the path analysis by eliminating variables with small paths.

In Model 2, percent white and urbanization are seen as factors explaining variation in literacy. The positive path from literacy to CIS is the correlation coefficient for these two variables. Three percent of the explained variance in CIS is lost (compare Model 1 with Model 2) when only literacy is used to explain variance in CIS. Both literacy and CIS have large negative paths to percent unmarried in consensual unions, and these two variables explain 80 percent of the variance—a loss of only 2 percent when compared with the four variables used to account for consensual marriages among the unmarried in Model 1. Finally, only literacy and the percent of unmarried women in consensual marriages are used to account for variation in illegitimacy rates. These two variables alone expain 79 percent of the variation, a loss of only 2 percent from the level expained using 5 predictors in Model 1.

The path from percent unmarried in consensual unions is .66 compared to a path of -.29 from literacy to illegitimacy rates. Considered together, then, both variables have large direct effects on illegitimacy rates. Part of the negative effect of literacy on illegitimacy rates (literacy alone accounts for 57 percent of the variance in illegitimacy rates) is caused by the direct effect literacy has in determining the level of CIS as well as the direct effect of literacy on consensual marriages. But literacy also has direct effects on illegitimacy rates independent of its effects on CIS or consensual-marriage levels. The negative path from literacy to illegitimacy is expected and may provide an estimate, independent of the effects of consensual marriages on illegitimacy rates, of the influence that literacy has on variation in abstinence and birth-control practice.

The .66 path from the percent in consensual unions to illegitimacy rates is more than double the path from literacy to illegitimacy. This larger path should be expected, given the fertility level of women in consensual unions and the impact that this variable should have on the illegitimacy rate. Interpreting this path requires knowledge of those factors that determine the percent unmarried in consensual unions—CIS and the exogenous variables. However, including a measure of consensual unions does add to the explained variance independent of the variables that precede it; clearly, the proportion of unmarried women in consensual marriages does affect Latin illegitimacy rates as defined in this paper.

There are, however, alternative illegitimacy rates that may be unrelated to the percent unmarried in consensual unions. For example, if we could calculate the illegitimacy rates for single, widowed, and divorced women, the status of percent unmarried in consensual unions in a path model would be conceptually unclear. It seems likely (in Table 13.4 compare "error" column with the percent of unmarried in consensual unions) that the illegitimacy rate to single, widowed, and divorced is positively correlated with the percent unmarried in consensual unions. If that were true, then the interpretation of percent unmarried in consensual unions would have to be expanded to include meanings beyond that which we have given to it—that is, a measure of coital activity among the unmarried. In sum, although we have been rather successful in accounting for variation in illegitimacy rates with the variables in our models, the same models might not work so well if alternative illegitimacy rates were considered. As they now stand, the models may or may not account for variation in illegitimate births to unmarried women *not* in consensual unions, and as we noted in Table 13.4, these births represent a substantial contribution to the illegitimacy rates of many Latin nations.

Conclusion

Although substantial measurement errors must remain in both the independent and the dependent variables used in this study, the high levels of explained variance and the high correlations between various measures testify to the fact that measurement errors are not excessive. For example, the .97 correlation between the consensual ratio (from census enumeration of marital status) and the illegitimacy ratio (from vital statistics) indicates little error. Fertility rates in a number of countries must be corrected for underregistration of births. These corrections are not perfect, but they appear to be adequate to the needs of this research. While exact equivalence among national measures of percent white, literacy, CIS, marital status, or even urbanization is unlikely, the power of these independent variables to account for variance in the dependent variables suggests a tolerable level of measurement error. In general, measurement error will reduce correlations and explained variance; improved measures would strengthen rather than weaken the relationships discussed.

The more serious problems in the analysis of Latin illegitimacy concern the selection and interpretation of independent variables, the interpretation of cross-sectional data, and the measurement of illegitimacy levels. Although we correctly rejected the illegitimacy ratio and measured illegitimacy by calculating a rate per 1000 unmarried women 15-49, the other problems remain.

We found that variation in Latin American illegitimacy rates is a function of both mating-marriage patterns and the level of fertility control. Since these factors are interrelated, a precise estimate of the contribution of each to the variation in Latin illegitimacy rates was not possible. The same characteristics of populations that affect their mating and marriage patterns also affect fertility control. These characteristics were first related to historical patterns of in-migration that resulted in nations having populations with different marriage patterns and different ideas and skills relevant to fertility control. Nations with few modern European in-migrants have maintained a pattern of high fertility similar to that found in many other underdeveloped nations.

The finding that only a part of the illegitimacy rate for women not in legal unions was caused by the fertility of women in consensual unions undercuts excessive reliance on consensual marriage as an adequate explanation of Latin illegitimacy rates. We rejected the view that consensual marriage is the sole key to understanding the high level of illegitimacy in Latin America. The extraresidential union, as well as the consensual union, should be explained both in historical terms (how these patterns of sexual behavior outside legal marriage began) as well as in contemporary terms (why they persist).

We suggested that the unusually high degree of sexual exploitation of women established by the Conquistadors and continued by their descendents, when accompanied by relatively low in-migration of peoples holding opposing views, may provide a plausible explanation of mating-marriage patterns that have resulted in high Latin illegitimacy levels. Structural characteristics that make it more or less likely for women to enter a legal rather than a consensual marriage are understandable on grounds other than the more remote and unmeasured changes in feelings of national integration and norms about legitimacy.

The effect of change in socioeconomic development on illegitimacy or marriage patterns did not appear to be strong. We did not place a strong emphasis on changes in literacy or urbanization over the past 40 to 60 years as factors that could explain 1960s variation in consensual marriage or fertility. Rather, we noted that the correlation between socioeconomic measures and consensual marriage or illegitimacy ratios in 1950 or 1960 seems to be largely a function of a similar set of relationships that have existed for a number of decades.

What can we say of future trends in illegitimacy rates in Latin nations? In European nations illegitimacy rates declined during the period of declining marital fertility—after about 1880 (Shorter, Knodel, and Van de Walle, 1971). The historical record of European populations prior to 1880 indicates that if continued modernization does not lead to a decline in marital fertility, then illegitimacy rates will tend to increase (Shorter, 1971). Thus, if future trends in Latin illegitimacy follow the trend expected from the European experience, one would expect a decline to occur when marital fertility rates decline. Given recent declines in fertility in a few Latin populations it should be possible to test this prediction in a few years.

Notes

1. This research was supported by Public Health Service grant MH 15567, the University of Nebraska, and Indiana University.

2. It is likely that a separate effect of colonization, as practiced by Europeans in Latin America, was to increase Indian fertility, an effect that would tend to boost illegitimacy rates without any change in Indian marriage or mating customs. Polgar (1971:3-8) reviews the impact of Western colonization on natality. Geertz (1963:69) specifies economic incentives from colonial rule on the indigenous population of Java that raised its fertility. No such inquiry exists for Latin populations, although Morner (1967) points out that the tax system used by the Spanish may have promoted miscegenation. Whether the tax system also provided economic incentives to increase Indian and mestizo family size is unknown but is worth investigation. If such incentives were at work the long-term effect would be to shatter traditional practices governing the control of natality, thus leaving the population poorly equipped to reduce fertility later when such a reduction might be "expected" to occur in response to rising socioeconomic development and declining mortality. The failure of Latin populations to follow the European model of fertility reduction has been reviewed by Arriaga (1970).

3. It may be argued that the exploitation of women is simply an index of cultural destruction and that all we have done is to make specific what was formerly vague. However, one problem that must be faced in accounting for Latin illegitimacy by focusing attention on the Indian population is that Latin nations with very high illegitimacy rates do not necessarily have many Indians in residence. For example, Costa Rica estimates 1 percent Indian but produces an illegitimacy rate of 106 per 1000 women who are 15-49 years old and not in legal unions (Tables 13.1 and 13.4). Such rates indicate that persons other than Indians are having illegitimate children.

From the scattered accounts in the various references cited in this article, we might guess that the mixed population in most Latin countries contributes disproportionately to national illegitimacy totals. Consider data for Argentina with only 9 percent mixed and 1 percent Indian persons. If whites in these countries have no illegitimate births, the rate per 1000 mixed and Indian women aged 15-49 would have to be 450 per year. If a more reasonable estimate of 100 per 1000 to the nonwhite population is assumed, then the rate to the white female population not in legal unions would be about 39 per 1000 aged 15-49. This rate is about double the highest European nation's illegitimacy rate around 1960 and is triple the average rate for white European and overseas whites outside Latin nations (Glass, 1968:143; Cutright, 1971b:Appendix 1). These data suggest a generalizing effect of Latin history on mating and marriage that affected not only the surviving Indians and the mixed population but whites as well.

4. The only quantitative analysis of the impact of changing levels of involuntary controls over conception and gestation on illegitimacy is reported by Cutright (1972a; 1972b). The major involuntary control appears to be spontaneous fetal loss rather than the level of adolescent or adult sterility. In the United States, changes in involuntary controls over conception and gestation due to improved health had a major impact on trends in nonwhite fertility in the 1880-1960 period. Similar large effects on the fertility of women in Latin nations seem unlikely. Future research may find some Latin populations with unusual levels of involuntary controls, but to judge from past and more recent fertility levels in Latin nations, the power of these controls in limiting fertility is relatively weak.

5. For example, rural women are more likely than urban women to be living in a consensual rather than a legal marriage (Miro, 1964:32). This finding is to be expected given rural-urban differences in (1) literacy (UNESCO, 1963, 1968); (2) female job opportunities and economic dependence on males (United Nations, 1962; Collver and Langlois, 1962; Gendell, 1967:150); (3) pressures to limit family size; (4) separation from kin who can "adopt" illegitimate children (Goode, 1960); (5) access to, and use of, birth control; and (6) differences in ethnicity and color, with the urban population tending to contain a higher share of the national white population than will be found in rural areas (Germani, 1970:323). One might expect that these factors would enable one to understand urban-rural differences in consensual marriage (and illegitimacy) without relying on possible differences in the level of community integration in rural or urban areas. Thus, one need not agree with Goode that the observed rural-urban differences in illegitimacy ratios provide evidence to support the integration theory of Latin illegitimacy. If rural-urban differences in illegitimacy ratios within nations can be seen as the result of factors other than community integration, then national differences in illegitimacy rates may also be explained by national characteristics other than the level of national integration.

6. The consensual ratio is the number of consensual marriages per 1000 legal and consensually married women. This measure correlates .97 with the illegitimacy ratio (see Table 13.6). However, this correlation is not evidence of the overwhelming importance of consensual marriages in determining illegitimacy, since the numerators and the denominators of the two ratios are so closely related.

7. The measurement of CIS was discussed by Johnson (1969:Appendix B). A total score for each nation was derived from measures of the numbers of persons included in each of seven categories of religious personnel—sisters, religious priests, diocesan priests, male religious nonpriests, major seminarians, minor seminarians, and priests that were foreigners. The religious personnel and population data relate to 1957 and 1960. Details on index construction are available from Johnson.

References

Adams, Richard N.

1957 Cultural surveys of Panama–Nicaragua–Guatemala–El Salvador–Honduras. Washington, D.C.: Pan-American Sanitary Bureau, *Scientific Publications* 33.

1960 An inquiry into the nature of the family. In Gertrude Dole and Robert L. Carneiro (Eds.), *Essays in the Science of Culture: In Honor of Leslie A. White.* New York: Thomas Y. Crowell. Pp. 30-45.

Arriaga, Eduardo E.

1968 Some aspects of family composition in Venezuela. *Eugenics Quarterly,* 15 (September):177-190.

1970 The nature and effects of Latin America's non-Western trend in fertility. *Demography,* 7 (November):483-501.

Arriaga, Eduardo E., and Kingsley Davis.

1969 The pattern of mortality change in Latin America. *Demography,* 6 (August):223-242.

Azevedo, Thales de.

1965 Family, marriage and divorce in Brazil. In Dwight B. Heath and Richard N. Adams (Eds.), *Contemporary Cultures and Societies of Latin America.* New York: Random House. Pp. 288-310.

Collver, Andrew.

1965 *Birth Rates in Latin America: New Estimates of Historical Trends and Fluctuations.* Berkeley and Los Angeles: University of California.

Collver, Andrew, and Eleanor Langlois.

1962 The female labor force in metropolitan areas: an international comparison. *Economic Development and Cultural Change,* 10 (July):367-385.

Cutright, Phillips.

1971a Illegitimacy: myths, causes and cures. *Family Planning Perspectives,* 3 (January):26-48.

1971b Economic events and illegitimacy in developed countries. *Journal of Comparative Family Studies,* 2 (Spring):33-53.

1972a The teen-age sexual revolution and the myth of an abstinent past. *Family Planning Perspectives,* 4 (January):24-31.

1972b *Illegitimacy in the United States: 1920-1968.* Background Papers, Commission on Population Growth and the American Future. Washington, D.C.: U.S. Government Printing Office.

In press. *Illegitimacy: Measurement and Analysis.*

Cutright, Phillips, and James A. Wiley.

1969- Modernization and political representation: 1927-1966. *Studies in*
1970 *Comparative International Development,* 5 (2):23-46.

Encyclopedia Britannica.

1953 Illegitimacy. Vol. XII, p. 85. Chicago: Encyclopedia Brittanica.

Geertz, Clifford.

1963 *Agricultural Involution.* Berkeley and Los Angeles: University of California.

Gendell, Murray.

1967 Fertility and Development in Brazil. *Demography,* 4(1):143-157.

Germani, Gino.

1970 Mass immigration and modernization in Argentina. In Irving Louis Horowitz (Ed.), *Masses in Latin America.* New York: Oxford University Press. Pp. 289-330.

Glass, D. V.

1968 Fertility trends in Europe since the Second World War. *Population Studies,* 22 (March):103-146.

Goode, William J.

1960 Illegitimacy in the Caribbean social structure. *American Sociological Review,* 25 (February):21-30.

1961 Illegitimacy, anomie and cultural penetration. *American Sociological Review,* 26 (December):910-925.

1967 A policy paper for illegitimacy. In Mayer N. Zald (Ed.), *Organizing for Community Welfare.* Chicago: Quadrangle. Pp. 262-312.

Guye, Roberto.

1967 Los paises de America Latina y sus diferentes characteristicos. *Estadistica,* 25 (September-December):461-486.

Hajnal, J.

1965 European marriage patterns in perspective. In D. V. Glass and D. E. C. Eversley (Eds.), *Population in History.* Chicago: Aldine. Pp. 101-146.

Hartley, Shirley M.

1970 Standardization procedures in the analysis of cross-national variations in illegitimacy measures. *Journal of Biosocial Science,* 2 (April):95-109.

Hutchinson, Harry.

1957 *Village and Plantation Life in Northeastern Brazil.* Seattle: American Ethnological Society, University of Washington Press.

Johnson, David R.

1969 Illegitimacy and national integration in Latin America. Mimeographed. Lincoln: Department of Sociology, U. of Nebraska.

Jones, Gavin W., and Dorothy Nortman.

1968 Roman Catholic fertility and family planning: a comparative review of the research literature. *Studies in Family Planning,* October:1-27.

Kiser, Clyde V., Wilson H. Grabill, and Arthur A. Campbell.

1968 *Trends and Variations in Fertility in the United States.* Cambridge, Mass.: Harvard University Press.

Kumar, Joginder.

1969 Demographic analysis of data on illegitimate births. *Social Biology,* 16 (June):92-108.

Kurtz, Seymour (Ed.).

1969 *The New York Times Encyclopedic Almanac, 1970.* New York: New York Times.

Leasure, J. William.

1963 Factors in the decline of fertility in Spain: 1900-1950. *Population Studies,* 16 (March):271-285.

Malinowski, Bronislaw.

1930 Parenthood—the basis of culture. In V. F. Calverton and S. D. Schmalhausen (Eds.), *The New Generation.* New York: Macaulay. Pp. 129-143. Repr. in R. W. Roberts (Ed.), *The Unwed Mother.* New York: Harper and Row, 1966. Pp. 25-41.

Miro, Carmen A.

1964 The population of Latin America. *Demography,* 1 (1):15-41.

Morner, Magnus.

1967 *Race Mixture in the History of Latin America.* Boston: Little, Brown.

Mortara, Giorgio.

1964 *Characteristics of the Demographic Structure of the American Countries.* Washington, D.C.: Pan American Union.

Polgar, Steven.

1971 Culture, history and population dynamics. In S. Polgar (Ed.), *Culture and Population: A Collection of Current Studies.* Cambridge, Mass.: Schenkman. Pp. 3-8.

Reh, Emma.

1946 *Paraguayan Rural Life.* Washington, D.C.: Institute of Inter-American Affairs.

Requena, Mariano B.

1965 Social and economic correlates of induced abortion in Santiago, Chile. *Demography,* 2:33-49.

1968 The problem of induced abortion in Latin America. *Demography,* 5 (2):785-799.

Rodman, Hyman.

1966   Illegitimacy in the Caribbean social structure. *American Sociological Review,* 31 (October):673-683.

Service, Elman R., and Helen S. Service.

1954   *Tobatl: Paraguayan Town.* Chicago: University of Chicago Press.

Shorter, Edward.

1971   Illegitimacy, sexual revolution and social change in modern Europe. *Journal of Interdisciplinary History,* 2 (Autumn):237-272.

Shorter, Edward, John Knodel, and Etienne Van de Walle.

1971   The decline of non-marital fertility in Europe, 1880-1940. *Population Studies,* 25 (November):375-393.

Smith, M. G.

1962   *West Indian Family Structure.* Seattle: University of Washington Press.

Stycos, J. Mayone.

1955   *Family and Fertility in Puerto Rico.* New York: Columbia University Press.

1968   *Human Fertility in Latin America: Sociological Perspectives.* Ithaca, N.Y.: Cornell University Press.

Thistlethwaite, Frank.

1964   Migration from Europe overseas in the nineteenth and twentieth centuries. In H. Moller (Ed.), *Population Movements in Modern European History.* New York: Macmillan. Pp. 73-92.

UNESCO.

1963   *Compendium of Social Statistics: 1963.* New York: United Nations.

1968   *Compendium of Social Statistics: 1967.* New York: United Nations.

Union Panamericana.

1963   *Estudio Economico y Social de America Latina, 1961: Segunda Parte: Aspectos Sociales,* vol. II. Washington, D.C.: Organization of American States.

United Nations.

1949- *Demographic Yearbook.* New York: United Nations.

1958   Recent trends in fertility in industrialized countries. In *Population Studies 27.* New York: United Nations.

1962   Demographic aspects of manpower. Report 1. Sex and age patterns of participation in economic activities. In *Population Studies 33.* New York: United Nations.

1965   *Population Bulletin no. 7-1963, with special reference to conditions and trends in fertility in the world.* New York: United Nations.

Woytinsky, W. S., and E. S. Woytinsky.

1968   World immigration patterns. In Charles B. Nam (Ed.), *Population and Society.* Boston: Houghton Mifflin. Pp. 298-313.

Discussion

Mr. Anderson.   The paper by Johnson and Cutright, like those by Schwirian and Finsterbusch, represents an attempt to generate quantitative analysis in comparative sociology. In doing so, these authors use aggregated data rather than individual data. Second, they take a multivariate approach to analysis. Johnson and Cutright use what we may refer to as a modern form of analysis, path analysis, which is a more recent version of multiple-regression analysis.

The analysis methods are based on correlation matrices, and they are particularly sensitive to the size of the correlation coefficients. That, in a sense, leads to one of the basic problems in using aggregated data rather than individual data. As Duncan indicates in *Statistical Geography* [1961], the size of the correlation coefficient varies with the size of the unit of aggregation.

Duncan's observation raises a central methodological problem which, as far as I can tell, is *not* faced in these papers. If you correlate the same two variables first at the aggregate level of townships, then at the country level, then at the state level, and then at the national level, you increase the size of the correlation coefficient. This change is presumably artificial, rather than substantive, in relation to the concepts that you are talking about, and the impact of this change on regression analyses is very hard to determine, but it should at least be discussed.

This problem may be more bothersome to Johnson and Cutright since they are dealing with a relatively small number of relatively large units. Consider the number of parameters that they are estimating relative to the number of original observations on which they base their analysis.

Mr. Strodtbeck. Can't you handle size differences simply with square root or log transformation so you have your variables roughly at the same magnitude? So long as you don't have greater magnitude than, say, 1 to 10, you can make whatever transformation is necessary in order to make the data equivalent. I don't think size should be an impediment.

Mr. Anderson. No, I don't agree with you. There is an actual transference of variance from "between" units to "within" units as you increase the level of aggregation that isn't just some sort of transformation of the results. You are putting more into the black box, in a sense, and I am presenting this simply to make the point that risks are involved in aggregating data.

Mr. Johnson. The size of the correlation coefficients we report is indeed large. These coefficients are always big in ecological analysis because when you aggregate people together, you cancel out random error due to individual differences. This reduction of random error adds a lot of variance, so naturally you have bigger correlations. That fact doesn't detract at all from the analysis we are doing. We are working at an aggregate level. We are not assuming that, because the Catholic Institutional Strength index correlates .86 with illegitimacy, that fact says anything about correlations of .86 at the individual level. This issue has been pursued since Robinson's [1950] article on the "ecological fallacy." I don't see the relevance of Anderson's point.

Mr. Southwood. There is one feature of the ecological fallacy which should be discussed. As Blalock [1964] points out, when you aggregate cases and get correlations between aggregates, you may be essentially transferring some of your variance inside the black box, as has already been said.

One of the ways in which we can examine what we have once we've done those correlations is to examine the relationship between the mean and the standard deviation of the dependent variable. We don't often do this. We look at a correlation, and we forget that we are explaining the difference between *units* on the dependent variable. We are not explaining the event per se.

Let me give a numerical example. Assume we have a dependent variable measured on a ratio scale—that is, we know where zero is. If the variable has a mean of 10 but the range of all our cases is limited from, say, 8 to 12, clearly nothing we do is going to explain that basic 8 which is common to all the cases. We can have a correlation of 1.00, but we have done nothing to explain that basic score which is common to all cases. On the other hand, if the variable has a range which goes all the way from zero up to 20, and we have a correlation of 1.00 with an independent variable, we have explained virtually everything about the event.

The ecological correlation using aggregated data is analogeous, in a sense, to a partial correlation, because we have now essentially removed the variance of certain independent variables which happen to have more or less equal means in all aggregated cases. But if those variables are in fact acting independently, then they should produce exactly the phenomenon that I mentioned before. In other words, they should restrict the variance in the dependent variable.

So this matter is rather important to consider when we do aggregate-data-correlation analysis; we should, in fact, look at the relationship of the standard deviation with the mean of the dependent variable, assuming that it is a true ratio scale. If there is a very wide range from zero on up, then we have an indication that those independent variables which have averaged out equally across cases are not producing any great effect.

Mr. Schnaiberg.   I think that point is very important. This problem is a general one regardless of what level of analysis you are dealing with, even the individual level. Very subtle changes in degrees of variation do produce artifacts.

Mr. Anderson.   When discussing Schwirian's paper, I noted two situations in which it is appropriate to aggregate data: when internal processes in subunits are subject to control at the aggregate level and when the time constants in the processes *within* the subsystems are much shorter than the time constants in the processes *between* the subsystems. Now with respect to Johnson and Cutright's paper, are either of these conditions met? Do nations in South America control illegitimacy in any national sense, or is the control lodged more in cultural systems which extend across national boundaries? How many subunits in South America are meaningful with reference to control devices affecting illegitimacy?

Johnson and Cutright argue that "national integration," which is a concept similar to national control of something involving a national control network, is in fact not a major explanatory variable in relation to illegitimacy. But that assertion raises a dilemma: If national integration is not an important explanatory variable, then in what respect is the nation an important and appropriate unit of aggregation? Put differently, how do we justify using national data to demonstrate that nations aren't important as a basis for the processes involving illegitimacy? If the control mechanism operating on illegitimacy is the level of fertility itself, then that is a much broader phenomenon, and there are really perhaps one or two cases of it within the domain of the South American or Latin American experience.

All I've done is to state one of the key problems that arises in relation to units of aggregation. I do not mean to imply that I know whether these are meaningful units or not, but I am suggesting that discussion might properly deal with whether or not they are.

Mr. Grimshaw.   Aaron Cicourel [cited in Grimshaw, 1969:20] had some very interesting things to say about the macro-micro question in connection with his research on fertility in Buenos Aires. We asked him, in a meeting a couple of years ago, what differences there would be between the findings he could report on the basis of quite intensive interviewing and reinterviewing of people as contrasted with those of more standard survey studies of fertility that had been done in the Caribbean.

He responded that the kinds of tables would be very similar; both he and other researchers had a set of independent variables for which they hypothesized a relation to various kinds of fertility outcomes. These tables might be useful to social planners by showing points of leverage at which social engineering might have some effect on fertility outcomes. Because of his more intensive work, though, Cicourel felt he knew something about the social behavior which brought people together into a single cell within a table even though the people and behaviors were actually quite different. He felt able to identify sociological dimensions which, in his view, were lost in some of the "microaggregated" studies.

Mr. Johnson.   Let me comment on whether we should aggregate things that don't have some kind of system property to them. It can be argued that if some variable in a model has system consequences—for example, illegitimate fertility has system consequences—then you can aggregate even though you cannot see that there is a contextual effect from location in a given country. In such a case it is very appropriate to aggregate variables.

Even though there are individual-level variables which don't have system-wide implications, we still have to consider them because they affect other factors which *may* have system implications. This situation actually happened in our analysis.

Further, all variables in every analysis aren't going to be of the kind that fit into systems and interrelated subsystems. Why can't one aggregate individuals even though they don't make any kind of system? Why can't they be put together in census tracts? If we do this, we are not in any sense testing individual behavior but rather making an index for a given region—for example, a census tract or the like.

Mr. Anderson.   Before we discuss this issue further, there are a variety of other problems that I would at least like to mention.

The first is a language or semantic problem. I think it is very unfortunate that path analysis has picked up a causal nomenclature. Path analysis is just another way of analyzing correlation. Its basic function is to provide a way of rationalizing the difference between zero-order correlations and nth-order correlations; it shows a path by which the differences between those correlations can be explained or accounted for. But the researcher is still dealing with correlations. If it is inappropriate to make causal inferences of correlations, it is equally inappropriate to make causal inferences of paths. I prefer to think of path analysis exclusive of any concept of cause.

Mr. Cutright.   I am sensitive to the misuse of path analysis, but I am not clear about your criticism. Are you saying that our models placed variables in an inappropriate order to each other? Are you talking about our specific models or are you talking about path analysis in general?

Mr. Johnson.   I am concerned about Anderson's statement that path analysis somehow needs to be separated from causal analysis. What I understand as path analysis *is* causal analysis—period. You can use correlation analysis and multiple R's and not have causal implications, but path analysis is a causal method. Look back at Duncan [1966] and the others who introduced path analysis to the discipline, or go back to the people who developed it; causality is what they specified.

I agree that the causal assumptions we made in our paper are very tenuous, and we are unfortunately relating things kind of arbitrarily. We did so because we are dealing with one point in time and no clear time sequence. But when you have independent variables and a dependent variable and you make a path model, you have causality. To deny causality and say, "Let's do path analysis," is impossible.

Mr. Anderson.   Let me raise a final problem concerning the arbitrary assumption of linearity in regressions. One unfortunate aspect of many discussions using multivariate systems is an automatic use of linear models without any attempt to justify the linearity of the relationships. The relationships may well be linear, but they may also be quite nonlinear. Anyone using linear systems, it seems to me, is under some obligation at least to be aware of this situation and to disclose the nature of the relationships.

This need is exceptionally great when a correlation matrix is being subjected to very complex forms of internal analysis, for example, path analysis or factor analysis; correlations *can* be affected to some extent by curvilinearity, and operations like partial correlation are even more affected. A little curvilinearity in a relationship can generate a big difference in the partial of one variable's relationship to another. In factor analysis, the effects with many variables may tend to cancel out and produce approximately the same factor structure you would have gotten had the relationship been linear. So far as I know, though, no evidence exists that this is the case in path analysis. In fact, I don't think this question has been extensively explored in relation to path analysis.

Mr. Schwirian.   I wonder about the assumption of the linear regression model that underlies most factor- and path-analytic models. I know you have worked a lot on this problem, but I wonder if there isn't an easier way out. In assuming linearity, might we not assume the results we obtained—let's say, in terms of multiple-correlation models such as path analysis? Might the results not be considered a conservative estimate of the independent variables' effect on the dependent variables? That is the only justification for the assumption that I can think of.

Mr. Johnson.   We have checked our results for linearity. We looked for errors in prediction to determine whether or not relationships were linear. What I normally do, and what everyone should do, to check for linearity is to run scattergrams. There are computer programs that will scatter all the variables against each other. The scattergrams immediately show curvilinear and other kinds of relationships.

Dealing more specifically with the paper, now, there have been very few comments on the validity of what we were trying to do. Our purpose is not to show that national variables don't in some way affect illegitimacy. Our concern, when examining Goode's research, is to demonstrate that the national integration measure he chose is a bad measure; not only is it bad, but it doesn't really add anything to our prediction of illegitimacy. Our concern is similar to that shown by Armer and Schnaiberg's work on individual modernity.

Mr. Anderson.   Your analysis clarifies matters. If, in fact, it is appropriate to analyze data at a national level in the way that you have, which is another question, the I certainly find your arguments sound. I think you have a good paper.

Mr. Southwood.   I would like to comment on the matter of curvilinearity, which you mentioned earlier. You didn't distinguish between two different types of curvilinearity—monotonic and nonmonotonic curvilinearity. For the most part, the theories that we have don't distinguish between linear relationships and monotonic curvilinearity. Since this is the case, then it may very well be that a monotonic curve—one that indicates a jump in B at some level of A—would be just as good at fitting a theory as a straight line. The pattern may be an artifact of our scales; we can't be sure that our scales are linearly related to whatever it is that we want to indicate. Our measures may show monotonic curvilinearity between linearly related theoretical concepts. Essentially, we don't have any distinct criteria for deciding whether a straight line or a monotonic curve is theoretically more parsimonious.

When we come to nonmonotonic curves, however, we are in a different ball game. We can no longer attribute a nonmonotonic relationship to some kind of monotonic curvilinear relationship between an indicator and the concept that we are trying to measure. I don't think we should accept a nonmonotonic curve without being quite sure that it is theoretically justified in some way. In other words, if a nonmonotonic curve does not explain significantly more than a monotonic curve, then we should not be prepared to change our theory to fit the nonmonotonic.

Mr. Anderson.   I am not too impressed with the process by which we reach decisions *after* we look at our data. It seems to me that the more we can get away from arbitrariness in the decision-making process—the more decisions we can put ahead of our data analysis—the better. So, for example, it isn't really so much of an issue to me whether a relationship is linear or not as whether it accounts for more or less variance.

If we want to organize our quantitative work more theoretically, I would suggest that we do the same thing the physicists used to do and conduct so-called conceptual experiments—take the regression that we think is the proper regression and extrapolate it. If in extrapolation we get an absurdity, then we do not have the correct regression. As a very simple example, if we cannot have, under any conditions, fewer than *no* people somewhere, then let's not use a regression that, when we extrapolate, gives us minus 100 people somewhere.

Mr. Chaplin.   I'd like to see Johnson and Cutright include data on prostitution. In a number of countries it is legal, and the women are registered. The data are not published in the UN *Demographic Yearbook* but are available if you have the right approach to local police departments, because the women have to get a health license. So the data are available, and they would fit into the model rather well.

I am disturbed by the vital-statistics information because it is much worse than the census data in general. Those who have dealt with it know of its qualitative irregularity over time with, of course, a general tendency to improve.

Another point that anthropologists would argue is that rural and urban illegitimacy mean very different things, particularly in Indian countries with no institutionalized arrangement for trial marriage. It is often expected that a woman has to be pregnant before she can get married. Although the extent to which this practice still exists in a legitimate cultural sense is open to debate, it is expected to differ between urban and rural areas. Also the availability of a priest to perform the ceremony may be less in rural areas. These are points which I think are relevant to the kind of comparative research conducted by Johnson and Cutright.

References

Blalock, H.M., Jr.

1964 *Causal Inferences in Nonexperimental Research.* Chapel Hill: University of North Carolina Press.

Duncan, O.D.

1961 *Statistical Geography.* Glencoe, Ill.: Free Press.

1966 Path analysis: sociological examples. *American Journal of Sociology,* 72 (July):1-16.

Grimshaw, Allen D.

1969 Language as obstacle and as data in sociological research. *Social Science Research Council,* 23 (June):17-21.

Robinson, W.S.

1950 Ecological correlations and the behavior of individuals. *American Sociological Review,* 15 (June):351-357.

United Nations.

1949- *Demographic Yearbook.* New York: United Nations.

CHAPTER FOURTEEN

The Sociology of Nation-States: Dimensions, Indicators, and Theory

KURT FINSTERBUSCH

University of Maryland

This paper is an effort to bring into focus the study of nation-states. Comparative macrosociology tends to examine either primitive societies, in total or by institutions, or the major institutions of nation-states such as the military, the polity, the economy, the educational system, and science. The study of nation-states as wholes, still a near monopoly of the historians, is relatively undeveloped as a sociological discipline. This paper suggests some key variables for the sociology of nations, discusses their measurement, constructs a causal theory that postulates their interrelationships, considers the validity of the theory, and finally reduces that theory to more manageable proportions. This effort has not been completely successful but is nevertheless instructive.

The list of possible variables to consider in the development of nation-states is almost endless; for example, the Dimensions of Nations Project (see Sawyer, 1967; and Rummel, 1972) selected 236 social, political, economic and other variables for study. The conceptual scheme proposed here includes only 48 variables (see Tables 14.1-3), which the reader will want to amend and expand according to his own interests and judgements.[1] Even the 48 variables included in the initial conceptual scheme are too many to handle conveniently at one time in theory construction, so we use instead a subset of 23 variables in the the causal theory of nation-states.[2]

A Conceptual Scheme for the Sociology of Nation-States

A nation is here conceived as a social system with inputs and outputs, structual characteristics, and activities occurring betweeen two points in time. To a large

417

extent inputs and outputs are the same basic items, changed only in quantity or quality by activities between time 1 and time 2; the output at time 2 often becomes the input for the next period. However, some output is traded to other nations in exchange for their output, and some is used to influence the behavior of other nations. These exchanges and interactions are the subject of another subfield of macrosociology: international relations. This paper holds the international situation (the net inputs from other nations) constant, for the most part, and focuses on relations among variables within nations.

Inputs and Outputs

The conceptual scheme includes two categories of inputs and outputs: assets and external conditions (see Table 14.1). Assets are outputs that have become inputs and are utilized by the nation-state to produce more outputs. External conditions are the natural environment or international situations that affect and are affected by the nation-state. Five assets are of prime importance as inputs: population (a natural asset), knowledge-skills and capital (produced assets), and organization and legitimacy (social assets). Natural resources and wealth have less important effects on the structure and functioning of nations. As outputs all assets are important, but knowledge-skills and wealth are emphasized in the literature. *Population, **natural resources, capital,*** and *wealth* have standardized meanings but knowledge-skills, organization, and legitimacy require clarification.

Table 14.1   Conceptual Scheme for the Study of Nation-States: Inputs into Nations as Social Systems at Time 1 and Outputs at Time 2

I. Quantity and quality of assets[a]
   A. Natural assets
      1. Population: number and characteristics[b]
      2. Natural resources: amount and value
   B. Produced assets
      1. Knowledge and skills: amount and level of science and technology[b]
      2. Capital: amount and productivity of productive goods[b]
      3. Wealth: value and durability of consumer goods[b]
   C. Social assets
      1. Societal organizations: the amount and effectiveness of organization in society[b]
      2. System legitimacy: extent and intensity of[b]
II. Degree of favorableness-unfavorableness of external conditions
   A. Of the natural environment
   B. Of the international environment: international danger[b]

[a]The aggregation of all of these assets equals the power of the society.
[b]Variables used in subsequent theoretical analysis

Knowledge and skills in this system of concepts does not include esoteric knowledge but refers to data (i.e., facts about events), understanding (i.e., reliable inferences from data), and learned skills. At the level of nation-states, knowledge-skills is approximately equal to the amount of science and technology.

Organization denotes an important but elusive societal input. Organizations are created to accomplish tasks more effectively. People working in an organization can do more than the same people acting singly. We note, therefore, that the amount of societal achievement or production is related to the amount and effectiveness of societal organization. The state itself is a large organization of which all citizens are members with duties (e.g., taxpaying and military service) and rights (e.g., voting and using governmental services). The basic instrumentality for coordinating actions in the state is the legal system. Nations vary in the degree to which the state is organized and even more in the amount and effectiveness of their various organizations.

To determine the amount of societal organization, one must consider the number of organizations within the society, the size of those organizations, and the extent of interorganizational coordination. The effectiveness of societal organization is what Weber called organizational rationality, which he equated with the degree of bureaucratization. Udy (1959:791-795), however, has shown that bureaucracy should not be equated with rationality, so other indicators of rationality are required.

Legitimacy, the third societal asset requiring clarification, is essential to a nation's effective functioning. Legitimacy refers to a population's degree of acceptance of the way in which society is organized.[3] Subdimensions of societal legitimacy are many, but the political and economic are the most important. The legitimacy of a political system is tarnished if its legal system is viewed as an instrument of oppression rather than of justice; if the decision-making system is seen as completely insensitive to the "will of the people"; and if the society's administration is felt to be incapable of achieving societal goals (especially security and prosperity). The legitimacy of an economic system rests upon (1) the effectiveness of its mechanisms for articulating production and consumption and for allocating labor; (2) the acceptance of its distribution of rewards and control over productive resources; and (3) the society's respect for its economic provisions for the maintenance of nonworkers. The legitimacy of the educational, religious, and family institutions seems to be of secondary importance for the analysis of the functioning of nation-states.

Structural Characteristics

The concepts utilized most heavily in this causal theory refer to the nation-state's structural characteristics. The following structural characteristics (see Table 14.2) are briefly discussed below: differentiation, integration of

Table 14.2   Conceptual Scheme for the Study of Nation-States: Structural
Characteristics of Societies

I.   Differentiation: division of labor and specialization of function[a]
II.   Integration of subgroups (the mixing of subgroups, not necessarily their elimination)[a]
    A. Casteness: height of ascribed group boundaries
    B. Classness (classes can be social strata or groups defined by market conditions)
       1. Amount of class organization and degree of class consciousness
       2. Extent of mutual opposition
III. Competition: the distribution of jurisdictions. Is access to a market or public the right of one, a few, or many organizations, groups, or persons?[a]
IV.   Scale of coordination
    A. Concentration (inverse of the number of organizations performing a function per million population)[a]
    B. Centralization (the level at which activities are coordinated and directed: local, state, or national)[a]
V.   Democracy: dispersion of policy decision-making
    A. Participation (the ratio of people participating in policy decisions to those who do not)[a]
    B. Pluralism (the number of groups and organizations that participate in policy decisions)[a]
VI.   Stratification: degree of inequality of the following:
    A. Income[a]
    B. Capital[a]
    C. Opportunity (mobility)[a]
    D. Justice[a]
    E. Prestige
VII. Ecology: the location of people and activities
    A. Urbanization[a]
    B. Density
    C. Commutation: work-living separation (mean daily commute)
    D. Network density (density of transportation and communication linkages)
    E. Regional inequality of people, activity, and development

---

[a]Variables used in subsequent theoretical analysis.

subgroups, concentration, centralization, democracy (participation, pluralism), competition, and stratification variables (inequality of income, capital, opportunity, prestige, and justice).[4] Some ecological variables are listed but, except for urbanization, are not used in the theory. *Differentiation* has been interpreted by Spencer (1893), Durkheim (1949), and, more recently, Smelser (1963), Eisenstadt (1964), and Parsons (1970) as the major sociological factor in the process of modernization. Related to increasing differentiation are the problems of coordination and social integration. The solution to the coordination problem in all existing nations has been to increase centralization and concentration so that more and more activity is coordinated and directed at the national level, by fewer and larger organizations.[5]

Increasing differentiation and the rise of capitalism in the West produced new, nonascriptive social groups and classes organized in varying degrees to pursue their interests in opposition to other groups. Meanwhile, the boundaries between ascriptive groups lessened. Except in utopian societies, subgroups have different interests and are in competition, if not overt conflict. The extent of subgroup formation, insulation, identification, organization, and opposition, however, varies considerably among societies. These structural components of society are classified under the term "the integration of subgroups."[6] Integration commonly has many other meanings including coordination, goal consensus, and the regulation of conflict, meanings that (except for goal consensus) are included elsewhere in the conceptual scheme. The meaning of the term "integration" in this theory is restricted to a single dimension, however, in order to make it more useful for theory construction.

Concomitant with differentiation and centralization in the development of the Western world was the evolution of democracy and the increase in equality. Democracy is often discussed in dichotomous terms (i.e., a government either is or is not a democracy) but should be treated in more variable terms (i.e., nations vary in their degree of democracy when policy decisons are made). The major dimension underlying the democracy category is the dispersion of policy decision-making (i.e., decisions that directly determine the distribution of rewards in a population). Here, following the recent tradition in political science literature, *participation* and *pluralism* are seen as two factors that disperse policy decision-making. The most common mechanism for such dispersion is voting, the major form of *participation* in decision-making by the average citizen in nations today. Voting can be for representatives and officials (as in elections) or for policies (as in referenda). The former is usually considered a minimum characteristic for classifying a country as a democracy, and few nations extensively use the latter. Most nations, therefore, are technically democracies, but none are *very* democratic. In part, this situation exists because people do not want to spend too much time and energy participating.

Pluralism, too, disperses policy decision-making. Pluralism, which refers to the number of groups and organizations participating in policy decisions, includes the dispersion of authority and the tendency for people to form groups and organizations for political action. The United States is noted for its dispersion of authority among three branches of government; among many agencies, departments, committees, positions, and persons in each branch; and among four or more levels of territorial government units. As a result, many government organizations and persons participate in the making and execution of most policy decisions. Furthermore, the dispersion of authority provides numerous points at which outside interest groups can and do exert pressure. The other aspect of pluralism is the propensity of citizens to organize to advance their political interests. Again the United States is noted for its citizens' involvement in such activity.

Competition is usually thought of as a process, but the degree of competition in society should rather be seen as a key structural characteristic of nations. Societies have mechanisms for determining the level of competition. They avoid chaos by regulating the means used to achieve ends: force and fraud are outlawed. Societies also specify jurisdictions to prevent chaos and inefficient competition and thus establish situations in which competition is appropriate or inappropriate. For example, most governmental functions are performed on a monopoly basis (e.g., those performed by the postal service and the courts). Other governmental functions are performed by near monopolies (e.g., public schools are district schools and do not compete with each other, although they do compete with private and religious schools; police departments at times compete with the FBI and private detectives in apprehending criminals and with private security guards in providing protection; on the whole, though, they have a near monopoly on policing). In the political sphere there is considerable competition between agencies with overlapping or imprecise jurisdictions and between parties and caucuses for constituencies and support.

Competition is most plentiful in the economy. Unlike mercantilistic economies, modern economies impose only modest legal limits (franchising) on the right to provide goods and services (more stringent limits are placed on the services provided by the utility, transportation, and communication industries). The degree of competition within nations, however, is not entirely a matter of law. The production of some goods and services is subject to substantial economies of scale when highly capitalized such that concentration acts to reduce competition substantially. A thorough analysis of competition would examine its prevalence not only in the polity and the economy but also in education, science, the communication of news, entertainment, health services, religion, and so on.

Stratification, a critical sociological variable, is usually thought of as hierarchy. It is here understood as the degree of inequality and thus the obverse of equality. This conceptual scheme uses five dimensions of inequality: income, capital, opportunity, prestige and justice. Inequality of income, opportunity (mobility), and prestige have traditional meanings but we need to comment on inequality of capital and of justice.

Inequality of capital (i.e., degree of concentration of the control over the means of production) is the crucial variable in Marx's sociology of nations and for this reason alone merits attention. It is a difficult variable to measure, however. One cannot be sure that the inequality of capital has declined in the United States in the past 150 years as individual ownership of small firms has been replaced by dispersed stock-ownership of large firms. There are few powerful stockholders, and one could argue for the growing inequality of capital. Yet another argument is that the managers control capital and do so for organizational more than for stockholders' interests (see especially Galbraith,

1967). Furthermore, "control" is increasingly being shared with the unions, governments, and action groups in a community. Although the small-scale capitalist was never permitted complete control over his capital, the capitalists' control over companies has become less and less exclusive. How do we add all these trends together to get a reading of changes in the inequality of capital?

Justice refers to the equality of rights and privileges before the law. Are all groups and classes of persons treated equally? What is the extent of discrimination against, and infringement of, the rights of various groups? We admit that this use of justice substitutes a part for the whole. Justice is the conjunction of at least five dimensions: equality of rights and privileges, merited unequal treatment, proof of guilt before sanctioning, penalties appropriate to the offenses, and honest enforcement. It may seem that the first two characteristics of justice are in contradiction—that is, equality and merited inequality. The latter refers to those situations in which equal treatment is inappropriate because all people are not, in fact, equal. On some rights and privileges children and adults, sane and insane, sick and well, intoxicated and sober, men and women are and should be treated unequally. These cases provoke surprisingly few complaints of injustice even from those who receive the less-than-equal treatment, because they accept the rationale for the inequality. For the sake of parsimony, this theory assumes that the societies in which people are treated equally also possess the other four characteristics of justice.

The distribution of rights in society is an important structural characteristic of a nation and is crucial to understanding a nation's development. If possible, this concept should be enlarged to cover the degree of justice prevailing in the judicial aspects of organizations.

Activities and Processes

The last variables in this scheme are the major activities occurring between times 1 and 2 (see Table 14.3). Foremost are the production and reproduction of societal assets—those activities that increase population, resources, knowledge-skills, capital, wealth, organization, and legitimacy. Next are the facilitating activities—communication, transportation, arranging-regulating-governing, commerce, and migration. Finally, transforming activities change aspects of the system, while stabilizing ones preserve other aspects. Assuming that the roles of production and facilitating activities are relatively self-evident, we will comment only on transforming and stabilizing activities.

Reforming and creating activities are transforming activities that are integral to modern nations and essential to their successful adaptation. Polity reform or change usually increases the political system's fit with the constantly changing distribution of power among groups. Businesses change to improve their market position, and all public and private organizations change to improve their situation, adapt to changing conditions, or improve their output. Some

Table 14.3   Conceptual Scheme for the Study of Nation-States: Societal
Activities and Processes

I.   Production activities (producing or reproducing the seven assets)
      A. Biological reproduction
      B. Agriculture, mining, and refining
      C. Research and training
      D. Investment
      E. Manufacturing and construction
      F. Organizational rationalization
      G. Legalization and legitimation
II.   Facilitating activities (facilitate the other activities)
      A. Communication[a]
         1. Public
         2. Private
      B. Transportation
         1. Of people
         2. Of goods
      C. Arranging, regulating, governing
      D. Commerce
      E. Migration (the movement of persons to locations of greater private utility
         and usually greater public utility)
III. Transforming activities
      A. Reforming and creating (the development of new products, organizations
         and institutions)[a]
      B. Disturbances[a]
         1. Disruptions (riots, protests, strikes, etc.)
         2. Rebellion
IV.   Stabilizing activities
      A. Socialization (a component of education)
      B. Coercion by the official coercive forces[a]
      C. Institutionalization

---

[a]Variables used in subsequent theoretical analysis.

organizations approach the cybernetic model, and others grow like Topsy, but reforming and creating are endemic in almost all organizations. Some efforts to change organizations, situations, institutions, and the polity, however, are not legitimate from the viewpoint of those in authority. Disruptions and rebellion are organized efforts to alter the system by illegal or extraordinary means favoring the interests or values of groups that consider themselves deprived of their due. Such disturbances usually indicate the need for some adaptive changes.

Nations transform themselves to achieve goals more fully, but they also act to preserve and maintain their systems through socialization, coercion, and institutionalization. In nations, persons are socialized into both their roles and the basic value system, which legitimates the social system. Disturbances and law violators are suppressed by means of coercion. New patterns are legitimized and institutionalized. Parents with their children, the educational system, the police and courts, and legislatures are largely devoted to stabilizing activities, but all organizations engage in them to some extent.

To summarize, three sets of variables (input-output, structural, and process) have been proposed for this conceptual scheme. While many of the most important variables for understanding the working of nations have been included, a major omission may prove to be a set of value or cultural variables. These have been excluded on the judgment that the sociology of nations should proceed as far as possible through analyzing input-output, structural, and process variables and have recourse to the value characteristics of nations only as a last resort.

A Theory of Nation-States

Formulation A (see Table 14.4) of a causal theory of nation-states postulates the interrelationships among the 23 footnoted variables of Tables 14.1-3. Of 506 possible direct causal relationships, the theory postulates (using a very minimal level of significance) that 219 exist and 287 do not. Confining this theory to the interrelationships among the 23 designated variables neglects some influences on some of the dependent variables. The purpose, however, was to spell out how this system of 23 variables operated when other variables were held constant. One technique for theory development, which is utilized later in this paper, is to relax this condition and incorporate the effects of additional variables into the model.

The postulates are not presented in propositional form in Table 14.4; the purpose there is simply to list all the independent variables (within the system of 23 variables) that directly affected a dependent variable in the system. As a start only, we assume that the independent variables are related to the dependent variable in the manner implied when one uses multiple-regression equations—additively and linearly. Table 14.4, therefore, provides the ingredients for 22 simultaneous multiple-regression equations hypothesized in the theory. For example, the row for capital in Table 14.4 can be translated into the following equation:

$$Ca = a + b_1(Po) + b_2(Co) + b_3(O) + b_4(CR) + b_5(D) + b_6(Cp) + b_7(Ce) + b_8(K) - b_9(Di) + e_{Ca}$$

(time lags, for the moment, being ignored).

The theory consists of the proposed conceptual scheme, the 219 proposed direct causal relationships (axioms), innumerable derived propositions (the indirect relationships), the assumptions of additivity and linearity (only as a start), and the scientists' talisman, "assuming that all other things are equal."

Table 14.4   A Causal Theory of Nation-States (Based on 23 Variables):
Formulation A

| Symbol | Effects: Dependent Variable | Causes: Independent Variables (ordered by importance) | |
		Positively Related	Negatively Related
Po	Population	W	U (K both helps [medicine] and hinders [contraception] Po)
K	Knowledge-skills	Po, D, O, Cm, CR, W, Pa, Cp, Ca (for research)	C, Di
Ca	Capital	Po, Co, O, CR, D, Cp, Ce, K	Di
W	Wealth	Ca, Po, O, D, Co, K, CR, Ce	Di (Po decreases per capita wealth)
O	Organization	D, Po, Co, Cp, Da, K, Ce, CR, Ca	
L	Legitimacy	Pa, J, I, W, Pl, E, CR, EO, EC, O	C
Da	International danger[a]	—	—
D	Differentiation	K, CR, Co, Po, Ca, Ce, O, W, U, Cp	
I	Integration	L, Da, E, EC, EO, J, Cm, Pa	Po, D, Di, U
Cp	Competition	Pl, U, EC, CR, Po, Cm	Da, Ca, Co, O, Ce
Co	Concentration	D, Ca, Ce, Cp, O, Po, U, K	
Ce	Centralization	Da, Co, D, U, O, K, Ca	Cp
Pa	Participation	E, J, Cm, Pl, K, W, D, EC, Cp, O	Po, Da, Ce, Co
Pl	Pluralism	D, Pa, Cp, E, Cm, W, K, Po, J, O	Da, Co, Ce
E	Equality of income	EC, Pa, CR, J, Pl, D	C
EC	Equality of Capital	Pa, Pl, Di, E	Ca, C, Co, Ce
EO	Equality of Opportunity	D, I, Ca, E, J, K, O, Pa, Cp, Cr	
J	Justice	EC, E, I, Pa, Pl, CR, Ce, Cm. O, K, EO	C
U	Urbanization	Po, Co, Ca, D, CR, Ce, O	
Cm	Communication	D, K, U, I, Pa, Po, E, O, Pl	Di, C
CR	Creation-reform	K, D, Pa, Cm, Po, Pl, Cp, E, O, EO	C
Di	Disturbances	Cp, U, Po	J, L, C, I, CR, Pa, Pl, EC, E, EO, O, W
C	Coercion	Da, Di	Pl, J, Pa, CR, Cm, L, I, O, E

[a]International Danger (Da) is caused mainly by variables outside the above system of variables and is not studied here as a dependent variable.

Thus far the indirect relationships have not been described; however, these can be deduced rather mechanically from the 219 direct causal relationships of Table 14.4 and need not be elaborated here. One example will suffice. We postulate that an increase in capital causes an increase in long-run wealth; an increase in wealth causes an increase in legitimacy; and an increase in legitimacy causes a decrease in disturbances. Therefore, an increase in capital, indirectly through the wealth it produces, causes an increase in legitimacy and a decrease in disturbances.

Having presented the direct causal relations postulated by the theory, and, by implication, the indirect causal relations as well as the assumptions underlying the theory, the next steps are to select indicators for these 23 variables and measure them for nations over time, hypothesize the appropriate time lags for the causative influences, correlate the variables pair by pair and in multiple-regression equations, and test for curvilinearity and nonadditivity. From the results of these steps the theory should be revised and reformulated into sets of more-accurate equations which constitute a mathematical model of change in these selected characteristics of nation-states. This last step requires (1) the unlikely assumption that error terms are uncorrelated and (2) the ability to determine the relative strength of reciprocal causes. In this theory, however, there is too much reciprocal influence and interaction among the variables to determine the relative strengths of reciprocal causes even if time-lag techniques are used.

Because of the probability of correlated error terms and the difficulties posed by reciprocal causality, the set of simultaneous equations cannot be solved nor will individual correlations and individual multiple-regression equations be interpretable. It is possible, however, to experiment with various sets of assumptions for the whole model or for parts of the model. Then by comparing predicted with actual results, one can differentiate between good and bad assumptions. Thus, through trial and error, limited model-testing is possible.

Since we have not yet collected data for this theory, we cannot test, revise, and develop it in the above manner. After discussing the problem of indicators, though, the theory is tested in a limited way by comparison with the findings of some prior empirical studies. The theory passes this limited test, so no revision results from this operation. Two further steps do produce some revision, however: (1) additional hypotheses from the literature are incorporated into the theory, and (2) variables are combined into factors in an effort to arrive at a set of solvable equations.

Indicators for Variables in the Theory of Nation-States

The measurement of concepts presents a problem almost as severe as the insolubility of the equations. Space does not allow detailed examination of the measurement problem here. Briefly, a major problem is the fact that most indicators for which quantitative data are available for a fair number of nations measure only one of several aspects of the concept being indicated. In addition, the scores for an indicator are not exactly comparable from nation to nation and from one time period to another. With these problems in mind, we suggest a list of tentative indicators for each of the 23 variables (see Table 14.5). Certainly this list is unsatisfactory in many ways. Some of the indicators have quite tenuous connections to their respective concepts. The indicators for wealth and organization, for example, do not literally measure these concepts. Nations do not measure wealth; thus, the portion of national income used to obtain durable goods has been chosen as a substitute indicator. If depreciation could be subtracted from the consumption of durable goods, then that indicator would measure the annual increment to wealth. Such a measure is as close as we can come, for many countries, to measuring the actual level of accumulated wealth. The extent of a society's organization is even more difficult to measure. Since all employees work in organizations, however, the total number of employees has been chosen as a crude indicator of organization until better indicators are available.

Some indicators, like those for centralization and competition, measure the variable in only one institutional area of society when other institutional areas are also important. Still other indicators capture only a small part of the concepts that they are supposed to measure. They need to be improved by adding measures for uncovered components. Such is the case especially for the indicators of organization, pluralism, equality of opportunity, justice, and communication. The proposed measure for organization overlooks effectiveness; the measure for pluralism, the degree to which authority is fragmented; the measure for equality of opportunity, mobility into the elite; the measure for justice, just enforcement of the laws; and the measure for communication, private communication. Still other indicators are embarrassingly crude (e.g., the indicators for differentiation, integration, and creation-reform). Finally, many indicators should, but do not, include weights in their construction because of the difficulty in determining legitimate weights.

The above indicators have many faults; one virtue, however, is that most are available for the United States and several other countries. Statistics are available for 12 of the 23 indicators from the *Statistical Abstract of the United States;* more specialized publications provide U.S. statistics for six additional indicators as well as the primary data from which the indicators for justice and integration can be constructed. The indicators for legitimacy, pluralism, and international danger require the generation of data, evaluations by national surveys, or the scorings of expert judges.

Socioeconomic Development and Our Theory of Nation-States

This theory needs testing and development. Although we cannot solve the 22 simultaneous equations, we can at least determine whether the hypothesized relationships are supported by empirical correlations. However, the hypothesized relationships assume that "all other things are equal," and such is not the case with nation-states. Analytically, one can approach this assumption through the use of statistical controls, but no study to date has collected enough data on enough indices at enough time points and for enough countries to allow the statistical control of these "other" variables. We are, therefore, forced to interpret correlations under less than optimal conditions.

The dominant trend in nation-states today is socioeconomic development. Figure 14.1 (below) shows that the theory is dominated by this factor, which includes the following nine intercorrelated variables: knowledge-skills, capital, wealth, organization, differentiation, equality of opportunity, urbanization, communication, and creation and reform.[7] The interrelationships and mutual causation among these variables focus much of the classical literature in sociology and inform nearly every discussion of modernization. This theory assumes that these intercorrelations are established and proceeds by briefly reviewing the literature on the correlations of socioeconomic development with all other variables in the scheme. This program tests only parts of the theory, but this test has been made vis-à-vis the dominant trend in nation-states today.

First, we examine the effect of the socioeconomic factor on the following eight structural characteristics: concentration, centralization, participation, pluralism, equality of income, equality of capital, justice, and competition. The conclusion is that much empirical evidence supports, and little contradicts, the conclusion that the socioeconomic factor is related to increasing participation, pluralism, centralization, concentration, equality of income, and justice.

The political-sociology literature relates socioeconomic development to participation and pluralism both theoretically and empirically (Lipset, 1959; Kornhauser, 1959; Cutright, 1963; Fitzgibbon, 1967). Spencer (1893) hypothesized the relationship of socioeconomic development with centralization, and Marx and Engels (1932), the same factor with concentration; in general, the historical record supports these observations. Kuznets's (1963) cross-national and historical data suggest that socioeconomic development is modestly related to increasing equality of income (Kuznets's series are correlated with indices of socioeconomic development in Russett et al., 1964), and Tocqueville (1945), on the basis of personal observations principally in France and the United States, associated these developments with increasing equality of privileges (i.e., justice).

The cross-sectional studies of nation states add further evidence of the association of participation, pluralism, concentration, centralization, and

Table 14.5   Tentative Indicators for Variables in the Theory of Nation-States

Concept	Indicator
Concepts with relatively good indicators	
Population	De facto population
Capital	Amount of capital
Equality of income	Inverse of the Gini index of income inequality
Urbanization	Percent urban (100,000 inhabitants)
Concepts with passable indicators (most do not cover all aspects of the concept)	
Knowledge-skills	Number of scientists and engineers
Concentration	Average size of productive organizations[a]
Centralization	Central government employees or labor force
Pluralism	Mean number of voluntary association memberships per adult[b]
Competition	Percent of economy involving products for which the principal producer supplies less than 20%
Communication	Index combining newspapers, TV, and radios
Disturbances	Gurr's index of civil strife[c]
Coercion	Index combining prisoners/population, degree of freedom of the press, and size of security forces/population
Concepts with inferior indicators	
Wealth	The value of all possessions is the appropriate indicator; we settle, instead, for national income minus capital formation; taxes; and consumption of services, fuel, and food
Differentiation	Degree of the division of labor among industries[d]
Integration	Index combining ascriptive homogeneity (measured by an index of religious, racial, and linguistic homogeneity) and class consciousness (measured by percent of vote cast for class-specific political parties)
Participation	Cutright's index of political development[e]

equality of income with the socioeconomic-development factor. Studies that present evidence for the association of socioeconomic development with participation and/or pluralism are Adelman and Morris (1965, 1967), Abrahamson (1969), Olsen (1968), Gregg and Banks (1965:602-614), Feierabend and Feierabend (1971), and Flanigan and Fogelman (1971a, 1971b). The large data-bank studies of Banks and Textor (1963), Russett and associates (1964), and Sawyer (1967) present correlations relating participation, pluralism,

Table 14.5 Continued

Concept	Indicator
Equality of opportunity	Rates of intergenerational mobility from blue-collar to white-collar
Justice	Number of laws discriminating against ethnic, racial, religious, and sex groups minus laws against discrimination
Creation-reform	Index combining patents and pieces of new legislation
Concept with acceptable indicators currently unavailable and with unsatisfactory substitutes	
Organization	Adequate Indicator: Employees times average size of employment organizations (substitute: total number of employees)
Legitimacy	Adequate indicator: national surveys (substitute: percent voting for parties advocating changing the organization of society)
International danger	Adequate indicator: military force of hostile nations weighted by degree of hostility (substitute: number of men in armed forces of nations judged hostile by experts)
Equality of capital	Adequate indicator: inverse of the Gini index of inequality of stockholdings and of agricultural landholding (substitute: inequality of landholding)[f]

[a] Gibbs and Browning (1966), p. 87.
[b] An alternative measure is found in Almond and Verba (1963). They estimated the percent of citizens in voluntary associations by surveying a national sample.
[c] See Gurr (1968).
[d] See Gibbs and Browning (1966), p. 87.
[e] See Cutright (1963).
[f] See Russett (1964), pp. 442-454, and Russett et al. (1964).

centralization, and equality with socioeconomic development. In the Russett and Sawyer data banks, development is modestly related to two variables that remotely indicate an aspect of justice—treatment of women versus treatment of men (female wage and salary earners/total wage and salary earners, and female primary and secondary school students/total primary and secondary students). The three data-bank studies have no measures of concentration, but Gibbs and Browning (1966) correlate concentration with the socioeconomic development factor.

If we agree that the above covariances between socioeconomic development and other variables are found in the historical and cross-sectional records, then we can have relatively definite expectations about the general direction of change for 15 of the 23 variables in the theory (at least until possible limits are approached). Of the remaining 8 variables, only population growth is clearly correlated with socioeconomic development, and this correlation is not predicted by the theory for the following reason: Population increase has been associated with socioeconomic development for centuries, because of increased food production and better health. Population is expected to increase for another generation, but many nations are seriously endeavoring to have both continuing socioeconomic development and population stability by the end of the century. For most nations population stability requires lowering the birthrate, and this task will require value changes by the populations involved.

The failure to find socioeconomic development correlated with four variables should be expected. International danger[8] is responsive to factors outside the system; and equality of capital, competition, and integration are both pushed and pulled by development variables and their correlates. Capital produces more capital; hence, the inequality of capital tends to develop still greater inequality unless people and groups act to countermand the trend. But countervailing acts do occur, spurred on by increasing participation, pluralism, and equality. Competition is reduced by concentration and centralization, while pluralism, equality, and differentiation keep it alive. Development increases classness at the same time that it reduces casteness, so the relation of development to integration is ambiguous.

According to the theory, development should be correlated positively with legitimacy and negatively with disturbances and coercion. Several quantitative, cross-sectional studies show that development has a modest negative correlation with disturbances (Russett et al., 1964:272, Gurr, 1969, 1970; Feierabend and Feierabend, 1966, 1971; Nesvold, 1969; Rummel, 1965:189-195, 1969, and 1972) and a modest negative correlation with coericion (Banks and Textor, 1963; Adelman and Morris, 1965; Feierabend and Feierabend, 1971). In one study, development has a modest correlation with a crude measure of legitimacy (the measure of legitimacy is the "legality of the last two governments," and its correlation with GNP per capita is .29; Sawyer, 1967).

This theory may be inadequate for predicting changes in legitimacy and disturbances. The 23 variables in the theory include most of the important causes of these two variables but omit a crucial one: levels of satisfaction among the citizenry.[9] Development is related to satisfaction, but that relationship is mediated by rates of change, standards of evaluation, and the degree of imbalance among variables. The following points suggest the influence of these additional variables on legitimacy and disturbances:

1. *Socioeconomic development causes uneven change.* Socioeconomic

development entails increases in the many variables that are components of it. The rate of change differs from variable to variable and from period to period throughout the process of socioeconomic development.

2. *The rate of change is curvilinear.* The rate of change in all development variables is very slow in traditional societies. With industrialization (or even colonization by industrial nations), the rate of change increases because of the large amount of mutual causation among the socioeconomic development variables. On the average the rate of change reaches its high point during the semideveloped stage when change is substantial, and the base upon which the rate is computed is still relatively small. Thereafter the amount of change continues to increase, but the rate of change (i.e., the ratio of the change to the base) gets smaller.

3. *The extent of imbalances is curvilinear.* The variance in the rates of change for different variables is perhaps greatest for the semideveloped countries. The disparities or imbalances between variables is greatest during the semideveloped stage.

4. *Imbalances cause disturbances.*[10]

5. *Socioeconomic development influences standards.* Socioeconomic development causes standards of evaluation to rise, so that increased well-being is necessary for the same degree of satisfaction and increased performance is necessary for the same level of legitimacy.

6. *The rate of socioeconomic development influences standards.* Socioeconomic development, since it is self-generating after a take-off point, leads to long periods of growth. Rising standards of living are then taken for granted. Legitimacy and satisfaction, therefore, are related not only to the level of progress but even to the rate of progress. A decline in the standard of living after a period of rising standards is particularly dissatisfying.[11]

7. *The level of satisfaction positively affects legitimacy and negatively affects disturbances.* The addition of the above considerations leads to different expectations regarding the correlation of development with legitimacy and disturbances. Some of the positive effect of development on legitimacy and negative effect on disturbances is cancelled out by the imbalances, tensions, and rising expectations that development produces. More precisely, then, we expect development to have a curvilinear relation with both legitimacy and disturbances. We would expect linear correlations, therefore, to be modest; and, in fact, they are.

Further Theory Development

If the causal propositions in Table 14.4 are valid, then it is legitimate to combine some variables into factors. Indeed we have already hypothesized that nine variables combine into a socioeconomic development factor. Now we shall combine several other groups of variables that tend to act in concert and cause each other. Accordingly, nine more variables can be collapsed into four factors: concentration and centralization combine into a scope-of-coordination factor; participation and pluralism into a "democracy" factor; equality of income, equality of capital, and justice into an equality factor; and legitimacy and integration into a legitimacy-integration factor (vertical and horizontal integration).

After 18 variables have been condensed into 5 factors plus 5 of the original variables, the result looks like Formulation B (Table 14.6), which hypothesizes the strong causative relations among the elements; that is, the 5 factors and 5 of the original variables. Figure 14.1 summarizes the changes involved in this and a subsequent reformulation. The table shows that the interrelated variables of democracy and equality relate logically to other variables in similar ways if our hypotheses are correct. This finding suggests that democracy and equality could be combined into a still more general factor, democratic-egalitarianism. Then, with somewhat less justification, the scope-of-coordination variable is absorbed into the socioeconomic-development variable; the resulting factor, which we will call "modernization," causes many other variables but is caused by few of them. Next, in an effort to arrive at solvable equations, modernization is converted from a growth factor to a per capita development factor in order to make modernization an exogenous factor. Standardizing by population removes population as a cause of modernization. At this point it is not unreasonable to treat modernization as a self-causing factor, exogenous to the remaining set of variables. It is true that disturbances can impede modernization when they become widespread and frequent (e.g., the destruction of war). If we limit the theory to more normal times, though, modernization is an exogenous variable.

Population likewise can be treated as an exogenous variable, causing, but not being caused by, other variables. For millenia, development has enabled population growth through an increase in food and health, but there is nothing about development that *inevitably* increases population. If individuals were to desire fewer children for whatever reasons, population would decline as a society modernized. So if we exclude periods of war from the theory, population becomes an exogenous variable along with modernization and international danger. Finally, competition can be removed. It has no strong causative influence on any other variable in the theory, it is unrelated to the other endogenous variables, and it is very inadequately explained by modernization and international danger.

The above changes produce Formulation C (see Figure 14.2), a theory having three exogenous variables (modernization, population, and international danger) and four endogenous variables (democratic-eqalitarianism, legitimacy-integration, disturbances, and coercion). This theory can be tested more stringently

Table 14.6 A Casual Theory of Nation-States (Based on 10 Variables): Formulation B[a]

Effects	Causes									
	Development	Centralization	Democracy	Equality	Legitimacy-Integration	Disturbances	Coercion	Competition	Population	International Danger
Development	+	+				−			+	
Centralization	+	+							+	+
Democracy	+	−	+	+						−
Equality	+		+	+						
Legitimacy-integration	+		+	+	+		−			+
Disturbances					−		−		+	
Coercion			−							+
Competition										−
Population										−

[a] Only causative relationships judged to be strong are indicated.

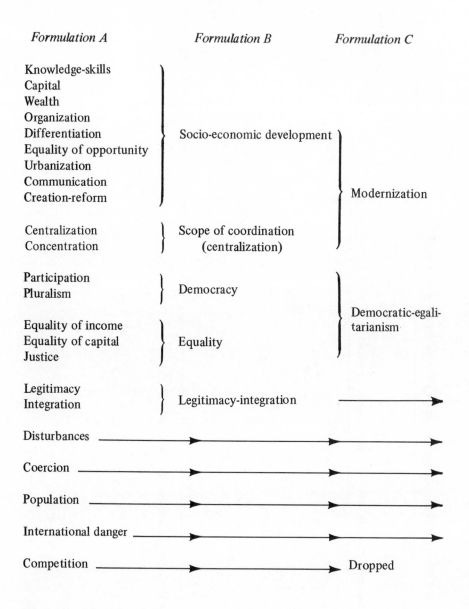

Figure 14.1 Variables used in three formulations of the casual theory of nation-states.

436

A. Matrix of causative relationships for three exogeneous and four endogeneous variables

Effects	Moderni-zation	Popula-tion	Danger	Demo-cratical egalitar-ianism	Legiti-macy Integra-tion	Dis-turb-ances	Coercion
Democratic-egalitarianism	+		−				−
Legitimacy-integration	+			+		−	−
Disturbances		+			−		−
Coercion			+	−		+	

Causes

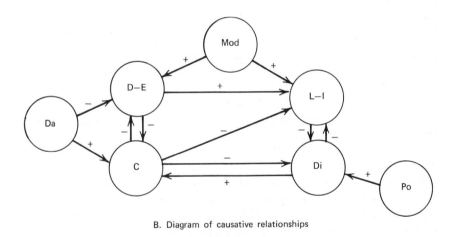

B. Diagram of causative relationships

Figure 14.2 A causal theory of nation-states (based on 7 variables): Formulation C.

than Formulation A in that its set of simultaneous equations can be solved, provided error terms are uncorrelated.[12]

In developing Formulation C from Formulation A by reduction (see Figure 14.1), we obtained a set of solvable equations, simplified the theory, and shifted the theoretical focus considerably. Formulation A emphasized the structural characteristics of nations and the production of assets. In Formulation C, modernization, which includes production, is not seen as problematic. Modernization is in large measure caused by itself because it involves many mutually reinforcing variables, including most of the input variables plus the structural variables of differentiation, concentration, and centralization. In Formulation C, the focus shifts to questions of equality, democracy, integration, coercion, and disturbances.

Before empirically testing the above set of equations, one additional operation should be performed. The model assumes that error terms are uncorrelated. How realistic is this assumption? We need to imagine the major influences on each variable from outside the theory and determine whether any two variables have a cause in common, thus violating the assumptions of the model. Listed below (Table 14.7) are hypothesized causes for the variables in the condensed theory.

Four variables affect more than one element in the condensed theory: education, imbalances, satisfaction, and goal consensus. Education presents no problem because it is really an aspect of modernization and just one more reason why modernization causes democratic-egalitarianism. Imbalances cause both an increase in disturbances and a decrease in legitimacy-integration. It is likely, though, that imbalances cause disturbances largely indirectly, through declining satisfaction, legitimacy, integration, and goal consensus. Controlling for these variables should remove most of the correlation of imbalances with disturbances. For this theory, therefore, we shall assume that the correlation in error terms for legitimacy-integration and disturbances due to imbalances is small and can be ignored at an acceptable risk.

Satisfaction increases legitimacy-integration and decreases disburbances. If the equations are to become solvable, we must enlarge the factor of legitimacy-integration to include satisfaction. This step is possible because all the causes of legitimacy-integration also cause satisfaction, and the effect of legitimacy-integration on other variables is the same as the effect of satisfaction. In other words, modernization, democratic-egalitarianism, (−) coercion and (−) disturbances increase both legitimacy-integration and satisfaction, and both legitimacy-integration and satisfaction decrease disturbances. Finally, legitimacy-integration causes satisfaction, and satisfaction causes legitimacy-integration. Including satisfaction in the legitimacy-integration factor, therefore, is theoretically appropriate. The only difficulty with this procedure is that it makes the resulting factor broader than any name for it would indicate. This problem afflicts most factor analyses, but analysts seem able to live with ıt.

Goal consensus, which causes all four endogenous variables, presents greater

Table 14.7 Additional Hypothesized Causes of Dependent Variables in Formulation C

Dependent Variables	Independent Variables
Modernization	*Education,* transportation, achievement, and work-oriented values and personalities (These variables should be viewed as aspects of modernization rather than as exogenous causes of modernization.)
Population	Factors affecting birthrates (e.g., [−] age of marriage), factors affecting death rates (e.g., [−] medicine), and factors affecting immigration rates (e.g., [−] immigration laws). Values regarding children are important influences on the birthrates.
International danger	(−) natural boundaries, (−) historical legitimacy of boundaries. (−) extent of mutually profitable exchanges with neighboring countries, (−) ideological compatibility with neighboring countries
Democratic–Egalitarianism	*Education,* democratic and egalitarian values, adequate levels of *goal consensus*
Legitimacy-integration	*Goal consensus,* public socialization, *satisfaction,* (−) *imbalances*
Disturbances	*Imbalances,* (−) *goal consensus,* (−) *satisfaction*
Coercion	(−) *goal consensus*

[a]Independent variables that affect more than one dependent variable are italicized.

difficulties. We would have no problem solving the equations if goal consensus could be added to the model as another exogenous variable, but this addition is not possible, since goal consensus is caused by democratic-egalitarianism, legitimacy-integration, and the inverse of disturbances. If we add goal consensus to the model as an endogenous variable, though, we still cannot solve the equations because the equation for legitimacy-integration would have six unknowns—that is, one more than the number of equations in the model when goal consensus is added. There is no certain way out of this difficulty.

Odd as it may seem, perhaps the model can be salvaged through finding an error in it. If, in fact, one of the hypothesized causes of legitimacy-integration turns out to have no *direct* impact on it, then the amended model, which includes goal consensus as an endogenous variable, would be workable. This possibility might be realistic when the variance on certain variables is kept within certain limits. For example, if only relatively developed nations are studied, then modernization might not increase legitimacy-integration. Or if very repressive nations are excluded from the sample, then the variations in coercion for the remaining nations might not be related negatively to legitimay-integration. If such steps are necessary to make the model work, then it will have limited applicability, but it will nevertheless be valuable. Most social science models, after all, are similarly limited but still very useful when properly applied.

There is another way to handle goal consensus. It could be made an aspect of legitimacy-integration-satisfaction, although with less justification than if we incorporated satisfaction into legitimacy-integration. This incorporation would result in another formulation of the theory (Formulation D) that would be identical to Formulation C except that satisfaction and goal consensus would be included in the legitimacy-integration factor. Goal consensus and legitimacy-integration *do* cause each other, both decrease disturbances, and both are caused by democratic-egalitarianism and negative disturbances. However, modernization can increase legitimacy-integration without necessarily increasing goal consensus; coercion decreases legitimacy-integration but might either increase or decrease goal consensus; and goal consensus contributes to democratic-egalitarianism, while legitimacy-integration does not. Since the two variables are closely related and do not have contradictory effects on other variables, the judgment has been made that the above discrepancies between the two variables are not serious enough to prohibit incorporating goal consensus along with satisfaction into the legitimacy-integration factor, which might then be renamed "national unity." Doing so would solve the problem of correlated error terms, allowing us to proceed with the empirical testing of equations. On the other hand, the extraordinary breadth of the ational-unity factor will make its measurement difficult, thereby complicating the model-testing.

The above represents the type of theoretical development presently required for analysis of the evolution of nation-states. A large number of variables is organized first into a conceptual scheme (Tables 14.1-3) and subsequently into a complex causal theory (Table 14.4). Third, the theory is tested against empirical findings in the literature and collected data. We were able to do the former to a small extent but not the latter. The fourth step is to revise the theory in the light of step three. Some theory development and reformulation has been done in this chapter (Table 14.6; Figures 14.1-2). The theory has been modified to make its equations solvable (Formulation C), and the question of correlated error terms has been considered.

The above is not the only possible model for theory construction. Some would prefer, quite legitimately, to start with five or six variables, hypothesize their interrelationships, and then hypothesize the additional variables that impinge upon the original variable system. Others would prefer to examine all the variables that significantly affect a single dependent variable—for example, the college aspiration studies of William Sewell and his colleagues[13]—and then to postulate the interrelationships among the independent variables. Still others would prefer combinations of these three styles of theory construction. The contention here is simply that the mode of theory construction demonstrated in this paper merits much wider use.

Notes

1. The dimensions of nations herein proposed are judged important on the basis of the author's experience in compiling a modest data bank on nations, his review of several literatures and factor analyses, and his efforts to arrive deductively at a parsimonious set of dimensions. The reader might want to compare the proposed conceptual scheme with that of Jerald Hage (1972) and that of Bertram Gross (1966).
2. In Tables 14.1-3, the 23 variables selected for the theory are footnoted. The variables used in the theory are found mainly at the subcategory and sub-subcategory levels in the conceptual scheme as shown in Tables 14.1-3; only three are at the major category level.
3. This definition of legitimacy is broader than most. For example, Lipset (1960) restricts it to belief in the appropriateness of the existing political institutions. It is difficult to measure legitimacy. First, one must decide how to aggregate the attitudes of individuals. On ethical grounds we would prefer to count everyone's opinion equally, but we know that the opinions of elites and media controllers have more weight in society than those of the average citizen. The second measurement problem is the considerable extent to which the legitimacy of a system is bound up with the legitimacy of its leadership. The two should be distinguished analytically even if it is often difficult to differentiate them empirically.
4. The major intellectual debt in developing this taxonomy of variables for nation-states is to Jerald Hage, whose work has been the foundation for this effort. Our taxonomies are most similar on structural characteristics. Differentiation, income equality, and justice are borrowed directly from him while scale and democracy expand on his concept of centralization. See Hage, "A General Theory of Society" (n.d.), and Hage (1972).
5. Increasing centralization and concentration have been discussed widely, expecially by Mills (1956) and his followers, but Eisenstadt's (1966) discussion is especially noteworthy for its breadth of perspective. An interesting conjecture occurs at this point. With further differentiation, will the most propitious scale of coordination increasingly become larger than the boundaries of most nation-states? If so, then the nation-state will become less independent and a less significant unit of analysis. The sociology of nation-states could well become eclipsed by the sociology of international systems.
6. The classic examination of this characteristic is Durkheim (1949). Measures of religious, ethnic, national, racial, and linguistic heterogeneity-homogeneity can be

found in one or more of the three major, large-scale, cross-national data-bank projects: Banks and Textor (1963); Russett et al. (1964); and Sawyer (1967).

7. Seven of the above nine variables are intercorrelated cross-nationally according to one or more of the three large-scale, cross-national data-bank studies cited in note 6. These studies, however, contained no measures for mobility or creation-reform. Adelman and Morris's (1965, 1967) cross-national studies show that social mobility is related to development.

8. If defense expenditures/GNP reflect the degree of international danger facing a nation, then the Russett and Sawyer data-bank studies find no correlation between development and international danger.

9. Bwy (1968:201-236) is able to account for over 90 percent of the variance in a turmoil factor and also in an internal-war factor for provinces in four Latin American nations by using indicators of dissatisfaction, legitimacy, and coercion or coercive force. Gurr (1968) has developed a similar, but more complex, model for disturbances in nations, using deprivations (dissatisfactions), legitimacy, coercion and three factors that capture aspects of participation (facilitation), pluralism (institutionalization), and satisfaction (past-strife levels). His model accounted for 65 percent of the variance in a "total magnitude of strife" (1961-1965) factor for 114 nations.

10. Points 3 and 4 are similar to the thesis of Deutsch (1960), who focused on the higher rate of increase in variables representing demands on national governments than in variables representing the capability of governments to meet demands.

11. Davies (1962) has made the classic statement of this thesis. He studied three revolutions that confirm his thesis, and Blasier (1967) found that it fit three others.

12. Because of the mutual dependence of three pairs of variables, simple least squares cannot be used in estimating the parameters.

13. Sewell (1971:793-809) presents a summary and bibliography of this work.

References

Abrahamson, Mark.

   1969   Correlates of political complexity. *American Sociological Review*, 34 (October):690-701.

Adelman, Irma, and Cynthia Taft Morris.

   1965   A factor analysis of the interrelationships between social and political variables and per capita gross national product. *Quarterly Journal of Economics*, 79 (November):555-578.

   1967   *Society, Politics and Economic Development: A Quantitative Approach.* Baltimore: Johns Hopkins.

Almond, Gabriel A., and Sidney Verba.

   1963   *The Civic Culture*. Princeton, N.Y.: Princeton University Press.

Banks, Arthur S., and Robert B. Textor.

   1963   *A Cross-Polity Survey.* Cambridge, Mass.: MIT. Press.

Blasier, Cole.

1967 Studies of social revolution: origins in Mexico, Bolivia, and Cuba. *Latin American Research Review,* 2 (Summer):28-64.

Bwy, Douglas.

1968 Dimensions of social conflict in Latin America. In Louis H. Musotti and Don R. Brown (Eds.), *Riots and Rebellions: Civil Violence in the Urban Community.* Beverly Hills, Calif.: Sage. Pp. 201-236.

Cutright, Phillips.

1963 National political development: measurement and analysis. *American Sociological Review,* 28 (April):253-264.

Davies, James C.

1962 Toward a theory of revolution. *American Sociological Review,* 27 (February):5-19.

Deutsch, Karl W.

1960 Social mobilization and political development. *American Political Science Review,* 55 (March):34-57.

Durkheim, Emile.

1949 *The Division of Labor in Society.* Glencoe, Ill.:Free Press.

Eisenstadt, S. N.

1964 Social change, differentiation, and evolution. *American Sociological Review,* 29 (June):375-386.

1966 *Modernization:Protest and Change.* Englewood Cliffs, N.J.: Prentice-Hall.

Feierabend, Ivo K., and Rosalind L. Feierabend.

1966 Aggressive behaviors within politics, 1948-1962, a cross-national study. *Journal of Conflict Resolution,* 10 (September):249-271.

1971 The relationship of systematic frustration, political coercion, and political instability: a cross-national analysis. In John V. Gillespie and Betty A. Nesvold (Eds.), *Macro-quantitative Analysis: Conflict, Development, and Democratization.* Beverly Hills, Calif.: Sage. Pp. 417-440.

Fitzgibbon, Russell H.

1967   Measuring democratic change in Latin America. *Journal of Politics,* 29 (February):129-166.

Flanigan, William, and Edwin Fogelman.

1971a   Patterns of political development and democratization: a quantitative analysis. In John V. Gillespie and Betty A. Nesvold (Eds.), *Macro-quantitative Analysis: Conflict, Development, and Democratization.* Beverly Hills, Calif.:Sage. Pp. 441-473.

1971b   Patterns of democratic development: an historical comparative analysis. In John V. Gillespie and Betty A. Nesvold (Eds.), *Macro-quantitative Analysis: Conflict, Development, and Democratization.* Beverly Hills, Calif.: Sage. Pp. 475-497.

Galbraith, John Kenneth.

1967   *The New Industrial State.* Boston: Houghton Mifflin.

Gibbs, Jack P., and Harley L. Browning.

1966   The division of labor, technology, and the organization of production in twelve countries. *American Sociological Review,* 31 (February):81-92.

Gregg, Phillip M., and Arthur S. Banks.

1965   Dimensions of political systems: factor analysis of a cross-polity survey. *American Political Science Review,* 59 (November): 602-614.

Gross, Bertram.

1966   The state of the nation. In Raymond Bauer (Ed.), *Social Indicators.* Cambridge, Mass.: Mit. Press. Pp. 154-271.

Gurr, Ted Robert.

1968   A causal model of civil strife: a comparative analysis using new indices. *American Political Science Review,* 62 (December): 1104-1124.

1969   A comparative study of civil strife. In Hugh Davis Graham and Ted Robert Gurr (Eds.), *Violence in America: Historical and Comparative Perspectives.* New York: Bantam. Pp. 572-632.

1970   *Why Men Rebel.* Princeton, N.J.: Princeton University Press.

Hage, Jerald.

    n.d.   A general theory of society. Mimeographed. Madison: University of Wicsoncin.

    1972   *Techniques and Problems of Theory Construction in Social Science,* New York: Wiley-Interscience.

Kornhauser, William.

    1959   *The Politics of Mass Society.* New York: Free Press.

Kuznets, Simon.

    1963   Quantitative aspects of the economic growth of nations: VIII. Distribution of income by size. *Economic Development and Cultural Change,* 11 (January): entire volume.

Lipset, Seymour Martin.

    1959   Some social requisites of democracy; economic development and political legitimacy. *American Political Science Review,* 53 (March):69-105.

    1960   *Political Man: The Social Basis of Politics.* Garden City, N.Y.: Doubleday.

Marx, Karl, and Friedrich Engels.

    1932   *Manifesto of the Communist Party.* New York: International Publishers. First published in 1848.

Mills, C. Wright.

    1956   *The Power Elite.* New York: Oxford University Press.

Nesvold, Betty A.

    1969   Scalogram analysis of political violence. *Comparative Political Studies,* 2 (July):172-194.

Olsen, Marvin E.

    1968   Multivariate analysis of national political development. *American Sociological Review,* 33 (October):689-712.

Parsons, Talcott.

    1970   Some considerations on the theory of social change. In S.N. Eisenstadt (Ed.), *Readings in Social Evolution and Development.* Oxford: Pergamon. Pp. 95-121.

Rummel, Rudolph J.

    1965   A field theory of social action and of political conflict within
           nations. *Yearbook of the Society for General Systems Research,*
           10:189-195.

    1969   Some empirical findings of nations and their behavior. *World
           Politics,* 21 (January):226-241.

    1972   *The Dimensions of Nations.* Beverly Hills, Calif.: Sage Publica-
           tions.

Russett, Bruce M.

    1964   Inequality and instability: the relation of land tenure to politics.
           World Politics, 16 (April):442-454.

Russett, Bruce M., Hayward R. Alker, Jr., Karl W. Deutsch, and Harold D.
Lasswell.

    1964   *World Handbook of Political and Social Indicators.* New Haven,
           Conn.: Yale University Press.

Sawyer, Jack.

    1967   Dimensions of nations: size, wealth, and politics. *American
           Journal of Sociology,* 73 (September):145-172.

Sewell, William H.

    1971   Inequality of opportunity for higher education. *American Socio-
           logical Review,* 36 (October):793-809.

Smelser, Neil.

    1963   Mechanisms of change and adjustment to change. In Bert F.
           Hoselitz and Wilbur E. Moore (Eds.), *Industrialization and
           Society.* New York: UNESCO.

Spencer, Herbert.

    1893   *The Principles of Sociology.* New York: Appleton.

Tocqueville, Alexis de.

    1945   *Democracy in America.* 2 vols. New York: Knopf.

Udy, Stanley H., Jr.

    1959   "Bureaucracy" and "rationality" in Weber's organization theory;
           an empirical study. *American Sociological Review,* 24
           (December):791-795.

Discussion

Mr. Anderson. I noted with respect to Johnson and Cutright's paper that data may be aggregated if we are dealing with a system which has relatively developed subsystems. If the transfer of information, goods, etc., occurs on a particular level in the form of aggregates, then that level is meaningful for aggregation. Finsterbusch proposes using national states as a unit of Finsterbusch proposes using national states as a unit of aggregation. It is very clear that national states represent subsystems of some larger regional, continental, etc., system and that, in fact, they contain control units. Therefore, one could well argue on these grounds that the national is a meaningful unit of aggregation. However, if we want an entirely general theory of national states that includes a large number of areas as is implied in Finsterbusch's analysis, we would have to determine that each variable is in fact subject to some sort of control at the national level. If some variables are *not* subject to any control at the national level, then the national may not be a particularly appropriate level on which to analyze the data.

Let me make a second general comment on Finsterbusch's paper. In constructing theory quantitatively, it seems most appropriate to do so in terms of a format through which we first identify a quantity and then the various settings in which we want to measure the level of that quantity. This approach contrasts with the more traditional procedure that is used in sociology of starting with the identification of concepts and then devising various ways to index or operationalize those concepts. I find severe logical problems in following the latter rather than the former path.

For example, one of the quantities that we can measure and identify is the number of people in different settings. One source of such counts can be historical registries of one kind or another. Indeed, right now a very hot area of comparative research is historical demography, which is fundamentally based on counting the number of people in many different settings. The resulting variables, then, all tend to have the same dimensional characteristic, namely, they are all counts of numbers of people. Slowly but surely a researcher can develop a meaningful body of substantive data out of material that is relatively comparable internally.

Economists, to take another example, count or measure amounts of money in many different settings. The ultimate result is an institution or intellectual structure built around the measurement of a particular kind of quantity.

If Finsterbusch wants to develop a general theory of national states or something comparable to it, I would suggest that he start with what he considers to be the key *quantities*, rather than the key concepts, that he wants to use in measuring things. He can then build concepts around the quantities.

Mr. Schnaiberg.   It seems to me that unless a researcher has a strong theoretical perspective that leads him to search for unconventional kinds of data, he may be denied some very important insights precisely because he takes only the conventional, easily available sources of data.

Mr. Anderson.   I hope you didn't read into my comments an isomorphism between my emphasis upon quantities and settings and an emphasis on working with the data that are available. In no sense did I intend that.

Mr. Schnaiberg.   You argued against working from concepts and then trying to develop approximate indexes of them which, in turn, may lead to new and unusual data sources. Furthermore, even when working from quantities based on readily available data, it is still necessary to go back and draw conceptual inferences from those data. These conceptual inferences are as often wrong as right. It seems to me that there is a continuous interplay between both the theory-conceptual level and the empirical-data level that is necessarily involved in the development of science. And it seemed to me you were ignoring that fact.

Mr. Anderson.   I hope not.

Mr. Finsterbusch.   In commenting on my paper I would emphasize the importance of using continuous variables, which should involve a single dimension. The dichotomies found so frequently in the comparative literature are multidimensional and contain continuous variables. For example, Johnson and Cutright's work took the concept of democracy and tried to dimensionalize it into a continuous variable. In particular, they used political participation, which doesn't cover democracy entirely but is an improvement on Lipset's [1959] democracy-nondemocracy dicho-tomy. I feel that we can only approach a sociology which is a generalizing science as we move away from dichotomies which contain very different entities on the same side of the dichotomizing line.

A second point is that I recommend the use of variable systems that are larger than the minimum necessary for the particular task at hand. I think it is important to map out a large variable space within which the specific problems under study are located. If somebody wants to study, say, revolutions or disturbances, turmoil, civil strife, or any of the particular variables that are suggested in my scheme, then it is important to consider not only the variables that are supposedly the principal causes but also to try and map out a larger system. If an investigator is dealing with revolution or civil strife, he is probably dealing with the nation-state unit.

Therefore, he should try to work out the principal variables operating in nation-states and do a mapping job which includes more than the particular eight or nine variables which might have very direct influence on revolution or disturbances. What will probably happen when an investigator does this (as exemplified in my paper) is that he will develop a conceptual scheme and then think in terms of the interrelationships among many variables. He is likely to posit a great deal of mutual causality as he thinks these relationships through, and possibly he will end up with equations which cannot be solved because of the extent of the mutual causality. But this result only suggests that it is inappropriate to work out a single multiple-regression equation to predict the dependent variable and to deduce therefrom the relative weights for the causal influences of the independent variables.

Third, my paper suggests that investigators should be alert to the extent to which variables are imbedded in factors. Very often analysts operate on the assumption that variables are distinct from each other. They look at correlation matrices, find that X is more highly correlated with Y than Z is, and conclude that X is a more important cause of Y than is Z. But the correlations might be influenced by many other variables, especially when the independent variables are components of factors like socioeconomic development, which in Sawyer's [1967] analysis, for example, has some 70 or 75 measured variables related to it. Clearly, there is an enormous amount of intercausality within factors like socioeconomic development. When the causal influence of individual variables cannot be ascertained because of the extent of mutual causality, then explanation of phenomena is usually done better when we use a factor rather than the variables which make it up.

Mr. Schnaiberg.   Let me ask Anderson a question related to the matter of goals and the aggregation problems he also discussed with respect to the Johnson-Cutright paper. In terms of societal goals one assumes that national integration is necessary for the future viability of a social system. There may be a policy or social engineering objective to develop changes in the nation-state such that national integration will, in effect, control illegitimate fertility and a whole host of other processes. In short, there are presumably societal objectives, and if, for example, we ultimately want national integration at the nation-state level to impinge on these processes, even though that condition doesn't exist at the present, the nation-state may still be a very critical unit of aggregation to deal with in our analysis.

Mr. Anderson,   It might be, but also it might not be. The only demurrer I think that I would have with reference to what you are saying is with regard to the idea that societal integration is necessarily connected to national integration. It may, in fact, be the case that the national would become the level at which control of that sort was introduced. On the other hand, it might be that control would occur at the international level. At some times in the past, for example, such control has occurred through church organization, a clearly international, rather than national, framework. In other settings, you could well imagine it occurring on a regional basis, not involving nations at all. In short, there is a difference between assuming some sort of large-scale integrative activity and assuming that such activity is occurring at the national level.

Mr. Schnaiberg.   The integration argument was not specific to the nation-state but rather to a larger aggregation.

Mr. Anderson.   The argument as a whole is well taken—right.

Mr. Schnaiberg.   Related to this problem is another that I detect in some of the discussion. We seem to be emphasizing a distinction in terms of macro- versus micro- or individual analysis. It seems to me, though, that the micro-macro dispute which underlies a lot of the statistical and substantive discussion is a false distinction.

A social system doesn't operate as a mechanical system; it operates via actors. We should be asking what impact the institution has on the actors as individuals and as collectivities or aggregates. What reaction, what feedback occurs, and what effect does it have on social-system change?

From this perspective, the nation-state level, particularly in the case of development, may turn out to be too low rather than too high a level of aggregation. Focus on the nation-state may be inappropriate in two ways. First, the nation-state does not clearly impinge equally upon all actors within the society. Second, the control we want to study may be located at a higher level because clearly there is an international stratification system even though a great many social scientists have not yet recognized these colonial and neocolonial influences.

There is a continuum involved here, between macro- and microlevels of analysis, and I don't think an either-or situation is the appropriate mode of response.

Mr. Anderson.   There is another problem that I would like briefly to put out for discussion. Systems of analysis that involve variable-variable relationships in which the quantity of X is related to the quantity of Y, whether the relationships are bivariate or multivariate in character, are relationships that presumably apply only in equilibrium or steady-state systems. If any *changes* are occurring, the relationship between X and Y is generated by the connection between the *change(s)* in X and/or Y rather than between X and Y alone. The effects of these changes should be included in our system of equations.

If we are going to ignore change variables, we should at least discuss whether or not the system is considered to be in or near a steady state. In some cases, it may be justifiable to use models which ignore change variables, but the issue should at least be considered.

Mr. Finsterbusch. Could you explain again how the analysis of steady states disallows the study of change variables?

Mr. Anderson. Because if you have a set of equations that relate the quantity of one variable to the quantities of various other variables and all the quantity changes are zero, you are left with sets of relationships among quantities but no statement about *changes* in quantity. That situation, by definition, is either an equilibrium state or a steady state.

Mr. Finsterbusch. I fail to understand why that has to be an equilibrium state. We could be "stopping the camera" at one point in time and then correlating variables cross-sectionally.

Mr. Anderson. Oh, no. If I take a picture when a process has been half completed, that picture hasn't stopped the process. It is true that I have a picture when the process is half completed, but you would certainly want to describe the position of that object as changing. You wouldn't say that it was somewhere even though you took a picture of it and in the picture it looked like it was somewhere.

Mr. Finsterbusch. Right.

Mr. Anderson. All right, it is changing.

Mr. Finsterbusch. My problem with your statement is that I don't see why you are assuming equilibrium.

Mr. Anderson. Because, if, in fact, you use a system of simultaneous equations that involves quantity-quantity relationships and you ask how, in terms of some social process, you get such relationships without any change-relationships existing, the only answer I know is that you get them in steady states or equilibrium.

Mr. Schnaiberg. Can I try to give a concrete example of what I think you are saying? Take the educational development process in a country like India as opposed to African countries. Suppose you do a survey on an individual basis in that developing society and you find a very high correlation between education and nonmanual occupational attainment. At that point in the society, let's say that 10 percent of the male adult population has been educated beyond the primary school level. Over the years, though, that condition changes to one in which, let's say, 40 percent of the male population has a primary level of education. Then you have overeducation developing, a condition which exists in parts of India today; there aren't enough nonmanual occupations in the labor market to occupy all those with a primary education. The original relationship between education and occupation no longer holds at t plus 25 years.

I think that you are saying that the context in which X and Y are related is itself changing, that the whole set of relationships between X, Y, and Z on a cross-sectional, correlational basis is dynamic and will change drastically when these variables change over time. Thus, arguing, for example, that one should invest scarce resources in education may be very important up to a certain point in nation development. Beyond that point, though, you get into diminishing returns because there is less absorption capacity.

Mr. Finsterbusch.   Are you saying that when you do cross-national correlations at a single point in time, the assumption is one of social-system equilibrium?

Mr. Anderson.   No. I don't know what "assumption" means in that context. What I am saying is that your interpretation of the correlations is an interpretation which makes sense *if* the system is in equilibrium but does not make much sense if the system is subject to rapid change.

Mr. Cutright.   I would disagree with that statement. When I began doing static correlations at a single point in time and found a huge relationship between measures of development and a measure of political structure of populations, I saw this correlation as confirming Lipset's [1959] hypothesis: Societies reached higher levels of political representation because of changes in literacy, which then elicited an inherent demand from the populations for a more representative political system.

I don't believe that anymore because I did a longitudinal study [Cutright and Wiley, 1969-1970] which, as far as I can see, proved that there was nothing at all to the hypothesis. The population in my sample that have a representative political structure do so simply because there isn't any reason for them not to have it. The economy is operating; things are functioning. When the economy stops operating, the government loses legitimacy; *then* the government changes. Even in a nonrepresentative political system, if the government performs at the levels demanded of it by the population, that system will remain. This is the case even though the hypothesis says that the government should be moving towards a regression line because of massive changes in literacy, massive changes in economic development, and so on. In short, I finally explained all the deviant cases in terms of what the government was doing in those countries.

Mr. Hill.   The point you are making is an excellent illustration of Anderson's methodological argument.

References

Cutright, Phillips, and James A. Wiley.

1969-   Modernization and political representation: 1927-1966. *Studies in*
1970   *Comparative International Development,* 5, no. 2:23-46.

Lipset, Seymour Martin.

1959   Some social requisites of democracy: economic development and
       political legitimacy. *American Political Science Review,* 53
       (March):69-105.

Sawyer, Jack.

1967   Dimensions of nations: size, wealth, and politics. *American*
       Journal of Sociology, 73 (September):145-172.

Conclusion

CHAPTER FIFTEEN

In Retrospect: A Brief Analysis
of the Confessions of Comparativists

RICHARD J. HILL

University of Oregon

Providing a critical summary of this volume's chapters and discussions demands a level of theoretical and methodological competence that would be claimed only by a charlatan or a fool. The variety of issues raised suggests that comparative sociology is a field that is congruent with the entire sociological enterprise. Thus, I begin with considerable uncertainty as to both the meaning of "comparative" and the professional self-identity of the "comparativist." Armer (pp. 49-50)[1] claims that there is general agreement about the conception of the field of comparative sociology, and Grimshaw provides an overview and history of comparative sociological concerns.[2] Despite such claims, I find the referent of "comparative sociology" impossible to specify. Consider the papers that constitute this volume as a collection of data to be described.

The substantive interests upon which the individual chapters focus range from the ecology of cities to power structures, class consciousness, organizations of industrial workers, to the child's production of responses to interrogation. The theoretical positions include institutional functionalism, neo-evolutionism, neo-Marxian conflict theory, and phenomenology. The methodological strategies employed are completely cosmopolitan: They include concerns with census procedures, historiography, responses to incomplete sentences, participant observation, and the detailed examination of videotape. This collection reflects, in surprising detail, the substantive, theoretical, and methodological interests and conflicts that characterize the total social science enterprise. I cannot deal with such diffuseness in a finite number of pages.

Being an occasional methodologist, I will therefore employ a strategy that has been of some utility to those of us who are given to statistical analyses: I will ignore certain variations that cause me some inconvenience. First, I shall not treat specific substantive issues. For example, I have no real appreciation of the importance of illegitimacy for the understanding of population dynamics. Hence, it would be totally inappropriate for me to discuss the demographic matters treated by Johnson and Cutright. Second, I will not consider many of the technical issues raised. Again, by way of illustration, the interpretive problems associated with the various factor-analytic strategies that Schwirian introduces deserve detailed analysis, but such an examination would be inappropriate to these circumstances.

Instead, my purpose will be to convey certain impressions that I have formed after considering these papers and exchanges as data. Some of my impressionistic conclusions have been more adequately treated in the discussions following the individual papers. Further, the introductory chapters by Grimshaw and Armer touch upon many of the same points that I shall address. I hope that my repetition of previously stated positions will be viewed as positive reinforcement rather than pedantic redundancy.

One of the distressingly dominant themes that run through these chapters has to do with the difficulties associated with assembling theoretically relevant, reliable, and valid data. Thus, Form, who understands the language of Italy and is well informed about the culture of that country, recounts a series of troubles that might be the equivalent of the Book of Job in a contemporary Bible of Sociological Method. Johnson and Cutright report that for Latin American nations records on vital statistics are often inadequate. Finsterbusch tells us that the available indicators for the variables incorporated in his taxonomy are less than satisfactory. The problems are particularly striking when we consider Schwirian's report. As a nonexperimental social psychologist, I frequently envy the hardness of the data available to the demographer and the ecologist. Typically, my data do not permit me to utilize the strategies that characterize the work of contemporary demographers and ecologists. Yet it is Schwirian (p. 347), a man employing factor-analytic techniques and path analysis, who writes, "Unfortunately for comparative ecological research, such data have not been collected for many of the world's cities, thereby precluding the possibility that their ecological structure may be identified through application of rigorous statistical procedures."

Given such a set of limitations, I am impressed by the compulsive perversity that drives the comparativist to deal with such difficulties. The comparativist apparently must be convinced that some variable of crucial importance to sociological understanding requires the researcher to tolerate such trouble. Perhaps this very obvious understanding provides a key to analyzing the nature of the work.

But what is the variable? Why, it is cultural difference or societal heterogeneity, of course. Clearly, if any single concern characterizes the comparativist, it is the conviction that cultural or societal variability is crucial to the explanation of social phenomena. It is only in this sense and at this level of abstraction that the chapters reported here have a common intellectual commitment. The comparativist, then, desires to be the sociologist who investigates a given substantive problem over a set of societies in order to evaluate the importance of cultural or societal heterogeneity as an explanatory variable.[3] This desire appears in different guises. Some comparativists seem to be searching for cultural universals. Others seek the cultural conditions that place limits on the generality of propositions that have emerged from the study of various Yankee cities or of American college sophomores. Grimshaw (Chapter 1 above) deals with these matters in considerable detail.

The conviction that cultural or societal heterogeneity is of crucial importance certainly cannot be debated profitably. However, I believe that this conviction is of only limited scientific utility; further, it is the basis for many of the troubles that beset the comparative enterprise.

Let me step back and approach this charge in a more cautious fashion. Whenever we attempt to establish a relationship between two variables, we are involved in a comparative logic. Thus, if I wish to know, given certain environmental conditions, the effects of different concentrations of nitrites on the productivity of a given type of corn, I must be concerned with making comparisons. The general nature of, and the problems associated with, comparative analysis are central to any empirically based attempt to understand relationships.

Walton begins his suggestive analysis by arguing that "systematic and distinctively comparative strategies" have not been developed by comparativists. However, unless we are concerned with detailed, technical developments, I would be amazed if a distinctive general strategy or logic were to emerge from attempts to compare what Walton terms "total societies." What is distressing is not the lack of ingenuity but rather the relative lack of rigor, precision, reliability, validity, and replication.

These latter problems, I believe, stem in considerable degree from the current status of the comparativist's major independent variable: cultural or societal heterogeneity. Clearly, that variable is N-dimensional, and comparative sociologists have not as yet agreed on the size of N, let alone on the conceptual nature of the dimensions that define that N-space. Here Finsterbusch's ambitious attempt to develop a taxonomy is illustrative. Forty-eight variables are contained in his initial conceptual scheme. From these, Finsterbusch selects a subset of 23 in an effort to construct a conceptual framework that he believes contains 219 causal relationships.

If it is assumed that the complexity of societal variability is approached (at least with respect to order of magnitude) by the Finsterbusch taxonomy, very serious difficulties follow. The nature of these difficulties is dependent upon the way in which the comparativist formulates his problem, but I am arguing that comparativists have a strong predilection to use societal or cultural variability as an *independent* variable. If the conceptual space is occupied by elements that can assume different locations on something between 23 and 48 dimensions, the intellectual demands required in utilizing the concept to formulate propositions become excessive. Furthermore, given the nature of the dimensions Finsterbusch identifies, there is little reason to believe that the space is orthogonal. Thus, not only must the original dimensions be considered, but the possibility of a host of higher-order interactions must be entertained.[4]

I believe that comparativists must devote much greater attention to the problem of delimiting the significant dimensions of cultural heterogeneity. Perhaps the concept of modernity constitutes one such dimension. Here Armer and Schnaiberg's chapter is suggestive of the hard, technical work that remains even when there appears to be some agreement about the components of the almost cosmic notion of cultural variability.

Hazelrigg's attack on the problem of measuring class consciousness suggests additional problems of an extremely vexing nature. Not only do societies vary on the dimension of class consciousness, but the nature of that dimension itself varies from society to society. The dilemma posed by such circumstances gives rise to conceptual and measurement tasks of excruciating complexity. Fortunately, Armer has relieved me of the need to review these matters. His distinction (see Chapter 2) between appropriateness and equivalence is addressed precisely to such problems, and the importance of that distinction is well illustrated by Hazelrigg's analysis.

There are other fundamental problems that follow from the above considerations. We can agree that sociologists should be concerned with cultural variability. My argument, however, is that such agreement is, at least currently, of limited scientific utility. Until the significant dimensions of cultural variability are further specified, the work of comparativists will not be integrated, and their efforts will lack the cumulative quality that is necessary to a science. I further believe that the failure to specify the fundamental dimensions of cultural variability leads to another serious limitation: the failure to agree on the basic unit of observation.

There seems to be some agreement that the nation-state is the appropriate unit. I suspect, however, that this decision is reached more on the basis of convenience than in terms of some theoretical conviction that such a unit is, in fact, the most appropriate. In some of these discussions, there is at least an implied uneasiness with the nation-state as a basic unit. For example, Johnson and Cutright (note 5) suggest that urban-rural differences are an important factor affecting such a basic demographic variable as the number of people legally married. It may well be that rural populations in different countries have more in common than do rural and urban populations in the same countries. Under such circumstances, comparing units comprised of nation-states would depress the relationships between many of the variables being investigated. Or consider Schwirian's data. The factorial differentiation of San Juan approximates that of Ottawa, Windsor, and Kingston more closely than it does that of Ponce. Schwirian speculates on the reasons for this finding, but his speculation also raises questions about using nation-states as fundamental units for comparative analysis.

To put the problem in slightly different terms, I believe that comparativists must consider how homogeneous collectivities need to be if comparisons are to have theoretical significance. Mehan compares children from different linguistic subpopulations of a particular school district of the United States; Form compares industrial units in different nation-states; Miller compares power structures in four different cities; Elder compares values in two different parts of India; Hazelrigg is concerned with comparing class consciousness in different societies. To what degree do the conclusions derived from these various studies depend upon the units selected for comparison? The attack on that question depends in part on prior analysis of the conceptual nature of cultural variability. Is linguistic difference required? If so, is that all? What about differences in value orientations, technological competence, and so on, and so forth?

With respect to the unit problem, there is a further difficulty that I shall term the problem of the "unit in context." Awareness of this issue is explicitly stated in several of the papers included in this volume. Finsterbusch asks, "With further differentiation, will the most propitious scale of coordination increasingly become larger than the boundaries of most nation states? If so, then the nation state will become less independent and a less significant unit of analysis. The sociology of nation states could well become eclipsed by the sociology of international systems" (note 5). Schwirian's analysis strongly suggests that the ecology of cities is significantly influenced by a nation's stage of development. Miller notes (p. 204) that the institutional power structure of a nation is the most important independent variable affecting the power structure of communities. In short, the relationships observed for the various units that have been compared are seen as being conditioned by more encompassing contextual variables. Until we can do more than recognize that such conditions operate, our conclusions will have only limited theoretical consequences.

Still another methodological problem addressed in these chapters concerns the issue of sampling. Obviously the solution of such technical matters requires appropriate decisions with respect to units of analysis, and no sampling expert can solve the technical issues involved unless the researcher can specify the units to be included in the sampling frame. However, let me ignore such details, for here the provocative paper by Portes introduces a different type of consideration, which I want to contrast with one of Miller's concerns.

In discussing research design, Miller takes a position that I would like to be able to defend. He employs standard research-design criteria, which include considerations regarding the selection of research sites and individuals residing within those sites. One cannot quarrel with his research paradigm from the standpoint of "scientific rigor." The argument, however, contains a pragmatic Achilles heel, for Miller's particular interests center on structures of community power, and this area, while not identical with the study of local politics, is certainly closely related to the study of political behavior. Portes concludes (p. 158) that "the area of study that comes closest to being universally sensitive is politics." If Portes is correct, we may infer that the image of the objective scientist selecting subjects solely on the basis of his theoretical concerns must depart from possible practice precisely in those areas in which Miller is interested. Thus, even if the nature of cultural variability was fully specified and even if the unit-of-comparison problems were solved, the use of certain sampling models might well be denied to us not for reasons of scientific applicability but rather as a partial consequence of other scientists' past behavior. This same set of limitations will operate even if we adopt the advice given by Walton and use theoretical sampling models rather than the inferentially stronger probability models. Again Armer's discussion of appropriateness and equivalence is pertinent to such decisions.

Given these difficulties, perhaps we should adopt alternative research strategies and seek other data sources. Turk persuasively argues for the use of historical materials not only as a reasonable, but as a necessary, sociological endeavor. The argument, in part, is that much of sociology is time-bound as well as culture-bound. I have not the slightest brief against the use of historiographic methods, provided the sociologist remains fully cognizant of the limitations and selectivity of archival materials, and some of Turk's concerns are obviously shared by those who point to the necessity for longitudinal investigations. Unfortunately, document search will not unearth the data required by the specific problems to which most of this volume's chapters are addressed. The necessary data will not be found in archives.

Given the unknown and unknowable selectivity of past clerks and scribes, then, sociologists, as one part of their professional obligation, should be future-oriented historians. Schwirian (p. 349) suggests such a function when he writes optimistically that "many nations are now collecting urban-subarea data that, in 20 to 30 years, will form a solid foundation for longitudinal investigations." We ought to be establishing research archives where field notes, research diaries, and other research materials can be available for future generations to inspect. We have begun this task with the establishment of data banks. Unfortunately, the operators of such banks are not particularly efficient documentarians. Code books frequently are incomplete; data on response rates are almost entirely unavailable; descriptions of interviewer-training practices are apparently considered unimportant; and detailed reviews of sampling decisions are suspiciously absent. Further, such banks are not now equipped to become archives for such materials as the field diary that Form found important as a data source for the analysis of his own research practices.

As a matter of fact, we are not even careful about the systematic organization of data that can be stored efficiently. Perhaps this situation results from the sociologist's here-and-now orientation. I have employed the adjective "stale" in describing data that I collected only 10 years ago. Others do the same, and we act on such definitions. Recently I wrote to a good friend who has a deserved national reputation as a research scholar. I asked him for the instruments he had employed in an earlier study of a problem I am currently investigating. His reply was, "I am sorry, but I threw all that material away when I moved from X." Thus, while we tend to be aware of the limitations of past archivists, we still have less than a firm professional commitment to perform such a service for future sociologists, who, after all, will be doing the really crucial work of the discipline if such work is ever to be done.

There is yet another theme that runs through some of these papers. Mehan's discussion suggested this problem to me, for he was concerned with the "demand characteristics" of the situation he was investigating. Portes addresses this issue directly at a number of points. Form's analysis of distrust is also related. The importance of demand characteristics is clearly recognized by experimental psychologists as crucial in their investigations. Further, they are usually dealing with subjects who share a common culture with the experimenter. This culture may even include a set of shared agreements on the value of science, the roles of experimenter and subject, and the obligation of a subject to be honest. Now, given that demand characteristics can affect the outcomes of controlled experiments in which a professor is observing rats under relatively simple conditions, it seems at least reasonable to believe that comparative sociologists, who are involved in much more complex situations, should devote serious attention to such matters.

Portes (p. 158) reminds us that the outcome of cross-national research can be defined as an interaction effect between the particular cultural setting in which the research is to take place and the general goals and specific techniques brought by the researcher. As a routine obligation, every field researcher ought to attend to that interaction and report the probable consequences. The point is that when such reports are lacking, it is impossible to evaluate the quality of information that *is* made public. Thus, while I might argue with Form about certain of the strategies he has employed, I must strongly reinforce his conclusion (p. 110) that "social scientists should publish their field experiences to enable scholars to profit from them prior to departure for the field."

The above recitation of troubles does not exhaust the difficulties that beset comparative sociology.[5] This situation may be uncomfortable, but as both Grimshaw and Armer point out, it is not unique to a given sociological specialty. Perhaps the problems faced by the comparativist are more acute than those confronting the student of middle-class Midwestern suburbanites, but the difference is only a matter of degree. Comparativists have performed a genuine service by reporting their difficulties and thereby calling the discipline's attention to matters that otherwise might not have come to our consciousness. If we are to achieve a science of society, that discipline cannot be limited by unknown cultural or temporal idiosyncrasies. To those who would protest that the enterprise is too difficult or the compexities too great, we ought to be candid. All of sociology is a tough business. The comparativists have clarified for all of us the intractable character of our quest. The problems confronting us can be solved only after they are clearly recognized. The papers in this volume move us in the desired direction. Let those who cannot tolerate the uncertainties, the ambiguities, and the high probability of failure pursue one of the simpler sciences.

Notes

1. Unless otherwise noted, references are to the conference papers included in this volume.

2. Grimshaw makes a distinction between "comparative" and other sociological specialties—he once referred to me as a "noncomparativist." I can take no offense because the meaning of that designation is not clear to me. This matter is further complicated because Grimshaw has described all "good sociology" as "comparative" in many senses, yet he seems to have some regard for my work.

3. This conclusion has been reached independently by a number of people who have attempted to integrate the comparative literature. See, for example, Straus (1968:565).

4. The possibility of interactions among variables in a set is not a problem that can be dismissed lightly. Finsterbusch (p. 427) recognizes this possibility when he questions the assumption of uncorrelated error terms. The literature on these matters is highly technical, but that literature must be mastered by those who wish to use models of the type suggested by Finsterbusch. See, for example, the various discussions of "disturbance terms" in Blalock (1971).

5. One particularly interesting issue arises when we examine the comparativist's perspective. Currently, comparative sociology is dominated by white males trained in institutions located within the United States. Further, these scholars now tend to be affiliated with U.S. universities. From a comparativist's viewpoint, certain consequences of this condition might be inferred. The successful professor at a university within the United States is at best an altruistic entreprneur. He is overburdened with a variety of expectations and must find acceptable mechanisms that permit him to steal time for his research. He feels guilty when he works less than a 60-hour week. He is torn by the conflicts between local and cosmopolitan pressures. If we adopt the comparativist's perspective, this set of conditions raises certain troublesome questions about our personal and professional qualifications to be truly comparative.

References

Blalock, H. M., Jr.

1971   *Causal Models in the Social Sciences.* Chicago: Aldine.

Straus, M. A.

1968   Society as a variable in comparative study of the family by replication and secondary analysis. *Journal of Marriage and the Family*, 30 (November):565-570.

Name Index

467

DATE DUE			
GAYLORD			PRINTED IN U.S.A